BEYOND OBJECTIVISM AND RELATIVISM

BEYOND OBJECTIVISM AND RELATIVISM:
SCIENCE, HERMENEUTICS, AND PRAXIS

RICHARD J. BERNSTEIN

UNIVERSITY OF PENNSYLVANIA PRESS

Philadelphia • 1983

PB 604

Design by Adrianne Onderdonk Dudden

Library of Congress Cataloging in Publication Data

Bernstein, Richard J.
  Beyond objectivism and relativism.

  Bibliography: p.
  Includes index.
  1. Hermeneutics.   2. Science—Philosophy.
3. Objectivity.   4. Relativity.   5. Practice (Philosophy)
I. Title.
BD241.B415   1983   121'.68   83-12439
ISBN 0-8122-7906-9

Printed in the United States of America

TO FOUR FRIENDS

Hannah Arendt
Hans-Georg Gadamer
Jürgen Habermas
Richard Rorty

ἔστι γὰρ ὁ φίλος ἄλλος αὐτός

Aristotle, *Nicomachean Ethics*

CONTENTS

PREFACE

Writing, for me, has always been an adventure of discovery. This book itself is a stage in a personal and intellectual odyssey—one which has opened new horizons of questioning. In *Praxis and Action* (1971), where I explored the meaning and centrality of the concepts of *praxis* and action in Marxism, Existentialism, Pragmatism, and Analytic Philosophy, I wrote in the introduction:

At first, it was the common negative stance of contemporary philosophers that most forcefully struck me. Most contemporary philosophers have been in revolt against the Cartesian framework. Descartes is frequently called the father of modern philosophy. If we are to judge by philosophy during the past hundred years, this title can best be understood in a Freudian sense. It is a common characteristic of many contemporary philosophers that they have sought to overthrow and dethrone the father.[1]

When writing *Praxis and Action*, I was aware that there is significant common ground in the diverse attacks on the Cartesian foundations of modern philosophy, the "spectator theory of knowledge," and in the new emphasis on the centrality of human agency and activity, but I did not at the time realize how much convergence and substantive agreement was to be discovered in the proposed alternatives to the Cartesian legacy. It was easier to isolate a common enemy than to discern a shared objective.

This concern was primary when I sought to make sense of the critiques and disputes about the social and political disciplines that were erupting during the 1960s and 1970s. In *The Restructuring of Social and Political Theory* (1976), I argued that a new sensibility and universe of discourse was in the process of emerging, one which sought to integrate dialectically the empirical, interpretive, and critical dimensions of a theoretical orientation that is directed toward practical activity. It was also becoming clear to me that the restructuring of social and political theory had much broader and deeper consequences. For it raised fundamental issues about the character and prospects of human rationality. I wrote at the time, "When individuals sense that they are living through a period of crisis, when foundations seem to be cracking and orthodoxies breaking up, then a public space is created in which basic questions about the human condition can be raised anew."[2]

Only when I was in the final stages of completing *The Restructuring of Social and Political Theory* did I fully and dramatically realize that the themes I had been pursuing in both of these books, as well as in my earlier studies of the pragmatic thinkers, were gravitating toward the complex network of problems concerning the character, dimensions, and texture of human rationality and irrationality. All the pathways of my thinking kept drawing me ineluctably to the question of rationality. I felt the need and urgency to work through the "rationality debates" that were becoming so central in a great diversity of cultural contexts, to sort out what were the underlying issues, to see how they might be related to each other, and to confront the specter of relativism that always seemed to be hovering in the background of these discussions.

As I began to work through these tangled debates in the philosophy of the natural and social sciences, in the confrontation between hermeneutics and critical theory, and in contemporary reflections on practical rationality, political judgment, and *praxis*, I kept having an uncanny sense of déjà vu. Let me illustrate what I mean with reference to three very different and apparently unrelated texts: Paul Feyerabend's *Against Method*; Hans-Georg Gadamer's *Truth and Method*; and Sheldon Wolin's essay "Political Theory as a Vocation." Whether we focus on the disciplinary matrices that characterize their investigations, their intellectual temperaments and styles, the traditions that inform their writings, or the specific issues they address, one's initial impression is that of radical differences. Feyerabend sharply criticizes prevailing orthodoxies in the philosophy of the natural sciences and attacks what he takes to be the myth of a determinate scientific method with fixed rational criteria. Gadamer focuses on the "happening" of understanding, especially as it pertains to tradition and the interpretation of works of art, literary texts, and history. Wolin's theme is the critique of contemporary political science and a defense of the vocation of the political theorist. But when one compares these three works, despite the manifest and real differences, fundamental latent similarities leap to the foreground. All three develop radical critiques of the intellectually imperialistic claims made in the name of Method. Feyerabend seeks to expose and ridicule the belief that there is a determinate scientific method that guides the way in which science and living scientists really work. He is critical of the "deification" of science in contemporary life. Gadamer, who barely discusses natural science, argues that the modern obsession with Method has distorted and concealed the ontological character of understanding. Wolin explicitly attacks the *vita methodi* (which he contrasts with the *bios theoretikos*) and argues that it has deformed our understanding of politics and political judgment. As they probe the various aspects of the tyranny of Method, it becomes increasingly clear that they are raising profoundly critical questions about the categories, distinctions, and biases that have shaped our culture and our everyday lives since the seventeenth century. Each, in his own way, seeks to come to grips with what he takes to be the fundamental intellectual crisis of our time. But the similarities revealed in these diverse texts go further than a common attack on the very idea of Method. Each of them opens the way to a more historically situated, nonalgorithmic, flexible understanding of human rationality, one which highlights the tacit dimension of human judgment and imagination and is sensitive to the unsuspected contingencies and genuine novelties encountered in particular situations. Their technical analyses are also animated by a practical-moral concern with the threats to, and the prospects for, human judgment and imagination. There are even similarities and shared resonances in their positive characterizations of human judgment, which emphasize its practical character. Indeed, in unsuspected ways, the juxtaposition of these three texts helps to illuminate the strengths and weaknesses of what each of these thinkers is struggling to articulate. The similarities and family resemblances that I was discovering had application to a much wider range of thinkers and texts. As I worked back and forth among the different "rationality debates," I kept noticing how similar issues were being raised, similar concerns were motivating these discussions, and how, despite diverse vocabularies, similar theses were being advanced and defended. My original hunches, conjectures, and hypotheses needed more careful explication, probing, and testing. At the time it was not entirely clear whether the interrelationships that I was discovering were only superficial and suggestive or whether they were a genuine indication of a more substantive convergence.

In the spring of 1976, I was invited to the University of Notre Dame to give a series of lectures in the Perspectives in Philosophy program. In this program a visiting philosopher is invited to share his or her work in progress. Prior to the visit, faculty and students read the philosopher's work. In addition to giving public lectures, meetings are arranged for informal discussion. Notre Dame's philosophy department is a congenial, lively, and critical community. The invitation to Notre Dame was an ideal opportunity to begin to expose and test ideas that were still in a formative stage. The experience at Notre Dame was exhilarating and sobering—exhilarating because I encountered wide sympathy for the project I was undertaking, sobering because I was made painfully aware of how much needed to be done to clarify and support what I was trying to say and to show.

The following fall, a felicitous event occurred which helped to bring my thinking into sharper focus. Jürgen Habermas accepted a visiting appointment at Haverford College, and Steven Lukes was a visiting professor at Temple University. For all three of us, issues about rationality and relativism were central to our philosophic interests. We had weekly meetings in which we discussed the relevant issues and sharpened our own theses in confrontation with each other. I sought to "detranscendentalize" Habermas and to persuade Lukes that there was something wrong with the moral relativism he was advocating at the time. Needless to say, I was incisively criticized from opposing directions.

When Habermas was at Haverford, he asked me to join him as a codirector with members of the Yugoslav *Praxis* group to organize a conference course to be given at the Inter-University Centre for Postgraduate Studies in Dubrovnik, Yugoslavia. Since 1977 I have served as a codirector of the conference course "Philosophy and Social Science" which is held each spring for two weeks. Participating in the Dubrovnik course has been one of my most stimulating, rewarding, and enjoyable intellectual experiences. Resource persons and participants from all over the world come together for a festival of talk and wide-ranging discussion. It has provided a unique opportunity to test stages of this book as it was taking on a determinate shape. I am especially indebted to Albrecht Wellmer, who has also been a codirector of the course. For the past ten years he has been working on the same problems that are central to this book. We have had an ongoing conversation about problems of rationality. Each spring when we meet in Dubrovnik, we begin our discussion where we left off.

From 1976 through 1978 I spent my time reading, musing, and writing exploratory essays. But I did not yet discern a unifying perspective for organizing the themes I was pursuing. In the spring of 1978, I was traveling on the long flight from New York to Dubrovnik with a group of colleagues. Nancy Fraser, a close friend and former student of mine, who at the time was beginning to become interested in poststructuralist French thought, was pressing me about my philosophic work and where I really stood on basic issues. As our conversation became more intense and heated (I felt I was being deconstructed), it turned to the question of objectivism and relativism. Challenged by Fraser's tenacious ability to get to the heart of issues, I blurted out that the dichotomy between objectivism and relativism was pernicious: one needed to get beyond objectivism and relativism. Suddenly I realized that this was the focal point for which I had been searching. I spent the rest of the night outlining this book. One of the highlights of the 1978 Dubrovnik course was the participation of Richard Rorty. He read parts of what was later published as *Philosophy and the Mirror of Nature*, including the sections where he is critical of Jürgen Habermas and Charles Taylor (both of whom were present at this session). I had already read earlier drafts of Rorty's book and was at once sympathetic with his critique of foundationalism and extremely dubious of the conclusions he drew from this critique. We spent several stimulating sessions trying to sort out the differences that really made a difference in our respective appropriations of the pragmatic tradition.

The following academic year (1978–79) I had a sabbatical leave from Haverford. With the help of an American Council of Learned Societies fellowship, I spent the year in England and had the opportunity to write the preliminary draft of this book. During the spring of 1979 I participated in a seminar on rationality and relativism given at Bailliol College, Oxford, which was organized by Steven Lukes, William Newton-Smith, and Charles Taylor. (Barry Barnes, David Bloor, Clifford Geertz, Martin Hollis, and Rom Harré also attended the seminar.) Since my year in England, this book has gone through numerous revisions.

Ever since my initial encounter with Hegel when I was a graduate student in the early 1950s, I have been attracted to, and at the same time skeptical of, Hegel's concept of *Geist*. In the spirit of Peirce and

Dewey, I have sought to pragmatically appropriate what still seems to me vital in Hegel's vision. While I have many critical reservations about some of Hegel's grand claims about *Geist* working itself out dialectically in the course of history, I believe there is a "truth" in Hegel's insight that there are dynamic movements of thinking that pervade, inform, and give direction to cultural life—movements that are concretely embodied by a great variety of individual thinkers. As I argue in this book, I do think that the spirit of our time is characterized by a movement beyond objectivism and relativism. At times I felt that this book was writing itself through me, and that what is expressed here are the thoughts, insights, and shared vision to which many individuals have contributed.

The book consists of four parts. The first part is an introduction and an overview. I explain what is meant by objectivism and relativism, why this dichotomy is helpful for drawing attention to the primary cultural conflicts of contemporary life, what is the basic anxiety that underlies the growing sense of intellectual crisis. I also describe the *prima facie* evidence for claiming that what is happening now is a movement beyond objectivism and relativism.

After this introductory statement, I begin my argument in part II by describing the outstanding themes in the postempiricist philosophy and history of science in order to show how developments in these disciplines have altered our understanding of science and of the character of rationality in scientific inquiry. Numerous lines of investigation interweave to delineate a type of rationality that is historically situated and practical, involving choice, deliberation, and judgment. What emerges in both the philosophy of the natural and social sciences is a recovery of the hermeneutical dimension of science. Finally, I grapple with the meaning and significance of incommensurability, arguing that when properly analyzed, it does not lead to, or entail, relativism. Rather, it clarifies the openness of language and communication, and the challenges we face in understanding different forms of life.

My conclusions in part II set the stage for a direct confrontation with hermeneutics. Concentrating on the work of Hans-Georg Gadamer, I present a sympathetic explication of the ontological turn in hermeneutics and an immanent critique of it. There is a to-and-fro movement here where I show how hermeneutics helps to clarify and deepen our understanding of lessons learned from the postempiricist philosophy and history of science. But at the same time Gadamer's inquiries keep drawing us toward the fusion of hermeneutics and *praxis*. Gadamer's model for hermeneutics is the tradition of practical philosophy that has its sources in Aristotle's *Nicomachean Ethics* and *Politics*. Understanding, according to Gadamer, is a form of *phronēsis*. But I also argue that while Gadamer opens new questions concerning *praxis* and *phronēsis*, he does not adequately answer and resolve these questions. Indeed, there is a radical *telos* in his questioning that requires us to move beyond philosophic hermeneutics. Throughout this part, my aim is to show how philosophic hermeneutics contributes to the movement beyond objectivism and relativism.

In the final part (part IV) I explore the interrelated concepts of *praxis, phronēsis, technē,* practical discourse, and judgment. Playing off the strengths and weaknesses of Gadamer, Habermas, Rorty, and Arendt, I show how an underlying common vision emerges, one that illuminates the dialogical character of our human existence and our communicative transactions, and that points to the practical need to cultivate dialogical communities. In the final analysis, the movement beyond objectivism and relativism is not just a perplexing theoretical quandary but a practical task that can orient and give direction to our collective *praxis*. There is a deep truth in Wittgenstein's remark, "The way to solve the problem you see in life is to live in a way that will make what is problematic disappear."[3]

A major theme running through the entire book is the reclamation and clarification of the interrelated concepts and experiences of dialogue, debate, conversation, and communication. These at once presuppose and foster solidarity and friendship (both personal and civic). The Greek philosophers were extraordinary insightful in exploring the varieties of friendship and in stressing its importance for ethics and politics. As I argue in part IV, the *experience* of solidarity and friendship is fundamental in the thought of Gadamer, Habermas, Rorty, and Arendt. I have come to appreciate the meaning and power of friendship and solidarity not only from their writings but also from my own conversations, debates, and dialogues with them.

I first met Richard Rorty when we were undergraduates in the late 1940s at the University of Chicago, and we were also together as graduate students at Yale University. Our intellectual development has intersected at numerous points, and over and over again Rorty's penetrating insights have forced me to rethink my own basic convictions. I started reading Habermas's work in the mid-1960s. The experience for me was one of a shock of recognition. Coming from the American pragmatic tradition, I had developed an early and abiding interest in the tradition of German thought from Kant through Hegel and Marx to the Frankfurt School. And Habermas, starting from this tradition of German thought, had expanded his horizon to embrace what is best in the pragmatic tradition. I have always believed that Habermas is very close to the spirit of Peirce, Dewey, and Mead. When we finally met in the early 1970s we both felt the bond of solidarity. We have worked closely together in the Dubrovnik course, and our continuous dialogue has moved back and forth from Dubrovnik, to Starnberg, to Haverford. When Gadamer made his first trip to the United States in 1969, he visited Haverford. I had begun reading his work earlier, and one of the first English reviews of *Wahrheit und Methode* appeared in the *Review of Metaphysics* when I was editor of the journal. He has visited Haverford several times since then, and each time has been a memorable occasion. Gadamer is the best listener and conversational partner that I have ever met.

My first personal encounter with Hannah Arendt in 1972 was stormy. We had a sharp debate about our different interpretations of Hegel and Marx. But that encounter was not only agonistic, it was also, in Plato's sense, erotic. We met several times during the few short remaining years of her life, and each time we passionately argued with each other. She is still very much a living presence for me, and I continue to argue with her.

This book is dedicated to these four friends who have influenced and shaped the thoughts expressed here.

ACKNOWLEDGMENTS

There is a prevailing bias in the United States that liberal arts colleges are primarily teaching institutions and that the university or multiversity is the place for serious scholarly research. But this bias (which, of course, contains some truth) can blind one to the unique advantages of the liberal arts college for humanistic inquiry and scholarship. Humanistic studies, as their long tradition reveals, require an ambience where talk and dialogue are cultivated, where one feels free to pursue issues and problems that transgress conventional academic boundaries, and where one directly experiences the challenges and encounters that come from colleagues and students with diverse intellectual concerns. One of the primary reasons why I joined the faculty of Haverford College in the mid-1960s was that at a time when so many institutions of higher learning were experiencing the deleterious effects of excessive bureaucratization and professionalization, Haverford was still an educational community that honored the ideal of the teacher–scholar in word and deed.

During the past fifteen years, Haverford College has fully supported my scholarly research, making it possible for me to write several books and to edit two very different journals, the *Review of Metaphysics* and *Praxis International*. The college has allowed me the time and provided the funds for me to go to Dubrovnik each spring to codirect the postgraduate conference course "Philosophy and Social Science." A fragile educational community could not thrive today unless it were guided by an enlightened administration. The chairman of the Board of Managers, John C. Whitehead (who recently retired as chairman), the president, Robert Stevens, and the provost, Robert Gavin, and members of the Haverford philosophy department have all provided encouragement for my intellectual work. I am convinced that the character of my scholarship during the past fifteen years has not only benefited enormously from Haverford's special quality but that it would have been qualitatively different if I had functioned in a less intellectually congenial environment.

Selections from three previously published articles has been modified and incorporated into this book. I am grateful to the editors and publishers for allowing me to use this material: "From Hermeneutics to Praxis," *Review of Metaphysics* 35 (1982):823–45; "Hannah Arendt: Judging—The Actor and the Spectator," in *Proceedings of History, Ethics, Politics: A Conference Based on the Work of Hannah Arendt,* edited by Robert Boyers (Saratoga Springs, N.Y.: Empire State College, 1982); "What Is the Difference That Makes a Difference? Gadamer, Habermas, and Rorty," in *PSA 1982,* vol. 2, Proceedings of the 1982 Biennial Meeting of the Philosophy of Science Association, edited by P. D. Asquith and T. Nickles (East Lansing, Mich.: Philosophy of Science Association, 1983).

I want to express my appreciation to the American Council of Learned Societies for granting me a fellowship for 1978–79, during which I wrote the first draft, and to the John C. Whitehead Fund for faculty development at Haverford, which enabled me to be free of teaching responsibilities when I was completing this book.

Many persons have helped with this book. Carol Bernstein, Fred Dallmayr, Heinz Lubasz, Richard Rorty, Charles Taylor, and Kathleen Wright have read earlier drafts. I have tried to answer their incisive criticisms. The present book is far better because of the care they gave in commenting on it. I have also benefited from my conversations with Hans-Georg Gadamer and Jürgen Habermas about the interpretation of their work.

Penny Coia typed the manuscript; Maggie Smith checked the accuracy of the quotations and notes; James Bohman translated the letter by Gadamer that appears as an appendix. I am especially grateful to Shirley Averill, who so efficiently and cheerfully helped with the final revisions.

John McGuigan of the University of Pennsylvania Press is an editor—all too rare—who still believes that as much care should be taken in producing a book as is taken in writing it. Christie Lerch has copyedited the manuscript with sensitivity and critical discrimination. Anne Cipriano Venzon has prepared the index.

Once again, my wife, Carol, took valuable time from her demanding academic career to discuss and criticize every aspect of this book from its inception to its completion.

BEYOND OBJECTIVISM AND RELATIVISM

PART ONE
BEYOND OBJECTIVISM
AND RELATIVISM:
AN OVERVIEW

I think that Aristotle was profoundly right in holding that ethics is concerned with how to live and with human happiness, and also profoundly right in holding that this sort of knowledge *("practical knowledge") is different from theoretical knowledge. A view of knowledge that acknowledges that the sphere of knowledge is wider than the sphere of "science" seems to me to be a cultural necessity if we are to arrive at a sane and human view of ourselves* or *of science.*

Hilary Putnam, *Meaning and the Moral Sciences*

THERE is an uneasiness that has spread throughout intellectual and cultural life. It affects almost every discipline and every aspect of our lives. This uneasiness is expressed by the opposition between objectivism and relativism, but there are a variety of other contrasts that indicate the same underlying anxiety: rationality versus irrationality, objectivity versus subjectivity, realism versus antirealism. Contemporary thinking has moved between these and other, related extremes. Even the attempts that some have made to break out of this framework of thinking have all too frequently been assimilated to these standard oppositions.

There are, however, many signs that the deep assumptions, commitments, and metaphors that have shaped these oppositions, and from which they gain their seductive power, are being called into question. For along with the disquietude that is provoked by these extremes, there is a growing sense that something is wrong with the ways in which the relevant issues and options are posed—a sense that something is happening that is changing the categorial structure and patterns within which we think and act—a sense that we have an urgent need to move beyond objectivism and relativism.

My purpose in this study is to probe this complex phenomenon, to clarify what is happening, to indicate what is wrong with the intellectual and cultural matrix that has shaped so much of modern life, to show why traditional oppositions are breaking down, what new directions are emerging, and what is the evidence for and the meaning of the move beyond objectivism and relativism. Specifically, I intend to examine a number of debates and controversies that have broken out recently among philosophers. While at first glance the debates may appear to have very different subjects and emphases, all of them, in essence, have a single concern and focus: to determine the nature and scope of human rationality.

A new conversation is now emerging among philosophers—a conversation about human rationality—and as a result of this dialogue we are beginning to gain a new understanding of rationality that has important ramifications for both theoretical and practical life. A true "conversation"—which is not to be confused with idle chatter or a violent babble of competing voices—is an extended and open dialogue which presupposes a background of intersubjective agreements and a tacit sense of relevance. There may be different emphases and stresses by participants in a conversation, and in a living conversation there is always unpredictability and novelty. The contours of the conversation about human rationality, especially as it pertains to science, hermeneutics, and *praxis*, have recently taken on a new and exciting shape. I want not only to reveal the common themes of this dialogue—the shared assumptions, commitments, and insights—but also to do justice to the different individual voices and emphases within it.

From a manifest perspective, many contemporary debates are still structured within traditional extremes. There is still an underlying belief that in the final analysis the only viable alternatives open to us are *either* some form of objectivism, foundationalism, ultimate grounding of knowledge, science, philosophy, and language *or* that we are ineluctably led to relativism, skepticism, historicism, and nihilism. Whether we focus on the origins of analytic philosophy or phenomenology, there was an earlier period of intellectual confidence and optimism, a conviction that we had finally discovered the secure path for philosophy, the right "method" for making genuine intellectual progress, for turning philosophy into a discipline that would yield knowledge (*epistēmē*), instead of being the endless battleground for competing and shifting opinions (*doxai*). In this respect the differences between such central figures as Russell and Husserl are less significant than what they shared. Both were at one time convinced that the "real" foundation or ground of philosophy had been discovered and that the methods and procedures for seriously advancing philosophic inquiry were at hand. The fact that such claims had been made over and over again in the past—and have become a persistent theme since the time of Descartes—was taken not as evidence for the dubiousness of the project of grounding philosophy but rather as a sign of the "scandal" of philosophy that demanded resolution. But as we follow the internal development in the twentieth century of both Anglo-American and continental philosophy, we can detect increasing doubts about the project of grounding philosophy, knowledge, and language.

The movement from confidence to skepticism about foundations, methods, and rational criteria of evaluation has not been limited to philosophy. The confusion and uncertainty in philosophy exhibits and reflects a phenomenon that is characteristic of our intellectual and cultural life. In the entire range of the human and social sciences, we have witnessed the playing out of bold attempts to secure foundations and the elaborations of new methods that promise genuine knowledge, followed by a questioning that reveals cracks and crevices in what had been taken to be solid and secure. There seems to be almost a rush to embrace various forms of relativism. Whether we reflect on the nature of science, or alien societies, or different historical epochs, or sacred and literary texts, we hear voices telling us that there are no hard "facts of the matter" and that almost "anything goes." Whether we focus on such cherished subjects in philosophy as rationality, truth, knowledge, reality, or norms, we seem to be confronted with incommensurable paradigms, theories, conceptual schemes, or forms of life. We have been told that it is an illusion and a deep self-deception to think that there is some overarching framework, some neutral descriptive language, some permanent standards of rationality to which we can appeal in order to understand and critically evaluate the competing claims that are made, and that we are limited to our historical context and to our own social practices. The dream or hope that many philosophers have had—to grasp the world *sub species aeternitatus*—is, we are told, a deceiving illusion that leads to dogmatism and even terror.

The problem is not just an intellectual one, nor is it restricted to parochial disputes about the meaning and scope of rationality. At issue are some of the most perplexing questions concerning human beings: what we are, what we can know, what norms ought to bind us, what are the grounds for hope. The malaise penetrates our everyday moral, social, and political experiences. The fashionable varieties of relativism that are spreading everywhere frequently lead to cynicism and a growing sense of impotence. The recent celebration of relativistic doctrines and the enthusiasm for an endless playfulness of interpretation that knows no limits has already elicited a strong reaction. It has been argued that regardless of the many errors of those who have been wedded to the concept of representation, the correspondence theory of truth, the doctrine that the function of the mind is to mirror nature, we cannot avoid the "primordial intuition" that there is a world that is independent of our beliefs and fancies that forces itself upon us willy-nilly and constrains what we can think, say, and do.[1]

Confusion is compounded not only by the complexity of the issues involved and the shifting meanings of such key concepts as rationality, objectivity, realism, and norms but by the different fundamental attitudes of philosophers toward opposing positions. Consider, for example, Karl Popper's horror at what he takes to be the rampant growth of subjectivism and relativism today. According to Popper, this is not simply an innocent epistemological deviation but an error that opens the floodgates to irrationalism and fanaticism.[2] Contrast this attitude with that of Paul Feyerabend, who at one time was intellectually quite close to Popper but has now turned against Popper and the "gang" of critical rationalists. Feyerabend gleefully champions "irrationality" against the type of rationality defended by critical rationalists. He claims that if one applies the standards of Popper and his followers one is forced to conclude that science itself is a thoroughly irrational discipline—and ought to be. In his recent work, Feyerabend, in ever more imaginative and wild ways, seeks to question and mock science itself and the role that it plays in our lives.[3]

At the heart of Popper's apology for "objective knowledge" is a practical-moral concern that informs all of his work and rhetoric. But this is also true of Feyerabend. These competing practical-moral concerns, which reflect Popper's and Feyerabend's different assessments of what is taking place in the contemporary world, are far more significant than many of the technical and professional issues that divide them. Popper thinks of himself as the public defender of the "open" society, which is being threatened. He is against all forms of dogmatism, irrationalism, and fanaticism. But Feyerabend accuses Popper and those sympathetic with his doctrines of being caught in a dangerous illusion. Popper's thinking, in Feyerabend's view, ultimately leads to further closure and fixity, to a new, masked form of dogmatism that is the enemy of human freedom, spontaneity, and creativity. Feyerabend ridicules and seeks to undermine the "puritanical seriousness" represented by Popper. The opposition between Popper and Feyerabend, especially in what I have called their practical-moral orientations, is an extreme example of a typical contrast that occurs in a variety of different contexts and domains of discourse. (Compare the style and content of Feyerabend's attack on "method" and "rationality" with Jacques Derrida's punning assaults on the "metaphysics of presence.")

Many professional philosophers, while they are critical of Popper and regard Feyerabend as irresponsible, nevertheless share the basic conviction of Descartes, Kant, Husserl, the early logical positivists, and indeed most modern philosophers, that philosophy has *now* finally discovered its "proper object" and the right way of going about solving philosophic problems. Michael Dummett, a leading (some would say *the* leading) British philosopher of our time has recently claimed:

Only with Frege was the proper object of philosophy finally established: namely, first, that the goal of philosophy is the analysis of the structure of *thought*; secondly, that the study of *thought* is to be sharply distinguished from the study of the psychological process of *thinking*; and, finally, that the only proper method for analysing thought consists in the analysis of *language.* . . . The acceptance of these three tenets is common to the entire analytical school . . . [but] it has taken nearly a half-century since his death for us to apprehend clearly what the real task of philosophy, as conceived by him, involves.

I know that it is reasonable to greet all such claims with scepticism, since they have been made many times before in the history of philosophy. Just because the scandal caused by philosophy's lack of a systematic methodology has persisted for so long, it has been a constant preoccupation of philosophers to remedy that lack, and a repeated illusion that they had succeeded in doing so. Husserl believed passionately that he at last held the key which would unlock every philosophical door; the disciples of Kant ascribed to him the achievement of devising a correct philosophical methodology; Spinoza believed that he was doing for philosophy what Euclid had done for geometry; and, before him, Descartes supposed that he had uncovered the one and only proper philosophical method. I have mentioned only a few of many examples of this illusion; for any outsider to philosophy, by far the safest bet would be that I was suffering from a similar illusion in making the same claim for Frege. To this I can offer only the banal reply which any prophet has to make to any sceptic: time will tell.[4]

But it is not only "outsiders" to philosophy who are skeptical. Such an insider as Richard Rorty has recently argued that the real scandal of philosophy is that we are still taken in and mesmerized by the very conception of philosophy that Dummett embraces. We still assume that there is such a thing as the "proper object" of philosophy; that philosophy identifies philosophic problems that are to be solved once and for all; and that there is "a systematic methodology" for doing this. According to Rorty, if we really want to overcome the scandal caused by "philosophy's lack of a systematic methodology," then what is needed is a form of philosophic therapy that will rid us of the illusion and the self-deception that philosophy is or can be the foundational discipline of culture. We need to abandon the very idea that philosophy is a form of inquiry that *knows* something about knowing, language, or thought that nobody else knows, and frankly admit that at its best, philosophy is just another voice in the conversation of mankind.

In contrast to Dummett's claims about the significance of Frege, Rorty interprets our contemporary situation in a radically different manner. According to Rorty, the three most important philosophers of the twentieth century are Dewey, Wittgenstein, and Heidegger. Rorty makes this claim for their importance precisely because they have helped us to overcome the very conception of philosophy that Dummett and so many professional philosophers accept.

Each tried, in his early years, to find a new way of making philosophy "foundational"—a new way of formulating an ultimate context for thought. Wittgenstein tried to construct a new theory of representation which would have nothing to do with mentalism, Heidegger to construct a new set of philosophical categories which would have nothing to do with science, epistemology, or the Cartesian quest for certainty, and Dewey to construct a naturalized version of Hegel's vision of history. Each of the three came to see his earlier effort as self-deceptive, as an attempt to retain a certain conception of philosophy after the notions needed to flesh out that conception (the seventeenth-century notions of knowledge and mind) had been discarded. Each of the three, in his later work, broke free of the Kantian conception of philosophy as foundational, and spent his time warning us against those very temptations to which he himself had once succumbed.

Thus their later work is therapeutic rather than constructive, edifying rather than systematic, designed to make the reader question his own motives for philosophizing.[5]

While Dummett likens himself to a prophet who will be vindicated by future developments, from Rorty's perspective he looks more like an arch reactionary who is desperately trying to hold on to what has been discredited and ought to be abandoned. The contrast between Dummett's and Rorty's views indicates not only the most divergent and antithetical understandings of the accomplishment of modern and recent analytic philosophy but of the self-understanding of philosophy itself.

The type of opposition represented by the contrast between Popper and Feyerabend is not localized to any school of philosophy, or even to philosophy itself; the same is true of the antithesis between Dummett and Rorty. The repeated stress on these oppositions, and the swinging back and forth of the pendulum of philosophic debate in relation to them, suggests that there is a different and more penetrating interpretation of what is happening in philosophy and more generally in the range of the cultural disciplines. Like Rorty, I think we are coming to the end—the playing out—of an intellectual tradition (Rorty calls it the "Cartesian–Lockean–Kantian tradition"). But I also think Rorty misses what is now in the process of emerging.[6] When we think and work through the most significant contemporary philosophic debates, we will discover that views which initially seem fragmentary, conflicting, and even contradictory ultimately converge and cohere. I do not want to make exaggerated claims for something that is still in the process of developing, sometimes in very tentative and hesitant ways, but I intend to show that there are now sufficient signs and evidence to reveal the shape and the *telos* of this new understanding of our human situation.

In order to set the context for this investigation, it is important to clarify in a preliminary manner what I mean by "objectivism" and "relativism" and why I take this to be the central cultural opposition of our time. Both terms have been used with shifting meanings. Furthermore, it might seem that the natural contrasts to pursue are those between "objectivism" and "subjectivism," or between "relativism" and "absolutism." I will be using the terms "objectivism" and "relativism" in an extremely broad sense which departs from some of the standard philosophic uses of these expressions. As I proceed, I will introduce further refinements and qualifications.

OBJECTIVISM AND RELATIVISM

By "objectivism," I mean the basic conviction that there is or must be some permanent, ahistorical matrix or framework to which we can ultimately appeal in determining the nature of rationality, knowledge, truth, reality, goodness, or rightness. An objectivist claims that there is (or must be) such a matrix and that the primary task of the philosopher is to discover what it is and to support his or her claims to have discovered such a matrix with the strongest possible reasons. Objectivism is closely related to foundationalism and the search for an Archimedean point. The objectivist maintains that unless we can ground philosophy, knowledge, or language in a rigorous manner we cannot avoid radical skepticism.

The relativist not only denies the positive claims of the objectivist but goes further. In its strongest form, relativism is the basic conviction that when we turn to the examination of those concepts that philosophers have taken to be the most fundamental—whether it is the concept of rationality, truth, reality, right, the good, or norms—we are forced to recognize that in the final analysis all such concepts must be understood as relative to a specific conceptual scheme, theoretical framework, paradigm, form of life, society, or culture. Since the relativist believes that there is (or can be) a nonreducible plurality of such conceptual schemes, he or she challenges the claim that these concepts can have a determinate and univocal significance. For the relativist, there is no substantive overarching framework or single metalanguage by which we can rationally adjudicate or univocally evaluate competing claims of alternative paradigms. Thus, for example, when we turn to something as fundamental as the issue of criteria or standards of rationality, the relativist claims that we can never escape from the predicament of speaking of "our" and "their" standards of rationality—standards that may be "radically incommensurable." It is an illusion to think that there is something that might properly be labeled "*the* standards of rationality," standards that are genuinely universal and that are not subject to historical or temporal change.

The *agōn* between objectivists and relativists has been with us ever since the origins of Western philosophy, or at least from the time of Plato's attack on the Sophists and on Protagoras's alleged relativism. But it is only in recent times that the complex issues that this debate raises have become almost obsessive and have spread to every area of human inquiry and life. Despite the many novel twists and turns in this ancient debate, it has exhibited a remarkable continuity. Each time that an objectivist has come up with what he or she takes to be a firm foundation, an ontological grounding, a fixed categorial scheme, someone has challenged such claims and has argued that what is supposed to be fixed, eternal, ultimate, necessary, or indubitable is open to doubt and questioning. The relativist accuses the objectivist of mistaking what is at best historically or culturally stable for the eternal and permanent. When the objectivist claims to come up with clear and distinct criteria or foolproof transcendental arguments to support his or her claims, the relativist argues that close examination reveals that there is something fraudulent and ingenuous about such claims. But ever since Plato objectivists have argued that relativism, whenever it is clearly stated, is self-referentially inconsistent and paradoxical. For implicitly or explicitly, the relativist claims that his or her position is true, yet the relativist also insists that since truth is relative, what is taken as true may also be false. Consequently, relativism itself may be true *and* false. One cannot consistently state the case for relativism without undermining it. As so frequently happens in philosophy, the argument tends to shift from substantive claims about what are the proper foundations and how we know them to who has the burden of proof. Objectivists argue, rather like Dummett, that even though we can frankly recognize the failures of past philosophers, this is not a sufficient or even a good reason for thinking that we cannot discover the "proper object" of philosophy and a "systematic methodology" for making genuine progress. Because philosophers like Rorty and the edifying thinkers that he admires see the trap of trying to *prove* that the objectivist is fundamentally mistaken, they employ a form of indirect communication and philosophic therapy that is intended to loosen the grip that objectivism has upon us—a therapy that seeks to liberate us from the obsession with objectivism and foundationalism.

It should be clear that I am using the term "objectivism" in a way that is far more inclusive than some of its standard uses. "Objectivism" has frequently been used to designate metaphysical realism—the claim that there is a world of objective reality that exists independently of us and that has a determinate nature or essence that we can know. In modern times objectivism has been closely linked with an acceptance of a basic metaphysical or epistemological distinction between the subject and the object. What is "out there" (objective) is presumed to be independent of us (subjects), and knowledge is achieved when a subject correctly mirrors or represents objective reality. This dominant form of objectivism is only one variety of the species. We can read Kant and the tradition of transcendental philosophy that he initiated as questioning the very possibility of making sense of the objectivity of knowledge by resorting to metaphysical realism—by appealing to a world or thing-in-itself that is completely independent of the ways in which we condition and constitute experience. But from my perspective, Kant is no less an objectivist and foundationalist than the empiricists and the rationalists he was criticizing. Kant does not question the need for an ahistorical permanent matrix or categorial scheme for grounding knowledge; he insists upon it more rigorously than many of his predecessors. He claims that his critical inquiry at once reveals and justifies the universal and necessary conditions for the possibility of experience and knowledge. Kant identifies the transcendental turn with the "proper way" of philosophy. To question the possibility and success of such a critical project would be to call philosophy itself into question. All those who share this commitment—all those who think that only by taking the transcendental turn and who claim that there is an a priori universal and necessary structure of human knowledge—share the objectivist bias.

Consequently even Husserl, who is at once sharply critical of Kant's understanding of transcendental philosophy and who argues that Kant was not radical enough in pursuing the questions that he raised, is an objectivist. Husserl thought of himself as pursuing the *telos* of transcendental philosophy in a more thoroughgoing way than any previous philosopher, and he understood himself as battling against all forms of objectivism in modern philosophy. He tells us that

what characterizes objectivism is that it moves upon the ground of the world which is pregiven, taken for granted through experience, seeks the "objective truth" of this world, seeks what, in this world, is unconditionally valid for every rational being, what it is in itself. It is the task of *epistēmē, ratio,* or philosophy to carry this out universally. Through these one arrives at what ultimately is; beyond this, no further questions would have a rational sense.[7]

He contrasts objectivism with transcendentalism, which claims that "the ontic meaning [*Seinssinn*] of the pregiven life-world is a *subjective structure [Gebilde]*, it is the achievement of experiencing, prescientific life."[8] Transcendentalism is not to be confused with the appeal to the "psychological subjectivity" of human beings, for "mature transcendentalism protests against psychological idealism" and claims to "have initiated a completely new sort of scientific procedure, the transcendental."[9] Husserl draws the contrast between objectivism and transcendentalism in the strongest possible manner in order to set the stage for his own investigation and defense of transcendental phenomenology. The fate of philosophy, and indeed the fate of European culture, is, he says, bound up with the fate of transcendental phenomenology. According to Husserl, the most consequential issues of modern philosophy and culture are involved in the battle between objectivism and the type of transcendentalism that he defends.

The whole history of philosophy since the appearance of "epistemology" and the serious attempts at a transcendental philosophy is a history of tremendous tensions between objectivistic and transcendental philosophy. It is a history of constant attempts to maintain objectivism and to develop it in a new form and, on the other side, of attempts by transcendentalism to overcome the difficulties entailed by the idea of transcendental subjectivity and the method it requires.[10]

But Husserl fails to stress the dialectical similarity between the objectivism that he attacks and the transcendentalism that he defends. *Au fond*, both share the aspiration to discover the real, permanent foundation of philosophy and knowledge—a foundation that will withstand historical vicissitudes, escape from "anthropologistic relativism," and satisfy the craving for ultimate constraints. In using the term "objectivism" to characterize both what Husserl calls "objectivism" and what he calls "transcendentalism," it is this common assumption about the objective of philosophic thought that I want to emphasize.[11]

It should be clear from the way I am using the term "relativism" that it must be carefully distinguished from "subjectivism." A relativist need not be a subjectivist, and a subjectivist is not necessarily a relativist. Husserl is a subjectivist, at least insofar as he claims that there are a priori structures of transcendental subjectivity that can be apodictically known—structures of transcendental subjectivity that ground both our scientific objective knowledge and the pregiven *Lebenswelt* of everyday experience. However, there is nothing relativistic about Husserl's conception of transcendental phenomenology; it is intended to be the definitive answer to all forms of relativism, skepticism, and historicism. Even if we think of subjectivism in its more common and mundane sense—using the term to call attention to whatever is "merely" a matter of personal opinion, taste, or bias, and consequently idiosyncratic—a relativist is not necessarily a subjectivist. As I have characterized the relativist, his or her essential claim is that there can be no higher appeal than to a given conceptual scheme, language game, set of social practices, or historical epoch. There is a nonreducible plurality of such schemes, paradigms, and practices; there is no substantive overarching framework in which radically different and alternative schemes are commensurable—no universal standards that somehow stand outside of and above these competing alternatives. But the relativist does not necessarily claim that there is anything subjective about these schemes, paradigms, and practices.

Given this characterization of objectivism and relativism, I can begin to explain why I am focusing on this opposition rather than on that between relativism and absolutism, or between objectivism and subjectivism. Although the quest for certainty and the search for absolute constraints continues to haunt philosophy, there is a sense in which "absolutism," to use William James's phrase, is no longer a "live" option. The dominant temper of our age is fallibilistic. If we focus on the history of our understanding of science during the past hundred years, from Peirce to Popper, or on the development of epistemology during this period, we discover that thinkers who disagree on almost everything else agree that there are no nontrivial knowledge claims that are immune from criticism. Even a philosopher like Husserl who claims to have discovered an entirely new science and believes that we can achieve apodictic knowledge of the structure of transcendental subjectivity nevertheless emphasizes the ways in which transcendental phenomenology is open, dynamic, cooperative, and fallible. Absolutism is therefore no longer a live option.

But neither is subjectivism. The type of transcendental subjectivism projected by Husserl has been extensively and devastatingly criticized. However great Heidegger's debt to Husserl, we can interpret Heidegger's philosophic journey as raising the profoundest questions about the very idea of a transcendental phenomenology.[12] Heidegger also probes the roots of the various forms of subjectivism that have pervaded modern thought. He questions the whole mode of thinking whereby we take the "subjective" and the "objective" as signifying a basic epistemological or metaphysical distinction. Despite some rearguard attempts to defend the type of transcendental phenomenology that Husserl elaborated, the entire program is in disarray. A pervasive skepticism about the possibility of a transcendental phenomenology is felt even by those who think of themselves as working within the phenomenological tradition. When we shift from this internal controversy within continental philosophy to more garden-variety notions of subjectivity, it becomes clear that the most plausible defenses of relativism have nothing to do with subjectivism. So while neither absolutism nor subjectivism is a live option for us now, the choice between a sophisticated form of fallibilistic objectivism and a nonsubjective conception of relativism does seem to be a live—and indeed a momentous—one.

Many thinkers want to distinguish between cognitive and moral relativism. They are convinced that while we can give strong arguments in favor of moral relativism, or at least cannot totally discredit it, cognitive relativism is indefensible. A combination of cognitive objectivism and moral relativism has been taken to be the most attractive and supportable option.[13] But recently even this has changed, and arguments have been advanced for showing that nothing, not even the "hard sciences," escapes the clutches of relativistic arguments. Relativism, a stream in the philosophy of the past two hundred years that began as a trickle, has swelled in recent times into a roaring torrent.

Although Kant was not explicitly concerned with battling relativists, he saw that there were already tendencies in the empiricist tradition that, if relentlessly pursued, would call into question the objectivity of knowledge, the foundations of morality, and indeed the very discipline of philosophy itself. The "Copernican Revolution" in philosophy—Kant's transcendental turn—was intended to show how we can account for and justify the *objectivity* of knowledge. In his *Critique of Practical Reason* and his *Foundations of the Metaphysics of Morals*, Kant sought to explain and establish the *objective* foundation of morality.

Kant's *Critiques* are not independent inquiries but stages of a single, comprehensive critical inquiry. As long as we fail to make a rigorous distinction between the Is and the categorical Ought, as long as we fail to realize that all attempts to ground morality on experience cannot possibly succeed, we are doomed to heteronomy (and, one might add, moral relativism). A primary aim of Kant's philosophy was to demonstrate once and for all that there is a basic, universal, objective moral law for all rational beings. In the background of Kant's inquiry into morals is a dramatic Either/Or. *Either* there is a universal, objective moral law, *or* the concept of morality is groundless and vacuous.

But once the concept of a sharp and rigorous distinction between the Is and the categorical Ought is pushed to its extreme, it is as if Kant had sowed the seeds for undermining his own project. Kant's intention in pressing and clarifying a rigorous distinction between the Is and the Ought was to show us what he took to be the only possible way of grounding the moral law itself. But almost immediately philosophers began questioning, probing, and even ridiculing the Ought side of this great divide. Hegel, Kierkegaard, Nietzsche, Schopenhauer, contemporary existentialists like Sartre, and logical positivists—with different emphases and philosophic motivations—have questioned Kant's categorical imperative. All agree that there is something basically wrong with the claim that there is an objective moral law that can be grounded by an appeal to pure practical reason. The specter that haunts this multifaceted critique of Kant is moral relativism.[14]

But it is not only the arguments, critiques, and failures of philosophers that have led us to a variety of types of moral relativism. With the growth of the social sciences, and especially cultural and social anthropology, many have interpreted the evidence gained from studying different societies and cultures as fresh support for cultural and moral relativism.

In the social disciplines, the despair about the grounding of ultimate moral norms is poignantly illustrated by Max Weber. Weber too insisted on an ultimate and unbridgeable gap between the Is and the Ought, between what science can teach us about the world and our ultimate moral norms. In this respect he was a follower of Kant, although his understanding of the Is and the Ought differs from Kant's. But although Weber held that there are varied and subtle ways in which our scientific knowledge of what Is can influence our basic moral norms, he thought that neither science nor any *rational* discipline could lessen the burden of responsibility and decision that we must assume in choosing the "gods" or "demons" that we follow. Weber was at once a passionate moralist and a defender of science as a vocation who despaired about the possibility—and indeed the intelligibility—of discovering a rational ground for ultimate moral norms.[15]

Although many of the thinkers who have criticized Kant certainly did not regard themselves as moral relativists and might have been horrified that this conclusion can be drawn from their critiques, nevertheless some form of relativism seems to be an ineluctable consequence of the lines of inquiry they have pursued.[16] Nietzsche himself thought of such a relativism as a form of nihilism, the prevailing sickness that was spreading throughout Western culture and that he explored with such acuity. Yet it is a deeply troubling and perplexing question whether Nietzsche shows us any way out—any way to escape the nihilism that is so characteristic of modernity.

Until recently this struggle about the status and nature of morality has been developed against the background conviction that at least in science—especially in the natural sciences—we have clear and rigorous standards of objectivity, truth, rationality, progress, and the growth of knowledge (although we can also find a questioning of this dogma in Nietzsche). But in our own time serious doubts have been raised about the meaning and warrant for these claims. Whether, and in what sense, Thomas Kuhn is a relativist is an intricate question that I will explore in part II. But it is undeniable that many thinkers, especially philosophers, have perceived him and others who have developed similar positions as being relativists. Kuhn's claims about the incommensurability of rival paradigms and about the "circular reasoning" involved in supporting these paradigms have been interpreted as leading straight to relativism, subjectivism, and irrationalism. Although Kuhn has consistently denied that this is what he has claimed or that it is entailed by what he says, Feyerabend feels no hesitancy about defending "Protagorean relativism," claiming that such relativism is *"reasonable* because it pays attention to the pluralism of traditions and values," a pluralism that includes Reason as merely one among many different traditions and as having "as much (or as little) claim to the centre of the stage as any other tradition."[17] We will look closely, in part II, at the work of Kuhn and Feyerabend, and the interpretations of their work, to see how controversies concerning relativism which originally focused on moral, social, and political issues have now spread to our very understanding of the "hard core" of scientific knowledge.

But how are we to account for the tangled controversies that have grown up between objectivists and relativists? Why is it that today variations of this opposition seem to turn up almost everywhere? Why have relativists been unconvinced when objectivists argue, as they almost invariably do, that relativism is self-referentially inconsistent, self-defeating, and incoherent?[18] Why have objectivists been unmoved when time and time again it is shown that they have failed to make the case for the objective foundations for philosophy, knowledge, or language, and that the history of attempts to reveal such foundations must be judged thus far to be a history of failures?

We might try to answer these questions in a variety of ways. Perhaps, despite the self-understanding of many philosophers that they are the defenders of rational argument, the positions they take are influenced more by social practices, metaphors, matters of temperament, and other nonrational factors than the arguments upon which they place so much emphasis. Perhaps, despite grand claims about clear and distinct ideas, transcendental proofs, conceptual necessities, philosophy never has been and never will be more than a shifting battleground of competing opinions. But even if we are dubious about what can and cannot be achieved by philosophic argumentation, this does not help us to understand why the controversies between objectivists and relativists have become so pervasive and dominant today, or why so much passionate energy and polemic are exhibited in these debates, or why it is felt that the choice is such a "forced" and "momentous" one.

THE CARTESIAN ANXIETY

We can begin to answer these questions by concentrating on what I shall call the "Cartesian Anxiety." I do not want to suggest that this anxiety begins with Descartes or even that thinkers after Descartes have accepted it in the form in which it is found in his work. To speak of the Cartesian Anxiety is to speak of a construct, but one that is helpful for getting a grip on the primary issues.

Descartes' *Meditations* is the *locus classicus* in modern philosophy for the metaphor of the "foundation" and for the conviction that the philosopher's quest is to search for an Archimedean point upon which we can ground our knowledge. The opening of the first *Meditation* introduces the metaphor.

It is now some years since I detected how many were the false beliefs that I had from my earliest youth admitted as true, and how doubtful was everything I had since constructed on this basis; and from that time I was convinced that I must once for all seriously undertake to rid myself of all the opinions which I had formerly accepted, and commence to build anew from the foundation, if I wanted to establish any firm and permanent structure in the sciences."[19]

And in the second *Meditation* Descartes tells us that

Archimedes, in order that he might draw the terrestrial globe out of its place, and transport it elsewhere, demanded only that one point should be fixed and immoveable; in the same way I shall have the right to conceive high hopes if I am happy enough to discover one thing only which is certain and indubitable.[20]

We know that Descartes claimed to have discovered something that could serve as a foundation upon which we could construct a "firm and permanent structure in the sciences." It is less clear what is the Archimedean point in Descartes' philosophy—whether it is the *cogito* or God himself.

The *Meditations* has been read as the great rationalist treatise of modern times. Its potentially radical implications have inspired many because of Descartes' demand that we should not rely on unfounded opinions, prejudices, tradition, or external authority, but only upon the authority of reason itself. Few philosophers since Descartes have accepted his substantive claims, but there can be little doubt that the problems, metaphors, and questions that he bequeathed to us have been at the very center of philosophy since Descartes—problems concerning the foundations of knowledge and the sciences, mind–body dualism, our knowledge of the "external" world, how the mind "represents" this world, the nature of consciousness, thinking, and will, whether physical reality is to be understood as a grand mechanism, and how this is compatible with human freedom. Philosophers have been primarily concerned with the precise character and cogency of Descartes' *arguments.*

But another pervasive theme in the *Meditations,* although it is seldom directly addressed by professional philosophers, has a greater relevance for clarifying what I mean by the Cartesian Anxiety. The *Meditations* portray a journey of the soul, a meditative reflection on human finitude through which we gradually deepen our understanding of what it really means to be limited, finite creatures who are completely dependent on an all-powerful, beneficient, perfect, and infinite God. If we practice these spiritual exercises earnestly, as Descartes urges us to do, if we follow the precarious stages of this journey without losing our way, then we discover that this is a journey that is at once terrifying and liberating, culminating in the calm reassurance that although we are eminently fallible and subject to all sorts of contingencies, we can rest secure in the deepened self-knowledge that we are creatures of a beneficient God who has created us in his image. The terrifying quality of the journey is reflected in the allusions to madness, darkness, the dread of waking from a self-deceptive dream world, the fear of having "all of a sudden fallen into very deep water" where "I can neither make certain of setting my feet on the bottom, nor can I swim and so support myself on the surface,"[21] and the anxiety of imagining that I may be nothing more than a plaything of an all-powerful evil demon. But the more I probe my finitude, and realize how completely dependent I am on a beneficient God, for he sustains me at every moment of my existence, the more I can be liberated from this dread, fear, and anxiety. It is a spiritual journey that culminates with the assurance that I can and ought to

set aside all the doubts of these past days as hyperbolical and ridiculous. . . . For because God is in no wise a deceiver, it follows that I am not deceived in this. But because the exigencies of action often oblige us to make up our minds before having leisure to examine matters carefully, we must confess that the life of man is very frequently subject to error in respect to individual objects, and we must in the end acknowledge the infirmity of our nature.[22]

Reading the *Meditations* as a journey of the soul helps us to appreciate that Descartes' search for a foundation or Archimedean point is more than a device to solve metaphysical and epistemological problems. It is the quest for some fixed point, some stable rock upon which we can secure our lives against the vicissitudes that constantly threaten us.[23] The specter that hovers in the background of this journey is not just radical epistemological skepticism but the dread of madness and chaos where nothing is fixed, where we can neither touch bottom nor support ourselves on the surface. With a chilling clarity Descartes leads us with an apparent and ineluctable necessity to a grand and seductive Either/Or. *Either* there is some support for our being, a fixed foundation for our knowledge, *or* we cannot escape the forces of darkness that envelop us with madness, with intellectual and moral chaos. Even those commentators who have claimed that there is a hidden message revealed in the *Meditations* that is the very opposite of what the book seems to say on the surface do not lessen the grip of this Either/Or.[24]

Despite the almost ritualistic attempts of succeeding philosophers to overthrow and murder Descartes as the father figure of modern philosophy, and despite the many attempts to discredit the foundation metaphor that so deeply affects modern philosophy, this underlying Cartesian Anxiety still haunts us and hovers in the background of the controversies waged by objectivists and relativists. It is reflected and extended in the counterpart to Descartes' metaphors with which Kant begins his *Critique of Pure Reason*, when, in the opening sentences, he speaks of *reason* precipitating itself into "darkness and contradictions," or again when Kant pauses to reflect upon his transcendental analytic of pure understanding before embarking on his critique of dialectical illusion.

We have now not merely explored the territory of pure understanding, and carefully surveyed every part of it, but have also measured its extent, and assigned to everything in it its rightful place. This domain is an island, enclosed by nature itself within unalterable limits. It is the land of truth— enchanting name!—surrounded by a wide and stormy ocean, the native home of illusion, where many a fog bank and many a swiftly melting iceberg give the deceptive appearance of farther shores, deluding the adventurous seafarer ever anew with empty hopes, and engaging him in enterprises which he can never abandon and yet is unable to carry to completion.[25]

It would be a mistake to think that the Cartesian Anxiety is primarily a religious, metaphysical, epistemological, or moral anxiety. These are only several of the many forms it may assume. In Heideggerian language, it is "ontological" rather than "ontic," for it seems to lie at the very center of our being in the world. Our "god terms" may vary and be very different from those of Descartes. We may even purge ourselves of the quest for certainty and indubitability. But at the heart of the objectivist's vision, and what makes sense of his or her passion, is the belief that there are or must be some fixed, permanent constraints to which we can appeal and which are secure and stable. At its most profound level the relativist's message is that there are no such basic constraints except those that we invent or temporally (and temporarily) accept. Relativists are suspicious of their opponents because, the relativists claim, all species of objectivism almost inevitably turn into vulgar or sophisticated forms of ethnocentricism in which some privileged understanding of rationality is falsely legitimated by claiming for it an unwarranted universality. The primary reason why the *agōn* between objectivists and relativists has become so intense today is the growing apprehension that there may be nothing—not God, reason, philosophy, science, or poetry—that answers to and satisfies our longing for ultimate constraints, for a stable and reliable rock upon which we can secure our thought and action.

Thus far, I have given a preliminary characterization of what I mean by objectivism and relativism; have explained why this dichotomy is helpful in making sense of many of the philosophic conflicts that have broken out recently; and have singled out what I take to be the basic anxiety that underlies these conflicts. But it is important to emphasize that I am not primarily concerned with taking sides on this grand Either/Or or with assessing the strengths and weaknesses of the varieties of objectivism and relativism. On the contrary, I view this dichotomy as misleading and distortive. It is itself parasitic upon an acceptance of the Cartesian persuasion that needs to be questioned, exposed, and overcome. We need to *exorcize* the Cartesian Anxiety and liberate ourselves from its seductive appeal. Only if we implicitly accept some version of Cartesianism does the exclusive disjunction of objectivism or relativism become intelligible. But if we question, expose, and exorcise Cartesianism, then the very opposition of objectivism and relativism loses its plausibility. In the course of this investigation both the meaning of these categorical assertions and the reasons supporting them will be explicated. But what does exorcising the Cartesian Anxiety mean? What is beyond

objectivism and relativism? Where is the evidence that such a movement is really taking place? What are the consequences of this transformation for theory and practice, for thought and action? In order
to begin to specify more concretely and to answer these questions,
let me briefly review some of the recent philosophic controversies
that I will be examining in greater detail later on in this book, and
suggest some of the ways in which they are intimately related.

POSTEMPIRICIST PHILOSOPHY AND HISTORY OF SCIENCE

In what initially appear to be quite disparate contexts, controversies
have broken out about the meaning, nature, and scope of rationality.
But why is there a problem here? We have to recognize that we do
use the expression "rational" to characterize beliefs, arguments,
actions, agents, societies, theories, and even philosophic positions.
So the question arises, does the use of "rational" in these disparate
contexts have a univocal meaning? Is there something like analogical
meaning in these different uses of the term? Is the situation here one
of family resemblances? Or is there some other way of explicating
the meaning(s) of the word?

Some philosophers have argued that the only clear sense of
"rational" is applicable to arguments and that what is meant is that
the arguments conform to logical canons. But such a severe restric-
tion does not help us to understand what appear to be other legitimate uses of "rational." For example, we frequently think of science,
especially natural science, as a rational form of conduct. When we
say this, we mean more than that science consists of arguments that
conform to the canons of logical reasoning. But the real difficulty
(and obscurity) begins when we try to specify precisely what is the
"more" that is intended. In recent debates, issues concerning the
meaning and scope of rationality have become even more complex
and tangled because of the conviction that there are incommensurable paradigms, language games, or forms of life.

In the philosophy of the natural sciences, these issues have been
in the foreground of discussion since the publication of Thomas Kuhn's
The Structure of Scientific Revolutions in 1962. Viewing this book
in its historical context, it is now clear that many of Kuhn's controversial theses that seemed so fresh and original had been anticipated
by others. This does not diminish the significance or the impact that

his monograph had (and continues to have). It helps to explain it. Kuhn gave expression to and helped to identify issues that were erupting from a wide variety of sources. It is as if Kuhn had touched a sensitive intellectual nerve, and it would be difficult to name another book published in the last few decades that has been at once so suggestive and provocative for thinkers in almost every discipline and so persistently attacked and criticized, frequently from antithetical perspectives. Kuhn even remarks about his book, "Part of the reason for its success is, I regretfully conclude, that it can be too nearly all things to all people."[26]

Kuhn argued that there is something fundamentally wrong and askew with the image or conception of science that had been elaborated by most mainstream or "orthodox" philosophers of science, a conception that was itself a blending of deeply entrenched dogmas inherited from traditional empiricism and rationalism. He attempted to sketch an alternative "image of science" which he claimed did far greater justice to the ways in which scientific inquiry is actually conducted. The typical pattern of development that he outlines can be divided into a series of stages. It begins with a preparadigmatic stage where there is little or no agreement about subject matter, problems, and procedures among competing "schools." This school phenomenon is followed by the emergence and acceptance of a dominant paradigm by scientists—"universally recognized scientific achievements that for a time provide model problems and solutions to a community of practitioners."[27] Paradigms guide "normal science," a type of "puzzle solving" through which the dominant paradigm is made more determinate and precise as it is applied to new phenomena. The pursuit of normal science, with its increasing specificity and precision, leads to the discovery of discrepancies and anomalies that resist solution. Although the "fit" between a paradigm and "nature" is never perfect—there are always some discrepancies that the paradigm cannot explain—a stage may be reached at which there is a growing sense of crisis, a questioning about the adequacy of the very paradigm that has guided normal science. This is the stage when "extraordinary science" begins and when rival paradigms are proposed. Scientists do not reject or abandon a dominant paradigm, even when discrepancies and anomalies are discovered. What appears to be an anomaly or a problem that resists solution may turn out to be only an obstacle that can be overcome and explained without abandoning the prevailing paradigm. This is one reason why Kuhn thinks the appeal to falsification can be so misleading. Evidence that may appear to falsify an existing paradigm theory may turn out to be accounted for by adjusting or modifying the paradigm without abandoning it.[28] Nevertheless the situation may become critical when a rival paradigm is proposed, one that may be able to explain the troubling anomaly but is incompatible and incommensurable with the entrenched paradigm. At this point a battle takes place between adherents of the entrenched paradigm and the advocates of the new paradigm. According to Kuhn, in the controversies that arise when new and rival paradigms are proposed—a situation that he compares with political revolutions—there are no criteria of logical proof or any straightforward appeals to evidence that are *sufficient* to resolve the dispute. The differences that arise during a scientific revolution may be so great that any common agreement is lacking about what counts as a decisive argument in favor of the competing paradigms.

When Kuhn denied that the choice of theories or paradigms in scientific revolutions is a matter of proof or appeal to evidence, when he insisted that "proponents of competing paradigms are always at least slightly at cross purposes,"[29] when he compared switching paradigms to "gestalt switches" and spoke of such a switch as a type of conversion through which one comes to see the world differently, and when he asserted that "after a revolution scientists work in a different world"[30] he touched off a storm of protest. Explicit discussion of rationality did not play a significant role in *The Structure of Scientific Revolutions*, but many of Kuhn's critics were quick to argue that Kuhn's image of science was one that made science into an irrational, subjectivistic, relativistic activity where "mob psychology" rules.[31]

When I try to untangle the major issues involved in the disputes between Kuhn and his critics in a later discussion, I will show not only that such accusations misrepresent Kuhn's intentions but that there is much more agreement among Kuhn and his critics than one might expect, given the fierce polemics that have characterized these debates. Many of the disagreements among the participants (including Popper, Feyerabend, Lakatos, and Toulmin), when reexamined, begin to look like differences of emphasis rather than absolute cleavages. I will be concentrating on the common ground that emerges in what has been called the "postempiricist philosophy and history of science"[32] and in doing so will bring to the fore features of scientific inquiry that have been neglected by many accounts of the nature of science from the seventeenth century until the present.

Part of the reason why Kuhn's book caused such a stir is the Cartesian Anxiety. Neither Kuhn nor his critics were defending or advocating foundationalism. Indeed, one of the most persistent and incisive critics of foundationalism and the misguided search for the origins of knowledge has been Karl Popper (who is also one of Kuhn's major critics).[33] Nevertheless the search for an algorithm of theory-choice, or for clear and explicit criteria for demarcating science from nonscience, or for reconstructing the permanent standards that it is believed ought to govern the validation of scientific hypotheses and theories are legacies of Cartesianism in contemporary analytic philosophy of science. They reflect the demand that the philosopher of science be able to state explicit, determinate, fixed criteria and standards. The task of the philosopher of science is to give a rational reconstruction of science which will clearly and unambiguously specify these decision procedures, criteria, and standards. Kuhn is right in detecting that this quest has been at the very heart of the project of giving a rational reconstruction of science. So it is little wonder that when Kuhn declared that there is "no neutral algorithm for theory choice, no systematic decision procedure which, properly applied, must lead each individual in the group to the same decision"[34] his critics, especially philosophers, took him to be challenging the very rationality and objectivity of science. One reason why these controversies seem to generate more heat than light is that the entire discussion is still infected with the legacy of the Cartesian Either/Or; many of the participants in these disputes argue as if we must choose between the alternatives of objectivism (e.g., scientific realism) or relativism. But this way of framing the key issues is misleading. We gain a better insight into the positive achievement of the postempiricist philosophy and history of science when we appreciate that what is really going on is that the whole framework of thinking that poses issues with reference to these and related dichotomies is being called into question. The most significant outcome of these discussions is the tentative steps taken toward a post-Cartesian and postmodern understanding of rationality and the way in which it is manifested in scientific inquiry.

I agree with many of Kuhn's critics that much of what he says is ambiguous, unclear, and unsatisfactory and that his rhetoric frequently invites conflicting interpretations. However, a fairer and more generous reading of even *The Structure of Scientific Revolutions* shows that his intention was never to claim that scientific inquiry is irrational but rather to show the way to a more open, flexible, and historically oriented understanding of scientific inquiry as a rational activity. He is suggesting that we need to transform both our understanding of scientific inquiry and our concept of rationality.

Consequently it was disingenuous of Larry Laudan, in 1977 (fifteen years after the appearance of *The Structure of Scientific Revolutions*), to write as if he were saying something startling new when he made these statements;

Confronted by the acknowledged failure of the traditional analysis to shed much light on the rationality of knowledge, three alternatives seem to be open to us:

1.   We might continue to hope that some as yet undiscovered minor variation in the traditional analysis will eventually clarify and justify our intuitions about the cognitive well-foundedness of science and thus prove to be a worthy model of rationality.

2.   We might, alternatively, abandon the search for an adequate model of rationality as a lost cause, thereby accepting the thesis that science is, so far as we know, blatantly irrational.

3.   Finally, we might begin afresh to analyze the rationality of science, deliberately trying to avoid some of the key presuppositions which have produced the breakdown of the traditional analysis.[35]

Laudan claims that Kuhn has pursued the second alternative, and he interprets Kuhn as arguing that "choices between competing scientific theories, in the nature of the case, *must be irrational.*"[36] Not only is this a gross distortion of Kuhn's position, but it blinds us to an idea that is central to Kuhn's work and that has also been at the heart of the controversies in the postempiricist philosophy and history of science—the third alternative listed.

To speak of a new model of rationality may be misleading, because it suggests that there is more determinacy than has yet been achieved (or can be achieved). Nevertheless, what is striking is the growing awareness and agreement about the components of an adequate understanding of rationality as it pertains to scientific inquiry. There has been a dramatic shift in what is taken to be the significant epistemological unit for coming to grips with problems of the rationality of science. In the philosophy of science, and more generally in contemporary analytic epistemology, we have witnessed an internal dialectic that has moved from the preoccupation (virtually an obsession) with the isolated individual term, to the sentence or proposition, to the conceptual scheme or framework, to an ongoing historical tradition constituted by social practices—a movement from logical atomism to historical dynamic continuity. Awareness has been growing that attempts to state what are or ought to be the criteria for evaluating and validating scientific hypotheses and theories that are abstracted from existing social practices are threatened with a false rigidity or with pious vacuity and that existing criteria are always open to conflicting interpretations and applications and can be weighted in different ways. The effective standards and norms that are operative in scientific inquiry are subject to change and modification in the course of scientific inquiry. We are now aware that it is not only important to understand the role of tradition in science as mediated through research programs or research traditions but that we must understand how such traditions arise, develop, and become progressive and fertile, as well as the ways in which they can degenerate.

Other questions about scientific inquiry also come into prominence as a result of this shift of orientation. What is it that constitutes a scientific community? How are norms embodied in the social practices of such communities, and how do such communities reach objective—intersubjective—agreement? We must do justice to the ways in which such communities are committed to the regulative ideal of achieving a *rational* consensus and discern how this is compatible with individual initiative and forms of dissent that may question a prevailing consensus. When I examine the controversies concerning "incommensurability" (and the meaning of this term) later in this book, we will discover that while some of the apparently extreme claims made about the significance of incommensurability must be rejected, nevertheless an important truth emerges from these controversies that must be preserved in an adequate understanding of scientific inquiry as a rational process.

These issues will be explored subsequently, but in this preliminary overview, I want to turn to another area of controversy that shows some remarkable and deep parallels with the issues raised, the positions taken, and the strategies of argumentation used in the postempiricist philosophy and history of the natural sciences.

THE IDEA OF A SOCIAL SCIENCE

A few years prior to the appearance of Kuhn's *Structure of Scientific Revolutions* in 1962, another monograph appeared, Peter Winch's *The Idea of a Social Science and Its Relation to Philosophy* (London: Routledge & Kegan Paul, 1958). Like Kuhn's book, it was short, polemical, provocative, and ambiguous; it too touched off a controversy that has continued until the present.

Winch was not primarily concerned with giving an analysis of the natural sciences but rather with drawing a strong conceptual contrast between the natural and the social disciplines. Ironically (and the significance of this will soon be apparent), in drawing his contrast Winch virtually accepted the empiricist image of science that Kuhn and others (including Polanyi, Feyerabend, and Hanson) were discrediting and deconstructing. Against the mainstream of social scientists, Winch sought to show the conceptual confusion involved in thinking that the object, methods, and aim of the social disciplines are the same as or even analogous to those of the natural sciences. As he put the issue in one of his subsequent clarifications, he was interested in giving an analysis and exhibiting the distinctive, nonreducible "logical grammar" of the "concept of the social."[37] One of the many influences on Kuhn was the work of the later Wittgenstein, especially the increasing importance for Wittgenstein of language games and forms of life. In Winch, this aspect of Wittgenstein's investigations is the dominant influence. Winch was one of the first to suggest and try to show that not only the work of Wittgenstein but the linguistic turn in analytic philosophy had significant consequences for understanding social life and for gaining a new insight into what is (or ought to be) distinctive about the social disciplines. Social life is a form of rule-following activity, using the term "rule" in the sense in which Wittgenstein, according to Winch, used it in his *Philosophical Investigations*.

Whatever one's final judgment of the adequacy of Winch's claims, he must be given credit for showing the close relations between concerns that had previously been thought of as independent and unrelated—the type of analysis of language games that we find in Wittgenstein and analytic philosophy, and the concrete understanding of social life that we find in the social disciplines.[38] Until the appearance of Winch's monograph, the main issues in analytic philosophy had appeared to be irrelevant to serious concern with questions pertaining to the social disciplines and social life. But this is not the only connection that Winch made. He realized that there were analogies and subterranean connections between the type of insights that could be appropriated from Wittgenstein and those that were at the center of the tradition of interpretative sociology, especially as formulated by Max Weber (even though Winch criticizes Weber for making too many concessions to a naturalistic, scientific model of the social sciences).

Winch was not only breaking new ground but was going against the mainstream of the Anglo-American understanding of the nature of the social sciences. The prevailing attitude at the time among professional social scientists was that their discipline was now on the secure path of becoming a genuine natural science of individuals in society, a natural science that differed in degree and not in kind from the rest of the natural sciences. Progress in the social sciences, they argued, required adopting and following those methods, procedures, and criteria for testing hypotheses and theories that had proven so successful in the natural sciences. They therefore scorned "interpretive sociology," with its appeal to "subjective meaning," *Verstehen* (understanding), and such concepts as empathy and interpretation. There was a prevailing dogma that while a concept like *Verstehen* might have some value in helping to clarify how social scientists make good guesses and invent hypotheses (and therefore was relevant to the context of discovery), it was irrelevant to questions about the validation and testing of social scientific hypotheses and theories which are formulated to explain and predict social phenomena.[39] Winch not only stressed the logical gap and the logical incompatibility between natural and social science; he questioned whether the interpretations required for understanding social life can be checked by the appeal to the type of data which many social scientists took to be vital for their scientific endeavors. Thus, in contrast to Weber, who claimed that we can check the validity of sociological interpretations by appealing to "statistical laws based on observations of what happens," Winch wrote: "Against this, I want to insist that if a proffered interpretation is wrong, statistics, though they may suggest that that is so, are not the decisive and ultimate court of appeal for the validity of sociological interpretations in the way Weber suggests. What is then needed is a better interpretation, not something different in kind."[40]

But perhaps the most controversial aspect of Winch's analysis of the "concept of the social" was that it seemed to entail a new, sophisticated form of relativism. This is indicated by the very appeal to notions like language games and forms of life. For Winch seems to be suggesting that forms of life may be so radically different from each other that in order to understand and interpret alien or primitive societies we not only have to bracket our prejudices and biases but have to suspend our own Western standards and criteria of rationality. We may be confronted with standards of rationality about beliefs and actions that are incompatible with or incommensurable with our standards. When Winch published his subsequent essay, "Understanding a Primitive Society" (1964), which develops the line of thought introduced in *The Idea of a Social Science*, he used the figure of speech of "our standards" and "their standards" of rationality when speaking of modern Western society and the "primitive" society of the Azande.[41] Winch, like Kuhn, was attacking positivist models of knowledge and rationality. Like Kuhn, he was protesting against the pervasive ethnocentricism whereby we measure and judge what is initially strange and alien to us by "our" present standards, as if they were the sole and exclusive measure of rationality.

In one respect Winch was far less radical than Kuhn. He seemed to accept an empiricist reconstruction of natural science. He argued, however, that such a reconstruction was totally inadequate for understanding social life. But in another sense he suggested something that was far more radical than Kuhn. Kuhn, for all his claims about incommensurability of paradigms and theories, never doubted that there is a proper sense in which we can speak of Aristotle, Galileo, Newton, and Einstein as scientists—that there was something common to them, even though Kuhn strongly objected to the ways in which philosophers of science tried to account for this commonality. Indeed, Kuhn's problem was to give an account of science which would make sense of why we consider inquirers as different as Aristotle and Einstein to be scientists. But Winch's claim about the way in which societies differ—that the point and meaning of their activities might differ—was far more extreme than anything that Kuhn suggested. Using Kuhn's language, we might say that the "conversion" required for understanding an alien or primitive society is far more extreme than the type of conversion involved in understanding a new scientific paradigm.

Winch's work, like Kuhn's, touched off a wide-ranging and tangled dispute about the meaning (meanings) of rationality and the sense (senses) in which there are (or are not) universal standards of rationality.[42] This dispute has raged not only among philosophers but has also spread rapidly to practicing social scientists, especially anthropologists, for the issues concern not just a philosophic understanding of the social disciplines but the practice of these disciplines—the types of questions that are addressed and the proper ways of explaining and understanding alien societies. But to construe the main issue as the problem of defining standards of rationality—which is how most of the participants in the debate construe it—is misleading and mystifying. The vital issue here is really the question of what is involved in understanding, interpreting, and explaining alien societies (and not just their rationality or lack of rationality). How are we to do justice to the strangeness that we discover when we encounter alien types of activities, beliefs, rituals, institutions, and practices, without falsifying or distorting them?

Initially the debates about the meaning and scope of rationality in the philosophy of the natural sciences and in reflection on the social disciplines were conducted almost totally independently of each other. But in looking back over these controversies, one is struck by the deep similarities in the underlying issues raised. For example, Kuhn was perceived as a relativist (although he denied this charge); so was Winch. And just as Kuhn was seen as questioning the very possibility of the objectivity of scientific endeavor, so Winch was accused of making social science a matter of subjective taste. There are structural parallels in the very arguments that were brought against Kuhn and against Winch. In both cases objectivists were alarmed by what they took to be the writer's blatant relativism and its pernicious consequences. The significance of the practical-moral concern that, as I have already suggested, is essential for understanding the controversies about the natural sciences becomes even more apparent in the controversies about understanding primitive societies, different cultures, or even early epochs of our own culture. It becomes clear that Winch's primary concern is a practical-moral and critical one. The basic problem that is at the center of his work is to determine what is the best way to try to understand and interpret different cultures and societies so that we can learn from them. Winch is seeking the type of practical wisdom whereby we grasp the point of institutions and practices that initially seem to be strange and alien and become more sensitive to the pointlessness of many institutions and practices that we take for granted in our own society. "My aim," he tells us,

is not to engage in moralizing, but to suggest that the concept of *learning from* which is involved in the study of other cultures is closely linked with the concept of *wisdom*. We are confronted not just with different techniques, but with new possibilities of good and evil in relation to which men may come to terms with life.[43]

In the controversy that has surrounded Winch's work, the Cartesian Anxiety also hovers in the background. After all, at the heart of Cartesian (and indeed most modern and ancient) philosophy has been the conviction of the universality of reason and the belief that there are universal standards and criteria of rationality (however extensive or narrow we take human rationality to be). To use a figure of speech such as "our standards" and "their standards" seems to fly in the face of this tradition and certainly looks like a version of the type of skepticism and relativism that Descartes sought to defeat. But in this controversy also, I shall try to show that posing issues in this manner, as many of the participants have done, obscures the areas in which there has been a significant movement beyond objectivism and relativism.

THE RECOVERY OF THE HERMENEUTICAL DIMENSION OF SCIENCE

One way to begin to appreciate how these discussions converge and help to illuminate each other is to view them from the perspective of hermeneutics. As I have already mentioned, Winch was attempting to show how themes concerning the nature of meaning and action that were emerging from analytic philosophy, especially Wittgenstein's *Philosophical Investigations,* were related to the major themes in the continental tradition of interpretative sociology. But if we consider this latter tradition, it was itself part of the general discussion that was taking place during the nineteenth century concerning the relation of the *Naturwissenschaften* and the *Geisteswissenschaften.* Insofar as one strand in this complex discussion had been the claim that these two types of sciences are conceptually distinct, requiring different methods, Winch's arguments about the logical gap between the social and the natural can be understood as a linguistic version of the dichotomy between the *Naturwissenschaften* and the *Geisteswissenschaften.* Even the arguments that he uses to justify his claims sometimes read like a translation, in the new linguistic idiom, of those advanced by Dilthey.[44] Dilthey drew upon hermeneutics, especially as it had been developed by Schleiermacher, to bring out what he took to be both the distinctive subject matter and the method of the *Geisteswissenschaften,* especially "historical reason." In the twentieth century, both the understanding and the scope of hermeneutics have been dramatically extended by Heidegger and other thinkers working in the phenomenological tradition, including Hans-Georg Gadamer and Paul Ricoeur.

In contemporary reexaminations of the social disciplines there has been a recovery of the hermeneutical dimension, with its thematic emphasis on understanding and interpretation. This is also what has been happening in the postempiricist philosophy and history of science. Kuhn himself remarks in the preface to his recent collection of articles,

What I as a physicist had to discover for myself, most historians learn by example in the course of professional training. Consciously or not, they are all practitioners of the hermeneutic method. In my case, however, the discovery of hermeneutics did more than make history seem consequential. Its most immediate and decisive effect was instead on my view of science.[45]

And he also states,

The early models of the sort of history that has so influenced me and my *historical* colleagues is the product of a post-Kantian European tradition which I and my *philosophical* colleagues continue to find opaque. In my own case, for example, even the term "hermeneutic," to which I resorted briefly above, was no part of my vocabulary as recently as five years ago. Increasingly, I suspect that anyone who believes that history may have deep philosophical import will have to learn to bridge the longstanding divide between the Continental and English-language philosophical traditions.[46]

Kuhn sometimes uses the term "hermeneutic" in a weak sense to mean the type of sensitive reading that has always been considered essential in the hermeneutical tradition. The maxim that he offers to his students is one that we could find in almost any discussion of hermeneutics:

When reading the works of an important thinker, look first for the apparent absurdities in the text and ask yourself how a sensible person could have written them. When you find an answer, I continue, when those passages make sense, then you may find that more central passages, ones you previously thought you understood, have changed their meaning.[47]

Such a maxim might lead one to think that what I am calling the "recovery" of the hermeneutical dimension of science is limited to the task of writing the history of science. There is, however, a much stronger and much more consequential sense in which the hermeneutical dimension of science has been recovered. In the critique of naive and even of sophisticated forms of logical positivism and empiricism; in the questioning of the claims of the primacy of the hypothetical-deductive model of explanation; in the questioning of the sharp dichotomy that has been made between observation and theory (or observational and theoretical language); in the insistence on the underdetermination of theory by fact; and in the exploration of the ways in which all description and observation are theory-impregnated, we find claims and arguments that are consonant with those that have been at the very heart of hermeneutics, especially as the discipline has been discussed from the nineteenth century to the present.

This point has been effectively made by Mary Hesse. She lists five contrasts that have typically been drawn in the past between the natural sciences and the human sciences (*Geisteswissenschaften*):

1. In natural science experience is taken to be objective, testable, and independent of theoretical explanation. In human science data are not detachable from theory, for what count as data are determined in the light of some theoretical interpretation, and the facts themselves have to be reconstructed in the light of interpretation.

2. In natural science theories are artificial constructions or models, yielding explanation in the sense of a logic of hypothetico-deduction: *if* external nature were of such a kind, *then* data and experience would be as we find them. In human science theories are mimetic reconstructions of the facts themselves, and the criterion of a good theory is understanding of meanings and intentions rather than deductive explanation.

3. In natural science the lawlike relations asserted of experience are external, both to the objects connected and to the investigator, since they are merely correlational. In human science the relations asserted are internal, both because the objects studied are essentially constituted by their interrelations with one another, and also because the relations are mental, in the sense of being created by human categories of understanding recognized (or imposed?) by the investigator.

4. The language of natural science is exact, formalizable, and literal; therefore meanings are univocal, and a problem of meaning arises only in the application of universal categories to particulars. The language of human science is irreducibly equivocal and continually adapts itself to particulars.

5. Meanings in natural science are separate from facts. Meanings in human science are what constitute facts, for data consist of documents, inscriptions, intentional behaviour, social rules, human artefacts, and the like, and these are inseparable from their meanings for agents.

It follows, so it is held, that in natural science a oneway logic and method of interpretation is appropriate, since theory is dependent on self-subsistent facts, and testable by them. In human science, on the other hand, the "logic" of interpretation is irreducibly circular: part cannot be understood without whole, which itself depends on the relation of its parts; data and concepts cannot be understood without theory and context, which themselves depend on relations of data and concepts.[48]

Hesse notes that these contrasts have not always been clearly formulated, particularly in relation to the crucial concepts of meaning and interpretation. But the point that she emphasizes, and the one that I want to emphasize in this context, is the "natural science half of the dichotomy." As she emphatically notes:

What is immediately striking about it to readers versed in recent literature in philosophy of science is that almost every point made about the human sciences has recently been made about the natural sciences, and that the five points made about the natural sciences presuppose a traditional empiricist view of natural science that is almost universally discredited.[49]

Hesse summarizes the new, postempiricist account of natural science with explicit parallels to the five points of the dichotomy.

1. In natural science data [are] not detachable from theory, for what count as data are determined in the light of some theoretical interpretation, and the facts themselves have to be reconstructed in the light of interpretation.

2. In natural science theories are not models externally compared to nature in a hypothetico-deductive schema, they are the way the facts themselves are seen.

3. In natural science the lawlike relations asserted of experience are internal, because what count as facts are constituted by what the theory says about their inter-relations with one another.

4. The language of natural science is irreducibly metaphorical and inexact, and formalizable only at the cost of distortion of the historical dynamics of scientific development and of the imaginative constructions in terms of which nature is interpreted by science.

5. Meanings in natural science are determined by theory; they are understood by theoretical coherence rather than by correspondence with facts.[50]

One must be careful not to draw the wrong conclusions from these observations. Hesse is not saying, and it does not follow from what she says, that there are no important differences between natural science and human science. Rather, she asserts that standard ways of making the dichotomy are suspect.[51]

It would be a mistake to think that postempiricist philosophers of science have been directly influenced by hermeneutics. In the main, as Kuhn indicates in the passages we have cited, they have been virtually ignorant of the hermeneutical tradition. It is primarily because of the internal dialectic of contemporary philosophy of science, by reflection on and argumentation about a correct understanding of scientific inquiry, that they have stressed those features of science (and not just the study of science and its history) that are hermeneutical. But this coincidence and convergence should at least, in the manner suggested by Kuhn, open us to a serious confrontation with hermeneutics. In hermeneutics and some of its critiques we discover still another rationality debate. And here, too, the central issues bear on the Cartesian Anxiety and can themselves be interpreted as further evidence of the movement beyond objectivism and relativism.

PHILOSOPHIC HERMENEUTICS: A PRIMORDIAL MODE OF BEING

In 1960 (at approximately the same time that Kuhn's and Winch's monographs appeared), Hans-Georg Gadamer published *Wahrheit und Methode*. (The English translation, *Truth and Method*, was published in 1975.) Gadamer was sixty years old then, and the book, his magnum opus, represents a life's work of philosophic and hermeneutical reflection. Building on the work of Heidegger, or rather drawing on themes that are implicit in Heidegger and developing them in novel ways, Gadamer's book is one of the most comprehensive and subtle statements of the meaning and scope of hermeneutics to appear in our time. Hermeneutics, for Gadamer, is no longer restricted to the problem of Method in the *Geisteswissenschaften*; it moves to the very center of philosophy and is given an ontological turn; understanding, for Gadamer, is a primordial mode of our being in the world. Acknowledging his debt to Heidegger, Gadamer tells us:

On the basis of Heidegger's existential analysis of *Dasein*, with the many new perspectives that it implies for metaphysics, the function of hermeneutics in the human sciences also appears in a totally new light. While Heidegger resurrects the problem of Being in a form which goes far beyond all traditional metaphysics—he secures at the same time a radically new possibility in the face of the classical [*aporias*] of historicism: his concept of understanding carries an *ontological* weight. Moreover, understanding is no longer an *operation* antithetic and subsequent to the operations of the constitutive life, but a primordial mode of being of human life itself.[52]

At first sight it may appear as if Gadamer's primary concerns are foreign to those that have been dominant in the postempiricist philosophy and history of natural science and to the rationality debate that followed Winch's controversial claims about the social sciences. Natural science is not explicitly analyzed in *Truth and Method* but enters only obliquely as a manifestation of "Method" that is contrasted with Gadamer's probing of the "hermeneutical phenomenon." In *Truth and Method* Gadamer does not discuss such social sciences as economics, political science, sociology, or anthropology. He concentrates primarily on the experience of works of art, the understanding and interpretation of literary texts, and the study of history.

Nevertheless the claims that Gadamer makes for the ontological primacy and universality of hermeneutics have important consequences for our understanding of the natural and social sciences. When I turn later to a detailed examination of Gadamer's contribution, we will see that there is a basis for a dialogue between hermeneutics and our current understanding of the natural and social sciences. Despite the contrasts that Gadamer wants to draw between modern science and the type of knowledge and truth that we can achieve through hermeneutics, his own understanding of hermeneutics helps to deepen our understanding of the natural and social sciences. At the same time we can also use insights gained from recent investigations of the natural and social sciences to test the limits of Gadamer's conception of philosophic hermeneutics.

Here we touch upon a crucial ambiguity caused by the disparity between the Anglo-American and the German understanding of the nature of the social sciences. In the Anglo-American tradition, intellectual disciplines fall into the trichotomy of the natural sciences, social sciences, and humanities, but on the Continent they are categorized according to the dichotomy between the *Naturwissenschaften* and the *Geisteswissenschaften* (the expression that was introduced into German as a translation for what Mill called the "moral sciences"). In the main tradition of Anglo-American thought—at least until recently—the overwhelming bias has been to think of the social sciences as *natural sciences* concerning individuals in their social relations. The assumption has been that the social sciences differ in the degree and not in kind from the natural sciences and that ideally the methods and standards appropriate to the natural sciences can be extended by analogy to the social sciences. But in the German tradition there has been a much greater tendency to think of the social disciplines as forms of *Geisteswissenschaften* sharing essential characteristics with the humanistic disciplines. One of the reasons why Gadamer's work has received so much attention is because it appeared at a time when many thinkers were arguing that a proper understanding of the range of the social disciplines requires us to recognize the essential hermeneutical dimension of these disciplines.

There is an affinity between Gadamer's probing of the hermeneutical phenomenon and Winch's reflection on the role of under-

standing and interpretation of social life, although Gadamer goes
much further than Winch in stressing the universality of hermeneutics and showing the historicity of all understanding and interpretation.[53] This affinity goes deeper than attempting to show that there
are ways of understanding alien cultures and texts without imposing
our blind prejudices, even prejudices about rationality. As I have
suggested, in order to grasp the point of Winch's claims we must be
sensitive to his primary aim. To quote him again,

> My aim is not to engage in moralizing, but to suggest that the concept of
> *learning from* which is involved in the study of other cultures is closely
> linked with the concept of *wisdom*. We are confronted not just with different
> techniques, but with new possibilities of good and evil in relation to which
> men may come to terms with life.

It is precisely in and through an understanding of alien cultures that
we can come to a more sensitive and critical understanding of our
own culture and of those prejudices that may lie hidden from us. We
will see that this theme, which Gadamer relates to dialogue, questioning, and conversation, stands at the very center of Gadamer's
philosophic hermeneutics. For him this is the type of practical wisdom
that is characteristic of the ongoing interpretation of our own tradition.

A pervasive theme in *Truth and Method,* and indeed in all of
Gadamer's writings, is the critique of the Cartesian persuasion. Here,
too, Gadamer is building on the work of Heidegger, who probed the
phenomenon of the modern turn to subjectivity and traced it back
to its Cartesian roots. The idea of a basic dichotomy between the
subjective and the objective; the conception of knowledge as being a
correct representation of what is objective; the conviction that human
reason can completely free itself of bias, prejudice, and tradition; the
ideal of a universal method by which we can first secure firm foundations of knowledge and then build the edifice of a universal science;
the belief that by the power of self-reflection we can transcend our
historical context and horizon and know things as they really are in
themselves—all of these concepts are subjected to sustained criticism. In this respect there are significant parallels (as well as striking
differences) between Gadamer's and Heidegger's critique of Cartesianism and the critique of a philosopher who might seem to have
little in common with them, Charles Sanders Peirce.[54]

The novel and distinctive element in Gadamer's challenge to
Cartesianism is his argument that the Cartesian tradition shaped

and distorted nineteenth-century hermeneutics. According to Gadamer's reading, Dilthey implicitly accepted the Cartesian ideal of "Method" and "objective knowledge." Dilthey sought to meet the challenge, so forcefully argued by John Stuart Mill, that the so-called moral or human sciences are to be understood as empirical, inductive sciences differing only in degree from the natural sciences. But as Dilthey interpreted this challenge it meant showing that there is a distinctive subject matter and method appropriate to the *Geisteswissenschaften* that can equal and even rival the claim of the natural sciences to achieve "objective knowledge." For Gadamer, Dilthey was not sufficiently radical in questioning whether the ideal of objectivity, or more accurately the Cartesian understanding of objectivity, is appropriate for understanding the *Geisteswissenschaften* and the hermeneutical phenomenon.

Gadamer tells us:

The understanding and the interpretation of texts is not merely a concern of science, but is obviously part of the total human experience of the world. The hermeneutic phenomenon is basically not a problem of method at all. It is not concerned with a method of understanding, by means of which texts are subjected to scientific investigation like all other objects of experience. It is not concerned primarily with the amassing of ratified knowledge which satisfies the methodological ideal of science—yet it is concerned, here too, with knowledge and with truth. (*TM*, p. xi; *WM*, p. xxv)

Gadamer argues that there is an "inconsistency at the heart of Dilthey's thought," a result of his "latent Cartesianism."[55] Gadamer, in his own way, is seeking to exorcise the Cartesian Anxiety and to elaborate a way of thinking that moves beyond objectivism and relativism. For relativism, he thinks, is not only the dialectical antithesis of objectivism; it is itself parasitic upon objectivism.[56] What is most important in Gadamer's work is the way in which, through his questioning of the hermeneutical phenomenon, he begins to elaborate a way of thinking that is beyond objectivism and relativism and that recovers and explores "an entirely different notion of knowledge and truth."[57] The understanding of reason and rationality itself undergoes a subtle transformation in Gadamer's work.[58] For he rejects the oppositions that have been so entrenched since the Enlightenment—between reason and tradition, reason and prejudice, reason and authority. Reason is not a faculty or capacity that can free itself from its historical context and horizons. Reason is historical or situated reason which gains its distinctive power always within a living tradition. For Gadamer this is not a limitation or deficiency of reason, but rather the essence of reason rooted in human finitude.

HERMENEUTICS AND PRAXIS

One of the most challenging, intriguing, and important motifs in Gadamer's work is his effort to link his ontological hermeneutics with the tradition of practical philosophy, especially as it is rooted in Aristotle's understanding of *praxis* and *phronēsis*. Gadamer is well aware that initially this may seem to be a strange connection. After all, hermeneutics has been primarily concerned with the understanding and interpretation of texts, and this was certainly not Aristotle's concern in his ethical and political writings. Gadamer tells us,

It is true that Aristotle is not concerned with the hermeneutical problem and certainly not with its historical dimension, but with the right estimation of the role that reason has to play in moral action. But precisely what is of interest to us here is that he is concerned with reason and with knowledge, not detached from a being that is becoming, but determined by it and determinative of it. (*TM*, p. 278; *WM*, p. 295)

Gadamer even claims that

if we relate Aristotle's description of the ethical phenomenon and especially of the virtue of moral knowledge to our own investigation, we find that Aristotle's analysis is in fact a kind of model of the problems of hermeneutics. (*TM*, p. 289; *WM*, p. 307)

The specific context in *Truth and Method* where Gadamer explores the relevance of Aristotle to hermeneutics is the investigation of the moment of "application" or appropriation in the act of understanding. According to an earlier tradition of hermeneutics, three elements were distinguished: *subtilitas intelligendi* (understanding), *subtilitas explicandi* (interpretation), and *subtilitas applicandi* (application). But Gadamer argues—and this is one of the central theses of *Truth and Method*—that these are not three distinct moments or elements of hermeneutics. They are internally related; every act of understanding involves interpretation, and all interpretation involves application. It is Aristotle's analysis of *phronēsis* that, according to Gadamer, enables us to understand the distinctive way in which application is an essential moment of the hermeneutical experience.

The intimate link that Gadamer seeks to establish between hermeneutics and the tradition of practical philosophy that has its origins in Greek philosophy is not an afterthought or merely incidental to his understanding of philosophic hermeneutics. It is a key for appreciating what he means by philosophic hermeneutics. Not only do we find in Gadamer an extraordinarily incisive interpretation of what Aristotle means by *phronēsis* and the ways in which he distinguishes *phronēsis* from both *epistēmē* and *technē;* the creative use Gadamer makes of Aristotle and the tradition of practical philosophy is far richer.[59] Gadamer's interpretation of Aristotle is an exemplification of what he means by opening ourselves to the truth that speaks to us through tradition. It is also the basis for his claim that the *Geisteswissenschaften* are genuine *moral* sciences. Furthermore, it is Aristotle's understanding of *praxis* and *phronēsis* that can enable us to come to grips with what Gadamer takes to be the most poignant problem in the modern world.

> When Aristotle, in the sixth book of the *Nicomachean Ethics*, distinguishes the manner of "practical" knowledge . . . from theoretical and technical knowledge, he expresses, in my opinion, one of the greatest truths by which the Greeks throw light upon "scientific" mystification of modern society of specialization. In addition, the scientific character of practical philosophy is, as far as I can see, the only methodological model for self-understanding of the human sciences if they are to be liberated from the spurious narrowing imposed by the model of the natural sciences.[60]

Or again, he writes:

> In my own eyes, the great merit of Aristotle was that he anticipated the impasse of our scientific culture by his description of the structure of practical reason as distinct from theoretical knowledge and technical skill. By philosophical arguments he refuted the claim of the professional lawmakers whose function at that time corresponded to the role of the expert in the modern scientific society. Of course, I do not mean to equate the modern expert with the professional sophist. In his own field he is a faithful and reliable investigator, and in general he is well aware of the particularity of his methodical assumptions and realizes that the results of his investigation have a limited relevance. Nevertheless, the problem of our society is that the longing of the citizenry for orientation and normative patterns invests the expert with an exaggerated authority. Modern society expects him to provide a substitute for past moral and political orientations. Consequently, the concept of '*praxis*' which was developed in the last two centuries is an awful deformation of what practice really is. In all the debates of the last century practice was understood as application of science to technical tasks. . . . It degrades practical reason to technical control.[61]

It would be a mistake to think that Gadamer is advocating some sort of nostalgic return to Aristotle. The thrust of his philosophic reflections moves in a very different direction. For the temporal distance between ourselves and Aristotle does not permit a return to Aristotle—Gadamer knows this is impossible—but rather a critical appropriation of Aristotle's insights about practical reason that we seek to make relevant to our questions and problems.[62] Philosophic hermeneutics is the heir of this tradition of practical philosophy:

I think, then, that the chief task of philosophy is to justify this way of reason and to defend practical and political reason against the domination of technology based on science. That is the point of philosophical hermeneutic. It corrects the peculiar falsehood of modern consciousness: the idolatry of scientific method and of the anonymous authority of the sciences and it vindicates again the noblest task of the citizen—decision-making according to one's own responsibility—instead of conceding that task to the expert. In this respect, hermeneutic philosophy is the heir of the older tradition of practical philosophy.[63]

With this interlacing of hermeneutics and *praxis*, the threefold interconnection of science, hermeneutics and *praxis* becomes explicit. Contemporary reflections on the character of the natural and the social sciences have led to a recovery of the hermeneutical dimension of these disciplines and to an encounter with the hermeneutical tradition. A common theme running through all these discussions is the movement beyond objectivism and relativism and the attempt to exorcise the Cartesian Anxiety. But thinking through the nature and grounds of hermeneutics as it has been probed by Heidegger and Gadamer leads to a confrontation with the understanding of *praxis* and *phronēsis*. According to Gadamer, not only is philosophic hermeneutics the proper heir of the tradition of practical philosophy, but the type of judgment and reasoning exhibited in all understanding is itself a form of *phronēsis*. I have suggested that we gain a more textured understanding of the postempiricist philosophy and history of science, as well as of the recent debates about the nature of the social and political disciplines, when we approach them from the perspective of the hermeneutical tradition. We gain an even more penetrating understanding when we pursue the intimate relations between hermeneutics and *praxis*. This will become clear when we see that the type of rationality that Kuhn has been struggling to articulate when dealing with the complex issues of theory-choice and paradigm switches—his insistence that reasons function as values which can be differently weighted and applied to concrete situations, and his defense of the role of judgment in making choices and decisions—are closely related to Gadamer's analysis of *phronēsis* and the role that it plays in all understanding and interpretation. There is a groping quality in Kuhn's several attempts to clarify the characteristics of the type of argumentation that is involved in choosing among rival paradigms. It is as if he has been searching for a proper model to express his awareness that such deliberation and choosing are rational activities, but not the sort of rational activity that has been characterized as deductive proof or empirical verification or falsification. I will argue that without being completely aware of what he is doing Kuhn is appealing to a conception of rationality that has been at the core of tradition of practical philosophy that Gadamer seeks to disclose and revive. In seeking to appreciate the basic orientation of Winch's work, too—an orientation that helps to set the context for his discussion of "our standards" and "their standards"—we need to be sensitive to his practical-moral stance. Here, too, we will discover latent affinities with the tradition of practical philosophy and wisdom.

The appearance of Winch's *Idea of a Social Science* in 1958 and the publication of Kuhn's *Structure of Scientific Revolutions* in 1962 were catalysts for complex, nuanced, and wide-ranging debates and controversies. Similar discussions occurred when Gadamer's *Wahrheit und Methode* was published in 1960. For heuristic purposes we can distinguish three closely related foci to the controversies that the book generated.[64] The first concerns the significance of philosophic or ontological hermeneutics for biblical interpretation and more generally for the interpretation of religious traditions. Since the time of the Reformation, one primary strand in the tradition of hermeneutics had been its relevance for the understanding and interpretation of sacred texts. The work of Heidegger, Gadamer, Ricoeur, and Bultmann provides new challenges to those concerned with biblical narrative, the interpretation of religious traditions, and the role that theology might play in the twentieth century.

The second focus concerns the significance of Heidegger's and Gadamer's reflections on hermeneutics for the understanding and interpretation of legal and literary texts. The Italian scholar Emilio Betti has been an arch rival to Gadamer as the interpreter of the hermeneutical tradition. In his major work, translated into German in 1962, *Die Hermeneutik als allgemeine Methodik der Geisteswissenschaften*, and in E. D. Hirsch, Jr.'s *Validity in Interpretation*, published in 1967 (which owes a great deal to Betti), it is forcefully argued that Heidegger and Gadamer lead us to a self-defeating historicism and relativism.[65] Against Gadamer, both argue that it is crucial to distinguish and separate the three traditional moments of hermeneutics that Gadamer blends together: understanding, interpretation, and application.

The third focus—and the one that I intend to explore in greater detail—concerns the significance and challenge of philosophic hermeneutics for understanding the nature of the social and political disciplines. From the beginning of his intellectual career Gadamer has always had an interest in the tradition of practical philosophy, especially as it emerges in Plato and Aristotle. It is also clear that a decisive intellectual event that deeply affected Gadamer's own distinctive practice and interpretation of hermeneutics was his participation in Heidegger's seminar (1923) on Aristotle's *Nicomachean Ethics*.[66] But it was as a result of criticism of Gadamer's work that this aspect of his thinking was brought into the foreground. In the twenty years since the publication of *Wahrheit und Methode*, Gadamer has returned again and again to the theme of the practical implications of hermeneutics and its significance for understanding the limits and role of the social and political disciplines.[67] It is not entirely inaccurate to claim that this aspect of Gadamer's thinking has come into so much prominence because it was at once underscored and sharply criticized by Jürgen Habermas.[68] But others besides Habermas drew attention to the significance and limitations of philosophic hermeneutics for the social and political disciplines. This is also a key idea in the work of Karl-Otto Apel and Albrecht Wellmer.[69] Since the initial confrontation between Gadamer and Habermas, beginning with Habermas's critical review of *Wahrheit und Methode*, there has been an extensive literature on what has come to be labeled the "Gadamer–Habermas debate."[70] I will be exploring some of the issues raised in this debate and will try to show how it is related to the other rationality debates in the philosophy of the natural and social sciences. My aim will be to show that the latent issues in this debate, and the responses and counter-responses by Gadamer and Habermas (and others), are a further contribution to the movement beyond objectivism and relativism. But in this preliminary overview I simply want to suggest why the interest in, and limitations of, philosophic hermeneutics was so important for Habermas. Quite independently of any direct influence by Heidegger or Gadamer, Habermas was already engaged in a critical reexamination of the social and political disciplines and the legacy of positivism in the twentieth century.[71] Working within a Hegelian-Marxist tradition, he argued that any adequate social and political theory must involve an interpretative or hermeneutical dimension. Habermas realized that Gadamer had developed one of the strongest and most persuasive arguments showing the importance of this dimension of human knowledge. But at the same time Habermas was skeptical of the universalistic claims of hermeneutics and argued that philosophic hermeneutics underestimated and distorted the role of a scientific understanding of social life. Philosophic hermeneutics lacked an explicit critical function, which is so vital for an adequate social theory. What was needed is a "depth hermeneutics" which would do justice to the role of *work* and *power* (not just language and communication) in the understanding of culture and society. Against Gadamer, who tended to contrast scientific method with the hermeneutical phenomenon, Habermas argued for the necessity of a dialectical synthesis of empirical-analytic science and hermeneutics into a critical theory that has a practical intent and is governed by an emancipatory cognitive interest.[72]

We can state the primary issue in a slightly different manner. Habermas thought that one of Gadamer's most significant contributions was the explicit linking of hermeneutics to application, or more generally to *praxis*.[73] But at the same time he argued that Gadamer's own understanding of *praxis* and his belief that Aristotle's conception of *praxis* is "the model for self-understanding of the human science" would not stand up to critical scrutiny.[74] Habermas certainly agreed with Gadamer's claim that "the concept of 'praxis' which was developed in the last two centuries is an awful deformation of what practice really is."[75] And Gadamer would certainly endorse the following statement by Habermas:

The real difficulty in the relation of theory and praxis does not arise from this new function of science as a technological force, but rather from the fact that we are no longer able to distinguish between practical and technical power. Yet even a civilization that has been rendered scientific is not granted dispensation from practical questions; therefore a peculiar danger arises when the process of scientification transgresses the limit of technical questions, without, however, departing from the level of reflection of a rationality confined to the technological horizon. For then no attempt is made to attain a rational consensus on the part of citizens concerning the practical control of their destiny. Its place is taken by the attempt to attain technical control over history by perfecting the administration of society, an attempt that is just as impractical as it is unhistorical.[76]

But while there is common agreement between Gadamer and Habermas about the pressures in modern society to confuse and deform genuinely practical questions with technical and strategic issues, and both seek to defend the autonomy and legitimacy of a *praxis* that is distinguishable from *technē*, they disagree about precisely what this means and its consequences. Many of their differences are related to their different understandings of *praxis*, the features of *praxis* that they highlight, and especially the nature and role of reason as it pertains to *praxis*.

POLITICAL JUDGMENT AND PRACTICAL DISCOURSE

The issues that come into prominence in the differing emphases of Gadamer and Habermas open us to a much broader dimension in the new conversation about human rationality. My purpose in introducing the "Gadamer–Habermas debate" is to emphasize the more general way in which the analysis of *praxis*, *phronēsis*, practical discourse, and political judgment (all of which are intimately related) has entered this new conversation. The critiques of the varieties of scienticism, positivism, behaviorism, and methodism are shared by a much larger group of thinkers who have sought in different ways to recover the meaning of *praxis* and to show its relevance to contemporary society. These have been major themes in the work of Hannah Arendt, whose investigation of the human condition focuses on the *vita activa*, with the threefold distinction of labor, work, and action (*praxis*).[77] She too warns us about the current danger of forgetting what action or *praxis* really is—the highest form of human activity, manifested in speech and deed and rooted in the human condition of plurality. She also argues that in the modern age a fabricating or means–end mentality (*technē*) and a laboring mentality have distorted and corrupted *praxis*. Her analysis of the public space of appearance in the *polis* has many parallels with Habermas's analysis of communicative action that is oriented toward mutual understanding.[78] Some dimensions of her analysis of political judgment have an affinity with Gadamer's own analysis of *phronēsis* and judgment.[79] But the common ground that is shared by Arendt, Gadamer, and Habermas enables us to appreciate the sharp and consequential differences among them in their reflections on the meaning and role of *praxis* in the contemporary world.

We find similar motifs in a variety of other political thinkers including Charles Taylor, Hanna Pitkin, and Sheldon Wolin.[80] Consider, for example, Sheldon Wolin's essay, "Political Theory as a Vocation." When we compare this essay with the writings of Gadamer and Feyerabend, structural similarities leap to view. All three examine and criticize the modern obsession with Method. All three trace this back to the Cartesian legacy. Feyerabend's attack on Method is directed against what he takes to be the invidious consequences that the obsession with Method has had for the understanding of the natural sciences. Gadamer is constantly battling against the intrusion of method into hermeneutics and the *Geisteswissenschaften*. Wolin seeks to show how "methodism" has infected and distorted the discipline of political science. Method is not innocent or neutral. It not only presupposes an understanding of what constitutes social and political life; it has become a powerful factor in shaping (or rather misshaping) human life in the modern world. Wolin makes fully explicit the practical–moral concern that lies at the heart of the writings of Feyerabend and Gadamer when he tells us that the *vita methodi* "avoids fundamental criticism and fundamental commitment," and that far from being an innocent, epistemological, neutral ideal it is a "proposal for shaping the mind"—a proposal that all three see as having ominous consequences.[81] Against the *vita methodi*, Wolin defends the *bios theoretikos*, and at the heart of his understanding of this form of life is judgment. The following passage by Wolin might have been written by Gadamer, for it approximates Gadamer's own understanding of the quintessence of political judgment.

What is political wisdom? Put in this vague form, the question is unanswerable, but it may be reformulated so as to be fruitful. The antithesis between political wisdom and political science basically concerns two different forms of knowledge. The scientific form represents the search for rigorous formulations which are logically consistent and empirically testable. As a form, it has the qualities of compactness, manipulability, and relative independence of context. Political wisdom is an unfortunate phrase, for . . . the question is not *what* it is but *in what* does it inhere. History, knowledge of institutions, and legal analysis [are relevant] . . . knowledge of past political theories might also be added. Taken as a whole, this composite type of knowledge presents a contrast with the scientific type. Its mode of activity is not so much the style of the search as of reflection. It is mindful of logic, but more so of the incoherence and contradictoriness of experience. And for the same reason, it is distrustful of rigor. Political life does not yield its significance to terse hypotheses but is elusive, and hence meaningful statements about it often have to be allusive and intimative. Context becomes supremely important, for actions and events occur in no other setting. Knowledge of this type tends, therefore, to be suggestive and illuminative rather than explicit and determinate. Borrowing from M. Polanyi, we shall call it "tacit political knowledge."[82]

SCIENCE, HERMENEUTICS, AND PRAXIS

It may seem that I have wandered quite far from the issues involved in the movement beyond objectivism and relativism. One may be genuinely perplexed about what political wisdom and the tradition of practical philosophy has to do with the character of rationality in the natural sciences and the type of argumentation required for theory-choice or paradigm switches. There may be legitimate suspicion that the interrelationships of science, hermeneutics, and *praxis* that I have been adumbrating are more suggestive than substantive. Finally, there may be a proper skepticism about my constant references to a new conversation, a feeling that this expresses more of a pious hope than a living reality. The reader rightly demands a working out or working through of the suggestions that I have been making that will clarify, test, and support my claims. My objective thus far has been to provide an orientation, to convey a sense of the underlying questions, and to suggest how I plan to go about probing and answering them.

In turning to the working out of this project, I begin with the self-understanding of the nature of science, its essential character and scope. It is our cultural understanding of science, especially the physical sciences, and the remarkable "success" of the scientific enterprise since its modern origins that has set the context for the intellectual and cultural problems in the modern world. Hermeneutics, as that discipline took shape in the nineteenth century, has been a defensive reaction against the universalistic and reductivistic claims made in the name of the sciences. Every defender of hermeneutics, and more generally the humanistic tradition, has had to confront the persistent claim that it is science and science alone that is the measure of reality, knowledge, and truth. As for *praxis* and *phronēsis*, these concepts are suspect once we are in the grips of the Cartesian legacy. There are deep cultural reasons and causes—as Gadamer, Arendt, and Habermas have argued—why in the modern world the only concept of reason that seems to make sense is one in which we think of reason as an instrument for determining the most efficient or effective means to a determinate end, and why the only concept of activity that seems viable is one of technical application, manipulation, and control. Once we are caught into thinking that the subjective–objective distinction is a fundamental one that arises as soon as anyone reflects and we pursue the variations of this distinction until the subjective becomes virtually synonymous with the private, idiosyncratic, and arbitrary, then the very idea of *phronēsis* seems like a confused concept. Knowledge must be objective— or else it is only pseudo-knowledge. When values enter, they must be treated as noncognitive emotional responses or private subjective preferences. From this perspective, especially in its positivist variants, talk of practical or political wisdom and *phronēsis* as a special type of rational activity may have a certain charm but fails to live up to the promise of serious scientific knowledge.

In contrast to the overwhelming bias which this invidious contrast between wisdom and science reflects and the obsession of many modern thinkers with *epistēmē* and science, the development that is becoming increasingly evident in the new conversation is an inversion.[83] It can be misleading to think of this inversion as the "primacy of the practical," insofar as we still accept traditional and modern contrasts between the "theoretical" and the "practical." One must be sensitive to and acknowledge the important differences between the nature of scientific knowledge and other forms of knowledge, but the more closely we examine the nature of this scientific knowledge that has become the paradigm of theoretical knowledge, the more we realize that the character of rationality in the sciences, especially in matters of theory-choice, is closer to those features of rationality that have been characteristic of the tradition of practical philosophy than to many of the modern images of what is supposed to be the character of genuine *epistēmē*.[84]

There is a deep irony in the tradition that Aristotle helped to initiate. Aristotle is at once one of the noblest defenders of the autonomy and integrity of *praxis* and *phronēsis* and also the philosopher who sowed the seeds for the denigration of practical philosophy. The expression "practical philosophy" is virtually self-contradictory, because philosophy as the love of *sophia* is something higher and more divine than *phronēsis*. In the tenth book of the *Nicomachean Ethics*, a book that has been so problematic for many scholars of Aristotle,[85] Aristotle, returning to the theme of happiness, states that "happiness consists in contemplation may be accepted as agreeing both with the results already reached and with the truth."[86] The life consisting of the pure *activity* of contemplation is more than truly human; it is godlike, divine. Compared to this, "the life of moral virtue . . . is happy only in a secondary degree."[87] *Praxis* in morals and politics is only second best to the highest form of activity, *theoria*, which is intimately related to *sophia*, *nous*, and *epistēmē*. Although the differences between modern conceptions of *epistēmē*, especially as shaped by the Cartesian legacy, and the more ancient understanding of *epistēmē* are as striking as similarities, the prejudice suggested by Aristotle's contrasts has worked itself out with a vengeance in modern thought. It has become a well-entrenched dogma of modern thought that only after we resolve the "hard" issues of epistemology and come to grips with scientific knowledge can we turn to the "softer" and "fuzzier" concerns of moral, social, and political philosophy. This is a prejudice that is being questioned in the new conversation about human rationality.

To conclude part I and set the context for my investigation of the postempiricist philosophy and history of science, let me summarize from a slightly different perspective. Ever since the origins of modern science, the typical strategy of scientifically minded philosophers, when confronted with the claim that there are other forms of knowledge in addition to those evidenced in the formal and natural sciences, has been to argue that whatever is legitimate, acceptable, or rational in these presumably "other" forms of knowledge can be assimilated, translated, or reduced to the canons of scientific discourse. What cannot be assimilated, translated or reduced must be rejected as pseudo-knowledge. In this respect, logical positivism and empiricism are continuous with the older traditions of empiricism and rationalism. But whenever the implicit scientism (science is the only measure of what counts as knowledge and reality) has been pressed to the extreme, there have always been those who have argued that such a scientism is deficient; it leaves out something vitally important, or it fails to recognize that there are other legitimate forms of experience and knowledge. But typically (although not universally), defenders of these other modes of knowledge and experience, whether they draw their inspiration from the classical humanistic disciplines or the tradition of practical philosophy and wisdom, have explicitly or implicitly accepted the self-understanding of the natural sciences that has been advocated by their "tough-minded" opponents. The tangled debates that we will examine have taken place within this framework of commonly shared assumptions about the characteristics of science and Method. Each time some philosopher comes up with what he or she takes to be a new argument or insight showing why one cannot assimilate or reduce all forms of knowledge to the canonical forms of the formal and natural sciences, there have always been an ample supply of tough-minded types who have countered with arguments that, at best, their opponents have noted some "practical" difficulties but certainly not any genuine "theoretical" obstacles to the essential unity of all science and the reduction of the several sciences to a single all-encompassing universal science.[88] The *dramatis personae* change: Descartes versus Vico, Comte or Mill versus Dilthey, positivists and logical empiricists versus ordinary language philosophers and phenomenologists. Although it is likely that this type of opposition will continue, a new pattern in the conversation concerning human rationality is now taking shape:

the very framework, the unacknowledged assumptions and metaphors that have kept these debates alive are now being called into question. With this questioning and probing, new continuities (and differences) among science, hermeneutics, and *praxis* are becoming increasingly manifest. It is now my task to show this in detail and to justify my central thesis that we are witnessing and participating in a movement beyond objectivism and relativism.

PART TWO
SCIENCE, RATIONALITY, AND INCOMMENSURABILITY

WITH elegant conciseness William James described "the classic stages of a theory's career. First, you know, a new theory is attacked as absurd; then it is admitted to be true, but obvious and insignificant; finally it is seen to be so important that its adversaries claim that they themselves discovered it."[1] Something like this has already occurred with the theory advanced by Thomas Kuhn in the twenty years since the publication of *The Structure of Scientific Revolutions*. The reaction to the book by its critics was immediate and sharp: Kuhn's leading ideas were absurd, contradictory, and wrong.[2] It was even suggested that they were immoral and irrational. His views were caricatured and ridiculed.[3] After the first flurry of heated polemic, calmer voices came to his defense and argued that although not without difficulties and ambiguities, many of his theses were warranted[4]—though some said that what was true in Kuhn was "obvious and insignificant." Finally, there are those who, while claiming that Kuhn has been refuted or is now passé, nevertheless go on to incorporate similar theses in their own distinctive contributions to the history and philosophy of science.[5]

THE PRACTICAL RATIONALITY OF THEORY-CHOICE

In the massive literature that has gathered around Kuhn's work, one theme has not been sufficiently stressed—the extent to which Kuhn was still caught in the idiom of positivism and logical empiricism that he sought to criticize and replace. Yet this positivist vestige helps us to understand some of the controversy that his work has generated. To put the issue simply and boldly, when Kuhn came to consider the character of scientific revolutions and the nature of the disputes that take place between adherents of rival paradigm theories, his fundamental insight was that traditional conceptions of such disputes break down; they are inapplicable and unilluminating. The type of argumentation that takes place at times of scientific crises and revolutions can be resolved neither by an appeal to the canons of deductive logic or proof nor by any straightforward appeal to observation, verification, confirmation, or falsification. This is the context within which Kuhn introduces the controversial notion of "persuasion" and its related concept of "conversion." He tells us that in the "battles" that are fought between adherents of rival paradigm theories (note the blending of provocative religious and political-military metaphors), "Though each may hope to convert the other to his way of seeing his science and its problems, neither may hope to prove his case. The competition between paradigms is not the sort of battle that can be resolved by proofs." And again, "the transfer of allegiance from paradigm to paradigm is a conversion experience that cannot be forced." If we ask how such "conversions" are induced, then we must turn to the "techniques of persuasion" and ask about "argument and counterargument in a situation in which there can be no proof."[6]

What has not been fully appreciated is how closely Kuhn's language and strategy parallel the reaction of the logical positivists when they were confronted by an analogous problem in a different context. Initially they thought that they could sharply distinguish analytic and synthetic propositions or sentences, and thereby clarify the only two types of cognitively meaningful discourse. But they realized that so-called ethical sentences do not fit into either of these neat categories. Consequently, when they sought to make sense of what takes place in ethical disputes (when questions of fact are not at issue), they claimed that such disputes can be properly understood only as a form of *persuasion* in which each of the disputants tries to *convert* an opponent to adopt his or her *noncognitive* attitude.[7] Just as there was a strong reaction against this strategy and against the underlying emotive theory of ethics with its blatant noncognitivism, so we find a parallel in those who accuse Kuhn of sanctioning some sort of irrationality, subjectivism, or mob psychology in the battle of rival paradigms. In effect, Kuhn has been charged with advocating noncognitivism in matters of scientific dispute, a view which to many seems patently absurd.

Despite those who claim that every time Kuhn has attempted to clarify his original meaning he is in effect rewriting his own history or changing his mind,[8] a sympathetic reading of *The Structure of Scientific Revolutions* shows that Kuhn always intended to distinguish forms of rational persuasion and argumentation that take place in scientific communities from those irrational forms of persuasion that he has been accused of endorsing.[9] In this respect there has been a move or clarification that reveals that Kuhn is much closer to the "good reasons" approach in ethics that came to replace the stark emotivism of the early logical positivists. I emphasize that this was (and is) Kuhn's intention, and not that he has successfully clarified how we are to make the distinction between good and bad reasons. Let me cite some relevant passages:

Nothing about that relatively familiar thesis [that theory-choice is not simply a matter of deductive proof] implies either that there are no good reasons for being persuaded or that those reasons are not ultimately *decisive for the group.* Nor does it even imply that the reasons for choice are different from those usually listed by philosophers of science: accuracy, simplicity, fruitfulness, and the like. What it should suggest, however, is that such reasons function as values and that they can thus be differently applied, individually and collectively, by men who concur in honoring them. If two men disagree, for example, about the relative fruitfulness of their theories, or if they agree about that but disagree about the relative importance of fruitfulness and, say, scope in reaching a choice, neither can be convicted of a mistake. Nor is either being unscientific. *There is no neutral algorithm for theory-choice, no systematic decision procedure which, properly applied, must lead each individual in the group to the same decision.* (Italics added, pp. 199–200)

Or, in a similar vein, he writes:

What I am denying then is neither the existence of good reasons nor that these reasons are of the sort usually described. I am, however, insisting that such reasons constitute values to be used in making choices rather than rules of choice. Scientists who share them may nevertheless make different choices in the same concrete situation. Two factors are deeply involved. First, in many concrete situations, different values, though all constitutive of good reasons, dictate different conclusions, different choices. In such cases of value-conflict (e.g., one theory is simpler but the other is more accurate) the relative weight placed on different values by different individuals can play a decisive role in individual choice. More important, though scientists share these values and must continue to do so if science is to survive, they do not all apply them in the same way. Simplicity, scope, fruitfulness, and even accuracy can be judged quite differently (which is not to say they may be judged arbitrarily) by different people. Again, they may differ in their conclusions without violating any accepted rule.[10]

Kuhn never clearly analyzes what he means by "values," but it is not accidental that he uses the language of practical discourse to clarify disputes about theories and rival paradigms. On the contrary, this is one of the major themes of his writings. Many of the features of the type of rationality that is exhibited in such disputes show an affinity with the characteristics of *phronēsis* (practical reasoning) that Aristotle describes. Aristotle, of course, was not addressing the problem of disputes about rival paradigm theories, and in his analysis of *phronēsis*, he contrasts it with *epistēmē* (scientific knowledge) as well as with *technē*. But *phronēsis* is a form of reasoning that is concerned with choice and involves deliberation. It deals with that which is variable and about which there can be differing opinions (*doxai*). It is a type of reasoning in which there is a mediation between general principles and a concrete particular situation that requires choice and decision. In forming such a judgment there are no determinate technical rules by which a particular can simply be subsumed under that which is general or universal. What is required is an interpretation and specification of universals that are appropriate to this particular situation. This corresponds to Kuhn's claim that the "universal" criteria scientists share are sufficiently open, that they require interpretation and judicious weighing of alternatives when specific choices are made between rival paradigms and theories. Like Aristotle, Kuhn insists that such choosing is a rational activity, although the reasons to which we appeal do not necessarily dictate a univocal choice. To expect or demand more precision than this is to misunderstand the character of such deliberation. There are further important similarities. As Aristotle explores the nature of *phronēsis* from a variety of perspectives, it becomes clear that we must understand the ways in which *phronēsis* is nurtured by the *polis* or community. For Kuhn, too, the character of our judgment and rational deliberation concerning the choice of rival paradigm theories is shaped by the social practices of the relevant scientific community.[11]

Kuhn returns to this theme and amplifies his discussion of the practical character of reasoning in choosing between theories in a lecture delivered in 1973 but published only in 1977 entitled "Objectivity, Value Judgment, and Theory Choice."[12] He reiterates his skepticism about the search for "an algorithm able to dictate rational, unanimous choice"[13] and emphasizes that criteria of choice "function not as rules, which determine choice, but as values, which influence it."[14] He lists five criteria of choice: "accuracy, consistency, scope, simplicity, and fruitfulness." He informs us that "I agree entirely with the traditional view that [these criteria] play a vital role when scientists must choose between an established theory and an upstart competitor."[15] But we must realize that "individually the criteria are imprecise: individuals may legitimately differ about their application to concrete cases." Furthermore, when the criteria are "deployed together, they repeatedly prove to conflict with one another."[16] Kuhn seeks to make sense of rational disagreement in theory-choice, disagreement that cannot be resolved by an appeal to precisely formulated determinate rules. Kuhn also claims that over time such disagreements can be and are rationally resolved by the force of arguments in the relevant scientific community. But even here it is misleading to speak of proof (if our model of proof is a deductive argument). Rather, the cumulative weight of the complex arguments advanced in favor of a given paradigm theory, together with its successes, persuade the community of scientists.

Such a mode of development, however, *requires* a decision process which permits rational men to disagree, and such disagreement would be barred by the shared algorithm which philosophers have generally sought. . . . What from one viewpoint may seem the looseness and imperfection of choice criteria conceived as rules may, when the same criteria are seen as values, appear an indispensable means of spreading the risk which the introduction or support of novelty always entails.[17]

But if criteria of choice understood as values are as open in their application and weighting as Kuhn suggests, it may still seem that Kuhn is relying on subjective and arbitrary factors as decisive elements in the making of a specific choice among theories. Kuhn tries to meet this persistent criticism by distinguishing two senses of "subjective": the first is typically contrasted with the "objective," while the second is contrasted with the "judgmental." "When my critics describe the idiosyncratic features to which I appeal as subjective, they resort, erroneously I think, to the second of these senses. When they complain that I deprive science of objectivity, they conflate the second sense of subjective with the first."[18]

What precisely is involved in this distinction between two senses of "subjective"? Consider the "subjective-judgmental" distinction.

Here Kuhn refers to *a* concept of taste where matters of taste, like sensation reports, are "undiscussable." When taste is understood in this sense, there can be no real dispute.[19] If I report that I like something (Kuhn's example is a film), short of claiming that I am lying or somehow deceiving myself no one can disagree with my subjective report. But if I claim that the film was a "terrible potboiler," then I am making a *judgment* which is discussable. If I am challenged in making this judgment, then I am expected to give *reasons* that support my judgment. According to Kuhn, the deliberations concerning the choices of theory have this judgmental character. They are "eminently discussable, and the man who refuses to discuss his own cannot expect to be taken seriously."[20] The crucial issue concerns the relation between the reasons given and my judgment. The reasons do not "prove" the judgment, they support it. In a concrete situation there can be better and worse reasons (even though there are no clear and precise rules for sorting out what is better and worse). There may be many situations where, even after the strongest reasons are given pro and con, we can recognize that the opponents who disagree are both rational; neither is making a mistake, being unscientific, or irrational. Employing this "subjective-judgmental" distinction, Kuhn claims that "if my critics introduce the term 'subjective' in a sense that opposes it to judgmental—thus suggesting that I make theory choice undiscussable [and consequently irrational—R.J.B.]—they have seriously mistaken my position."[21]

Concerning the "subjective-objective" distinction, Kuhn thinks that it does not fit the process he has been characterizing any better.

When my critics say I deprive theory choice of objectivity, they must, therefore, have recourse to some very different sense of subjective, presumably the one in which bias and personal likes or dislikes function instead of, or in the face of, the actual facts. But that sense of subjective does not fit the process I have been describing any better than the first. . . . Objectivity ought to be analyzable in terms of criteria like accuracy and consistency. If these criteria do not supply all the guidance that we have customarily expected of them, then it may be the meaning rather than the limits of objectivity that my argument shows.[22]

The dominant theme that emerges from this discussion is that if we are to understand the type of rationality that is involved in theory-choice we must recognize that theory-choice is a judgmental activity requiring imagination, interpretation, the weighing of alternatives, and application of criteria that are essentially open. But such judgments also need to be supported by reasons (reasons which

themselves change and vary in the course of scientific development).
It is not a deficiency but an intrinsic characteristic of this judgmental process that rational individuals can and do disagree without
either of them being guilty of making a mistake. While the "balance
of argument and counterargument" in support of conflicting judgments "can sometimes be very close indeed" (p. 157), in the course
of further scientific development the force of the arguments in support
of one of these conflicting judgments does become decisive for the
community of relevant scientists.

The shift from a model of rationality that searches for determinate rules which can serve as necessary and sufficient conditions, to
a model of practical rationality that emphasizes the role of *exemplars* and judgmental interpretation, is not only characteristic of
theory-choice but is a leitmotif that pervades all of Kuhn's thinking
about science.[23] This shift even helps to clarify one of Kuhn's original
motivations for introducing the slippery and controversial notion of
a paradigm. The primary sense of a paradigm is that of a concrete
exemplar that is open to differing interpretations. Yet "paradigms
may be prior to, more binding, and more complete than any set of
rules for research that could be unequivocally abstracted from them."[24]
Kuhn has been maligned when it is claimed that this contrast is to
be understood as a contrast between the cognitive and the noncognitive. The real point is to show what is wrong with a theory or
understanding of the "cognitive" which restricts this honorific term
to what can be explicitly formulated in a series of propositions.[25]
Like Polanyi, Kuhn is arguing that the tacit knowledge of the scientist may be more important for understanding science as it is practiced than what can be explicitly formulated into propositions and
rules.[26] Alasdair MacIntyre beautifully expresses the practical character of such rationality when he writes:

Objective rationality is therefore to be found not in rule-following, but in
rule-transcending, in knowing how and when to put rules and principles to
work and when not to. Consider how practical reasoning of this kind is
taught, whether it is the practical reasoning of generals, of judges in a common
law tradition, of surgeons or of natural scientists. Because there is no set of
rules specifying necessary and sufficient conditions for large areas of such
practices, the skills of practical reasoning are communicated only partly by
precepts but much more by case-histories and precedents. Moreover the
precepts cannot be understood except in terms of their application in the
case-histories; and the development of the precepts cannot be understood
except in terms of the history of both precepts and case-histories. *The teaching of method is nothing other than the teaching of a certain kind of history.*[27]
(italics added)

However sympathetic we may be with Kuhn's portrayal of scientific activity, there are many questions that Kuhn does not satisfactorily answer. On the one hand he claims that the criteria he lists are open to differing interpretations and that these criteria can be differently weighted and applied. On the other hand he claims that "roughly speaking, but only very roughly," the "criteria or values deployed in theory choice are fixed once and for all."[28] But it is never clear precisely what is fixed (even "roughly speaking"). Thus, for example, when Kuhn speaks of accuracy as a criterion, he says "accuracy, as a value, has with time increasingly denoted quantitative or numerical agreement, sometimes at the expense of qualitative. Before early modern times, however, accuracy in that sense was a criterion only for astronomy, the science of the celestial region. Elsewhere it was neither expected nor sought."[29] This suggests that not only the application and weight of these values are open to interpretation but also that the sense in which they are taken or the domain to which they apply can vary. One might even accuse Kuhn of backsliding here, because many of the arguments he has advanced about incommensurability of paradigms apply, *mutatus mutandis*, to criteria and values.

Even more important, Kuhn never squarely answers the question, What is the epistemological status of the values that he isolates? Echoing the type of question that Socrates asks of Euthythro, we can ask Kuhn, Are the criteria or values accepted by scientific communities rational because these are the values *accepted* by scientific communities, *or* are they accepted by scientific communities because they are *the criteria of rationality?* Even if one thinks that there is something wrong with this disjunction, Kuhn never really confronts this question. So, if we read Kuhn's remarks about criteria, reasons, and values as a proposed solution to an extremely complicated set of problems, then we have to judge them a failure. His comments raise many questions about the nature and status of the relevant values, their specific content, and the ways in which such values do and do not change in the course of scientific development that he does not answer. But we can also interpret Kuhn's remarks differently—not as proposed solutions but rather as the opening up of questions to be pursued if we are to gain an adequate understanding of scientific inquiry and the sense(s) in which it is a rational activity—questions that have been in the foreground of discussion ever since the publication of *The Structure of Scientific Revolutions*.

In defense of Kuhn, it may be said that those who accuse him of advocating an image of science that presents it as an irrational activity have missed the main point of his argument. His claim is that many traditional or standard theories of what constitutes the rationality of science are inadequate and need to be revised if we are to make sense of how science functions and in what sense it is a rational activity. He himself conceives of this as a hermeneutical task where one tries to clarify and interpret the type of rationality exhibited in scientific inquiry in light of the ways in which science is practiced. Thus, in commenting on Feyerabend, he tells us that while he agrees with much of what Feyerabend says, nevertheless

to describe [Feyerabend's] argument as a defence of irrationality in science seems to me not only absurd but vaguely obscene. I would describe it, together with my own, as an attempt to show that existing theories of rationality are not quite right and that we must readjust or change them to explain why science works as it does. To suppose, instead, that we possess criteria of rationality which are independent of our understanding of the essentials of the scientific process is to open the door to cloud-cuckoo land.[30]

Kuhn makes a similar point when commenting on Lakatos.

Scientific behavior, taken as a whole, is the best example we have of rationality. Our view of what it is to be rational depends in significant ways, though of course not exclusively, on what we take to be the essential aspects of scientific behavior. That is not to say that any scientist behaves rationally at all times, or even that many behave rationally very much of the time. What it does assert is that, if history or any other empirical discipline leads us to believe that the development of science depends essentially on behavior that we have previously thought to be irrational, then we should conclude not that science is irrational but that our notion of rationality needs adjustment here and there.[31]

This way of approaching Kuhn—focusing on the questions that he has opened up for discussion rather than on those that he has fully answered—allows us to see how he joins issue with Popper, Feyerabend, Lakatos, Toulmin, Hesse, Shapere, McMullin, and Laudan (to mention only some of the figures in what have become raging polemical debates).[32] The most significant aspect of these debates is the emergence of common agreements and insights about the nature of scientific inquiry, which collectively indicate a dramatic shift in our understanding of scientific inquiry. This does not mean that the differences among the disputants are less important than their agreements. Nevertheless, once we become clearer about implicit agreements and shared understandings, many of these differences begin to look like differences of emphasis rather than absolute cleavages. It is natural, in any living debate, that differences will be emphasized and even exaggerated. But focusing exclusively on these differences has obscured the common ground that is the basis for disagreement. When we stand back and view the cumulative results of the postempiricist philosophy and history of science, we realize that there has been a major transformation in our understanding of science, when compared to older rationalist, empiricist, and logical empiricist images of science.

Before attempting to uncover these shared agreements, let us consider how Kuhn's work (and more generally the postempiricist philosophy and history of science) is related to the Cartesian Anxiety and to the movement beyond objectivism and relativism. Kuhn's persistent attacks on the idea of an algorithm for theory-choice, his criticism of the idea of a permanent, neutral observation language, and his undermining of the notion of a determinate set of scientific criteria that can serve as rules or necessary and sufficient conditions for resolving scientific disputes can all be interpreted as calling into question the Cartesian Anxiety. While no contemporary philosopher of science has wanted to claim that there is a determinate decision procedure or method for advancing scientific discovery, many have been firmly convinced that there are (or ought to be) permanent procedures for testing and evaluating rival theories. This is the basis for the "orthodox" distinction between the context of discovery and the context of justification.[33] The latter has been taken to be the proper domain of the philosopher of science. His or her task is to discover, specify, and reconstruct the criteria. Moreover, it has been assumed that to deny that there are such determinate, unambiguous criteria is to open the way to subjectivism, relativism, and irrationalism. These are the very charges initially brought against Kuhn. The fierceness of the attacks on Kuhn is indicative of the grip of the Cartesian Either/Or. But it is more illuminating, and closer to Kuhn's intent, to see that he has, in effect, been urging us to set aside this Either/Or and to find a way of understanding the varieties of rational disagreement that cannot be eliminated in the frontiers of scientific inquiry. For even what we take to be good reasons in support of rival paradigms or theories are open to historical change and differing interpretations. Many of Kuhn's critics might agree that it is true (indeed, trivially true) that scientists have "rational disagreements," but they would claim that what is characteristic about science is that "in principle" all such disagreements can be rationally resolved. We can know in advance what kind of information or evidence is needed to rationally resolve any important disagreement. At the most fundamental level, this assumption is just what Kuhn is calling into question.

This point has been concisely expressed and generalized by Richard Rorty when he seeks to root out the bias "that all contributions to a given discourse are commensurable" and shows how fundamental this bias has been not only for the philosophy of science but for modern epistemology.

> By "commensurable" I mean able to be brought under a set of rules which will tell us how rational agreement can be reached on what would settle the issue on every point where statements seem to conflict. These rules tell us how to construct an ideal situation, in which all residual disagreements will be seen to be "noncognitive" or merely verbal, or else merely temporary— capable of being resolved by doing something further. What matters is that there should be agreement about what would have to be done if a resolution *were* to be achieved.[34]

Rorty claims that this has been the fundamental bias of epistemology since Descartes. One of the reasons why this bias has been so entrenched is that it has been taken to be the essential characteristic of "scientific method." Kuhn's work can be seen as challenging the claim that this assumption is fundamental for scientific activity. Or, to put it more cautiously, while Kuhn thinks that such an assumption is warranted and necessary for normal science, it does not apply at times of scientific crises. To give up such an assumption about commensurability is not to call into question the rationality of science but rather to change our understanding of the character of rationality in scientific disputes and conflicts—an understanding that highlights the practical character of scientific rationality. In this respect, then, Kuhn (although at times still caught in the language of "objectivism" and "relativism") seeks to move beyond this Either/Or.

KUHN AND HIS CRITICS: THE COMMON GROUND

I want to return to showing how much common ground there is between Kuhn and his critics. Consider Paul Feyerabend, who has been the enfant terrible in the postempiricist philosophy of science. Any interpretation of Feyerabend is fraught with dangers, because he not only delights in his own inconsistencies but also warns the reader against taking his arguments "seriously." In *Against Method*, he teases us by saying he hopes the reader will remember him "as a

flippant Dadaist and *not* as a serious anarchist."[35] Feyerabend relishes
the extremism of his shifting positions and thoroughly enjoys mock-
ing and knocking down any claim to stability, fixity, or "puritanical
seriousness." I do not want to claim to be representing his "true
beliefs."[36] (It is not even clear what this means.) But I do find a
persistent theme or voice in his work (especially in *Against Method*)
that is relevant to our discussion. Although Feyerabend might deplore
the fact, there is an underlying thematic coherence in the style and
content of his claims. Given Feyerabend's own assessment of what
is happening not only in the philosophy of science but in society
itself—that we are threatened by closure, fixed method, and social
rigidity, all of which are enemies of life, spontaneity, creativity,
imagination, and individual freedom—then the task of the critic is
to use any rhetorical means available to undermine and ridicule those
who think that there are or ought to be fixed rational criteria in
scientific inquiry (or any other domain of life). In the spirit of the
"opportunistic" strategy that he employs, Feyerabend informs us that
"there may, of course, come a time when it will be necessary to give
reason a temporary advantage and when it will be wise to defend its
rules to the exclusion of everything else. I do not think that we are
living in such a time today" (p. 22).

But although ostensibly, rationality is the great enemy for Feyerabend, especially as it is employed by those whom he calls "critical
rationalists," some of his other comments reveal a very different
attitude: "We are here dealing with a situation that must be analysed
and understood if we want to adopt a more *reasonable* attitude towards
the issue between 'reason' and 'irrationality' than is found in the
school philosophies of today" (italics added, p. 154). Despite the
exuberance of Feyerabend's style and the self-conscious outrageous-
ness of some of his claims, he has an eminently serious and important purpose. Although he wants to claim much more, one of his
central themes might be expressed as follows: Name any rule, algorithm, decision procedure, method, or value that is supposed to guide
scientific inquiry, whether it be accuracy, verification, falsification,
or some other standard, and I will show you that it has been violated
not only in advancing and discovering new hypotheses and theories
but in supporting and justifying them. Name anything that you think
is or ought to be irrelevant to scientific inquiry, whether it be social
context, metaphysical beliefs, or personal idiosyncrasies, and I will
show you cases in which it is relevant to a scientist's investigations.
I think Feyerabend is right, and the point is an important one, but it
is not very different from the one that Kuhn makes. Although Feyer-

abend would strongly object to Kuhn's reference to "good reasons" (and might consider this to be little more than "verbal ornament"), Kuhn and Feyerabend are in substantial agreement that the search for necessary and sufficient conditions or rules of theory-choice is a project doomed to failure. Furthermore, both assert that any statement of rules, procedures, and methods fails to capture the wit, imagination, and judgment required for the invention, testing, and evaluation or justification of scientific hypotheses and theories. Feyerabend's main target of attack and ridicule is a false (and he would add a pernicious) conception of what constitutes the rationality of science. And he attacks his target in the name of what even he calls a more "reasonable" attitude.

Feyerabend (almost inadvertently) displays a remarkable perspicacity about his own polemical stance when he writes:

A society that is based on a set of well-defined and restrictive rules so that being a man becomes synonymous with obeying these rules, *forces the dissenter into a no-man's-land of no rules at all and thus robs him of his reason and his humanity.* It is the paradox of modern irrationalism that its proponents silently identify rationalism with order and articulate speech and thus see themselves forced to promote stammering and absurdity. . . . Remove the principles, admit the possibility of many different forms of life, and such phenomena will disappear like a bad dream. (pp. 218–19)

The passage is revealing because it not only characterizes the "no-man's-land" into which Feyerabend has wandered but also underscores the rationale for his polemical stance.[37] At times it does seem as if Feyerabend is promoting "stammering and absurdity" and is forced to take extreme positions of "irrationalism," because he implicitly accepts the characterization of reason and rationality that he ostensibly seeks to overthrow. His rhetoric and tropes make it appear as if the choice is between rationalism and a new, playful, hedonistic form of irrationalism and relativism. But this dichotomy obscures what is really at issue—a proper understanding of man's "reason and humanity" which stresses its practical character. Feyerabend plays a double game with us. The effectiveness of his polemic presupposes the very concept of rationality (and the implicit contrast with irrationality) that he is attacking.[38] The voice in Feyerabend that I want to recover is the one that urges us to set aside the Cartesian Anxiety (and not simply to take sides on the Either/Or). At his best, Feyerabend is a satirist, and the point of his satire is to ridicule, root out, and exorcise the entrenched bias for commensuration that Rorty stresses.

We gain a subtler grasp of what Feyerabend is emphasizing when we compare his work to that of Lakatos. Presumably there are sharp differences between Feyerabend and Lakatos, the "prodigal sons" of Karl Popper (both studied with and were deeply influenced by Popper). But Feyerabend is right when he stresses how much substantive agreement there is between himself and Lakatos, despite their manifest differences. Lakatos, especially in some of his early papers, took himself to be the great defender of Popper (or at least of Popper properly understood, who turns out to be identical with Lakatos).[39] Lakatos calls his approach a "methodology of research programmes."

The distinctive feature of Lakatos' theory of progressive and degenerating research programs is that he wants to do justice to the openness and options in living scientific inquiry (at least in the short run) without going so far as to maintain that "anything goes" or denying that we can give a rational reconstruction of "the growth of scientific knowledge."[40] Increasingly (and I take this to be one of his most important contributions) Lakatos came to realize that all theories of "instant rationality" fail. If we want to understand the rationality of scientific inquiry, it is misleading to focus exclusively on a specific choice in a specific situation and ask whether such a choice is rational (if this suggests that we must be able to discover clear, explicit criteria which will tell us whether the choice is rational or irrational). The unit that we need to examine is the research program, a program which develops and changes over time and is consequently historical.

Feyerabend notes two important points of agreement between himself and Lakatos.

The first suggestion is that methodology must grant "a breathing space" to the ideas we wish to consider. Given a new theory, we must not at once use the customary standards for deciding about its survival. . . . It is the *evolution* of a theory over long periods of time and not its shape at a particular moment that counts in our methodological appraisals. . . .

Secondly, Lakatos suggests that methodological standards are not beyond criticism. They can be examined, improved, replaced by better standards. The examination is not abstract, but makes use of *historical data:* historical data play a decisive role in the debate between rival methodologies.[41] (p. 183)

But Feyerabend, as well as Musgrave, has effectively shown that there is an ambiguity in Lakatos' "methodology of research programmes."[42] Lakatos sometimes writes as if such a methodology is essentially retrospective, implying that it is possible to go over a slice of history and give a rational reconstruction of why one research program came to replace a rival one. The point of calling such a reconstruction "rational" is that we can isolate the reasons why the new program did replace (and ought to have replaced) the degenerating program. This is the basis for Lakatos insisting that his methodology is normative (and not merely descriptive). But sometimes, especially in his late papers, Lakatos so qualifies his position that it is difficult to see that his concept of methodology has any bite. Insofar as the core of the idea of methodology is that it can guide and direct research, Lakatos seems to be abandoning this prescriptive and prospective aspect of methodology. Thus he writes:

My "methodology," older connotations of the term not withstanding, only *appraises* fully articulated theories (or research programmes) but it presumes to give advice to the scientist neither about how to *arrive* at good theories nor even about which of the two rival programmes he should work on. My "methodological rules" explain the rationale of the acceptance of Einstein's theory over Newton's, but they neither command nor advise the scientist to work in the Einsteinian and not in the Newtonian research programme.
. . . .
Also when it turns out that, on my criteria, one research programme is "progressing" and its rival is "degenerating," this tells us only that the two programmes possess objective features but does not tell us that scientists must work only in the progressive one.[43]

According to Lakatos, "one may rationally stick to a degenerating programme until it is overtaken by a rival *and even after*."[44] The situation is made even more complicated and ambiguous when Lakatos also concedes that we may be mistaken or too hasty in our judgment about a research program; a program can get out of "degenerating troughs" and reverse directions.[45] Musgrave reluctantly concludes that "the abdication of the Lakatosian methodologist is complete,"[46] and Feyerabend gleefully states that there is no " 'rationally' describable difference between Lakatos and myself" (p. 187). "Lakatos' philosophy appears liberal only because it is an *anarchism in disguise*" (p. 14). So, Feyerabend suggests that while there may be no rationally describable difference, there is a "great difference in rhetorics" (p. 187).

But the difference between Lakatos and Feyerabend is more than a matter of rhetoric; there is a significant difference in emphasis, although these differences are compatible. Feyerabend typically focuses on the individual creative scientist when he or she is proposing some new hypothesis or theory that is incompatible with the accepted wisdom of scientific communities. He does not deny that in concrete situations there are accepted canons, procedures, standards, and methods for testing and evaluating new hypotheses and theories. He says that these are neither necessary nor sufficient to provide objective standards of evaluation and that they may and should be violated to advance scientific inquiry. He challenges the idea that the task of the philosopher of science is to come up with a set of standards that are fixed and permanent and that presumably have some transhistorical or transcendental status. For Feyerabend this is the road to dogmatism.

Lakatos does not really disagree with Feyerabend. But Lakatos is primarily concerned with a different set of questions: Can we give a rational reconstruction of the growth of scientific knowledge? Can we give an account of what has happened in which we isolate the reasons (and not just the causes) that explain why one research program or theory has replaced a rival one? Even Lakatos' distinction between the actual history of a research program and the rational reconstruction of this history is intended to emphasize that we can discriminate the reasons (indeed the good reasons) that are involved in the growth of scientific knowledge. Although Feyerabend sometimes writes as if he is challenging even this claim, this is belied by what he does. For when Feyerabend addresses himself to what he takes to be significant creative advances in the history of science—as he does in his extended discussion of Galileo in *Against Method*—he is in effect arguing for an alternative reconstruction of what Galileo achieved and how he achieved it, a reconstruction that claims to be true and that can be (and has been) contested on rational grounds.[47]

I have been arguing that despite the polemical differences between Kuhn and his critics there is much more common ground and convergence than may initially be apparent. But still it may be felt that I am glossing over a major point of disagreement between Kuhn and his critics. Rorty highlights this point when he considers the case of the arguments advanced by Cardinal Bellarmine against Galileo and the Copernican theory.

But can we then find a way of saying that the considerations advanced against the Copernican theory by Cardinal Bellarmine—the scriptural descriptions of the fabric of the heavens—*were* "illogical or unscientific?" This, perhaps, is the point at which the battle lines between Kuhn and his critics can be drawn most sharply. Much of the seventeenth century's notion of what it was to be a "philosopher," and much of the Enlightenment's notion of what it was to be "rational," turns on Galileo's being absolutely right and the church absolutely wrong. To suggest that there is room for rational disagreement here—not simply for a black-and-white struggle between reason and superstition—is to endanger the very notion of "philosophy." For it endangers the notion of finding "a method for finding truth" which takes Galilean and Newtonian mechanics as paradigmatic. A whole complex of mutually reinforcing ideas—philosophy as a methodological discipline distinct from the sciences, epistemology as the provision of commensuration, rationality as possible only on the common ground which makes possible commensuration—seems endangered if the question about Bellarmine is answered in the negative.[48]

While Rorty notes that Kuhn does not give an explicit answer to this question, he thinks that Kuhn's writings provide an "arsenal of argument in favor of a negative answer."[49] At any rate, this is the way in which Rorty thinks the question should be answered:

The "grid" [to use Foucault's expression—R.J.B.] which emerged in the later seventeenth and eighteenth centuries was not there to be appealed to in the early seventeenth century, at the time that Galileo was on trial. No conceivable epistemology, no study of the nature of human knowledge, could have "discovered" it before it was hammered out. The notion of what it was to be "scientific" was in the process of being formed.[50]

In giving a sharply negative answer, Rorty is in agreement with Feyerabend. Feyerabend has been most incisive and effective in ridiculing the notion that there are free-floating standards of rationality detached from actual historical practices to which we can appeal in order to decide who is scientific, logical, and rational and who is not. But when Rorty asserts that the very notion of what it is to be scientific and rational was being "hammered out," he is making the same point that both Kuhn and Lakatos emphasize—that we can give a correct narrative account of why certain reasons and modes of argumentation prevailed and others did not.[51] In giving such an account, we are not appealing to permanent, atemporal standards of rationality that are (or ought to be) available but to those reasons and practices that are "hammered out" in the course of scientific inquiry. What a given scientist, or even what a community of scientists, takes to be "good reasons" may turn out later to be no longer accepted as good reasons. But when this happens it is not a matter of "mere" rhetoric or of arbitrarily endorsing one set of values in preference to another set. Cardinal Bellarmine did not just state personal subjective preferences but offered a number of sophisticated arguments in support of his views, arguments which made the claim to validity. Rorty rightly claims that it is an illusion to think that there is a permanent set of ahistorical standards of rationality which the "philosopher" or epistemologist can discover and which will unambiguously tell us who is rational and who is not. But it is illusory to suggest, as Rorty sometimes does, that it is simply an accident of history that we now judge the types of reasons and arguments advanced by Bellarmine to be deficient. Lurking in the background here is a false dichotomy: either permanent standards of rationality (objectivism) *or* arbitrary acceptance of one set of standards or practices over against its rival (relativism). We need to alter our understanding of how rational argumentation (and the history of forms of argumentation) works, to realize that there are times when there are disagreements that we cannot immediately resolve by appeal to fixed standards, to admit that at such times we may not even know in advance "how to construct an ideal situation, in which all residual disagreements will be seen to be . . . capable of being resolved by doing something further."[52] Nevertheless, in the course of the evolution of scientific development we can come to see the force of the better practices and arguments and why certain historical practices and modes of argumentation are abandoned.

But here a critic, infected by the spirit of Humean skepticism, might well ask, What is it that happens in a historical span that does not occur in a given temporal moment or instant? The very question shows the stance that needs to be abandoned, the implicit atomism which claims that there is nothing more to a historical development than the repetition and aggregation of isolated events. This atomism prevents us from seeing that "good reasons," and the social practices in which they are embedded, are not discrete and separable but are always parts of larger networks (the expression "holism" can be misleading here insofar as it suggests a single seamless continuity).[53] Both Galileo and Bellarmine offered complex reasons, considerations, and evidence to support their respective positions. Each was claiming validity that would presumably stand up to further critical tests. The "reasons" that they offered themselves had implications, entailments, and ramifications with other sorts of reasons and considerations. When we now claim it was right that Galileo *should* have won out over Bellarmine (at least insofar as claims were being made about the natural and physical world), it is because we can now give strong arguments showing why the type of reasons Bellarmine gave were deficient. A scientist is always under the obligation to give a rational account of what is right and wrong in the theory that is being displaced and to explain how his or her theory can account for what is "true" in the preceding theory (when adequately reconstructed) and what is "false" or inadequate. Of course, we do this with reference to what we now take to be the best possible scientific reasons that can be given—reasons embedded in the social practices

that have been "hammered out." To admit (or rather insist) the like-
lihood that in the future there will be modifications of the standards,
reasons, and practices we now employ does not lead to epistemological skepticism but only to a realization of human fallibility and the
finitude of human rationality. (The skeptic is always playing on the
fear that unless we achieve finality we have not achieved anything
and that we might discover someday that we have been totally
mistaken in what we take to be warranted. The point is not so much
to refute this variety of skepticism as to see through it, to see that
the seduction of such skepticism depends on accepting a notion of
what counts as knowledge and what counts as rationality that needs
to be abandoned.)[54]

The philosopher who most carefully and penetratingly distinguishes epistemological skepticism from human fallibilism is Charles
Sanders Peirce. Peirce criticizes the picture of scientific reasoning
that represents it as a linear movement from premises to conclusions
or from individual "facts" to generalizations. In its place he emphasizes the multiple strands and diverse types of evidence, data, hunches,
and arguments used to support a scientific hypothesis or theory. Any
one of these strands may be weak in itself and insufficient to support
the proposed theory, but collectively they provide a stronger warrant
for rational belief than any single line of argument—like a strong
cable that is made up of multiple weak strands. This shift in characterizing scientific argumentation is one of the reasons Peirce so
emphasized the community of inquirers—for it is only in and through
such a critical community that one can adequately test the collective
strength of such multiple argumentation.

The movement beyond objectivism and relativism in describing
the character of scientific arguments is also evidenced when we
examine the dispute between Popper and Kuhn. Popper thinks that
Kuhn's understanding of science leads straight to relativism, and
Popper—in part, as a reaction to Kuhn and other "relativists"—has
increasingly defended an objectivist account of science, appealing to
what Popper calls the Third World, or World 3, a growing, objective
world of knowledge that cannot be reduced to World 1 (the physical
world) or World 2 (the subjective world).[55] Popper's main target of
attack is what Kuhn calls "normal science." Popper tells us that
"what Kuhn has described does exist, and . . . must be taken into
account by historians of science,"[56] but this phenomenon of so-called
normal science is one that Popper "dislikes," and the normal scientist "is a person one ought to be sorry for."[57] Popper singles out for
criticism the aspect of normal science that Kuhn speaks of as "puzzle

solving," and Popper underscores the "dogmatism" of this form of scientific activity.

But there is something askew in Popper's criticism, even though Kuhn is in part responsible for this caricature of what he means by normal science. Two faces of normal science stand out in Kuhn's description of it. The first is the one that Popper exaggerates: normal science is seen as a narrow-minded, closed form of activity in which novelty and fundamental challenges to the dominant paradigm are avoided. Although this aspect of the portrayal of normal science has come under heavy attack, it is less significant than the other face of normal science. If we examine Kuhn's descriptions of normal science, we see that he views it, at its best, as a highly imaginative and creative form of inquiry involving new procedures for gathering facts and making them more precise, as well as making sophisticated theoretical advances in the development and extension of a paradigm. What is most essential for Kuhn in normal science is the degree of precision and subtlety that can be achieved in working out the promise of a paradigm (not its dogmatism), for without this we would never be aware of the precise character of anomalies that can be used to challenge a paradigm. The issue of liking or disliking normal science, or praising or denigrating it, is beside the point. Without the development of normal science, in which precision and accuracy are all-important, there would never be a scientific revolution. Popper (and others who have made a similar point) correctly note that the line between normal science and revolutionary science is not nearly as sharp as Kuhn sometimes suggests. Normal science is more like revolutionary science, and revolutionary science is more like normal science than Kuhn (at times) leads us to believe.

But despite these skirmishes about normal science, Popper's primary purpose is to defend the idea of a rational growth of knowledge. He constantly stresses that all scientific hypotheses and theories are open to and invite sharp criticism. Kuhn does not really dispute these claims. The more interesting issues that divide them concern how we are properly to understand scientific progress and the growth of knowledge and how we are to understand the role that criticism plays in scientific inquiry. Popper frequently writes as if we always know in advance what will count as a good argument or criticism against a conjecture. The basic idea behind the appeal to falsification as the demarcation criterion between science and nonscience is that there are clear criteria for determining under what conditions a conjecture or hypothesis is to be rejected—that we know in advance what are the proper standards of criticism. But as Kuhn,

Feyerabend, and Lakatos have argued, the situation is not nearly as clear and as determinate as Popper suggests: we frequently do not know, in a concrete scientific situation, whether we are confronted with an obstacle to be overcome, a counterinstance that can be tolerated because of the enormous success of the theory, or with evidence that should be taken as falsifying our claim. Data or evidence do not come marked "falsification"; in part, it is we who decide what is to count as a falsification or refutation, and this judgment is one that is eminently fallible. What count as the effective standards of criticism and refutation (and not just nominal standards) is itself open to interpretation and disputation, a point which Popper (in theory and practice) tends to slight. But even when these points are made against Popper, he is right in reminding us that in cases of a serious scientific dispute we are always explicitly or implicitly making validity claims, claims that call for further specification, testing, and criticism.

THE DEVELOPMENT OF THE PHILOSOPHY OF SCIENCE

Let me draw together the several strands of my argument, which highlights the common features of the image of science that is emerging in the postempiricist philosophy of science.

1.   We can interpret this movement of thought as contributing to the demise of the Cartesianism that has dominated and infected so much of modern thought. The Cartesian dream or hope was that with sufficient ingenuity we could discover, and state clearly and distinctly, what is the quintessence of scientific method and that we could specify once and for all what is the meta-framework or the permanent criteria for evaluating, justifying, or criticizing scientific hypotheses and theories. The spirit of Cartesianism is evidenced not only by rationalists but by all those who subscribe to strong transcendental arguments that presumably show us what is required for scientific knowledge, as well as by those empiricists who have sought for a touchstone of what is to count as genuine empirical knowledge.

One of the first great attacks on this Cartesian framework, especially in regard to characterizing scientific knowledge, was made by Peirce. Nevertheless it has taken more than a hundred years for us to become fully aware of how the Cartesian view distorts the way in which science is actually practiced. There has been a continuous development from Peirce through the other pragmatists to Quine, Sellars, and Popper that not only challenges the characteristic Cartesian appeal to foundations but adumbrates an alternative understanding of scientific knowledge without such foundations.[58] One substantive result of recent work in the philosophy of science has been to show us that any abstract statement of what are supposed to be the permanent rules, methods, or standards of scientific inquiry turns out to be untrue to actual scientific inquiry or consists merely of "pious generalities." This is one reason why it is so important to turn to a concrete examination of historical practices and standards that have been "hammered out" in the course of scientific inquiry.

2.   Although the types of argumentation involved in advancing new hypotheses and theories, as well as those employed in appraising them, are in fact much more complex than has frequently been acknowledged, it is not literally true, as Feyerabend once said, that "anything goes." The "cash value" of this slogan (Feyerabend says he meant it as a "joke") is that no statement of rules for advancing, testing, and evaluating competing hypotheses and theories is sufficient to dictate what is acceptable or unacceptable in concrete situations of research. But this does not mean that there are not better or worse arguments in support of a hypothesis or theory. There is a difference between hitting someone over the head or exercising thought control and engaging in open, rational persuasion. Ironically, Feyerabend himself makes this point forcefully. For while his "anything goes" includes wit, deviousness, imagination, daring, and propaganda, it excludes anything that might inhibit or limit the spontaneity, creativity, pluralism of traditions, and individual freedom.

However, as soon as it is recognized that there is a difference between better and worse arguments, it must be admitted that it can be extremely difficult to recapture and articulate the distinctive modes of argumentation in any interesting cases of scientific dispute and change. As Feyerabend and Rorty argue, it is an illusion to think that there is or must be a permanent, neutral matrix to which we can appeal that will tell us once and for all what is to count as better and worse substantive arguments or even what is properly a scientific argument. But Feyerabend's "epistemological anarchism" needs to be counterbalanced by the truth implicit in Lakatos' "methodology of research programmes"—that at least retrospectively we can give a rational reconstruction which singles out the reasons (not just the causes) why a specific research program has won out over its rival. To emphasize that any appeal to reasons and arguments is contestable and/or fallible and that our idea of what we consider to be good reasons and arguments can change is not to call into question the rationality of this process but rather to characterize the rationality of the self-corrective nature of scientific inquiry. It is true, of course, that any rational criticism implicitly appeals to standards and criteria and that we cannot call everything into question at once. Something must be *taken* as fixed. But even methodological standards may (and have) been subject to criticism. As Peirce, Quine and Sellars, and Wittgenstein show us (in very different ways), there is no need to presuppose that there is some ultimate foundation or ultimate standards that must be presupposed to make this activity intelligible.

3. It becomes clear why the study of the history of science, and more generally the history of human inquiry, is so vital if we want to understand the continuity and differences in human rationality. This is how we can escape from the parochialism of assuming that what we now take to be paradigmatic forms of argumentation are the only legitimate forms. But here two important warnings are necessary.

First, although the charge of irrational historicism and relativism is bandied about, none of the figures that I have discussed (not even Feyerabend) have claimed that different epochs of human inquiry are so totally different that they cannot be compared or that it is impossible to find any standards, criteria, or shared agreements for comparing them. Kuhn claims to have been shocked that his critics could have interpreted him as making or even suggesting such a view. Instead of the total breakdown of communication between the advocates of different paradigms, he now speaks of a partial breakdown of communication. Feyerabend keeps dancing around this issue: it is never quite clear how radical or incommensurable he thinks alternative theories, forms of life, and traditions really are, but, as MacIntyre has noted, when Feyerabend cites examples of progress in science, they are typically the same examples that everyone else cites: Galileo, Einstein, quantum physics.[59] Here, too, there is a reasonable way of phrasing what I take to be Feyerabend's main substantive point: it is possible to compare different scientific theories in *multiple ways*, and we must avoid the Whiggish prejudice that there is a single ultimate "grid" for making comparisons.

The second warning concerns the very appeal to the history of science. Paradoxically, we find here a vestige of Cartesianism. What Descartes hoped to achieve by the appeal to foundations, or what empiricists hoped to achieve by the appeal to simple impressions—some sort of basic touchstone—is what is sometimes explicitly or implicitly assumed the history of science can provide. Kuhn, Lakatos, Feyerabend, Popper, Toulmin, Shapere (and many others) all appeal to selected moments of the history of science, or more accurately to interpretations of selected moments of the history of science, as evidence for their views about what is characteristic of or most vital for understanding science. But the appeal to history is not sufficient to bear the weight that is being placed upon it. It is an illusion to think that there is some straightforward way in which we can appeal to selected aspects of the history of science in order to justify global assertions about the nature of science. If observation is theory-laden, or at least influenced by the preconceptions we bring to it, as has so frequently been emphasized, so too is the study of the history of science. One will not find in the history of science whatever one seeks to find. But the study of the history of science, like any form of intellectual inquiry, is far more complex and open to conflicting interpretations than has sometimes been acknowledged.[60] Furthermore, when we turn to the specific details of the historical evidence cited by Kuhn, Feyerabend, Lakatos, Popper, and others in support of their claims about the nature or image of science, we find that deep and troubling questions have been raised about the accuracy of their reading of this history. We must be wary of the temptation to escape from epistemological varieties of the "myth of the given" by appealing to historical varieties of the same myth.[61]

4.   As a result of recent work in the philosophy and history of science, an appreciation of the practical character of rationality in science has been emerging. In speaking of the "practical" character, I want to underscore the role of choice, deliberation, conflicting variable opinions, and the judgmental quality of rationality. The search for method (when this is conceived of as a set of permanent, unambiguous rules) needs to be abandoned. The sharing of criteria by communities of scientists allows for, and indeed requires, interpretation, weighing, and application of these criteria to specific choices and decisions. Scientific argumentation, especially at those moments of "scientific revolution," requires rational persuasion, rational persuasion which cannot be assimilated to models of deductive proof or inductive generalization. We need to balance this consideration with the realization that in the course of scientific development the cumulative weight of evidence, data, reasons, and arguments can be rationally decisive for scientific communities. While social practices, criteria, and standards are hammered out in the course of scientific inquiry, there is nothing sacrosant about these; they can (and have been) changed, modified, and even abandoned. Thus, for example, there are considerations and modes of argumentation that Copernicus or Kepler employed to support their claims that we no longer (for good reasons) would now consider appropriate in scien-

tific inquiry. Our successors may make the same claims about what we now regard as exemplars of the best scientific argumentation.

Let me now suggest a slightly different perspective for understanding the dialectical coherence of the development of the philosophy of science in the twentieth century. For the story of this development has been dialectical, and indeed closely resembles the stages that Hegel discriminated in the dialectical development of knowledge.[62] For heuristic purposes, we can isolate four stages.

The first stage was marked by the attempt to ground—or rather the obsession with grounding—scientific knowledge with reference to the single term as the primary epistemological unit. This was reflected in the preoccupation with "ostensive definition" and the highly artificial attempts to isolate "logical proper names." One reason why this consumed so much intellectual energy and technical finesse was the underlying conviction that this was the proper way of grounding knowledge or language in "reality."

The second stage was characterized by the shift to the proposition, statement, or descriptive sentence as the primary epistemological unit for grounding empirical knowledge. This set off the search for a criterion of cognitive meaning that would once and for all distinguish empirically meaningful propositions from those that paraded as cognitively meaningful propositions but failed to meet a "rigorous" criterion of empirical meaning. But with the failure of all such attempts and the increasing realization of the futility of the entire project, there was a shift away from isolated propositions, statements, and sentences to a focus on the conceptual scheme or framework as the proper unit of epistemological analysis.[63]

This third stage has proved to be highly unstable, for a variety of reasons. There are deep difficulties in trying to clarify just what is a conceptual scheme, how we demarcate one conceptual scheme from another, and how radical are the differences among various conceptual schemes. But an even more fundamental difficulty concerns what these so-called conceptual schemes are supposed to be *about*.

As some philosophers, such as Davidson and Rorty, have shrewdly argued, the very idea that there is a distinction between "something" that is known (uncontaminated by different conceptual schemes) and the various schemes for conceiving or knowing it is suspect.[64] Rorty argues that this "new" distinction is a successor of the Kantian distinction of a sensible manifold "given" to us and our conceptual conditioning of "it" and consequently also entails the Kantian problem of how we can account for our knowledge of a world that is essentially conditioned by our understanding. In Rorty's view, the fashionable talk of alternative conceptual schemes is a linguistic, pluralistic development of Kant's claim that there is only *one* human conceptual scheme which is specified by *the* table of categories. As long as we stay within a quasi-Kantian perspective, there seems to be no satisfactory way of dealing with the question, What is the "it" or "world" that is conceived or known by these alternative conceptual schemes? There is a fundamental tension between the various critiques of the "myth of the given" and the claim that there is an "it" or "world" that has some meaning independent of any mode of conceptual description. Davidson concludes his critique, "On the Very Idea of a Conceptual Scheme," by telling us:

> It would be wrong to summarize by saying we have shown how communication is possible between people who have different schemes, a way that works without need of what there cannot be, namely a neutral ground, or a common coordinate system. For we have found no intelligible basis on which it can be said that schemes are different. It would be equally wrong to announce the glorious news that all mankind—all speakers of language, at least—share a common scheme and ontology. For if we cannot intelligibly say that schemes are different, neither can we intelligibly say that they are one.
>
> In giving up dependence on the concept of an uninterpreted reality, something outside all schemes and science, we do not relinquish the notion of objective truth—quite the contrary. Given the dogma of a dualism of scheme and reality, we get conceptual relativity, and truth relative to a scheme. Without the dogma, this kind of relativity goes by the board. Of course truth of sentences remains relative to language, but that is as objective as can be. In giving up the dualism of scheme and world, we do not give up the world, but reestablish unmediated touch with the familiar objects whose antics make our sentences and opinions true or false.[65]

Rorty, using Davidson's arguments for his own purposes, draws different conclusions and tends to historicize the issue. He recognizes that what he has to say sounds very much like a "naturalized" Hegel (in the manner in which Dewey naturalized Hegel). Hegel, of course, was not struggling with the problem of the intelligibility of alternative conceptual schemes, but he was perhaps the most incisive and penetrating critic of the latent ambiguity in Kant that can be seen as the origin for the contemporary dilemma. Hegel argued that Kant cannot have his cake and eat it too; Kant cannot insist that there is a given or "unsynthesized manifold" that grounds all phenomenal knowledge and also insist that what plays this vital epistemological role is intrinsically nonconceptual and unknowable in itself (because all knowledge and conception involves synthesis). In epistemology, and especially in the epistemology of the sciences, there has been something altogether too facile in the "dogma of a dualism of scheme and reality."

The fourth stage of development in the philosophy of science in this century is characterized by the increasing realization that when it comes to interesting questions about the rationality of scientific inquiry we must focus on the conflict of theories, paradigms, research programs, and research traditions in their *historical development.* To repeat Lakatos' telling phrase, all theories of "instant rationality" fail. The unit of appraisal becomes the research program, "a series of theories rather than an isolated theory." And, as McMullin rightly points out, what Lakatos calls a research program is what many practicing scientists themselves call a "theory"—something which is not static but which develops and changes over time.[66] With this shift to the study of the historical development of conflicting research programs or theories, many new characteristics and problems of scientific inquiry come into the foreground. For example, we can begin to see how in scientific development we have an historical phenomenon that is analogous to that of tradition, and indeed competing traditions, which can inform practice and are modified by further practice. A tradition, as MacIntyre has noted, "not only embodies the narrative of an argument, but is only to be recovered by an argumentative retelling of that narrative which will itself be in conflict with other argumentative retellings. Every tradition therefore is always in danger of lapsing into incoherence and when a tradition does so lapse it sometimes can only be recovered by a revolutionary reconstitution."[67] It is a false dichotomy to oppose tradition and reason, or even tradition and revolution, for "it is traditions which are the bearers of reason, and traditions at certain periods actually require and need revolutions for their continuance."[68]

Not only do we need to reexamine the ways in which traditions are vital for understanding scientific development; we must also consider the nature, function, and dynamics of *communities of inquirers.* Peirce claimed that the "very origin of the conception of reality shows that this conception essentially involves the notion of a COMMUNITY, without definite limits, and capable of a definite increase of knowledge."[69] One can make a similar claim about scientific rationality: that it essentially involves the notion of a community.[70]

When we concentrate on the nature and role of community in scientific inquiry, on the ways in which rationality is essentially dialogic and intersubjective, then we must not only clarify the descriptive aspects of actual scientific communities but their normative dimensions as well. While it is possible for certain purposes to distinguish the descriptive and the normative dimensions of such communities, it is crucial to realize how intimately and dialectically these dimensions are interrelated. One of the primary weaknesses of Kuhn's image of science is that at times he obscures the subtle ways in which these two dimensions are interrelated. This is reflected in his ambiguity about the epistemological status of those values that he takes to be the criteria for theory-choice or paradigm choice. Many critics, including Popper, Feyerabend, and Lakatos, have noted this weakness in Kuhn. In this respect, too, Peirce saw long ago that an adequate analysis (even an adequate descriptive analysis) must take account of the norms embedded in intersubjective communication, norms which serve as regulative and critical ideals of such inquiry (and which themselves can be subject to further interpretation and criticism). In other words, if we want to understand what science is, it is not sufficient simply to describe what scientists do (in some restrictive, empiricist sense of "description"), but we must also take account of the norms constitutive of scientific inquiry, even when scientists violate these norms.[71]

Focusing on the structure and dynamics of scientific communities can help to make sense of some of the important differences among Kuhn, Popper, Lakatos, and Feyerbend, revealing these as differences of emphasis. Kuhn, for example, has in his work made a particular point of the role of the community of scientists and their shared values. The existence of such community, he argues, is what guarantees that while there can be a breakdown of communication among defenders of rival paradigms, nevertheless scientific communities are ultimately persuaded by the complex forms of argumentation—and there is scientific progress.[72] Although the point that rivets Feyerabend's attention is typically the individual creative scientist, he has been particularly sensitive to the ways in which communities, even those that are considered to be enlightened and open-minded, nevertheless become closed, rigid, and intolerant to new ideas and alternatives. Popper's slogan, "conjectures and refutations," implicitly acknowledges individual spontaneity and communal criticism. He wants to leave the broadest latitude for scientific conjectures (in the proposing of hypotheses and theories Popper would have no difficulty with the principle "anything goes"), but any conjecture must be subjected to the most rigorous intersubjective criticism. But Popper has not always been sufficiently sensitive to the issue of how much the effective standards of criticism are themselves open to rational debate and disagreement. Lakatos' methodology of research programs gains its plausibility from his confidence that while in the short run we must provide for a breathing space that allows for a variety of choices and options, in the long run there can be and are collective or communal rational choices and decisions. Grünbaum puts the matter succinctly when he declares, "Since scientific inquiry is conducted by a *community* of scientists—practices that would be considered irrational if adopted by that community as a whole or by a majority of it need not necessarily be irrational when only a certain gifted minority engages in them."[73]

INCOMMENSURABILITY AND THE NATURAL SCIENCES

In my discussion of the postempiricist philosophy and history of science, I have alluded several times to what has been taken to be the most exotic, controversial, and perhaps the vaguest theme in these discussions—incommensurability. The term gained prominence in the writings of both Kuhn and Feyerabend (who were colleagues at the University of California at Berkeley during the 1950s). In 1977, in a review of Stegmüller, Feyerabend wrote, "Apparently everyone who enters the morass of this problem comes up with mud on his head, and Stegmüller is no exception."[74] One is tempted to add that neither is Feyerabend an exception. However, it is undeniable that the heady talk about incommensurability has captured the imagination of many thinkers who have had strong opinions about it, both pro and con. Why? The answer, I believe, is that here the *agōn* between objectivism and relativism seems to come into sharp focus. For those attracted by the new varieties of relativism, the alleged incommensurability of language games, forms of life, traditions, paradigms, and theories has been taken to be the primary evidence for the new relativism. For those who have a "pro" attitude towards incommensurability, it has been viewed as a liberating doctrine, one that releases us from the false parochialism of regarding our familiar language games and standards as having some sort of transcendental permanence. And for those who have a characteristic "anti" attitude, the "thesis of incommensurability" opens the door to everything that is objectionable—subjectivism, irrationalism, and nihilism.

Trying to sort out what is involved in these heated controversies is extraordinarily difficult, for a variety of reasons. First, one simply will not find a single well-defined characterization of what "incommensurability" is supposed to mean that all parties to the disputes share. Or rather one finds so many differing characterizations that it is difficult to distinguish what is essential and nonessential, what is important and unimportant. Moreover, if we consider some of the subsequent "clarifications" by Kuhn and Feyerabend of what they meant by "incommensurability," they are poor and misleading guides. Kuhn betrayed his own best insights when he wrote in 1976:

Most readers of my text have supposed that when I spoke of theories as incommensurable, I meant that they could not be compared. But 'incommensurability' is a term borrowed from mathematics, and it there has no such implication. The hypotenuse of an isosceles right triangle is incommensurable with its side, but the two can be compared to any required degree of precision. What is lacking is not comparability but a unit of length in terms of which both can be measured directly and exactly. In applying the term 'incommensurability' to theories, I had intended only to insist that there was no common language within which both could be fully expressed and which could therefore be used in a point-by-point comparison between them.[75]

Nobody thinks that the incommensurability of the hypotenuse of an isosceles triangle with its sides offers new insights about the nature or image of mathematics (although the discovery of this incommensurability was a significant event in the history of geometry). Furthermore, it is not clear who denies that scientific theories may be incommensurable in this minimal sense.

Feyerabend is no better a guide to what he meant. In 1977, he distinguished three aspects or types of incommensurability, the first of which he described as one in which different paradigms "use *concepts* that cannot be brought into the usual logical relations of inclusion, exclusion, overlap."[76] He goes on to claim that it is this aspect of incommensurability that he always meant when using the expression. "When using the term 'incommensurable' I always meant deductive disjointedness, *and nothing else.*"[77] But when we look at the most extended discussion of incommensurability that Feyerabend provides in *Against Method*, this claim is simply false.

My aim is not to criticize Kuhn and Feyerabend for verbal inconsistency or for confusion about what they did and did not mean. Rather, I want to try to recover or reconstruct what this controversy about incommensurability signifies—what, if anything, is the "truth" implicit in the varied claims and counterclaims. To begin with, it may be helpful to go back to Kuhn's original text, to see how and where he introduces the expression and what claims he makes about incommensurability.

The term is used only about a half-dozen times in *The Structure of Scientific Revolutions*. When discussing the phenomenon of competing schools of thought in the early developmental stages of most sciences, he writes, "What differentiated these various schools was not one or another failure of method—they were all 'scientific'—but what we shall come to call their incommensurable ways of seeing the world and of practicing science in it" (p. 4). Much later in his discussion, when he analyzes the nature and the necessity of scientific revolutions, he tells us that "the normal-scientific tradition that emerges from a scientific revolution is not only incompatible but often actually incommensurable with that which has gone before" (p. 103).

But the main (although very brief) discussion of incommensurability occurs in the context of Kuhn's analysis of the resolution of revolutions. Kuhn seeks to clarify why proponents of competing paradigms "may [each] hope to convert the other to his way of seeing his science and its problems [but] neither may hope to prove his case" (p. 148). He isolates three reasons why "the proponents of competing paradigms must fail to make *complete* contact with each other's viewpoints" (italics added, p. 148). These are the reasons for claiming that there is "incommensurability of the pre- and post-revolutionary normal-scientific traditions" (p. 148). "In the first place, the proponents of competing paradigms will often disagree about the list of problems that any candidate for paradigm must resolve. Their standards or their definitions of science are not the same" (p. 148). However, "more is involved than the incommensurability of standards" (p. 149). Secondly, then, "within the new paradigm, old terms, concepts, and experiments fall into new relationships one with the other" (p. 149). Thus, for example, to make the transition from Newton's universe to Einstein's universe, "The whole conceptual web whose strands are space, time, matter, force, and so on, had to be shifted and laid down again on nature whole" (p. 149). But there is a third, and for Kuhn this is the "most fundamental, aspect of the incommensurability of competing paradigms."

In a sense that I am unable to explicate further, the proponents of competing paradigms practice their trades in different worlds. One contains constrained bodies that fall slowly, the other pendulums that repeat their motions again and again. In one, solutions are compounds, in the other mixtures. One is embedded in a flat, the other in a curved, matrix of space. Practicing in different worlds, the two groups of scientists see different things when they look from the same point in the same direction. Again, that is not to say that they can see anything they please. Both are looking at the world, and what they look at has not changed. But in some areas they see different things, and they see them in different relations one to the other. That is why a law that cannot even be demonstrated to one group of scientists may occasionally seem intuitively obvious to another. Equally, it is why, before they can hope to communicate fully, one group or the other must experience the conversion that we have been calling a paradigm shift. Just because it is a transition between incommensurables, the transition between competing paradigms cannot be made a step at a time, forced by logic and neutral experience. Like the gestalt switch, it must occur all at once (though not necessarily in an instant) or not at all. (p. 150)

I have cited virtually all of the passages in which Kuhn speaks explicitly of incommensurability (though, of course, much of what he says in other places is relevant to his discussion). These passages are instructive not only for what they mention but for what they omit. The primary emphasis here is not on a "theory of meaning," which is what many commentators and critics have mistakenly assumed that Kuhn was suggesting in making his claims about incommensurability. Rather, he stresses the incommensurability of *problems* and *standards*, and asserts that scientists with competing allegiances "practice their trades in different worlds" and, *in some areas*, "see different things."[78]

Furthermore, if we are to sort out what is and what is not involved in the incommensurability of paradigm theories, we must carefully distinguish among *incompatibility, incommensurability*, and *incomparability*. Frequently these three notions have been treated as synonyms by Kuhn's critics, and even by his defenders. For example, Kuhn's (and Feyerabend's) remarks about incommensurability have been taken to mean that we cannot *compare* rival paradigms or theories. But such a claim, I will argue, is not only mistaken but perverse. The very rationale for introducing the notion of incommensurability is to clarify what is involved when we do compare alternative and rival paradigms.

Before turning directly to incommensurability, let us consider the meaning and significance of the claims about *incompatibility*. The concept of incompatibility is a logical one. Two or more statements or theories are logically incompatible if they entail a logical contradiction. When Kuhn and Feyerabend (in some of his earlier papers) spoke of the incompatibility of different theories, they were making an important critique of what has come to be called the "received" or "orthodox" view of the development of scientific theories.[79] The specific thesis under attack was the claim that the relation of a more comprehensive theory to a less comprehensive one could be properly analyzed in strictly logical terms, since a less comprehensive theory can be logically derived from the laws and primitive terms of the more comprehensive theory. Thus, to take a standard case of the relation of Newton's dynamics to Einstein's dynamics, there was a tendency, especially among logical empiricists, to state that what Einstein showed is not that Newton was wrong but only that his theory was incomplete. Consequently, Newtonian theory is supposedly "derivable from Einsteinian, of which it is therefore a special case."

This asymmetrical, logically compatible relation was taken to be a model—indeed the model—for how a more comprehensive and adequate theory stands in relation to a less comprehensive one. This conception of the "derivability" of less comprehensive theories from more comprehensive theories supports the picture of science (all science and not just normal science) as a cumulative linear process— the very picture that Kuhn (and Feyerabend) attack. Such a process of "rational reconstruction" omits the element of conflict and the destruction of paradigms and theories that Kuhn and Feyerabend take to be so vital in scientific development. This is why Kuhn argues that "the relation between contemporary Einsteinian dynamics and the older dynamic equations that descend from Newton's *Principia*" is *"fundamentally incompatible"* (p. 98). What Einstein showed is not that Newton's dynamical equations are partial or incomplete but that they are wrong. It is false to believe that Newtonian dynamics can be logically *derived* from relativistic dynamics. It is because this type of incompatibility and conflict is neglected that "scientific revolutions" frequently appear to be invisible.

We must not misinterpret Kuhn's claim. He is fully aware that it is certainly possible to reconstruct or transform "Newton's laws" so that we can derive an *approximation* of these laws from Einsteinian mechanics. But this is precisely the point: it is just an approximation that is derived, and one that is not, strictly speaking, identical with Newton's laws. It is only because we can give a translation and a transformation from the perspective of Einstein that we are enabled *now* to speak of a transformed Newtonian theory as a special case of Einsteinian theory. "Though an out-of-date theory can always be viewed as a special case of its up-to-date successor, it must be transformed for the purpose. And, the transformation is one that can be undertaken only with the advantages of hindsight, the explicit guidance of the more recent theory" (pp. 102–3). From Kuhn's perspective, the perspicuous way of putting the positivist's point

about derivability is that one powerful reason for accepting a successor theory or paradigm over its rival is that it can explain what is
"true" and "false" in the replaced theory; it has a richer content and
at the same time can account for what is still taken as valid in the
earlier theory, a transformation that becomes possible only because
of the new theory.

This point, so vital for Kuhn's new image of science, which stresses
the element of conflict, incompatibility, and destruction of earlier
paradigms, bears a very strong resemblance to one aspect of Hegel's
understanding of dialectic, his concept of *Aufhebung*. For *Aufhebung*
is at once negation, preservation, and overcoming or synthesis. So,
in the instance of Einsteinian and Newtonian theory, we can say
that Einstein's theory at once negates Newton's (shows that it is
false); preserves it (can reconstruct the "truth" implicit in Newton's
theory by explaining a transformation of it); and both negates and
preserves Newtonian theory by offering a new, rival theory that goes
beyond what Newton achieved.

Kuhn's assertions about incompatibility and Feyerabend's assertions about "deductive disjointedness" were directed at helping us to
understand the role of serious conflict in the development of science.
But it is also clear that if we are to speak of logical *incompatibility*,
we are presupposing a common *logical* framework within which we
can show that two theories are logically incompatible. In making the
claim for *incommensurability*, however, Kuhn wants to make a very
different sort of point. To quote him again, "The normal-scientific
tradition that emerges from a scientific revolution is not only *incompatible* but often actually *incommensurable* with that which has
gone before" (italics added, p. 103). One way to appreciate what is
being said here is to return to the logical empiricist or positivist
understanding of the structure of scientific explanation and theory.
Even if one accepted the minority view that there is a logical incompatibility between two such rival theories as Einstein's and Newton's,
this does not call into question other tenets of the received view that
there is a permanent neutral observation language, or common
framework of scientific standards by which we can evaluate rival and
competing theories. But it is just this dogma of empiricism that
Kuhn is challenging in his appeal to incommensurability.

It is true that Kuhn's rhetoric and metaphors sometimes suggest
what Popper has called the "Myth of the Framework," a metaphor
which suggest that "we are prisoners caught in the framework of our
theories; our expectations; our past experiences; our language,"[80]
and that we are so locked into these frameworks that we cannot

communicate with those encased in "radically" different frameworks or paradigms.[81] But this is not an accurate representation of what Kuhn means, nor is it compatible with many of the claims that he makes. There is always some overlap between rival paradigms—overlap of observations, concepts, standards, and problems. If there were not such overlap, rational debate and argumentation between proponents of rival paradigms would not be possible. Kuhn's detractors have criticized him for failing to realize this, but there is plenty of textual evidence to show that Kuhn himself effectively makes this point.[82] In fact, what he wants to single out in his talk about incommensurability is an important feature of this overlap. He seeks to root out the objectivist bias that we can only make sense of this overlap, and of the rational comparison of rival theories, if we assume that there is something permanent and determinate that stays the same in all such cross-paradigmatic comparisons. He denies that there is a "third," completely neutral language or framework within which rival paradigmatic theories "could be *fully* expressed and which could therefore be used in a point-by-point comparison between them" (italics added).[83] Furthermore, Gerald Doppelt, who carefully reconstructs Kuhn's "incommensurability thesis," has shown it is the incommensurability of *problems* and *standards*—not the incommensurability of *meanings*—that constitutes the most basic thesis for Kuhn,[84] and that in Kuhn's view "there is insufficient overlap in the problems and standards of rival paradigms to rank them on the same scale of criteria."[85] Interpreted in this manner, Kuhn's claims about incommensurability are far less exotic than the suggestion that proponents of rival paradigms are so locked into their frameworks that they cannot communicate with each other, but one should not underestimate the importance of his claims. For he does call into question one of the pillars of a common variety of objectivism—the idea that there is (or must be) a single, universal framework of commensuration.

We can now better understand why Kuhn's claims about incommensurability have provoked such a storm of protest. Implicitly or explicitly, many philosophers of science have maintained that the progressive development of science offers overwhelming support for the belief that such commensuration is the basis for distinguishing rationality from irrationality. What Kuhn (and others) have done is to explode the myth that scientific development offers firm and unambiguous evidence for the dogma that there is a "set of rules which will tell us how rational agreement can be reached on what would settle the issue on every point where statements seem to conflict." They have not shown that science is *irrational*, but rather that something is fundamentally wrong with the idea that commensurability is the essence of scientific rationality.

I stated earlier that Kuhn did not introduce the incommensurability thesis in order to call into question the possibility of *comparing* theories and rationally evaluating them, but to clarify what we are *doing* when we compare theories. The first and most important point is that there are multiple ways in which we can compare theories: we can even compare them to see what is lost when a successor paradigm wins out over and destroys an earlier paradigm.[86] This point is badly distorted when some of Kuhn's critics say that he is denying scientific progress. On the contrary, Kuhn consistently maintains that one of the distinctive characteristics of science is that it does progress.[87] Kuhn is not suggesting that we abandon the notion of scientific progress, but rather that we reinterpret it. Simplistic (or even sophisticated) empiricist theories of what constitutes scientific progress are inadequate.

Observing Kuhn's emphasis on the multiple ways in which rival scientific theories can be *compared* places his discussion of reasons or criteria as values in a new perspective. When clarifying what is involved in argumentation about theory-choice, he is analyzing the various ways in which theories can be rationally compared. Although he denies that there are fixed rules for doing this, or a permanent calculus for rating different theories, he still presents the making of comparative judgments for the purpose of supporting rival theories or paradigms as a rational activity. In summary, we can say that for Kuhn rival paradigm theories are logically *incompatible* (and, therefore, really in conflict with each other); *incommensurable* (and, therefore, they cannot always be measured against each other point-by-point); and *comparable* (capable of being compared with each other in multiple ways without requiring the assumption that there is or must always be a common, fixed grid by which we measure progress).

This last point, about the multiple ways of comparing rival theories, paradigms, and traditions is, as we have seen, one that is also underscored (and perhaps exaggerated) by Feyerabend. In his early papers he was primarily concerned with the incompatibility, or logical disjointedness, of theories, since his primary object was to attack the received view that there is a smooth, linear, progressive development in science. But incompatibility is not the primary point in his most extended discussion of incommensurability, in chapter 17 of *Against Method*. There he tells us,

As incommensurability depends on covert classifications and involves major conceptual changes it is hardly ever possible to give an explicit definition of it. Nor will the customary "reconstructions" succeed in bringing it to the fore. The phenomenon must be shown, the reader must be led up to it by being confronted with a great variety of instances, and he must then judge for himself. This will be the method adopted in the present chapter. (p. 225)

It becomes clear as he proceeds that the aspect of incommensurability that he is stressing is close to what Kuhn claimed was "the third and most fundamental aspect of incommensurability"—that aspect in which we speak of scientists as "practicing in different worlds" and seeing "different things."

Feyerabend, especially in his more recent work, presses his views much further than Kuhn. Kuhn tends to restrict himself primarily to incommensurability as it pertains to the natural sciences. But Feyerabend argues that the conclusions can be generalized and that we can speak of the incommensurability of different traditions ("Rationalism" and "Western Science" are only two of the great variety of traditions) from which we can learn and all of which should have equal rights.[88] Let me outline Feyerabend's position briefly. He begins by speaking about perception, and moves on to a discussion of styles in art. In particular, he seeks to show us the distinctive features of the world view that is expressed in archaic Greek art. He tells us that "the modes of representation used during the early archaic period in Greece are not just reflections of incompetence or of special artistic interests, they give a faithful account of what are felt, seen, thought to be fundamental features of the world of archaic man" (p. 248). One may wonder what this has to do with the philosophy of science and, specifically, the incommensurability thesis as applied to rival scientific theories. Feyerabend concludes his discussion by repeating its results in three theses:

The *first thesis* is that *there are* frameworks of thought (action, perception) which are incommensurable. (p. 271)

....

Secondly, we have seen that incommensurability has an analogue in the field of perception and that it is part of the history of perception. This is the content of my *second thesis* on incommensurability: the development of perception and thought in the individual passes through stages which are mutually incommensurable. (pp. 273–74)

....

My *third thesis* is that the views of scientists, and especially their views on basic matters, are often as different from each other as are the ideologies that underlie different cultures. Even worse: there exist scientific theories which are mutually incommensurable though they apparently deal "with the same subject matter." (p. 274)

Neither in his three summary theses nor in any other place in chapter 17 does Feyerabend explicitly define what he means by incommensurability. But in light of his initial claim that "the phenomenon must be shown" rather than defined, this is not necessarily an objection. Something does emerge here that will directly connect with our discussion of an analogous problem in the social sciences, especially social anthropology, and with our more general discussion of hermeneutics. Feyerabend claims that "the method that has been used for establishing the peculiarities of the archaic cosmology" is, in principle, "the method of an anthropologist who examines the world-view of an association of tribes" (p. 249). He contrasts this method with what he calls the method of "logical reconstruction," which he takes to be the misguided obsession of philosophers of science. It is instructive to see how Feyerabend characterizes "the anthropological method."[89]

An anthropologist trying to discover the cosmology of his chosen tribe and the way in which it is mirrored in language, in the arts, in daily life . . . first learns the language and the basic social habits; he inquires how they are related to other activities, including such *prima facie* unimportant activities as milking cows and cooking meals; he tries to identify *key ideas*. . . .

Having found the key ideas the anthropologist tries to *understand* them. This he does in the same way in which he originally gained an understanding of his own language, including the language of the special profession that provides him with an income. . . .

Having completed his study, the anthropologist carries within himself both the native society and his own background, and he may now start comparing the two. The comparison decides whether the native way of thinking can be reproduced in European terms (provided there is a unique set of "European terms"), or whether it has a "logic" of its own, not found in any Western language. In the course of the comparison the anthropologist may rephrase certain native ideas in English. This does not mean that English *as spoken independently of the comparison* is commensurable with the native idiom. It means that languages can be *bent* in many directions and that understanding does not depend on any particular set of rules. (pp. 250–51)

Feyerabend's account of "the anthropological method" closely parallels many of the standard descriptions of hermeneutics. This is further confirmed in his own version of the hermeneutical circle:

Each item of information is a building block of understanding, which means that it is to be clarified by the discovery of further blocks from the language and ideology of the tribe rather than by premature definitions.

In the process of understanding, there may be

preliminary attempts to anticipate the arrangement of the totality of all blocks. They are then to be tested and elucidated by the discovery of further blocks rather than by logical clarifications (a child learns the meaning of a word not by logical clarification but by realizing how it goes together with things and other words). Lack of clarity of any particular anthropological statement indicates the scarcity of the material rather than the vagueness of the logical intuitions of the anthropologist.[90] (pp. 251–52)

It seems that Feyerabend has wandered from what is supposed to be the problem at hand—the nature of incommensurability in science. But he emphatically tells us,

Exactly the same remarks apply to my attempt to explore incommensurability. Within the sciences incommensurability is closely connected with meaning.[91] (p. 252)

Let us pause and reflect on Feyerabend's description of "the anthropological method," which, he states, is "the correct method for studying the structure of science (and, for that matter, of any other form of life)" (p. 252).

Feyerabend is not recommending that this is the method to be pursued by practicing scientists. Sometimes critics of Feyerabend and Kuhn have interpreted them as saying that physicists ought to be historians or hermeneuticians, but this is silly. On the contrary, both are acutely aware that a major difference between science and other disciplines lies precisely in the attitude that the practicing scientist takes toward the history of his discipline. In comparing art and science, Kuhn tells us:

In no area is the contrast between art and science clearer. Science textbooks are studded with the names and sometimes with portraits of old heroes, but only historians read old scientific works. In science new breakthrough[s] do initiate the removal of suddenly outdated books and journals from their active position in a science library to the desuetude of a general depository. Few scientists are ever seen in science museums, of which the function is, in any case, to memorialize or recruit, not to inculcate craftsmanship or enlighten public taste. Unlike art, science destroys its past.[92]

Knowledge of science's past and study of its history are essential for philosophers and historians who want to understand the nature or image of science but are not necessarily relevant for developing the skills required to be a practicing scientist (except, of course, in the minimal sense that it is necessary for such a scientist to know the relevant literature pertaining to specific scientific problems).

But consider more closely what Feyerabend does in order to show us the phenomenon of incommensurability. In his example of the Greek archaic style, he does not, as some critics have claimed, tell us that because this style (and the world view that it embodies) is incommensurable with later styles we must dumbly contemplate it. We are not confronted with forms of life that are so self-contained that we cannot compare them. If this were really the case, the appropriate response would be silence. On the contrary, he attempts to understand what is distinctive about this style—and the procedure for bringing out what is distinctive depends on a skillful use of *comparison* and *contrast*. The basic presupposition here is that we can understand what is distinctive about this incommensurable style and form of life—and we do not do this by jumping out of our own skins (and language) and transforming ourselves, by some sort of mystical intuition or empathy, into archaic Greeks. Rather, the analysis proceeds by a careful attention to detail—to the various "building blocks"—working back and forth in order to appreciate and highlight similarities with and differences from other styles and forms of life.

In doing this, Feyerabend employs what Clifford Geertz calls "experience-near" and "experience-distant" concepts.

An experience-near concept is roughly, one which an individual—a patient, a subject, in our case an informant—might himself naturally and effortlessly use to define what he or his fellows see, feel, think, imagine, and so on, and which he would readily understand when similarly applied by others. An experience-distant concept is one which various types of specialists—an analyst, an experimenter, an ethnographer, even a priest or an ideologist—employ to forward their scientific, philosophical, or practical aims.[93]

We need to employ both sorts of concepts in a subtle dialectical interplay if we are to come to an understanding of the incommensurable phenomena that we are studying. We need to realize that experience-distant concepts are not simply blind prejudices that get in the way of understanding but can be enabling concepts that allow us to understand. Thus, for example, when Feyerabend tells us,

Instead of looking for the psychological *causes* of a "style" we should therefore rather try to discover its *elements*, analyse their *function*, compare them with other phenomena of the same culture (literary style, sentence construction, grammar, ideology) and thus arrive at an outline of the underlying *world view* including an account of the way in which this world view influences perception, thought, argument, and of the limits it imposes on the roaming about of the imagination. (p. 232)

he is primarily using experience-distant concepts.

The skill or the art here (and it is a rare art) is to do this in a manner that avoids two extremes—the extreme of mutely contemplating something without any understanding, and the extreme of too easily and facilely projecting our own well-entrenched beliefs, attitudes, classifications, and symbolic forms onto the alien phenomenon. While this is an art that requires patience, imagination, attention to detail, and insight—and cannot be completely captured by the specification of rules of procedure—it is certainly a rational activity in which we can discriminate better and worse understandings and interpretations of the phenomenon. Feyerabend is implicitly claiming to give us *a* correct (not necessarily *the* correct) interpretation of Greek archaic art, just as he claims to give a correct interpretation of what Galileo achieved and of the structure of a field of discourse such as quantum physics. Any understanding or interpretation may be challenged and criticized and supplanted by a better, more perspicuous, more adequate one. We must avoid the fallacy of thinking that since there are no fixed, determinate rules for distinguishing better from worse interpretations, there is consequently no rational way of making and warranting such practical comparative judgments.

There is another point to be emphasized here. Whether we are studying the history of science, or different styles, or alien societies, and seeking to elicit what is distinctive and unique about them, we can learn from such a study, we can come to a more sensitive and critical understanding of our own biases and prejudices. Here, too, we must avoid two extremes—the extreme of a type of romanticism that assumes that what is alien or past is necessarily superior, and the ethnocentrism of thinking that there is nothing more to the world than lies within our own "philosophy"—that is, our own well-entrenched beliefs, attitudes, standards, methods, and procedures.

Our discussion of incommensurability leads to a conclusion that is the very opposite of (or an inversion of) the one that many commentators have drawn. Popper is not alone in thinking that the incommensurability thesis is meant to support the Myth of the Framework, where we are enclosed in the prison house of our own frameworks and forms of life. The inversion that I want to stress is that the "truth" of the incommensurability thesis is not closure but *openness*. For at their best, Kuhn and Feyerabend show us that we can understand the ways in which there are incommensurable paradigms, forms of life, and traditions and that we can understand what is distinctive about them without imposing beliefs, categories, and classifications that are so well entrenched in our own language games that we fail to appreciate their limited perspective. Furthermore, in and through the process of subtle, multiple comparison and contrast, we not only come to understand the alien phenomenon that we are studying but better come to understand ourselves. This openness of understanding and communication goes beyond disputes about the development of the natural sciences; it is fundamental to all understanding. When I discuss Gadamer's philosophic hermeneutics, in part III, we will see how crucial this openness is for his analysis of understanding.

I can now relate this discussion of incommensurability to the movement beyond objectivism and relativism, as well as to the Cartesian Anxiety. The misunderstanding of incommensurability is an example of how new insights get submerged and deformed because of the weight of old dichotomies and distinctions. The incommensurability thesis has been rightly taken as an attack on objectivism (not, however, on objectivity). The thesis calls into question that modern version of objectivism which assumes that there is or must be a common, neutral epistemological framework within which we can rationally evaluate competing theories and paradigms or that there is a set of rules (which the philosopher or the epistemologist can "discover") that will tell us "how rational agreement can be reached on what would settle the issue on every point where statements seem to conflict."

But the alternative to such an objectivism has been taken to be relativism, and the incommensurability thesis has been all too easily assimilated and entangled with relativism. In part, this is due to the underlying Cartesian Anxiety—the apprehension that if we give up objectivism, then there is only one real alternative (whatever label we give it). But what is sound in the incommensurability thesis has *nothing to do* with relativism, or at least that form of relativism which wants to claim that there can be no rational comparison among the plurality of theories, paradigms, and language games—that we are prisoners locked in our own framework and cannot get out of it. What is sound in the incommensurability thesis is the clarification of just what we are doing when we do compare paradigms, theories, language games. We can compare them in multiple ways. We can recognize losses and gains. We can even see how some of our standards for comparing them conflict with each other. We can recognize—especially in cases of incommensurability in science—that our arguments and counter-arguments in support of rival paradigm theories may not be conclusive. We can appreciate how much skill, art, and imagination are required to do justice to what is distinctive about different ways of practicing science and how "in some areas" scientists "see different things." In underscoring these features, we are not showing or suggesting that such comparison is irrational but opening up the types and varieties of practical reason involved in making such rational comparisons.

INCOMMENSURABILITY AND THE SOCIAL DISCIPLINES

In discussing the incommensurability thesis with regard to the natural sciences, we have seen, especially in Feyerabend's work, how the discussion spills over to issues of understanding the social disciplines and hermeneutics. This becomes obvious in Feyerabend's appeal to, and description of, what he calls "the anthropological method." It is also clear how closely related Feyerabend's and Winch's concerns are.

But before turning to Winch, I want to consider the contribution of Clifford Geertz, who has combined important field work in anthropology with sophisticated reflection on the discipline of anthropology. He also has the great virtue of being a gifted writer who is able to communicate his insights without lapsing into jargon. (Sometimes in reading the debates of philosophers about anthropology one has the impression that the only anthropologist that they have ever skimmed is Evans-Pritchard—or, less charitably, that the only source of their knowledge of what goes on in anthropology is what philosophers have said about Evans-Pritchard.) The reason why anthropology is (or should be) important for philosophers is that it is in this wide-ranging discipline that many of the issues touched upon in discussions of incommensurability come into sharp focus. One task of the anthropologist who engages in field work is to try to understand alien, or what are sometimes called "primitive," societies, and in doing this he or she must both do justice to the phenomenon being studied and make claims that are intelligible and illuminating to those who have not had direct experience with the societies that are studied. The history of anthropology provides plenty of evidence for the two pervasive temptations that we mentioned as problems in understanding alien phenomena: the temptation to impose, read into, or project categories and moral standards that are well entrenched in our own society onto what is being studied, and the dialectical antithesis of this—the temptation to go native, to suppose that we only really understand the Azande, Neur, or Balinese when we think, feel, and act like them.

This is the set of issues that Geertz explores in his article "From the Native's Point of View: On the Nature of Anthropological Understanding" (1976). There is, he says, a "general problem" that has been exercising methodological discussion in anthropology.

The formulations have been various: "inside" versus "outside," or "first person" versus "third person" descriptions; "phenomenological" versus "objectivist," or "cognitive" versus "behavioral" theories; or, perhaps most commonly, "emic" versus "etic" analyses, this last deriving from the distinction in linguistics between phonemics and phonetics—phonemics classifying sounds according to their internal function in language, phonetics classifying them according to their acoustic properties as such.[94]

The problem is, How is anthropological knowledge of the way natives think, feel, and perceive possible? It is in the context of this general problem that Geertz introduces the distinction between experience-near and experience-distant concepts. The best way to deal with the general problem, he asserts, is to focus on "how anthropological analysis is to be conducted and its results framed, rather than what psychic constitution anthropologists need to have" (p. 227).[95] Of course, anthropologists need to be sensitive and imaginative, need to really listen and to see, but Geertz incisively criticizes the bias that what is special about the anthropologist is that he or she can achieve some sort of psychic unity with the people that he or she is studying.

The trick is not to achieve some inner correspondence of spirit with your informants; preferring, like the rest of us, to call their souls their own, they are not going to be altogether keen about such an effort anyhow. The trick is to figure out what the devil they think they are up to. (p. 227–28)

What is required of the anthropologist is close attention to

searching out and analyzing the symbolic forms—words, images, institutions, behaviors—in terms of which . . . people actually represent themselves to themselves and to one another. (p. 228)

But Geertz is acutely aware that this cannot be done by using only experience-near concepts—by using only those concepts that a person from the culture studied might "naturally and effortlessly use to define what he or his fellows see, feel, think, imagine, and so on" (p. 227). Rather, to gain understanding, the experience-near concepts must be balanced by the appropriate experience-distant concepts, concepts that are not necessarily familiar to the people being studied but that enable us to understand the distinctive symbolic forms of their culture.[96]

In examples drawn from his own field work in Java, Bali, and Morocco, Geertz compares the concepts of a person that are embodied in these cultures (or, more cautiously, those villages that Geertz studied). The concept of a person is a good example of an experience-distant concept. Geertz shows us that these three cultures have three very different concepts of what a person is, each of which, "from our point of view," may seem "more than a little odd." But he is not saying that the "concept of a person" is one that these natives use in thinking about themselves. This concept or vehicle is one that the anthropologist (as a professional) uses to make intelligible the symbolic forms that he or she is studying. Reflecting on these three very different concepts of a person, Geertz asks:

What do we claim when we assert that we understand the semiotic means by which, in this case, persons are defined to one another? That we know words or that we know minds? (p. 239)

In a manner reminiscent of Feyerabend's appropriation of the hermeneutical circle, Geertz makes his own appropriation of it, focusing on the intellectual movement or conceptual rhythm of the anthropologist who engages in

a continuous dialectical tacking between the most local of local detail and the most global of global structure in such a way as to bring both into view simultaneously. . . . Hopping back and forth between the whole conceived through the parts which actualize it and the parts conceived through the whole which motivates them, we seek to turn them, by a sort of intellectual perpetual motion, into explications of one another. (p. 239)

Geertz himself recognizes that he is describing and using the hermeneutical circle, arguing that it is central for ethnographic interpretation. He concludes his article by telling us:

Whatever accurate or half-accurate sense one gets of what one's informants are "really like" comes not from the experience of that acceptance as such, which is part of one's own biography, not of theirs, but from the ability to construe their modes of expression, what I would call their symbol systems, which such an acceptance allows one to work toward developing. Understanding the form and pressure of, to use the dangerous word one more time, natives' inner lives is more like grasping a proverb, catching an allusion, seeing a joke—or, as I have suggested, reading a poem—than it is like achieving communion. (p. 241)

Although Geertz never mentions "incommensurability," his discussion of ethnographic interpretation helps to further our understanding of this concept. The Javanese, Balinese, and Moroccan senses of self are not only very different from our own conception(s) of self; they are incommensurable with ours, in the sense that we cannot make a point-by-point comparison or translation or discover something which is *the* generic concept of self of which these are exotic species with clearly defined differentia. (Geertz, in this context, does not systematically distinguish between the concept of a person and the concept of a self.) But such incommensurability does not get in the way of understanding and comparing the concepts—it rather sets a challenge to us of finding out how to understand and compare them, a challenge that is met by the artful employment of hermeneutical skills.

Suppose we ask what we can learn from such descriptions, other than being able to collect and classify interesting varieties of notions of selfhood. Although Geertz does not explicitly make the point here, it is clear that comparing concepts of the person from other cultures is a way to come to a better and more critical understanding of our own concept of a person. Because the concept of a person is so important in all social groups, we can learn not only about others but about ourselves. And we come to a deeper understanding of ourselves precisely in and through the study of others.[97] By concrete, detailed understanding of other cultures, we can come to realize that

the Western conception of the person as a bounded, unique, more or less integrated motivational and cognitive universe, a dynamic center of awareness, emotion, judgment, and action organized into a distinctive whole and set contrastively both against other such wholes and against a social and natural background is, however incorrigible it may seem to us, a rather peculiar idea within the context of the world's cultures. (p. 229)

We can gain the type of self-knowledge that is achieved whenever we realize that something that we have thought was obvious, universal, and intuitive may not have this epistemological character at all. We may even begin to ask new sorts of questions about our own concept of a person. How did it come to be? What is its history? What institutions, practices, behaviors reinforce it? How is it changing? What poses threats and challenges to it?[98]

An awareness of Geertz's views will help to direct our attention to what is sound and most illuminating in Winch. I do not intend to give a full-scale analysis of Winch or of the many debates that have taken place between him and his critics.[99] Winch is ambiguous and, at times, ambivalent. His style, like Kuhn's, is frequently provocative and all too easily lends itself to conflicting interpretations. The critics' preoccupation with and extensive criticism of Winch's remarks about rationality tend to obscure his primary concern—to determine what is required for and what is involved in the understanding and interpretation of alien or primitive societies. (Winch, of course, particularly in choosing to speak of "our standards" of rationality and "their standards," is partly responsible for this turn in the debate.) I want to pursue a single theme in Winch—his concepts of "learning from" and practical "wisdom."

Winch does not use the term "incommensurability" in elaborating his views. But it is not difficult to detect the family resemblances between what he has to say about different forms of life and the type of incommensurability that Kuhn describes. There is, however, a striking difference. Kuhn, as we have seen, deals with the problems of incommensurability in a very circumscribed context: he is exclusively concerned with the incommensurability of paradigm theories in the natural sciences. He never doubts that Aristotle, Copernicus, Galileo, Newton, Dalton, Priestley, and Einstein are scientists. The problem is to work out an adequate image of science that will account for, and make intelligible, their scientific activities while doing justice to the wide differences among them. We have seen in Feyerabend (and Rorty) an attempt to generalize the type of claims and insights that Kuhn presents, in a much broader context. Both Feyerabend and Rorty want to show that different forms of life, or traditions which extend far beyond science, can be seen as incommensurable. Winch, too, is dealing with this broader problem. Many comparisons with, and understandings of, primitive societies have gone astray, he thinks, because they are frequently insensitive to the different "point" or "meaning" of activities and beliefs that are customary in cultures so different from our own.

What we may learn by studying other cultures are not merely possibilities of different ways of doing things, other techniques. More importantly we may learn different possibilities of making sense of human life, different ideas about the possible importance that the carrying out of certain activities may take on for a man, trying to contemplate the sense of his life as a whole.[100]

Let me begin with a brief discussion of Winch's alleged relativism. Like Kuhn, Winch has explicitly denied that he is advocating or endorsing relativism. In "Understanding a Primitive Society," he explicitly states:

We should not lose sight of the fact that the idea that men's ideas and beliefs must be checkable by reference to something independent—some reality—is an important one. To abandon it is to plunge straight into an extreme Protagorean relativism, with all the paradoxes that involves. (p. 11)

But like Kuhn, Winch has constantly been interpreted as, and criticized for, endorsing the very sort of relativism he disclaims. Comparing the critical literature on Winch with that on Kuhn and his critics, one has a strong sense of déjà vu. One finds the same reiterated interpretations and the same points of criticism. It is not surprising that I. C. Jarvie (who was a student of Popper) makes many of the same points about Winch that Popper and other Popperians have made about Kuhn. Jarvie, in effect, accuses Winch of being committed to Popper's "Myth of the Framework": "[Winch] maintains in [*The Idea of a Social Science*] that understanding a society is a kind of conceptual empathy which imprisons you in a universe of discourse that cannot evaluate itself." Winch's position, Jarvie claims, denies the possibility of ever understanding a form of social life very different from one's own.[101] Again the picture here is one of forms of life so radically different from one another that they cannot be compared. While I do not want to deny that there are passages in Winch that can be extracted to support such an interpretation, it is, nevertheless, a distortion. Reference to the Either/Or of objectivism or relativism can help us to understand why there is an enormous temptation to assume that Winch must be supporting relativism (or that this is what his views really amount to in the end).

The basic issue, according to Winch, is not whether we can *compare* alien societies with our own. This is exactly what he is doing in his discussions of Zande witchcraft. "The question," he argues, "is not *whether* we can do this, but *what sort* of comparison is involved." (This is a precise analogue to the point that Kuhn makes in speaking of the comparison of incommensurable paradigms.) Winch might have helped to forestall some of the misinterpretations of his views if he had been as emphatic in his earlier writings as he is in his reply to Jarvie.

Jarvie shares . . . a tendency which I criticized . . . to speak of the standards of "our scientific culture" in this connection in a way which suggests that the only standards available to us against which to compare Zande standards are the standards involved in the practice of *scientific* work. Now it is of course true that the role played by such work in the culture of western industrialized societies is an enormously important one and that it has had a very far-reaching influence on what we are and what we are not prepared to call instances of "rational thought." But it was an essential part of my argument . . . to urge that our own conception of what it is to be rational is certainly not exhausted by the practices of science; . . . one of the main thrusts of my argument was an attempt to show (a) that misunderstandings of the sense and purport of an institution like Zande magic arose from insisting on just *this* comparison; and (b) that an understanding of such an institution may be furthered by comparing it with quite other sectors of the kind of life we are familiar with.[102]

Winch alerts us here to the error of thinking that our culture is a seamless whole. In trying to understand Zande magic and witch-craft, it may be a mistake to compare witchcraft with the institution of Western science.[103] If, for example, we think that the primary purpose or point of witchcraft is to control and predict events in the environment (just as this is a primary purpose of some aspects of Western science), then we can easily be led to view witchcraft as an irrational or poor form of what we are able to do so much better. But the brunt of Winch's critique is to question whether science is the appropriate standard of comparison for understanding Zande witch-craft. Evans-Pritchard, whose writings are the basis for the claims and counter-claims about Zande witchcraft, made this point himself.

It may have occurred to many readers that there is an analogy between the Zande concept of witchcraft and our own concept of luck. When, in spite of human knowledge, forethought, and technical efficiency, a man suffers a mishap, we say that it is his bad luck, whereas Azande say that he has been bewitched. The situations which give rise to these two notions are similar. If the misfortune has already taken place and is concluded Azande content themselves with the thought that their failure has been due to witchcraft, just as we content ourselves with the reflection that our failure is due to our hard luck. In such situations there is not a great difference between our reactions and theirs. But when a misfortune is in process of falling upon a man, as in sickness, or is anticipated, our responses are different to theirs. We make every effort to rid ourselves of, or elude, a misfortune by our knowledge of the objective conditions which cause it. The Zande acts in a like manner, but since in his beliefs the chief cause of any misfortune is witchcraft, he concentrates his attention upon this factor of supreme impor-tance. They and we use rational means for controlling the conditions that produce misfortune, but we conceive of these conditions differently from them.[104]

Some of Winch's critics have taken him as denying that we and the Azande have anything in common. If this were his position, one could scarcely make any sense of his entire project of trying to understand the language, customs, institutions, and practices of primitive societies. More particularly, however, Winch's talk of "our" standards of rationality and "their" standards suggests that there may be nothing in common between "our" standards and "their" standards—as if, for example, the rules by which they reason and draw logical inferences are radically different from our own rules or as if the procedures by which they identify and reidentify molar objects in their environment are radically different from the ways in which we do this.

I do not think that Winch is making either of these claims or that they follow from what he says. On the contrary, Winch agrees with Evans-Pritchard that the patterns of inference used by the Azande in their famous poison oracle follow the same logical rules, especially of *modus ponens* and *modus tollens*, that we use in reasoning.[105] Furthermore, he assumes that the Azande, like us, identify molar objects. The results of the poison oracle depend on the questions put to the oracle and whether the fowls who are given the Benge (poison) do or do not die in the two tests that are given. "In the two tests one fowl must die and the other must live if the verdict is to be accepted as valid. If both live or both die the verdict is invalid and the oracle must be consulted on the matter a second time on another occasion."[106] Evans-Pritchard and Winch are clearly assuming that we can know with reasonable confidence that the Azande are capable of identifying such a "molar object" as a fowl. If we did not (or could not) know this, we could not even begin to describe the practice of consulting the poison oracle. The two points—that there are patterns of logical inference that we share with the Azande and that there is a range of common objects that both the Azande and we identify in similar ways—may seem so obvious that one may wonder why I note them. I do so because some of Winch's critics claim he is denying this.[107] But if this is not what Winch is claiming, what is his point?

The following passages give us a clue.

We must, if you like, be open to new possibilities of what could be invoked and accepted under the rubric of "rationality"—possibilities which are perhaps suggested and limited by what we have hitherto so accepted, but not uniquely determined thereby.

The point can be applied to the possibilities of our grasping forms of rationality different from ours in an alien culture. First . . . these possibilities are limited by certain formal requirements centering round the demand for consistency. But these formal requirements tell us nothing about what in particular is to *count* as consistency, just as the rules of the propositional calculus limit, but do not themselves determine what are the proper values of *p*, *q*, etc. We can only determine this by investigating the wider context of the life in which the activities in question are carried on. (p. 34)

Or again,

I never of course denied that Zande witchcraft practices involve appeals to what we can understand as standards of rationality. *Such appeals also involve behavior which we can identify as "the recognition of a contradiction." What I was urging, though, was that we should be cautious in how we identify the contradiction, which may not be what it would appear to be if we approach it with "scientific" preconceptions.* Against the background of such preconceptions Zande standards might indeed seem "rather poor," but whether they really are rather poor or not depends on the point of the activity within which the contradictions crop up. My claim was that this point is in fact very different from the point of scientific investigations.[108] (italics added)

Although there are some ambiguities and overstatements in these passages (e.g., "these formal requirements tell us nothing about what in particular is to *count* as consistency"), we can extract Winch's main point, which concerns the *genres* of interpretation. We can begin to understand his point by imagining a sophisticated Zande anthropologist who has learned the language and some of the strange practices of the West. He might, for example, when studying Christian beliefs about God, come across the statements that "God is one" and "God (the same God) is three" and declare that this is or entails a blatant contradiction and, consequently, shows what poor thinkers or how irrational the strange folk from the West really are. Even though there are some Western thinkers who themselves might make this claim, we would be inclined to say that such a judgment is philistine, or at least misses the point of what is expressed in the conjunction "God is one" and "God is three." We might try to explain—to give various theological interpretations of the doctrine of the Trinity (without necessarily denying it as a mystery). But certainly any sympathetic defender of Christianity would object simply to the procedure of extracting these two statements from Christian beliefs and practices, declaring them to be contradictory, and concluding in some straightforward manner that Christianity (and the West) are irrational.

We can make the same point, using the example of science, to show what is wrong with a simplistic understanding of falsification in science. Suppose our Azande is studying the Western institution of science and discovers that there are scientific theories accepted as true, when in fact there are anomalies or evidence that contradicts what would be expected if the theory is true. If the Zande anthropologist concluded that Western science is therefore irrational, we would not hesitate to say that he or she misunderstands how science works. We would say that if this anthropologist better understood the practice of science, he or she would discover that there are many good reasons for accepting a theory as a true theory even when not all the evidence "fits" it and some contradicts it. Winch's argument might have been clearer if he had said that unless we understand and grasp the point of an activity, we are not yet in a position to assess the significance of what appears to be a contradiction. Evaluating what appears to be contradictory is open to interpretation—interpretation that requires a knowledge of what are taken to be *defeasible* conditions, whether this be in understanding the doctrine of the Trinity, Western science, or Zande witchcraft.

Ironically, it is one of Winch's most acute critics, Alasdair MacIntyre, who lucidly expresses Winch's main point. The primary issue is not whether the Azande make logical inferences according to the same rules that we use or are able to identify some of the same or similar molar objects in their environment. Rather, Winch's central concern is with how we *classify* what they are doing—what *genres* we employ in understanding their activities.

Speaking of the anthropologists Frazer and John Beattie, MacIntyre writes:

To a Frazer, who classified primitive rites as inept technology, we are apt to reply that such rites are not science but, for example, a kind of poetry or drama. Thus John Beattie asserts that magic is not technology but "the acting out of the expression of a desire in symbolic terms." . . . I am not competent to question Beattie's ethnographic findings, insofar as these are empirical. It is, however, right to wonder whether, sophisticated as we are, we may not sometimes at least continue to make Frazer's mistake, but in a more subtle way. For when we approach the utterances and activities of an alien culture with a well-established classification of genres in our mind and ask of a given rite or other practice "Is it a piece of applied science? Or a piece of symbolic and dramatic activity? Or a piece of theology?" we may in fact be asking a set of questions to which any answer may be misleading. . . . For the utterances and practice in question may belong, as it were, to all and to none of the genres that we have in mind. . . . Questions of rationality and irrationality cannot be appropriately posed until in a given culture the relevant utterances are given a decisive interpretation in terms of genres. Myths would then be seen as perhaps potentially science *and* literature *and* theology; but to understand them as myths would be to understand them as actually yet none of these. Hence the absurdity involved in speaking of myths as misrepresentating reality; the myth is at most a possible misrepresentation of reality; for it does not aspire, while still only a myth, to be a representation.[109]

To use MacIntyre's terms, Winch's main efforts have been directed against the bias or prejudice that our "genre" of science is the right one for understanding Zande witchcraft. The specific standards of rationality that may be appropriate for scientific activity are not necessarily relevant for understanding the standards of rationality and irrationality in Zande witchcraft.

It is in this context that claims about incommensurability have some bite. In cultures that differ from ours, genres that also differ from ours may be available, embedded in social practices, and these genres may not lend themselves to translation in any simple or direct way into those with which we are familiar. The task of understanding an alien culture may require the imaginative elaboration of new genres, or the stretching of familiar genres, in order to *compare* what may be *incommensurable*. The art here is one of knowing what are the right questions to ask in approaching the strange practices of an alien culture.

But still we want to know *how* to do this. We have good reason to be suspicious of a method (or, more accurately, the concept of method) that leads us to think that there is a set of determinate rules to be followed in understanding and interpretation. But once this negative point is made, there are still plenty of appropriate questions to ask about how we are to proceed—and frankly, Winch is not very helpful in guiding us. In fairness to Winch, it should be noted that he disclaims any effort to provide such a methodology.[110] But we can still ask, How does Winch account for what Geertz called "experience-near" and "experience-distant" concepts, both of which are required for understanding alien societies? Here, too, there is unfortunate ambiguity and vagueness. Winch concentrates on the need to employ "experience-near" concepts. This is even one of the bases he uses for sharply distinguishing the natural from the social sciences. He tells us:

The concepts and the criteria according to which the sociologist judges that, in two situations, the same thing has happened, or the same action performed, must be understood *in relation to the rules governing sociological investigations*. But here we run against a difficulty; for whereas in the case of the natural scientist we have to deal with only one set of rules, namely those governing the scientist's investigation itself, here *what the sociologist is studying*, as well as his study of it, is a human activity and is therefore carried on according to rules. And it is these rules, rather than those which govern the sociologist's investigation, which specify what is to count as "doing the same kind of thing" in relation to that kind of activity.[111]

Winch asserts that we do not have to stop at the kind of unreflective understanding that participants have of their actions, but claims that

any more reflective understanding must necessarily presuppose, if it is to count as genuine understanding at all, the participant's unreflective understanding.[112]

Several problems arise here. There is something a bit too facile about the use Winch is making of this distinction between the unreflective understanding of the participants that we are studying and our reflective understanding; it suggests that we can achieve such an unreflective understanding first, without being influenced by our own reflective categories. (We will see that there was a parallel move in nineteenth-century hermeneutics and historiography, where it was thought that we can somehow jump out of our skins, concepts, and prejudgments and grasp or know the phenomenon as it is in itself.) Geertz's remarks about the dialectical interplay of "experience-near" and "experience-distant" concepts warn us that there are many pitfalls in thinking that we can sharply distinguish between a reflective and unreflective understanding. Furthermore, while one can find some evidence that Winch also believes in the importance of experience-distant concepts, such as when he indicates that psychoanalytic concepts may be helpful in gaining a better understanding of the beliefs and activities of the participants we are studying, he does not squarely face the many issues that arise here. Which experience-distant concepts are most relevant? Weber's? Durkheim's? Freud's? Marx's? How are we to decide? We do not have to assume that there is or can be a univocal answer to such questions, but at least one should recognize that most serious disputes about understanding and interpreting alien phenomena—whether they are primitive societies, sacred or literary texts, or different historical periods and stages of our own society—involve serious disputes about the reflective understanding or experience-distant concepts that are appropriate for understanding and interpretation. By failing to deal directly with the issues involved, Winch neglects a vital dimension in all understanding and interpretation.

This failure has important consequences. As we saw in part I, for Winch the ultimate goal of studying alien societies is to learn from such studies and increase our (practical) wisdom. The study of alien societies throws light on alternative possibilities of good and evil that are reflected in the practices, rituals, beliefs, and institutions. Such learning involves not merely a "disinterested" attitude toward the subject matter that we study. Rather, it has (or can have) consequences for our own self-understanding. It is the beginning of wisdom to realize that what *we* take to be intuitive, natural, obvious, or universal may not be so at all but is only one historical social possibility among several alternatives. But Winch does not clarify what critical standards are to be used in evaluating our culture or an alien one.

More specifically, Winch seeks to deal with the problem of the universal and the particular in regard to the study of alien societies in a manner that is quite different from one of the traditional ways in which this has been approached. A pervasive framework for dealing with the universal and the particular has been to think we must first specify what is universal or generic (for example, the supposedly universal "categories" of rationality) and then treat the specific differentia that distinguish particular societies. (Or, if one accepts this way of posing the issue, one may deny that there is anything that is genuinely and generically universal.) Winch's alternative approach is contained in some sketchy but suggestive remarks at the end of the essay "Understanding a Primitive Society." He speaks of "limiting notions"—certain fundamental notions involved in the very conception of human life, "which have an obvious ethical dimension, and which indeed in a sense determine the 'ethical space', within which the possibilities of good and evil in human life can be exercised" (p. 43). He invokes the name of Vico in making this claim and lists such "limiting notions" as "birth, death, sexual relations." One might add the concept of a person that Geertz examines. Winch himself notes that "unlike beasts, men do not merely live but also have a conception of life [and death]" (p. 44). We can compare and understand different societies by seeking to elicit the distinctive ways in which these societies treat these "limiting notions"—how different attitudes and approaches to them are reflected in concrete practices, institutions, beliefs, and linguistic habits. This does not mean that we study only the forms of reflective thought embodied in different cultures but that we also pay close attention to the details and minutiae of the people's everyday lives, searching for clues as to how such "limiting notions" are reflected and concretely embodied.

Geertz, in his essay "The Impact of the Concept of Culture on the Concept of Man," deals with the issue raised here in a far more incisive manner than Winch does, and Geertz's argument can be directly related to the movement beyond objectivism and relativism.

He criticizes what he calls the *"consensus gentium* approach" which has plagued not only the study of anthropology but the whole range of the social sciences. This approach, he says, is obsessed by the search for abstract cross-cultural universals. But the failure to come up with informative, rich, substantive universals leads right to the antithesis—cultural relativism. (Here, too, the failure of a form of objectivism seduces one into thinking that the only viable alternative is relativism.)

Geertz perceptively shows the way out of, or beyond, this Either/ Or when he writes:

> If we want to discover what man amounts to, we can only find it in what men are; and what men are, above all other things, is various. It is in understanding that variousness—its range, its nature, its basis, and its implications—that we shall come to construct a concept of human nature that, more than a statistical shadow and less than a primitive dream has both substance and truth.[113]

Becoming aware of our own "blind prejudices," learning that there is more to the "world" and to different forms of life than is captured by our own entrenched forms of life and genres, is only the beginning—not the end—of wisdom. There is very little unambiguous evidence that even those anthropologists who have practiced what Winch advocates have become *better persons* as a result of their studies or that reading the works of anthropologists has had this practical consequence for others. There is a gap or void at the center of Winch's analysis. Even if we concede everything that Winch wants to claim about how we can learn from the study of alien cultures and forms of life, he has not given us the slightest clue about what *critical* standards we are to employ in doing this, how we are to assess and evaluate new and alternative "possibilities of good and evil, in relation to which men may come to terms with life" (p. 42).[114] In raising this question, we do not have to assume that there are or must be universal critical standards that transcend all local cultures and are ahistorical. But Winch does not really confront this issue; he avoids it. Or rather, he suggests, without argument, that all answers must be ad hoc and piecemeal. (When I examine the Gadamer–Habermas debate, we will see that an analogous issue stands at the crux of their most important differences.)

Winch might reply that the questions raised in speaking of critical standards of evaluation are indeed important ones but that it is unfair to criticize him on this point; that it misses the main purpose of his work. He might even claim that in some of the essays written after "Understanding a Primitive Society" he has attempted to approach these questions from a variety of perspectives.[115] After all, he might add, there has been so much confusion about the concept of the social and the proper way to study alien societies that the first task is to clear up these confusions and clarify what we can learn from such studies.

Without contesting these claims, such a reply is inadequate. We are learning to appreciate the pitfalls of the various forms of objectivism and relativism. Winch's work, as we have seen, contributes to an understanding of how we can perceive the incommensurability of different forms of social life without denying that we can compare them with each other. The judicious understanding of alien societies requires a type of practical judgment and reasoning in which we do justice to such "universals" as the "limiting concepts" that are involved in all forms of human life but are nevertheless particularly and concretely textured in the different cultural forms of human life. And from what Winch says about the "ethical space" of such limiting concepts, it also becomes evident that practical wisdom is required when we critically compare different possibilities of good and evil.

But our problem today—and it is a problem that emerges from Winch's own analyses and reflections—is to find out what standards and criteria we can legitimately appeal to in assessing and evaluating what we learn. How can we critically understand, and perhaps modify, our own entrenched "possibilities of good and evil"? Winch enables us to gain a better understanding of some of the wrong ways of engaging in such a practical critique but offers us very little in the way of positive guidance. We will return to this issue when we take up the question of the nature and varieties of *praxis*.

Throughout part II, and especially in the discussion of incommensurability (whether in the more localized sense of the incommensurability of scientific paradigm theories or the more global sense of the incommensurability of forms of life, cultures, and traditions), we have witnessed the beginnings of the recovery of the hermeneutical dimension of experience. It is implicit in Kuhn, explicit in Feyerabend's account of the anthropological method, and dominant in Geertz and Winch. Several features of hermeneutics have been touched upon: the significance and role of tradition in human understanding; the recognition that different traditions or forms of life may be incommensurable but can nevertheless be rationally compared; an awareness of the intimate connection between understanding and interpretation, and of the essential role of practical judgment in making such comparisons; the belief that the study of alien phenomena can create a subtle dialogue or dialectic through which we can come to a deeper, more critical understanding of our own forms of life and even uncover our prejudices. The core of the incommensurability thesis, we have seen, is not closure and being encapsulated in self-contained frameworks but the openness of experience, language, and understanding. All of this contributes to the movement beyond objectivism and relativism and to liberating us from the Cartesian Anxiety. But our approach to hermeneutics thus far has been indirect—witnessing how it arises from internal reflection on the nature of science and the understanding of society. We need to confront hermeneutics directly, to understand understanding itself and how it is related to interpretation and application. These are the issues that we now need to address in order to further our exploration of rationality.

PART THREE
FROM HERMENEUTICS
TO *PRAXIS*

THE term "hermeneutics," with its ancient lineage, has only recently begun to enter the working vocabulary of Anglo-American thinkers. Its novelty is indicated in a passage cited earlier from Thomas Kuhn's *The Essential Tension* (1977) in which he confesses that "the term 'hermeneutic' . . . was no part of my vocabulary as recently as five years ago. Increasingly, I suspect that anyone who believes that history may have deep philosophical import will have to learn to bridge the longstanding divide between the Continental and English-language philosophical traditions."[1]

We can trace the paths by which interest in hermeneutics has spread and deepened among Anglo-American thinkers. One of the primary traditions that feeds into contemporary hermeneutics has been that of biblical hermeneutics. The meaning and scope of hermeneutics was significantly extended in the nineteenth century by such German thinkers as Schleiermacher and Dilthey, who in turn influenced Heidegger and Bultmann. Some of the earliest discussions of hermeneutics in an Anglo-American context were by biblical scholars, theologians, and students of the history of religions who were influenced by or reacting against the claims of Schleiermacher, Dilthey, Heidegger, and Bultmann. But the problems of the interpretation of sacred texts, as Frank Kermode has most recently argued, have analogues with the problems of the interpretation of literary texts.[2] It is not surprising in an age when the question of interpretation has become so fundamental for literary history and literary criticism that interest in hermeneutics should become so prominent.[3]

A significant event focusing attention on hermeneutics in the United States in recent times occurred at a symposium held in 1970 in which Charles Taylor, Paul Ricoeur, and Hans-Georg Gadamer participated. Taylor, although he was trained at Oxford at a time when the work of Wittgenstein and J. L. Austin were the dominant influences, has always had a long-standing interest in bridging "the divide between Continental and English-language philosophical traditions." He began his paper with the question,

Is there a sense in which interpretation is essential to explanation in the sciences of man? The view that it is, that there is an unavoidably "hermeneutical" component in the sciences of man, goes back to Dilthey. But recently the question has come again to the fore, for instance, in the work of Gadamer, in Ricoeur's interpretation of Freud, and in the writings of Habermas.[4]

Taylor's question and the positive answer that he develops in his paper have had extensive resonances because they appeared at a time when important developments were taking place within the sciences of man and the social sciences. This was a period when there were increasing doubts about the methodological self-understanding of the social disciplines that had been shaped by logical positivism and empiricism. Three factors contributed to the uneasiness about the nature of the social disciplines and to the receptivity to hermeneutics. There was a growing awareness that themes in analytic philosophy, and especially insights of the later Wittgenstein and the theory of speech acts developed by Austin, were relevant to a critical understanding of social life. This was complemented by the realization that the tradition of interpretive sociology was neither dead nor passé, and more generally that hermeneutics could be used to criticize positivist strains in the social disciplines and open the way to a more penetrating understanding of them. Anglo-American thinkers became more receptive to the type of hermeneutical critiques developed by Ricoeur, Gadamer, and Habermas. Finally, many practitioners of the social disciplines themselves began to question the adequacy of the notion of social science as a fledging natural science.

Because hermeneutics, as it was shaped in the nineteenth century, was intimately related to the study of history and the nature of historical knowledge, it is only natural that discussions of hermeneutics began to appear among historians who were reflecting on the status of their discipline. In this respect the work of Hayden White and Quentin Skinner should be mentioned.[5] Although both have been sharply critical of some of the claims made by hermeneutics, nevertheless both have entered into serious dialogue with this tradition. A key influence on Skinner has been Collingwood. One can only speculate about the hearing that hermeneutics might have received from Anglo-American philosophers if the work of Collingwood had had the influence it so eminently deserves.[6] The major themes of Collingwood's investigations of art and history are those which have been at the very center of hermeneutical discussion. We have already seen how Mary Hesse began exploring the significance of hermeneutics for the study of the history and philosophy of science and how Clifford Geertz characterizes anthropological research as a hermeneutical inquiry.

From the perspective of professional Anglo-American analytic philosophers, the several fields that I have mentioned—the study of sacred and literary texts, the study of the nature of history, and the range of the sciences of man—have been seen as peripheral to the "hard core" of serious philosophy. Although there were some preliminary skirmishes, it was only with the appearance of Richard Rorty's *Philosophy and the Mirror of Nature* (1979) that a philosopher who had a reputation for making serious contributions to analytic philosophy dared to suggest that the lessons of hermeneutics might be essential for the understanding of philosophy itself. The title of the penultimate chapter of his book, "From Epistemology to Hermeneutics," might have served as the subtitle for the entire book. Rorty argues that it is epistemology that has been the basis for and stands at the center of modern philosophy. But he portrays the death of epistemology, or, more accurately, shows why it should be abandoned. It is in the aftermath of epistemology (and its successor disciplines) that hermeneutics becomes relevant—not as leading to a new "constructive" foundational discipline but as "an expression of hope that the cultural space left by the demise of epistemology will not be filled—that our culture should become one in which the demand for constraint and confrontation is no longer felt."[7] It is not surprising that the publication of Rorty's book has provoked so much controversial discussion.

In speaking of the spread of interest in hermeneutics, we should not exaggerate the degree of change. There are still many, perhaps the majority of thinkers in the several fields that I have mentioned, who view hermeneutics as some sort of woolly foreign intrusion to be approached with suspicion. But I believe that the recent concern with hermeneutics reflects more than a faddish interest in the exotic. On the contrary, what has happened is that thinkers in diverse fields, working on a variety of problems, have come to share many of the insights, emphases, and concerns of contemporary philosophic hermeneutics.

The above sketch of the growing interest in hermeneutics during the past decade or so has been presented from an Anglo-American perspective. The narrative would be very different if told from a continental point of view, especially that of German philosophy.[8] It was in the nineteenth century, the great age of the rise of historical consciousness, that the exploration of hermeneutics deepened on the Continent and was seen to have consequences for the entire range of the human sciences. As Gadamer tells us,

In the nineteenth century, the old theological and literary ancillary discipline of hermeneutics was developed into a system which made it the basis of all the human sciences. It wholly transcended its original pragmatic purpose of making it possible, or easier, to understand literary texts. It is not only the literary tradition that is estranged and in need of new and more appropriate assimilation, but all that no longer expresses itself in and through its own world—that is, everything that is handed down, whether art or the other spiritual creations of the past, law, religion, philosophy and so forth—is estranged from its original meaning and depends, for its unlocking and communicating, on that spirit that we, like the Greeks, name Hermes: the messenger of the gods. It is to the development of historical consciousness that hermeneutics owes its central function within the human sciences. (*TM*, pp. 146–47; *WM*, p. 157)

Schleiermacher, who was one of the first to argue for the general significance of hermeneutics, drew upon this tradition to meet the challenge of the skepticism about religious understanding. But by the time of Dilthey, this interest had been extended to deal with two of the great intellectual problems of the age: the study of history and the nature of historical knowledge; and the rival claims of the *Naturwissenschaften* and the *Geisteswissenschaften*. Nineteenth-century hermeneutics developed as a reaction against the intellectual imperialism of the growth of positivism, inductivism, and the type of scientism that claimed that it is the natural sciences alone that provide the model and the standards for what is to count as genuine knowledge. The character of hermeneutics was shaped by the assault on the integrity and autonomy of the human sciences. The primary task was seen, especially by Dilthey, as that of determining what is distinctive about humanistic and historical knowledge and of revealing its characteristic subject matter, aims, and methods in a manner that would meet and challenge the belief that only the natural sciences can provide us with "objective knowledge." Dilthey's dream was to do for the historical human sciences what Kant presumably accomplished for mathematics and the natural sciences: to write a *Critique of Historical Knowledge* that would show at once the possibility, nature, scope, and legitimacy of this type of "objective knowledge."

But what were the sources of the nineteenth-century interest in hermeneutics? Gadamer mentions the "development of historical consciousness," which certainly was a major factor in the development of the entire range of the cultural disciplines in Germany. Historians of hermeneutics have argued that there are many diverse sources reaching back to the tradition of classical and medieval rhetoric, whose last great representative was the prophetic thinker Vico; the tradition of practical philosophy that took shape as a result of Aristotle's reflections on *praxis* and *phronēsis;* legal history and jurisprudence; the humanism of the Renaissance, and the post-Reformation discipline of biblical interpretation. It is clear from the way in which Gadamer begins *Truth and Method* with a review of the "leading humanistic concepts"—including *Bildung, sensus communis,* judgment, and taste—that hermeneutics is closely intertwined with the entire history of humanistic studies.

But only in the twentieth century, primarily due to the influence of the phenomenological movement and, in particular, Heidegger's *Being and Time,* has hermeneutics moved to the very center of continental philosophy. Implicit in Heidegger, and explicit in Gadamer, are two interrelated fundamental claims: the claim for the *ontological* significance of hermeneutics, and the claim for its *universality.* Hermeneutics is no longer conceived of as a subdiscipline of humanistic studies or even as the characteristic Method of the *Geisteswissenschaften,* but rather as pertaining to questions concerning what human beings are. We are "thrown" into the world as beings who understand and interpret—so if we are to understand what it is to be human beings, we must seek to understand understanding itself, in its rich, full, and complex dimensions. Furthermore, understanding is not one type of activity, to be contrasted with other human activities. (We will see that, for Gadamer, understanding is misconceived when it is thought of as an activity of a *subject;* it is a "happening," an "event," a *pathos*). Understanding is universal and may properly be said to underlie and pervade all activities. One of my main objectives in part III will be to clarify and explore what is meant by the claim that hermeneutics is ontological and universal. But it should already be clear that hermeneutics conceived in this manner is no longer thought of as the method of the *Geisteswissenschaften*. It is presumably more fundamental than Method, and sharply critical of imperialistic claims made in the name of Method.

If one were to try to tell the complete story of the developments, variations, and vicissitudes of twentieth-century hermeneutics, it would require nothing less than a study of the whole of continental philosophy in recent times. Fortunately my task is a more limited one, for I am interested in the ways in which philosophic hermeneutics contributes to overcoming the Cartesian Anxiety and helps us to move beyond objectivism and relativism. In exploring the fusion of hermeneutics and *praxis*, I intend to show how the implicit *telos* within philosophic hermeneutics requires us to move beyond hermeneutics itself. While I will refer to a range of thinkers, I will concentrate on the work of Gadamer. For although Gadamer's views are not shared by all those working in this tradition (and have been sharply criticized), he has presented one of the most comprehensive, powerful, and subtle explanations of philosophic hermeneutics.

Treating Gadamer in an Anglo-American philosophic context presents special problems. Gadamer's understanding of philosophic hermeneutics emerged from his own practice of the interpretation of texts. Typically, and especially in *Truth and Method*, Gadamer does not simply state the theses that he seeks to defend, and argue for them in the usual manner of analytic philosophers. He proceeds in what, from an analytic perspective, looks like indirect, oblique, "suggestive" discourse—by interpreting, questioning, and conversing with texts. Because the range of his interpretations is staggering in its scope and subtlety, one sometimes feels that in order to understand him one must already have the *Bildung* that he talks about. Yet Gadamer beautifully orchestrates *Truth and Method* so that what at first might appear to be only a display of erudition is not that at all. Themes, concepts, and interpretations enter and interweave in his reflections so that they mutually support each other and exhibit a textured vision of philosophic hermeneutics, and how it is revelatory of human finitude.

Several commentators have queried the significance of the very title of Gadamer's *Wahrheit und Methode*, questioning not only the precise meaning of *Wahrheit* and *Methode* but also how one is to understand the conjunction *"und." ("Wahrheit und Methode"* was not Gadamer's original choice for the title.) At times it seems as if Gadamer is emphasizing not the *con*junction but the *dis*junction between Truth and Method, so that a more apt title might have been "Truth *versus* Method." Gadamer has denied that it was his intention to play off Truth against Method, although when we examine what Gadamer means by "play," we will see that there is indeed, throughout the work, a "play" of Truth and Method. A more appropriate title or subtitle of the book, and indeed of Gadamer's entire philosophic project, might have been "Beyond Objectivism and Relativism." Gadamer's primary philosophic aim is to expose what is wrong with the type of thinking that moves between these antithetical poles and to open us to a new way of thinking about understanding that reveals that our being-in-the-world is distorted when we impose the concepts of objectivism and relativism.

To appreciate what is distinctive about philosophic hermeneutics, we need to discuss the Cartesian legacy that serves as the backdrop for the drama that Gadamer unfolds. Gadamer builds upon the work of Heidegger, who himself engaged in a thoroughgoing critique of modern subjectivism that stems from Descartes (and can even be traced back to earlier motifs in Platonism). In speaking of the Cartesian legacy, one must be careful to distinguish the historical Descartes from Cartesianism. Recent historical scholarship, which itself has been partially influenced by a hermeneutical sensibility, has revealed how much disparity there is between what Descartes' texts say and the interpretation of his work by later thinkers. We can nevertheless discriminate the main features of Cartesianism that did enter the mainstream of philosophy. By listing these salient characteristics and relating them to Gadamer's thinking, we can gain a proper orientation for appreciating the nature of philosophic hermeneutics.

THE CARTESIAN LEGACY

First, Descartes introduces a rigorous distinction between *res cogitans* and *res extensa*. This distinction is the basis for the sharp separation of two types of quasi substance, mind and body. I speak of mind and body as "quasi substances" because they lack one essential characteristic that was traditionally associated with the doctrine of substance: independence or self-sufficiency. As Descartes makes clear in the *Meditations*, both mind and body are ultimately dependent for their sustained existence on God. Consequently, one might say that implicit in Descartes' "dualism" is the suggestion that there is only one completely self-sufficient substance—God himself. Although Descartes does not employ the expressions "subject" and "object" in the ways in which they have come to be used by post-Cartesian philosophers (he still draws on the scholastic tradition), nevertheless his metaphysical and epistemological dichotomies provide the basis for this systematic distinction. Even those post-Cartesian philosophers who have challenged metaphysical dualism have generally accepted some version of the subject–object dichotomy as being basic for understanding our knowledge of the world.

Second, if one is to achieve clear and distinct knowledge, the "I" (the subject) must engage in the activity of intellectual self-purification. By the procedure of methodical doubt, I must bracket or suspend judgment in everything that can be doubted in order to discover the Archimedean point that can serve as a proper foundation for the sciences. I must suspend judgment in all my former opinions and prejudices. This is essentially a solitary, monological activity (although it is likened to an internal dialogue), in the sense that I, in the solitude of my study, can by self-reflection discover the groundlessness of former opinions and prejudices. Descartes never really doubts that one can achieve this self-transparency and self-understanding by proper meditative reflection.

Third, Descartes understands human finitude in a distinctive way. For although we are finite, we are not imperfect. In the fourth Meditation, when Descartes seeks to explain his errors, he tells us

that they depend on a combination of two causes, to wit, on the faculty of knowledge that rests in me, and on the power of choice or free will—that is to say, of the understanding and at the same time of the will. For by the understanding alone I [neither assert nor deny anything, but] apprehend the ideas of things as to which I can form a judgment.[9]

It is by virtue of this "ample" and "unconstrained" free will that I have the capacity to assert *or* to deny—that is, to *judge*. There is no intrinsic defect or imperfection in my will or my understanding. Human error (and sin) results from the misuse of these capacities—a misuse for which I alone, and not God, am responsible. We are created in the image of God, with whom we share such an "infinite" will. However, our understanding, while containing no intrinsic imperfection, is limited and finite. We cannot understand everything that an omniscient being understands. We err when we affirm or deny that which we do not understand clearly and distinctly—when we allow our will to outstrip the domain of what we truly understand. Human finitude is most sharply expressed in the realization of our complete dependence on a beneficent God for our sustained existence, but in the realm of knowledge our finite knowledge is related to God's knowledge as a part to a (infinite) whole.

Fourth, truth is primarily ascribed to *judgments.* Although Descartes speaks of the "material falsity of ideas," the primary source of error and falsity is misjudgment, when I allow myself to affirm or deny what I do not understand clearly and distinctly. And because judging is an activity of the will, it is always within my power (at least when meditating) to withhold my judgment. It is I who am responsible for making false judgments, although because of the "exigencies of action" and the "infirmity" of my nature, I cannot hope to altogether avoid making errors.

Fifth, once we discover the Archimedean point that can serve as a foundation, then we can build a solid edifice of knowledge by following strict rules and Method. These rules can be specified, and they serve two closely related functions. They enable us to extend our knowledge systematically, and they ensure that nothing will be admitted as knowledge (and consequently as true) unless it satisfies the rigorous requirements of the specified rules.

Sixth, when *justifying* claims to knowledge, there should be no appeal other than the appeal to reason itself. We must be skeptical about any claims to knowledge that are based solely on the testimony of the senses, former opinions, prejudices, tradition, or any authority other than reason. There may be many sources for our coming to know something, but the court of appeal to validate claims to knowledge is reason—a reason which is universal, not limited by historical contingencies, and shared by all rational beings.

Seventh, one of the important consequences of Cartesianism was to forge a close link between experience and the senses and to focus almost exclusive attention on the *epistemological* role of experience. Of course, it was not due solely to Descartes that the senses have been thought of as the primary source of experience. This is also fundamental to the empiricist tradition. But despite major differences between rationalists and empiricists in their understanding of the senses and their contribution to knowledge, both traditions are dominated by an epistemological interest in the senses and experience.

Given these seven points, it should be clear why Descartes is so suspicious of any claims to knowledge that are based upon appeals to authority, tradition, or opinions. We even find here the seeds for the typical Enlightenment contrasts between reason and tradition, reason and authority, reason and superstition. We can also understand why Descartes (despite his own traditional education) was so skeptical about and even hostile to the study of history, classical languages, and texts. While the erudition achieved may be an innocent adornment, it can get in the way of, and divert us from, the serious project of discovering the foundations and building the edifice of objective knowledge.

Gadamer's critique of Cartesianism (like that of Heidegger and Peirce) is radical in the sense of "getting at the roots." Gadamer does not merely raise objections about the epistemological, methodological, or even the metaphysical claims of Cartesianism. The basis of his critique is *ontological*; he thinks that Cartesianism is based on a misunderstanding of being, and in particular upon a misunderstanding of our being-in-the-world. But while Gadamer's critique is radical, it is not frontal. On the contrary, it is indirect and almost oblique, butnevertheless—orperhapsbecauseofthisindirectness—devastating.

TRUTH AND THE EXPERIENCE OF ART

In the first part of *Truth and Method,* which is entitled "The Question of Truth as It Emerges in the Experience of Art," Gadamer explores a topic that is barely mentioned by Descartes and might even seem peripheral to Cartesianism. Gadamer's main concern is with the "subjectivisation of aesthetics in the Kantian critique," but it is here that he also begins his assault on the Cartesian legacy. The questions that preoccupy Gadamer here are these: How are we to account for the typically modern denigration of the idea of the truth of works of art? How are we to deal with the modern embarrassment in even speaking about truth in regard to works of art? What is the source for the deep prejudice that the appreciation of art and beauty has nothing to do with knowledge and truth? Gadamer examines the sources of this modern prejudice because he wants to question and challenge it. He finds that Kant's *Critique of Judgment* (especially the first part of this critique) and its decisive influence played a key role in the emergence of aesthetics and the concepts of "aesthetic consciousness" and "aesthetic differentiation."

It is important to appreciate the problem Kant confronts in his analysis of aesthetic judgment. Kant, after completing the first two critiques, in which he sought to reveal the a priori foundations of knowledge and morality, now faced the task of not only unifying the critical project through a study of judgment, but also of demonstrating the legitimacy of judgments of taste, and in particular the type of *reflective judgment* characteristic of aesthetic judgment. He sought to provide an *analytic* and a *deduction* that would reveal the a priori foundations of this distinctive type of judgment. Aesthetic judgments are not to be confused or identified with knowledge of the phenomenal world or with the activity of pure practical reason. But this does not mean that for Kant aesthetic judgments are merely arbitrary or idiosyncratic. They do make a distinctive claim to universality (or more accurately, generality or communicability).[10] Throughout Kant maintains a basic dichotomy between the subjective and the objective, although the meaning of these concepts is transformed because of Kant's Copernican Revolution.

The specific problem for him was to explain how aesthetic judgment is related to a distinctive type of subjective aesthetic pleasure (to be carefully distinguished from other sorts of pleasure) and at the same time to account for the communal validity of such judgments. Kant tells us that the cognitive powers are here in "free play, because no definite concept limits them to a definite rule of cognition. . . . This state of *free play* of the cognitive faculties in a representation by which an object is given must be universally communicable."[11] Using a more contemporary idiom, Kant's project was to show that aesthetic judgments are grounded in human subjectivity and yet are not merely *relative* to an individual subject. Taste is communal, not idiosyncratic.

Aesthetic judgments, however, are not judgments of truth or falsity. Gadamer locates the same tendency—to exclude completely the question of truth—in Kant's analysis of genius. Anticipating what happened after (and partly as a result of) Kant, Gadamer tells us:

The radical subjectivisation involved in Kant's new basis for aesthetics was a completely new departure. In discrediting any kind of theoretical knowledge apart from that of natural science, it compelled the human sciences to rely on the methodology of the natural sciences in self-analysis. But it made this reliance easier by offering as a subsidiary contribution the "artistic element," "feeling," and "empathy." (*TM*, p. 39; *WM*, p. 38)

It is this "radical subjectivisation" of aesthetic judgment that Gadamer calls "aesthetic consciousness," and he claims that it no longer left any room for speaking of knowledge or of claims to truth by a work of art. Such a notion of "aesthetic consciousness" goes hand-in-hand with what Gadamer calls the abstraction of "aesthetic differentiation," according to which we are to disregard everything in which a work of art is rooted, such as its original context and its secular or religious function, in order for the "pure work of art" to stand out. We can call this the "museum" conception of art, which assumes that by isolating the work of art from its original context and placing it in a museum we abstract it from everything that is extraneous to it in order to appreciate and judge it aesthetically. And Gadamer does claim that the growth of the modern museum as the repository of works of art is closely related to the growth of aesthetic consciousness and aesthetic differentiation.

Given these tendencies that are implicit in Kant's understanding of aesthetic judgment, it is not difficult to see how they lead to consequences that undermine what he sought to accomplish. Once we begin questioning whether there is a common faculty of taste (a *sensus communis*), we are easily led down the path to relativism. And this is what did happen after Kant—so much so that today it is extraordinarily difficult to retrieve any idea of taste or aesthetic judgment that is more than the expression of personal preferences. Ironically (given Kant's intentions), the same tendency has worked itself out with a vengeance with regard to all judgments of value, including moral judgments.

Gadamer draws out these consequences of Kant's "radical subjectivisation" in order to begin to show what is wrong with this entire way of approaching works of art. At this stage in his inquiry, he raises a series of questions which indicate the direction of his thinking.

Is there to be no knowledge in art? Does not the experience of art contain a claim to truth which is certainly different from that of science, but equally certainly is not inferior to it? And is not the task of aesthetics precisely to provide a basis for the fact that artistic experience is a mode of knowledge of a unique kind, certainly different from that sensory knowledge which provides science with the data from which it constructs the knowledge of nature, and certainly different from all moral rational knowledge and indeed from all conceptual knowledge, but still knowledge, i.e., the transmission of truth? (*TM*, p. 87; *WM*, p. 93)

If such questions are not to be taken as merely rhetorical but as questions that can be given, as Gadamer thinks they can, affirmative answers, then we need to find a way of thinking that overcomes this "radical subjectivisation." In this regard we can appreciate the introduction of a concept that might at first seem incidental, and even fanciful—the concept of *play*. Its importance, however, is indicated when Gadamer speaks of play as "the clue to ontological explanation" and claims that it points the way toward understanding "the ontology of the work of art and its hermeneutical significance" (*TM*, p. 91; *WM*, p. 97).

Many philosophers who identify themselves with the phenomenological movement have a tendency to talk constantly about phenomenology and what it can achieve, rather than to *do* phenomenological analysis. But Gadamer's rich description of play and games is an example of phenomenological analysis at its best. But why introduce the concept of play here? And what does it mean to say that play is the "clue to ontological explanation"? To anticipate, Gadamer is searching for a phenomenon or model that provides an alternative to the Cartesian model that rivets our attention on "subjective attitudes" (*Vorstellung*) toward what is presumably "objective." If he is to succeed in moving beyond objectivism and relativism (and the entire cluster of dichotomies associated with this opposition), then he needs to show us—to point the way to the alternative. This is what he seeks to accomplish by introducing the concept of play. Gadamer not only gives a subtle phenomenological description of play; he also draws upon Huizinga's penetrating analysis of play and upon the crucial role of "free play" in Kant's analysis of aesthetic judgment.[12]

Beginning with ordinary games and children's play, Gadamer stresses the primacy of the game or the play that we participate in. "Play fulfills its purpose only if the player loses himself in his play" (*TM*, p. 92; *WM*, p. 97). Gadamer calls attention to the internal buoyancy, the to-and-fro movement that belongs to play itself. Play is a "happening."

Play obviously represents an order in which the to-and-fro motion of play follows of itself. . . . The structure of play absorbs the player into itself, and thus takes from him the burden of the initiative, which constitutes the actual strain of existence. This is seen also in the spontaneous tendency to repetition that emerges in the player and in the constant self-renewal of play, which influences its form. (*TM*, p. 94; *WM*, p. 100)

Gadamer seeks to show us that there is a distinctive "mode of being" of play. For play has its own essence (*Wesen*), independent of the consciousness of those who play. According to Gadamer, "The players are not the subjects of play: instead play merely reaches presentation [*Darstellung*] through the players" (*TM*, p. 92; *WM*, p. 98). Furthermore, play is not even to be understood as a kind of activity; the actual subject of play is not the individual, who among other activities plays, but instead the play itself.

As we explore Gadamer's understanding of philosophic hermeneutics, we will see just how central this concept of play is for him;

it turns out to be the key or the clue to his understanding of language and dialogue.

> Now I contend that the basic constitution of the game, to be filled with its spirit—the spirit of buoyancy, freedom and the joy of success—and to fulfill him who is playing, is structurally related to the constitution of the dialogue in which language is a reality. When one enters into dialogue with another person and then is carried along further by the dialogue, it is no longer the will of the individual person, holding itself back or exposing itself, that is determinative. Rather, the law of the subject matter [*die Sache*] is at issue in the dialogue and elicits statement and counterstatement and in the end plays them into each other.[13]

But at this point one might be inclined to object. If we are really speaking about human games and play, then there is no play without players—the *subjects*. And the *objects* here, insofar as we are speaking about games (and not just "free play"), are the rules of the game and the objective to be achieved—for example, scoring the most points. Gadamer, of course, knows this as well as anyone else. But such an objection is likely to miss the point of Gadamer's phenomenological description. There is a not-so-innocent *epistemological* sense of what is "subjective" and what is "objective" (which is basic to Kant's understanding of aesthetics) that Gadamer is seeking to undermine. If we recognize the distinctive features of play that Gadamer is highlighting—the primacy of the play itself, the to-and-fro movement of play, the sense in which play has a rhythm and structure of its own—then we may begin to realize that trying to analyze play in terms of the attitudes of subjects toward what is objective or "out there" distorts the very phenomenon that we are trying to describe. But still we may ask, what does the concept of play have to do with the ontology of a work of art, truth, and with hermeneutical understanding? If asked to answer in a word, I think Gadamer would say, "Everything"—but let us see how this unfolds.

As Gadamer develops and enriches his analysis of play, it becomes clear that he is showing that the concept of play provides an understanding of the ontological status of works of art—how they are related to us and we are related to them. It is not as if we are somehow detached or disinterested spectators simply looking upon "objects" and seeking to purify our "aesthetic consciousness" by "aesthetic differentiation." Rather there is a to-and-fro movement, a type of participation characteristic of our involvement with works of art.

My thesis, then, is that the being of art cannot be determined as an object of an aesthetic awareness because, on the contrary, the aesthetic attitude is more than it knows of itself. It is a part of the essential process of representation [*Seinsvorganges der Darstellung*] and is an essential part of play as play. (*TM*, p. 104; *WM*, p. 111)

A work of art is not to be thought of as a self-contained and self-enclosed object (something *an sich*) that stands over against a spectator, who, as a subject, must purify himself or herself in order to achieve aesthetic consciousness of the work of art. There is a dynamic interaction or transaction between the work of art and the spectator who "shares" in it.[14]

Even this way of speaking can obscure the fact that a work of art is essentially incomplete, in the sense that it requires an interpreter. And the interpreter is not someone who is detached from the work of art but is someone upon whom the work of art makes a claim. The spectator, then, is present to the work of art in the sense that he or she participates in it. This even has an affinity, as Gadamer notes, with the early Greek idea of the *theoros*, the *witness* to sacred festivals (and is source of the later philosophic notion of *theoria*). "Theoria is a true sharing, not something active, but something passive (*pathos*), namely being totally involved in and carried away by what one sees" (*TM*, p. 111; *WM*, p. 118).[15] This also helps to explain why Gadamer characterizes a work of art not as a thing or object but as an event or happening of being. "A work of art belongs so closely to that to which it is related that it enriches its being as if through a new event of being" (*TM*, p. 130; *WM*, p. 140).

In order to further clarify the distinctive ontological character of a work of art, Gadamer discusses dramatic and musical performances—what he calls "the reproductive arts." He introduces a theme here that plays a major role in his understanding of hermeneutics.

It is thus of the nature of dramatic or musical works that their performance at different times and on different occasions is, and must be, different. Now it is important to see that, *mutatis mutandis*, this is also true of the plastic arts. But in the latter it is not the case either that the work exists *an sich* and only the effect varies: it is the work of art itself that displays itself under different conditions. The viewer of today not only sees in a different way, but he sees different things. (*TM*, p. 130; *WM*, pp. 140–41)

If it is true that "we" are as deeply involved in the ontological event of a work of art as Gadamer suggests, and also true (as Gadamer maintains) that "we" are always changing because of our historicity, then it begins to look as if Gadamer's understanding of works of art and their interpretation leads straight to relativism. This is the criticism that has most frequently and persistently been brought against Gadamer. I have already indicated that this is to misunderstand what he is doing and saying. (Later we will consider whether Gadamer in fact avoids historical relativism.) But if we are to escape such a blatant relativism, then our task is to comprehend what it means to claim that works of art do not exist *an sich* but are events involving spectators or interpreters in a manner that avoids relativistic consequences. The problem becomes even more acute when we turn to the written word (which has always been the primary subject of hermeneutics), and specifically to literary works of art, for Gadamer tells us "to be read is an essential part of the literary work of art" (*TM*, p. 143; *WM*, p. 153).

Summarizing (and generalizing), Gadamer again raises a series of questions.

As we were able to show that the being of the work of art is play which needs to be perceived by the spectator in order to be completed, so it is universally true of texts that only in the process of understanding is the dead trace of meaning transformed back into living meaning. We must ask whether what was seen to be true of the experience of art is also true of texts as a whole, including those that are not works of art. We saw that the work of art is fully realised only when it is "presented," and were forced to the conclusion that all literary works of art can achieve completion only when they are read. Is this true also of the understanding of any text? Is the meaning of all texts realised only when they are understood? In other words, does understanding belong to the meaning of a text just as being heard belongs to the meaning of music? (*TM*, p. 146; *WM*, p. 156)

This passage also indicates the movement of Gadamer's own thinking. Although Gadamer begins with a discussion of works of art, he moves to the question of the interpretation of texts, to history, to anything that is "handed down to us" through a living tradition. What is now required is to understand understanding itself and to do this in a manner that permits us to make sense of the claim that understanding *belongs* to the meaning of a text. Gadamer has already given us a hint about how to approach this question by his comments on the reproductive or performing arts. Consider a musical or a dramatic performance. Here the original score or text needs to be understood and interpreted by those engaged in the performance. In this context we do not have any difficulty in speaking of the original score or text making claims upon the interpreter and in realizing that all interpretation involves highlighting. Furthermore, it makes no sense to speak of *the* single or *the* correct interpretation. We recognize that there can be a variety of interpretations, and we can even discriminate distinctive interpretations, such as Schnabel's interpretations of Beethoven's sonatas. We can also distinguish between better and worse performances—the brilliant interpretations of a distinguished performer from those of the novice. Here, too, it is quite easy to grasp what is meant by saying that the work of art is fully realized only when it is performed. Of course, a Beethoven sonata consists of the notes written down by Beethoven, but the sonata is also the realization of the written score. We not only recognize that different musicians will perform a work differently but even that on each occasion the performance of a given artist will itself be different. But in this instance, acknowledging the variety of different interpretations does not invite us to speak of relativism or to think that all performances are of equal merit. And we certainly judge better and worse performances, making judgments that are not to be assimilated to the expression of private likings (even though we do acknowledge that there can be conflicting judgments).

Now it may be objected that while this is true when speaking about different performances, the analogy breaks down as soon as we shift to literary texts and start talking about the claims to truth that they make upon us. But we can see where Gadamer is leading us when we realize that in drawing an analogy between interpretation in the reproductive arts and interpretation of texts he is not punning or making some sort of "category mistake." We are dealing with the same phenomenon: the phenomenon of understanding.

The classical discipline concerned with the art of understanding texts is hermeneutics. If my argument is correct, however, then the real problem of hermeneutics is quite different from its common acceptance. It points in the same direction in which my criticism of the aesthetic consciousness has moved the problem of aesthetics. In fact, hermeneutics would then have to be understood in so comprehensive a sense as to embrace the whole sphere of art and its complex of questions. Every work of art, not only literature, must be understood like any other text that requires understanding, and this kind of understanding has to be acquired. This gives to the hermeneutical consciousness a comprehensive breadth that surpasses even that of the aesthetic consciousness. Aesthetics has to be absorbed into hermeneutics. . . . Conversely, hermeneutics must be so determined as a whole that it does justice to the experience of art. *Understanding must be conceived as a part of the process of the coming into being of meaning, in which the significance of all statements—those of art and those of everything else that has been transmitted—is formed and made complete.* (italics added, TM, p. 146; WM, p. 157)

UNDERSTANDING AND PREJUDICE

As the passage just cited suggests, the "radical subjectivisation" that Gadamer ascribes to Kant's aesthetics is not limited to aesthetic phenomena, or even to Kant, but pervades all of modern thought.[16] It is itself a reflection of the modern obsession with objectivism. Gadamer has already indicated this when he claims that the unintended consequences of Kant's critical inquiry was to leave the human sciences in an unhappy disjunction. Either they must model themselves on the natural sciences, if they are to provide us with objective knowledge, or they must give up any claim to objective knowledge and be resigned to dealing with what is "left over"—with the "merely" subjective, with "private" feelings. One of Gadamer's most striking criticisms of nineteenth-century German hermeneutics is that although it intended to demonstrate the legitimacy of the human sciences as autonomous disciplines, it implicitly accepted the very dichotomy of the subjective and the objective that was employed to call into question the cognitive legitimacy of these disciplines.

As a consequence, a new concept of inner experience (*Erlebnis*) was elaborated, and a concept of psychological empathy was developed, according to which the aim of "understanding" is to grasp the subjective intentions of the author of a work of art or a text, or (in the case of historical understanding) to grasp the subjective intentions of historical agents.[17] But Gadamer's statement that "understanding must be conceived as a part of the process of the coming into being of meaning" indicates that neither meaning nor understanding are to be identified with psychological states of mind. This, for Gadamer, is still a vestige of the Cartesian legacy that plagued nineteenth-century hermeneutics. The task of hermeneutical understanding is not to (deceptively) convince us that we can somehow abstract ourselves from our own historical context, or that it is even conceivable to think that by some pure act of empathy we can leap out of our situation and "into" the minds of the creators of works of art or historical subjects. Meaning and understanding are not psychological processes, discrete events, or states of mind; they are essentially and intrinsically *linguistic*.[18] It is the work of art or text itself that possesses meaning. And furthermore, this meaning is not self-contained—simply "there" to be discovered; meaning comes to realization only in and through the "happening" of understanding.

Once again, despite Gadamer's warnings to the contrary, a skeptical critic might claim that we seem to be on the brink of a new, sophisticated version of relativism. For it would *seem* that if the meaning of a work of art or text is affected by or conditioned by the understanding of its meaning, then there does not *seem* to be any meaning that has "objective" integrity, that is "there" in the work of art or text to be understood. Such a relativism (which *seems* to make meaning dependent on our changing understanding of this meaning) is a misinterpretation of Gadamer. Indeed, it is just this type of relativism that he seeks to refute. But the possibility of misunderstanding his argument in this way points to a problem that needs to be confronted if we are to escape from such relativistic consequences—the question of the nature and role that prejudice plays in all understanding. One of the boldest and most controversial aspects of Gadamer's philosophic hermeneutics is his defense of prejudice and his argument with the Enlightenment's "prejudice against prejudice" (*TM*, p. 240; *WM*, p. 255).

We might try to make Gadamer's position more intellectually palatable by substituting the more neutral term "prejudgment" for "prejudice," because the latter term suggests something that is negative, unfounded, and false.[19] But such a substitution (while not entirely inaccurate) tends to weaken the strong claims that Gadamer wants to make.

It is not so much our judgments as it is our prejudices that constitute our being. This is a provocative formulation, for I am using it to restore to its rightful place a positive concept of prejudice that was driven out of our linguistic usage by the French and the English Enlightenment. It can be shown that the concept of prejudice did not originally have the meaning we have attached to it. Prejudices are not necessarily unjustified and erroneous, so that they inevitably distort the truth. In fact, the historicity of our existence entails that prejudices, in the literal sense of the word, constitute the initial directedness of our whole ability to experience. Prejudices are biases of our openness to the world. They are simply conditions whereby we experience something—whereby what we encounter says something to us. This formulation certainly does not mean that we are enclosed within a wall of prejudices and only let through the narrow portals those things that can produce a pass saying, "Nothing new will be said here." Instead we welcome just that guest who promises something new to our curiosity.[20]

Gadamer emphatically tells us that "this recognition that all understanding inevitably involves some prejudice gives the hermeneutical problem its real thrust" (*TM*, p. 239; *WM*, p. 255). If we are not simply to dismiss these claims about prejudice, then we must carefully tease out what Gadamer is telling us and pursue the rich implications of this passage.

If Gadamer is right in claiming that not only understanding but all knowing "inevitably involves some prejudices," then it is difficult to imagine a more radical critique of Cartesianism, as well as of the Enlightenment conception of human knowledge. For in these traditions there are sharp dichotomies ·between reason and prejudice, or between knowledge and prejudice. To gain knowledge we must bracket and overcome all prejudices. Gadamer might have drawn support for his provocative formulation from the tradition in the philosophy of science that runs from Peirce to Popper. Here too we find an attack on the Cartesian misunderstanding of the nature of science and knowledge. There is no knowledge without *pre*conceptions and *pre*-judices. The task is not to remove all such preconceptions, but to test them critically in the course of inquiry. Peirce tells us:

We cannot begin with complete doubt. We must begin with all the prejudices which we actually have when we enter upon the study of philosophy. These prejudices are not to be dispelled by a maxim, for they are things which it does not occur to us *can* be questioned.[21]

It is clear, however, that Gadamer does want to make the all-important distinction between *blind* prejudices and "justified [*berechtigte*] prejudices productive of knowledge" (*TM*, p. 247; *WM*, p. 263), or what might be called *enabling* prejudices. But this does not diminish the significance of his thesis that both types of prejudice are constitutive of what we are. But then how are we to make this crucial distinction? How are we to discriminate which of our prejudices are blind and which are enabling?

One answer is clearly ruled out. We cannot do this by an act of pure self-reflection, such as Descartes claimed, in which we bracket all prejudices, for there is no knowledge and no understanding without prejudices. We even have dramatic evidence of this in the case of Descartes, who prided himself on doubting everything that can be doubted. For it is evident, in retrospect, that Descartes himself was filled with all sorts of prejudices and prejudgments that he inherited from the very tradition that he was battling. Gadamer's answer to the question of how we come to make this distinction among our prejudices is the very one that Descartes ruled out of serious consideration. For Gadamer, it is in and through the encounter with works of art, texts, and more generally what is handed down to us through tradition that we discover which of our prejudices are blind and which are enabling. In opposition to Descartes' *monological* notion of purely rational self-reflection by which we can achieve transparent self-knowledge, Gadamer tells us that it is only through the *dialogical* encounter with what is at once alien to us, makes a claim upon us, and has an affinity with what we are that we can open ourselves to risking and testing our prejudices.

This does not mean that we can ever finally complete such a project, that we can ever achieve complete self-transparency, that we can attain that state which Descartes (and in another way, Hegel) claims is the *telos* of such a project, the attainment of perfect or absolute knowledge. To think that such a possibility is a real possibility is to fail to do justice to the realization that prejudices "constitute our being": that it literally makes no sense to think that a human being can ever be devoid of prejudices. To risk and test our prejudices is a constant task (not a final achievement). This is one way of understanding what Gadamer means by human finitude (a conception which is strikingly different from the Cartesian notion of a finite but perfect knowledge). We can also see the affinities between what Gadamer is saying and our earlier discussion of the "truth" of the incommensurability thesis. For I argued that the "truth" of this thesis, as developed by Kuhn, Feyerabend, Rorty, and even Winch, is to point to the openness of experience, not to the type of closure where "we are enclosed within a wall of prejudices." Gadamer makes a similar point when he declares that "prejudices are biases of our openness to the world."

The concept of prejudice is closely related to two other concepts that Gadamer seeks to restore and defend against Enlightenment prejudices: authority and tradition. Gadamer argues that Enlightenment thinkers not only denigrated the concept of authority, they deformed it. They thought of authority as a matter of blind obedience to persons in positions of power.

But this is not the essence of authority. It is true that it is primarily persons that have authority; but the authority of persons is based ultimately, not on the subjection and abdication of reason, but on recognition and knowledge [*der Anerkennung und der Erkenntnis*]—knowledge, namely, that the other is superior to oneself in judgment and insight and that for this reason his judgment takes precedence, i.e., it has priority over one's own. . . . Authority in this sense, properly understood, has nothing to do with blind obedience to a command. Indeed, authority has nothing to do with obedience, but rather with knowledge. (*TM*, p. 248; *WM*, p. 263)

And Gadamer makes explicit the connection between authority and positive, enabling prejudices.

Thus the recognition of authority is always connected with the idea that what authority states is not irrational and arbitrary, but can be seen, in principle, to be true. This is the essence of the authority claimed by the teacher, the superior, the expert. The prejudices that they implant are legitimised by the person himself. Their validity demands that one should be biased in favour of the person who presents them. But this makes them then, in a sense, objective prejudices, for they bring about the same bias in favour of something that can come about through other means, e.g., through solid grounds offered by reason. Thus the essence of authority belongs in the context of a theory of prejudices free from the extremism of the enlightenment. (*TM*, p. 249; *WM*, p. 264)

Thus far we (and Gadamer) have emphasized two dimensions of the temporality of prejudices and prejudgments. They are always constitutive of what we are now (although this is, of course, a changing now). But if we ask what are the sources of our prejudices, and especially those prejudices which open us to experience, then we must turn to the past, to tradition, and to the proper authority (based on knowledge) which "implants" these prejudices. Shortly we will see that a comprehensive analysis of prejudice must also recognize its anticipatory, or future-oriented, dimension.

Just as Gadamer questions the typical Enlightenment contrasts between reason and prejudice, or between reason and authority, he also questions what lies behind these contrasts—the opposition between reason and tradition. He has been preparing the ground for showing us that there is something fundamentally wrong with this opposition. All reason functions *within* traditions. Here, too, there has been a deformation of the concept of tradition when we think of it as the "dead weight" of the past. A living tradition not only informs and shapes what we are but is always in the process of reconstitution.[22] When tradition is no longer open in this manner, we can speak of it as "dead," or as no longer a tradition. Even the Romantic reaction against the Enlightenment tended to misconceive the concept of tradition as "something historically given, like nature" (*eine geschichtliche Gegebenheit von der Art der Natur*) (*TM*, p. 249; *WM*, p. 265). Consequently both the Enlightenment and the Romantic reaction to it tended to reify tradition, to think of it as something "given" and determinate which is to be overthrown or celebrated. And both tended to contrast tradition with the autonomy of reason.

It seems to me, however, that there is no such unconditional antithesis between tradition and reason. . . . The fact is that tradition is constantly an element of freedom and of history itself. Even the most genuine and solid tradition does not persist by nature because of the inertia of what once existed. It needs to be affirmed, embraced, cultivated. It is, essentially, preservation, such as is active in all historical change. But preservation is an act of reason, though an inconspicuous one. For this reason, only what is new, or what is planned, appears as the result of reason. But this is an illusion.

Even where life changes violently, as in ages of revolution, far more of the old is preserved in the supposed transformation of everything than anyone knows, and combines with the new to create a new value. At any rate, preservation is as much a freely-chosen action as revolution and renewal. This is why both the enlightenment's critique of tradition and its romantic rehabilitation are less than their true historical being. (*TM*, p. 250; *WM*, p. 265)

Gadamer pursues the analysis of prejudice, authority, and tradition in the context of probing what is distinctive about hermeneutical understanding, but one cannot help being struck by his rapprochement with insights gleaned from the postempiricist philosophy and history of science, where the importance of tradition has also been recognized. As we have traced the stages of development in recent philosophy of science, we have seen the importance of the concept of research traditions in the practice of science. This was anticipated by the Kuhn's emphasis on the historical dimension of what he called "normal science," was refined by Lakatos' analysis of research programs, and was further elaborated by Laudan's analysis of research traditions. In these analyses of science, the concept of tradition is employed to give us a better grasp of the way in which scientific rationality must be situated within living traditions. It is important to be sensitive to differences among various types of tradition and to the ways in which they are reconstituted, criticized, and even overthrown. But any attempt to distinguish scientific practice from other forms of human conduct by employing the opposition between reason and tradition is inadequate and misleading.

But we want to know how Gadamer's reflections on prejudice, authority, and tradition enable us to increase our comprehension of what understanding is, and how they help to clarify the central thesis that "understanding must be conceived as part of the process of coming into being of meaning." We can see how Gadamer weaves these themes together by turning to his discussion and transformation of the hermeneutical circle.

THE HERMENEUTICAL CIRCLE

At several earlier stages of our inquiry we have anticipated the discussion of the hermeneutical circle, witnessing how thinkers working in different contexts have discovered for themselves its centrality. Kuhn even records "a decisive episode in the summer of 1947" when he made this discovery in his struggle to make sense of

Aristotle's physics. He reports that he was deeply perplexed about how Aristotle, who had been "an acute and naturalistic observer" and who "in such fields as biology or political behavior" had given penetrating interpretations, could have said so many absurd things about motion. "How could his characteristic talents have failed him so when applied to motion? . . . And, above all, why had his views been taken so seriously for so long a time by so many of his successors?" The more Kuhn read, the more perplexed he became. But "one memorable (and very hot) summer day those perplexities suddenly vanished." Kuhn discovered the

rudiments of an alternative way of reading the texts with which I had been struggling. For the first time I gave due weight to the fact that Aristotle's subject was change-of-quality in general, including both the fall of a stone and the growth of a child to adulthood. In his physics, the subject that was to become mechanics was at best a still-not-quite-isolable special case. More consequential was my recognition that the permanent ingredients of Aristotle's universe, its ontologically primary and indestructible elements, were not material bodies but rather the qualities which, when imposed on some portion of omnipresent neutral matter, constituted an individual material body or substance.[23]

In Gadamerian terms, we can say that Kuhn's initial perplexity was the result of his approaching Aristotle's physics through the prejudices of modern mechanics. Aristotle's claims seemed not only false but absurd. In effect, Kuhn was asking the wrong sorts of questions, and what he had to learn was to ask the right questions—and to come to understand the questions that Aristotle was seeking to answer. Kuhn tells us that this episode changed his intellectual career and became "central to my historical research." In trying to transmit the lesson he learned to his students, he, in effect, formulates his own version of the hermeneutical circle, in a passage that I quoted in part I:

When reading the works of an important thinker, look first for the apparent absurdities in the text and ask yourself how a sensible person could have written them. When you find an answer, I continue, when those passages make sense, then you may find that more central passages, ones you previously thought you understood, have changed their meaning.[24]

This maxim is extremely abstract and sketchy. It would not be very helpful unless one had had some experience in the *practice* of interpretation. We know that to be able to do this well requires a great deal of background knowledge that can enable us to understand what the texts are saying. In order to make sense of "apparent absurdities," we need to try out alternative readings that themselves can only be tested by seeing how they make sense (or do not quite fit) with other parts of the text we are seeking to understand. Whatever "subjective processes" take place in an interpreter—whether this happens in a flash on a hot summer day or is the result of a laborious struggle—the essential question is the adequacy of the interpretation, which can be judged only by returning to the texts themselves.

But it is not only in Kuhn that we detect the importance of the hermeneutical circle; it is just as vital for Feyerabend and is evident in his characterization of the "anthropological method" which he thinks is appropriate not only for understanding science but for understanding any "form of life." It is especially prominent when Feyerabend tells us that "each item of information is a building block of understanding, which means that it is to be clarified by the discovery of further blocks from the language and ideology of the tribe."[25] Here Feyerabend, too, is characterizing a type of understanding that constantly moves back and forth between "parts" and the "whole" that we seek to understand. This is the very process that Geertz so eloquently characterizes (and explicitly relates to the hermeneutical circle), "namely, a continuous dialectical tacking between the most local of local detail and the most global of global structure in such a way as to bring both into view simultaneously."[26]

We have also seen how important the hermeneutical circle is for Winch. Although he does not explicitly mention it, the tracing of the circle is the procedure that he follows in seeking to understand Zande witchcraft. And Charles Taylor explicitly defends the importance of the hermeneutical circle when he argues that there is an unavoidably hermeneutical component to the sciences of man. Taylor is acutely aware that the appeal to the hermeneutical circle challenges the biases of those schooled in empiricism who demand some method of definitive empirical verification in testing hypotheses. He states the typical objection to the hermeneutical circle—that it is really a *vicious* circle. For if we "validate" our interpretations by appealing to other interpretations of the "parts," then we fail to break out of the circle of interpretations. When Taylor seeks to meet this objection, he introduces a "suggestion" that becomes thematic for Gadamer's own understanding and transformation of the hermeneutical circle. According to Taylor, a hermeneutical science of man

would not be founded on brute data; its most primitive data would be readings of meanings, and its object would have the [following] three properties. . . : the meanings are for a subject in a field or fields; they are, moreover, meanings which are partially constituted by self-definitions, which are in this sense already interpretations, and which can thus be re-expressed or made explicit by a science of politics. In our case, the subject may be a society or community; but the intersubjective meanings . . . embody a certain self-definition, a vision of the agent and his society, which is that of the society or community.[27]

Such a science

cannot but move in a hermeneutical circle. A given reading of the intersubjective meanings of a society, or of given institutions or practices, may seem well founded, because it makes sense of these practices or the development of that society. But the conviction that it does make sense of this history itself is founded on further related readings[28]

Here the empiricist or positivist objects. For he or she demands some clear procedure, some method that can break out of the circle of interpretations and serve as a touchstone for determining which interpretations or readings are correct and which are not.

Taylor does not try to meet this demand (and the implied criticism) by claiming that there are clearly formulizable rules or procedures for sorting out better and worse interpretations. Rather, he tells us,

Some claims of the form "If you don't understand, then your intuitions are at fault, are blind or inadequate," some claims of this form will be justified; . . . some differences will be nonarbitrable by further evidence, but . . . each side can only make appeal to deeper insight on the part of the other.[29]

I do not want, at this stage, to evaluate the adequacy of this response but only to note that according to Taylor the circularity of such a hermeneutical understanding is neither vicious nor to be judged as a defect.[30] It is seen as such only when judged by the mistaken and unwarranted epistemological demands for empirical verification— the appeal to some "brute data." But toward the conclusion of his analysis Taylor suggests an idea that is crucial to Gadamer's understanding of the hermeneutical circle—that "the practical and the theoretical are inextricably joined here."

It may not just be that to understand a certain explanation one has to sharpen one's intuitions, it may be that one has to change one's orientation—if not in adopting another orientation, at least in living one's own in a way which allows for greater comprehension of others. Thus, in the sciences of man insofar as they are hermeneutical there can be a valid response to "I don't understand" which takes the form, not only "develop your intuitions," but more radically "change yourself." This puts an end to any aspiration to a value-free or "ideology-free" science of man. A study of the science of man is inseparable from an examination of the options between which men must choose.[31]

And Taylor concludes his paper by explicitly relating his discussion to Aristotle.

There are thus good grounds both in epistemological arguments and in their greater fruitfulness for opting for hermeneutical sciences of man. But we cannot hide from ourselves how greatly this option breaks with certain commonly held notions about our scientific tradition. We cannot measure such sciences against the requirements of a science of verification: we cannot judge them by their predictive capacity. . . . These sciences cannot be "*wertfrei*": they are moral sciences in a more radical sense than the eighteenth century understood. Finally, their successful prosecution requires a high degree of self-knowledge, a freedom from illusion, in the sense of error which is rooted and expressed in one's way of life; for our incapacity to understand is rooted in our own self-definitions, hence in what we are. To say this is not to say anything new: Aristotle makes a similar point in Book I of the *Ethics*. But it is still radically shocking and unassimilable to the mainstream of modern science.[32]

Up until this last "radically shocking" suggestion that calls into question the very possibility of a *wertfrei* science of man and that links interpretation with practical choice, there has been a consistent theme in these several formulations of the hermeneutical circle. The circle of understanding is "object" oriented, in the sense that it directs us to the texts, institutions, practices, or forms of life that we are seeking to understand. It directs us to the sensitive dialectical *play* between part and whole in the circle of understanding. Many standard (and pre-Heideggerian) characterizations of the hermeneutical circle focus exclusively on the relation of part to whole in the texts or phenomena which we seek to understand. No essential reference is made to the interpreter, to the individual who is engaged in the process of understanding and questioning, except insofar as he or she must have the insight, imagination, openness, and patience to acquire this art—an art achieved through practice. There is no determinate method for acquiring or pursuing this art, in the sense of explicit rules that are to be followed. Or we might say that rules here function as heuristic guides that gain their concrete meaning by appealing to exemplars of such hermeneutical interpretation. But a full statement and defense of the hermeneutical circle requires us to ask the Kantian question, How is such understanding and interpretation possible? What presuppositions are we making about ourselves, and what we are trying to understand if we are to show the legitimacy of the hermeneutical circle? These are the questions that Gadamer seeks to answer.[33]

From his perspective, the understanding of the hermeneutical circle primarily as the Method of the *Geisteswissenschaften*, and as a rival and alternative to the Method of the *Naturwissenschaften*, still is wedded to a Cartesian framework, with its acceptance of the categorial distinction between what is objective and what is subjective. But Heidegger transformed the meaning, scope, and significance of the hermeneutical circle. Gadamer quotes the central passage from Heidegger's *Being and Time* in which he comments on the hermeneutical circle.

[The hermeneutical circle] is not to be reduced to the level of a vicious circle or even a circle which is merely tolerated. In the circle is hidden a positive possibility of the most primordial kind of knowing. To be sure, we genuinely take hold of this possibility only when, in our interpretation, we have understood that our first, last, and constant task is never to allow our fore-having [*Vorhabe*], fore-sight [*Vorsicht*], and fore-conceptions [*Vorgriffe*] to be presented to us by fancies and popular conceptions, but rather to make the scientific theme secure by working out these fore-structures in terms of the things themselves.[34]

Gadamer makes the following claim about this passage:

Just as they stand, these lines announce not only the conditions imposed on the practice of understanding; they also describe the manner in which interpretation always proceeds when it intends an understanding tempered to the "thing itself." For the very first time the *positive ontological meaning* of the circle that understanding implies is explicitly affirmed. . . . In order to be authentic the inquiring gaze must be focused on the "thing itself," and in such a manner that it may be grasped, as it were, "in person." Likewise it is evident that an understanding faithful to the meaning of the text, for example, is not a matter of a simple, more or less vague wish nor of "good and pious intentions," but rather has the same meaning as the program Heidegger designated as the "first, last, and constant task" of interpretative understanding. Now, the circular character of understanding is precisely the outcome of the effort which leads the interpreter to strictly abide by this program, despite any errors he might commit in the course of his investigations.[35]

This dense passage has several implications. The reference to the *positive* ontological meaning of the circle indicates that the hermeneutical circle is not "second best"; it is not an intellectual stepsister to the methods of the natural sciences. The statement indicates the positive role that fore-having, fore-sight, fore-conception, and prejudgment play in all understanding. The reference to the *ontolog-ical* character of the circle indicates something basic about our very being-in-the-world—that we are essentially beings constituted by and engaged in interpretative understanding. The reference to the "things themselves" is not to be misunderstood as suggesting that these "things" exist *an sich* and that we must "purify" ourselves of all forestructures and prejudgments in order to grasp or know them "objectively." On the contrary, the meaning of the "things them-selves" can only be grasped through the circle of understanding, a circle that presupposes the forestructures that enable us to understand.

The most important consequence of Gadamer's understanding of the hermeneutical circle is that it clarifies the relation between the interpreter and what he or she seeks to understand. And here again we can detect the significance of Gadamer's phenomenological analysis of play as a "primordial mode of being." We must learn the art of being responsive to works of art, texts, traditions (and, we can now add, other persons or forms of life) that we are trying to under-stand. We must participate or share in them, listen to them, open ourselves to what they are saying and to the claims to truth that they make upon us.[36] And we can accomplish this only because of the forestructures and prejudgments that are constitutive of our being. When Gadamer says that works of art, texts, or tradition "speak to us," he is not referring to a loose, metaphorical way of "speaking" that we ourselves "project" onto the texts; rather, he is expressing what he takes to be the most fundamental ontological character of our being-in-the-world. We can also better appreciate why Gadamer thinks it is misleading to characterize understanding as an "activity of a subject." It is true, of course, that understanding requires effort and care, imagination and perceptiveness, but this is directed to the *pathos* of opening ourselves to what we seek to understand—of allowing it to "speak to us." And such receptiveness is possible only by virtue of those "justified prejudices" that open us to experience. Gadamer emphasizes this point when he tells us:

But do not make me say what I have not in fact said; and I have *not* said that when we listen to someone or when we read we ought to forget our own opinions or shield ourselves against forming an anticipatory idea about the content of communication. In reality, to be open to "other people's opin-ions," to a text, and so forth, implies right off that they are *situated* in my system of opinions, or better, that I situate myself in relation to them. . . .

The authentic intention of understanding, however, is this: in reading a text, in wishing to understand it, what we always expect is that it will *inform* us of something. A consciousness formed by the authentic hermeneutical attitude will be receptive to the origins and entirely foreign features of that which comes to it from outside its own horizons. Yet this receptivity is not acquired with an objectivist "neutrality": it is neither possible, necessary, nor desirable that we put ourselves within brackets. The hermeneutical attitude supposes only that we self-consciously designate our opinions and prejudices and qualify them as such, and in so doing strip them of their extreme character. In keeping to this attitude we grant the text the opportunity to appear as an authentically different being and to manifest its own truth, over and against our own preconceived notions.[37]

What might, on first appearance, strike one as extraordinarily paradoxical brings us to the heart of Gadamer's understanding and transformation of the hermeneutical circle. On the one hand, Gadamer stresses that we must always temper our understanding to the "things themselves"; we must listen to them and open ourselves so that they can "speak to us"; we must be receptive to the claims to truth that they make upon us. But on the other hand, we do not do this by bracketing or forgetting all our prejudgments and prejudices. On the contrary, it is only because of the play of these prejudgments that we are enabled to understand the "things themselves." In contrast, then, to many standard characterizations of the hermeneutical circle that focus exclusively on the text, tradition, or practices to be understood, Gadamer (following Heidegger) thematizes the forestructures of the interpreter. By opening ourselves to the "newness" of what is handed down to us, through the play of our forestructures and the "things themselves," we can become aware of those prejudices that blind us to the meaning and truth of what we are trying to understand and those prejudices that enable us to understand.

This shift in the significance of the hermeneutical circle, involving the recognition that prejudices enable us to understand, and that hermeneutical understanding is constitutive of what we are in the process of becoming, has some very strong consequences. Thus far we have not distinguished between *understanding* and *interpretation*. If we want to interpret a Shakespearean tragedy, we must be sure that we understand Shakespeare's English, and especially the ways in which it differs from contemporary English. But contrary to that tradition within hermeneutics that seeks to draw a rigorous distinction between understanding and interpretation (and to relegate these activities to different subdisciplines), Gadamer maintains that there is no essential difference between understanding and interpretation. All understanding involves interpretation, and all interpretation involves understanding. (This claim scandalizes those who think that there is or can be "objective understanding," freed from all prejudices and not "contaminated" by interpretation.) The continuity of understanding and interpretation is evident in the phenomenon of translation, Gadamer points out. For there is no translation without highlighting, and all highlighting involves interpretation.[38] We can, of course, speak of and discriminate misinterpretations and misunderstandings, but this does not mean that we do this by reaching some level in which no interpretation is involved.

We can see why for Gadamer the process of understanding can never (ontologically) achieve finality, why it is always open and anticipatory. We are always understanding and interpreting in light of our anticipatory prejudgments and prejudices, which are themselves changing in the course of history. This is why Gadamer tells us that to understand is always to understand *differently*. But this does not mean that our interpretations are arbitrary or distortive. We should always aim (if informed by an "authentic hermeneutical attitude") at a correct understanding of what the "things themselves" say. But what the "things themselves" say will be different in light of our changing horizons and the different questions that we learn to ask. Such an analysis of the ongoing and open character of all understanding and interpretation can be construed as distortive only if we assume that a text possesses some meaning in itself that can be isolated from our prejudgments. But this is precisely what Gadamer is denying, and this play between the "things themselves" and our prejudgments helps us comprehend why "understanding must be conceived as part of the process of the coming into being of meaning." Meaning is always *coming into being* through the "happening" of understanding.

Gadamer's point is brought into sharp focus in his characterization of the "classical." He defines it as

that which speaks in such a way that it is not a statement about what is past, a mere testimony to something that still needs to be interpreted, but says something to the present as if it were said specially to it. What we call "classical" does not first require the overcoming of historical distance, for in its own constant communication it does overcome it. *The classical, then, is certainly "timeless," but this timelessness is a mode of historical being.* (*TM*, p. 257; *WM*, p. 274, italics added)

TEMPORAL DISTANCE, EFFECTIVE-HISTORICAL CONSCIOUSNESS, AND THE FUSION OF HORIZONS

Gadamer's claims that timelessness is a mode of historical being opens up a new dimension of philosophic hermeneutics. For Gadamer's reflections on philosophic hermeneutics can be approached (as is also true of Heidegger) as a meditation on temporality and historicity. I want to consider only those aspects of temporality that can help to forestall a common misinterpretation of Gadamer. To put it very simply, we might be inclined to say that because Gadamer's thinking is oriented toward tradition, he expresses a nostalgia for what has been destroyed by the onslaught of modernity. But it is vital to see that his thinking moves us in a very different direction. Gadamer has been sharply critical of the romantic infatuation with a past that is frequently an imaginative construction of our own present concerns. This is only another version of the false belief that we can escape or bracket all our prejudices and enter into a radically different world.

Temporal distance is not something that must be overcome. This was, rather the naive assumption of historicism, namely that we must set ourselves within the spirit of the age, and think with its ideas and its thoughts, not with our own, and thus advance towards historical objectivity. In fact the important thing is to recognise the distance in time as a positive and productive possibility of understanding. It is not a yawning abyss, but is filled with the continuity of custom and tradition, in the light of which all that is handed down presents itself to us.

....

[Temporal distance] lets the true meaning of the object emerge fully. But the discovery of the true meaning of a text or a work of art is never finished; it is in fact an infinite process. Not only are fresh sources of error constantly excluded, so that the true meaning has filtered out of it all kinds of things that obscure it, but there emerge continually new sources of understanding, which reveal unsuspected elements of meaning. (*TM*, pp. 264–66; *WM*, pp. 281–82)

Another aspect of temporality needs to be emphasized: the temporality of those prejudgments that are the conditions for understanding. Where do these prejudices come from? They are themselves handed down from the traditions that shape us and that are constitutive of the historicity of our being. And as we have seen, a tradition is only alive when it is freely appropriated. But there is also an *anticipatory* or future-oriented dimension to all prejudgments. This is already indicated by Heidegger's linguistic emphasis on fore-having, fore-sight, and fore-conceptions. All understanding is *projective*. To accomplish "an understanding is to form a project [*Entwurf*] from one's own possibilities." In short, prejudgments and prejudices have a threefold temporal character: they are handed down to us through tradition; they are constitutive of what we are now (and are in the process of becoming); and they are anticipatory—always open to future testing and transformation.

Gadamer is laying the groundwork for his own version of the thesis that there is an "inextricable connection of the theoretical and the practical" in all understanding and interpretation—that hermeneutical understanding shapes our practical lives (and is not a purely disinterested, theoretical activity). This signals the third element that Gadamer seeks to integrate into all understanding and interpretation—the moment of *application*. All understanding, as we noted in part I, involves not only interpretation but also application. And Gadamer tells us that recognizing the intrinsic role of application in all understanding represents "the rediscovery of the fundamental hermeneutic problem" (*Wiedergewinnung des hermeneutischen Grundproblems*) (*TM*, p. 274; *WM*, p. 290). It is here that we discover the fusion of hermeneutics and *praxis*, which becomes the most central theme in Gadamer's analysis of philosophic hermeneutics. This is the reason why Gadamer believes that philosophic hermeneutics is the heir to the older tradition of practical philosophy. But before examining this crucial stage of Gadamer's argument, I want to consider briefly two other concepts that will help round out the discussion of philosophic hermeneutics and set the stage for exploring the centrality of *praxis* and *phronēsis: effective-historical consciousness* (*wirkungsgeschichtliches Bewusstsein*) and the *fusion of horizons* (*Horizontverschmelzung*).

Both of these themes have been in the background of our discussion, but we need to bring them into the foreground. We can introduce these interrelated themes by reminding ourselves of what underlies Gadamer's analysis of works of art, texts, and history. The characteristic of anything that is "handed down to us" that elicits the need for understanding is the tension between strangeness or alienness and familiarity. This is one more way in which hermeneutics relates to the discussion of incommensurability. For the problem that Kuhn, Feyerabend, Rorty, Winch, and Geertz are all struggling with is how to understand and do justice to something that at once strikes us as so strange and alien and yet has sufficient affinity with us that we can come to understand it. The problem is structurally similar, whether we are trying to make sense of Aristotle's physics, Greek archaic art, Zande witchcraft, or the embodied concepts of a self in Javanese, Balinese, or Moroccan cultures. The hermeneutical task is to find the resources in our language and experience to enable us to understand these initially alien phenomena without imposing blind or distortive prejudices on them. If we were confronting some-thing so alien and strange that it had nothing in common with our language and experience, no affinity whatsoever, then it would no longer be intelligible to speak of understanding. This point is just as fundamental for Gadamer as it is for Davidson.

I have used the term "affinity" to indicate the relationship that exists between us and the alien text or tradition that we seek to understand and appropriate. But the German word that Gadamer employs (*Zugehörigkeit*) is much stronger, and it is better translated as "belongingness." As Gadamer sees it, we belong to a tradition before it belongs to us: tradition, through its sedimentations, has a power which is constantly determining what we are in the process of becoming. We are *always already* "thrown" into a tradition. We can see how far Gadamer is from any naive form of relativism that fails to appreciate how we are always shaped by effective-history (*Wirkungsgeschichte*). It is not just that works of art, texts, and tradi-tion have effects and leave traces. Rather, what we are, whether we are explicitly aware of it or not, is always being influenced by tradi-tion, even when we think we are most free of it. Again, it is impor-tant to reiterate that a tradition is not something "naturelike," some-thing "given" that stands over against us. It is always "part of us" and works through its effective-history.

This sets the task for effective-historical *consciousness* (*wirkungsgeschichtliches Bewusstsein*), and explains its possibility. According to Gadamer, "historical objectivism," which treats the "object" as if it were ontologically independent of the "subject," "conceals the involvement of the historical consciousness itself in effective-history" (*TM*, p. 268; *WM*, p. 285). The task of effective-historical *consciousness* is to bring to explicit awareness this histor-ical affinity or belongingness.

True historical thinking must take account of its own historicality. Only then will it not chase the phantom of an historical object which is the object of progressive research, but learn to see in the object the counterpart of itself and hence understand both. The true historical object is not an object at all, but the unity of the one and the other, a relationship in which exist both the reality of history and the reality of historical understanding. A proper hermeneutics would have to demonstrate the effectivity of history within understanding itself. (*TM*, p. 267; *WM*, p. 283)

Effective-historical consciousness influences what we consider worthy of investigation and how we go about investigating it. It is "already operative in the choice of the right question to ask" (*TM*, p.

268; *WM*, p. 285). Effective-historical consciousness does not indicate a final state of self-knowledge. Rather, we are always "on the
way" to such self-knowledge, a self-knowledge achieved with the
dialectical interplay with the "other." But if the movement toward
such *consciousness* of effective-history is the primary task of philosophic hermeneutics, how is this to be achieved? In asking and
answering this question, Gadamer does not specify procedural rules,
but instead clarifies what it means to achieve effective-historical
consciousness. This is the context in which Gadamer introduces his
notion of the "fusion of horizons" (*Horizontverschmelzung*).

Drawing on Nietzsche and Husserl, Gadamer characterizes a
horizon as follows:

Every finite present has its limitations. We define the concept of "situation"
by saying that it represents a standpoint that limits the possibility of vision.
Hence an essential part of the concept of situation is the concept of "horizon." The horizon is the range of vision that includes everything that can
be seen from a particular vantage point. (*TM*, p. 269; *WM*, p. 286)

A horizon, then, is limited and finite, but it is *essentially* open. For
to have a horizon is not to be limited to what is nearest but to be
able to move beyond it. Indeed the very idea of a closed horizon is a
false abstraction.

The closed horizon that is supposed to enclose a culture is an abstraction.
The historical movement of human life consists in the fact that it is never
utterly bound to any one standpoint, and hence can never have a truly closed
horizon. The horizon is, rather, something into which we move and that
moves with us. Horizons change for a person who is moving. Thus the
horizon of the past, out of which all human life lives and which exists in
the form of tradition, is always in motion. It is not historical consciousness
that first sets the surrounding horizon in motion. But in it this motion
becomes aware of itself. (*TM*, p. 271; *WM*, p. 288)

Horizons are limited, finite, changing, and fluid.

The question then arises, What are we doing (or rather what is
happening to us) when we try to understand a horizon other than
our own? We already know that the answer that others have given—
the idea that we can escape our own standpoint and leap into the
horizon of the past—is not the right answer. For this is impossible,
and violates Gadamer's claim that we are always ontologically
grounded in our situation and horizon. Rather, what we seek to achieve
is a "fusion of horizons," a fusion whereby our own horizon is enlarged
and enriched. Gadamer's main point becomes even sharper when we

realize that for him the medium of all human horizons is linguistic, and that the language that we speak (or that rather speaks through us) is essentially open to understanding alien horizons. It is through the fusion of horizons that we risk and test our prejudices. In this sense, learning from other forms of life and horizons is at the very same time coming to an understanding of ourselves. "Only through others do we gain true knowledge of ourselves."[39] Applying this to history and historical consciousness, Gadamer writes:

> When our historical consciousness places itself within historical horizons, this does not entail passing into alien worlds unconnected in any way with our own, but together they constitute the one great horizon that moves from within and, beyond the frontiers of the present, embraces the historical depths of our self-consciousness. It is, in fact, a single horizon that embraces everything contained in historical consciousness. Our own past, and that other past towards which our historical consciousness is directed, help to shape this moving horizon out of which human life always lives, and which determines it as tradition. (*TM*, p. 271; *WM*, p. 288)

For Gadamer, there is nothing which is in principle beyond the possibility of understanding. This is one of the primary senses in which hermeneutics is universal, although we can never exhaust the meaning of that which we seek to understand or bring understanding to final closure. To use the language of incommensurability, we can say that the incommensurability of different forms of life or different historical epochs always presents a challenge to us, a challenge that requires learning to ask the right questions and drawing on the resources of our own linguistic horizon in order to understand that which is alien. For Gadamer, it is not a dead metaphor to liken the fusion of horizons that is the constant task of effective-historical consciousness to an ongoing and open dialogue or conversation.

APPLICATION: THE REDISCOVERY OF THE FUNDAMENTAL HERMENEUTICAL PROBLEM

With this outline of Gadamer's philosophic hermeneutics, we can understand what it means to claim that hermeneutics is both onto-logical and universal. It is ontological in the sense that understand-ing "denotes the basic being-in-motion of [*Dasein*] which constitutes its finiteness and historicity"; understanding is the primordial mode of being of what we most essentially are. Understanding is universal in several senses. It is not just one activity which is to be distin-guished from other human activities, but underlies all human activities. It is universal in the sense that nothing is in principle beyond understanding, even though we never exhaust the "things themselves" through understanding. The universality of understanding can also be approached through the "linguistic turn" of Gadamer's philosophic hermeneutics. Language is the medium of all understanding and all tradition. And language is not to be understood as an instrument or tool that we use; rather it is the medium in which we live. Like play itself, which reaches presentation (*Darstellung*) through the players, so language itself reaches presentation through those who speak and write.[40]

We have also laid the groundwork for exploring Gadamer's fusion of hermeneutics and *praxis*. This leitmotif has appeared from the very beginning of our analysis and becomes thematic when Gadamer claims that understanding, interpretation, and application (or appropriation) are not three independent activities to be relegated to three different subdisciplines but rather are internally related. They are all moments of the single process of understanding.[41] This integration of the moment of application into understanding brings us to the truly distinctive feature of philosophic hermeneutics. And we will also see that it reveals some deep problems and tensions within Gadamer's hermeneutics.

As I have indicated in part I, the issue of "application" is taken up in *Truth and Method* at the stage of his argument when Gadamer questions an older tradition that divided hermeneutics into *subtilitas intelligendi* (understanding), *subtilitas explicandi* (interpretation), and *subtilitas applicandi* (application). It is here that Gadamer explicitly discusses the relevance of Aristotle's analysis of *phronēsis* in book 6 of the *Nicomachean Ethics*. Gadamer's own understanding, interpretation, and appropriation of Aristotle has rich philosophic consequences and is itself a model of what he means by hermeneutical understanding. It is an exemplar of effective-historical consciousness; the fusion of horizons; the positive role of temporal distance; the way in which understanding is part of the process of the coming into being of meaning; the way in which tradition "speaks to us" and makes a "claim to truth" upon us; and what it means to say that "the interpreter dealing with a traditional text seeks to apply it to himself." Furthermore, when we see how Gadamer appropriates what Aristotle says, we can understand why the *Geisteswissenschaften* are practical disciplines in the sense that Aristotle's *Ethics* and *Politics* are practical and why Gadamer thinks that "hermeneutic philosophy is the heir of the older tradition of practical philosophy" whose chief task is to "justify this way of

reason and defend practical and political reason against the domination of technology based on science." Gadamer's own understanding
of philosophic hermeneutics can itself be interpreted as a series of
footnotes on his decisive intellectual encounter with Aristotle.

We can see why *phronēsis* is so important to Gadamer by returning to the apparent paradox that we find at the heart of Gadamer's
elucidation of the happening of understanding. Hermeneutic understanding is always tempered to the "thing itself" (*die Sache selbst*)
that we are seeking to understand. We seek nothing less than to
understand the same text or the same piece of tradition. But the
meaning of what we seek to understand comes into being only through
the happening of understanding. And such understanding is possible
because of the prejudgments that are constitutive of what we are and
that come into play in understanding. *Phronēsis* is a form of reasoning and knowledge that involves a distinctive mediation between the
universal and the particular. This mediation is not accomplished by
any appeal to technical rules or Method (in the Cartesian sense) or
by the subsumption of a pregiven determinate universal to a particular case. The "intellectual virtue" of *phronēsis* is a form of reasoning, yielding a type of ethical know-how in which what is universal
and what is particular are codetermined. Furthermore, *phronēsis*
involves a "peculiar interlacing of being and knowledge, determina-
tion through one's own becoming, *Hexis*, recognition of the situational Good, and *Logos*."[42] It is not to be identified with the type of
"objective knowledge" that is detached from one's own being and
becoming. Just as *phronēsis* determines what the *phronimos* becomes,
Gadamer wants to make a similar claim for all authentic understanding—that it is not detached from the interpreter but becomes
constitutive of his or her *praxis*. Understanding, for Gadamer, is a
form of *phronēsis*.

We can comprehend what this means by noting the contrasts
that Gadamer emphasizes when he examines the distinctions that
Aristotle makes between *phronēsis* and the other "intellectual
virtues," especially *epistēmē* and *technē*. Aristotle characterizes all
of these virtues (and not just *epistēmē*) as being related to "truth"
(*alētheia*).[43] *Epistēmē*, scientific knowledge, is knowledge of what is
universal, of what exists invariably, and takes the form of scientific
demonstration. The subject matter, the form, the *telos*, and the way
in which *epistēmē* is learned and taught differ from *phronēsis*, the
form of reasoning appropriate to *praxis*, which deals with what is
variable and always involves a mediation between the universal and
the particular that requires deliberation and choice.

For Gadamer, however, the contrast between *epistēmē* and *phronēsis* is not as important for hermeneutics as the distinctions between *technē* (technical know-how) and *phronēsis* (ethical know-how). Gadamer stresses three contrasts.

1. *Technē*, or a technique,

is learned and can be forgotten; we can "lose" a skill. But ethical "reason" can neither be learned nor forgotten. . . . Man always finds himself in an "acting situation" and he is always obliged to use ethical knowledge and apply it according to the exigencies of his concrete situation.[44]

2. There is a different conceptual relation between means and ends in *technē* than in *phronēsis*. The end of ethical know-how, unlike that of a technique, is not a "particular thing" or product but rather the "*complete* ethical rectitude of a lifetime."[45] Even more important, while technical activity does not require that the means that allow it to arrive at an end be weighed anew on each occasion, this is precisely what is required in ethical know-how. In ethical know-how there can be no prior knowledge of the right means by which we realize the end in a particular situation. For the end itself is only concretely specified in deliberating about the means appropriate to a particular situation.[46]

3. *Phronēsis*, unlike *technē*, requires an understanding of other human beings. This is indicated when Aristotle considers the variants of *phronēsis*, especially *synēsis* (understanding).

It appears in the fact of concern, not about myself, but about the other person. Thus it is a mode of moral judgment. . . . The question here, then, is not of a general kind of knowledge, but of its specification at a particular moment. This knowledge also is not in any sense technical knowledge. . . . The person with understanding does not know and judge as one who stands apart and unaffected; but rather, as one united by a specific bond with the other, he thinks with the other and undergoes the situation with him. (*TM*, p. 288; *WM*, p. 306)

For Gadamer, this variation of *phronēsis* provides the clue for grasping the centrality of friendship in Aristotle's *Ethics*.

We can gain a concrete understanding of what Gadamer means by the distinctive codetermination of the universal and the particular that is characteristic of *phronēsis* by considering how he weaves legal hermeneutics into his analysis of application. To Gadamer, the hermeneutical process used in making a legal judgment exemplifies the hermeneutical process as a whole. Gadamer argues that the judge does not simply "apply" fixed, determinate laws to particular situations. Rather the judge must interpret and appropriate precedents and law to each new, particular situation. It is by virtue of such considered judgment that the meaning of the law and the meaning of the particular case are codetermined. "We can, then, bring out as what is truly common to all forms of hermeneutics the fact that the sense to be understood finds its concrete . . . form only in interpretation, but that this interpretative work is wholly committed to the meaning of the text" (*TM*, p. 297; *WM*, p. 315).

But what does this analysis of *phronēsis* and the ways in which it differs from *epistēmē* and *technē* have to do with the problems of hermeneutics? The analogy that Gadamer draws is that just as application is not a subsequent or occasional part of *phronēsis* in which we relate some pregiven determinate universal to a particular, this, Gadamer claims, is characteristic of *all* authentic understanding and interpretation.

The interpreter dealing with a traditional text seeks to apply it to himself. But this does not mean that the text is given for him as something universal, that he understands it as such and only afterwards uses it for particular applications. Rather, the interpreter seeks no more than to understand this universal thing, the text; i.e., to understand what this piece of tradition says, what constitutes the meaning and importance of the text. In order to understand that, he must not seek to disregard himself and his particular hermeneutical situation. He must relate the text to this situation, if he wants to understand at all. (*TM*, p. 289; *WM*, p. 307)

The striking thing about this passage is that it applies perfectly to the way in which Gadamer himself understands, interprets, and appropriates Aristotle's text. That is what I meant earlier when I said that Aristotle's analysis of *phronēsis* is not only a model of the problems of hermeneutics but that Gadamer's interpretation of Aristotle is also itself a model or exemplar of what is meant by hermeneutical understanding. Gadamer tells us that if we are to understand what a text or a tradition says, then we must not seek to disregard ourselves and our hermeneutical situation. Gadamer brings his own awareness of our hermeneutical situation to his interpretation of Aristotle's text, emphasizing (as the essence of our hermeneutical situation) that we are confronted with a world in which there has been "a domination of technology based on science," a "false idolatry of the expert," "a scientific mystification of the modern society of specialization," and a dangerous "inner longing . . . to find in science a substitute for lost orientation." This is the problem that orients Gadamer's questioning of Aristotle's text; Gadamer's central claim is that we have deformed the concept of *praxis* and forgotten what *praxis* really is.[47]

Through a dialogical encounter with Aristotle's text, we risk and test our own entrenched prejudices that prevent us from grasping the autonomy and integrity of *phronēsis*. This does not mean that we approach Aristotle without any prejudgments. We can understand Aristotle and appropriate the truth of what he is saying because we ourselves have been shaped by this effective-history. Gadamer is not advocating a nostalgic return to Aristotle but rather an appropriation of Aristotle's insights to our concrete situation. Gadamer's interpretation of Aristotle illustrates what he means by the fusion of horizons. We are, of course, questioning Aristotle's text from our own historical hermeneutical horizon. But in coming to understand what Aristotle is saying, our prejudices are challenged and we enlarge our own horizon. This fusion of horizons provides a critical perspective on our own situation, enabling us to see how *praxis* has been deformed. Every encounter with tradition is intrinsically critical. By being sensitive to Aristotle's own confrontation with the "professional lawmakers whose function at that time corresponded to the role of the expert in modern scientific society," we can better understand the problems we confront in our own situation. We can learn from Aristotle what practice really is, and why it is not to be identified with the "application of science to technical tasks." Gadamer realizes that in modern society *technē* itself has been transformed, but this only highlights the importance of what we can learn from Aristotle about *praxis* and *phronēsis*. He tells us:

In a scientific culture such as ours the fields of *technē* and art are much more expanded. Thus the fields of mastering means to pre-given ends have been rendered even more monological and controllable. The crucial change is that practical wisdom can no longer be promoted by personal contact and the mutual exchange of views among citizens. Not only has craftmanship been replaced by industrial work; many forms of our daily life are technologically organized so that they no longer require personal decision. In modern technological society public opinion itself has in a new and really decisive way become the object of very complicated techniques—and this, I think, is the main problem facing our civilization.[48]

The temporal distance between ourselves and Aristotle is not a negative barrier but is, rather, positive and productive for understanding. By opening ourselves to what Aristotle's text says to us, and to the claim to truth that it makes upon us, we bring to life new meanings of the text. And this understanding, as a form of *phronēsis*, is a practical-moral knowledge which becomes constitutive of what we are in the process of becoming. Gadamer seeks to show us that authentic hermeneutical understanding becomes integral to our very being and transforms what we are in process of becoming, just as *phronēsis* determines the being of the *phronimos.*

This stress on the moment of appropriation in hermeneutical understanding enables us to see why Gadamer believes that the *Geisteswissenschaften*, when truly practiced, are practical-moral disciplines. As hermeneutical disciplines, they are not primarily directed toward amassing theoretical, "objective" knowledge. Rather, while hermeneutical understanding does require theoretical distancing, it also involves the type of appropriation characteristic of *phronēsis.*[49] The type of knowledge and truth that hermeneutics yields is practical knowledge and truth that shapes our *praxis* (we will soon explicitly examine the question of truth). This also helps to explain why for Gadamer the "chief task" of philosophic hermeneutics is to "correct the peculiar falsehood of modern consciousness" and "to defend practical and political reason against the domination of technology based on science." It is the scientism of our age and the false idolatry of the expert that pose the threat to practical and political reason. The task of philosophy today is to elicit in us the type of questioning that can become a counterforce against the contemporary deformation of *praxis.* It is in this sense that "hermeneutic philosophy is the heir of the older tradition of practical philosophy."

THE MOVEMENT BEYOND PHILOSOPHIC HERMENEUTICS

I have indicated that Gadamer's appropriation of the tradition of practical philosophy is not without tensions and problems. If we take Gadamer seriously and press his own claims, they lead us beyond philosophic hermeneutics. But before I begin my immanent critique— a critique that takes Gadamer's arguments seriously and draws out their conclusions—it is important to remember that in *Truth and Method* Gadamer's primary concern is with the understanding and interpretation of works of art, texts, and tradition, with "what is handed down to us." Ethics and politics are not in the foreground of his investigations. Even his discussion of Aristotle is introduced only insofar as it helps to illuminate the hermeneutical phenomenon. But it is also clear that if we pay close attention to Gadamer's writings before and after the publication of *Truth and Method*, we will see that from his very earliest to his most recent writings he has consistently shown a concern with ethics and politics, especially with what we can learn from Greek philosophy. In his writings since the publication of *Truth and Method*, Gadamer has returned again and again to the dialectical interplay of hermeneutics and *praxis*. When we enlarge our horizon and consider the implications of what he is saying for a contemporary understanding of *praxis*, a number of difficulties come into sharp relief.

Let me begin with a consideration of the meaning of *truth* for Gadamer, then move to his conception of *criticism*. This will allow us to take a close look at some of the difficulties with his appropriation of *phronēsis*. Finally, we can turn to Gadamer's reflections on dialogue and freedom.

Although the concept of truth is basic to Gadamer's entire project of philosophic hermeneutics, it turns out to be one of the most elusive concepts in his work. After all, a primary intention of *Truth and Method* is to elucidate and defend the legitimacy of speaking of the "truth" of works of art, texts, and tradition. Gadamer tells us that it was not his aim to play off Method against Truth, but rather to show that there is "an entirely different notion of knowledge and truth"[50] which is not exhausted by the achievements of scientific method and which is available to us through hermeneutical understanding. The appeal to truth—a truth that enables us to go beyond our own historical horizon through a fusion of horizons—is absolutely essential in order to distinguish philosophic hermeneutics from a historicist form of relativism. Gadamer concludes *Truth and Method* with strong claims about this distinctive type of truth.

Thus there is undoubtedly no understanding that is free of all prejudices, however much the will of our knowledge must be directed towards escaping their thrall. It has emerged throughout our investigation that the certainty that is imparted by the use of scientific methods does not suffice to guarantee truth. This is so especially of the human sciences, but this does not mean a dimunition of their scientific quality, but, on the contrary, the justification of the claim to special humane significance that they have always made. The fact that in the knowing involved in them the knower's own being is involved marks, certainly, the limitation of "method," but not that of science. Rather, what the tool of method does not achieve must—and effectively can—be achieved by a discipline of questioning and research, a discipline that guarantees truth [*die Wahrheit verbürgt*]. (*TM*, pp. 446–47; *WM*, p. 465)

But what precisely does "truth" mean here? And what does it mean to say that there is a discipline of questioning and research that "guarantees truth"? It is much easier to say what "truth" does not mean than to give a positive account. It might seem curious (although I do not think it is accidental) that in a work entitled *Truth and Method* the topic of truth never becomes fully thematic and is discussed only briefly toward the very end of the book. (The word "truth" is not even listed in the index.) It is clear, however, that like Hegel and Heidegger, Gadamer rejects the notion of truth as correspondence, as *adequatio intellectus et rei*, at least in regard to the distinctive type of truth that is achieved through hermeneutical understanding. What Gadamer means by "truth" is a blending of motifs that have resonances in Hegel and Heidegger. Like Hegel, Gadamer seeks to show that there is a truth that is revealed in the process of experience (*Erfahrung*) and that emerges in the dialogical encounter with tradition. Even the passage just quoted echoes the typical Hegelian movement from certainty (*Gewissheit*) to truth (*Wahrheit*). And like Heidegger, Gadamer also seeks to recover the notion of *alētheia* as unconcealment (*Unverborgenheit*). There is even a parallel between Heidegger's claim that *Dasein* is "equally in truth and in untruth" and Gadamer's claim that prejudices (both blind and enabling ones) are constitutive of our being. But Gadamer also distances himself from both Hegel and Heidegger. He categorically rejects what Hegel himself took to be the ground of his conception of truth—that "truth is the whole" that is finally revealed in *Wissenschaft*, the absolute knowledge that completes and overcomes experience.[51] Gadamer also stands in an uneasy relation with Heidegger. He draws back from the "radical" thinking (*Denken*) of Heidegger. With implicit reference to Heidegger Gadamer writes, "When science expands into a total technocracy and thus brings on the 'cosmic night' of the 'forgetfulness of being', the nihilism that Nietzsche prophesied, then may one look at the last fading light of the sun that is set in the evening sky, instead of turning around to look for the first shimmer of its return" (*TM*, p. xxv; *WM*, p. xxv). And with explicit reference to Heidegger, he tells us, "What man needs is not only a persistent asking of ultimate questions, but the sense of what is feasible, what is possible, what is correct, here and now" (*TM*, p. xxv; *WM*, p. xxv).[52] But even if we play out the similarities and differences with Hegel and Heidegger, the precise meaning of truth in Gadamer's philosophy still eludes us. Even more problematic and revealing, if we closely examine the way in which Gadamer appeals to "truth," we see that he is employing a concept of truth that he never fully makes explicit. Typically he speaks of the "claim to truth" (*Anspruch auf Wahrheit*) that works of art, texts, and tradition make upon us. Gadamer never says (and it would certainly pervert his meaning) that something is true simply because it is handed down to us. This is just as evident in his claims about the tradition of practical philosophy as it is in his criticism of the Enlightenment's prejudice against prejudice. In saying, for example, that "when Aristotle, in the sixth book of the *Nicomachean Ethics,* distinguishes the manner of 'practical' knowledge . . . from theoretical and technical knowledge, he expresses, in my opinion, one of the greatest truths by which the Greeks throw light upon the 'scientific' mystification of modern society of specialization," Gadamer is not telling us that this is one of the "greatest truths" simply because it is what Aristotle's text says. Furthermore, in this context, he is clearly referring to a *discursive* truth which needs to be justified or warranted by argumentation. Rather, Aristotle's doctrine is true because Gadamer thinks we can now give convincing arguments and reasons to show why it is true. The emphasis here is not simply on what tradition says to us or even on the "claim to truth" that it makes upon us but on the validation of such claims by our own thinking and argumentation. Gadamer has warned us against reifying tradition and taking it as something simply given. Furthermore, tradition is not a seamless whole. There are conflicting traditions making conflicting claims of truth upon us—for example, a tradition of Enlightenment thinking, as well as the older tradition of practical philosophy. If we take our historicity seriously, then the challenge that always confronts us is to give the best possible reasons and arguments that are appropriate to our hermeneutical situation in order to validate claims to truth.

Gadamer himself makes this point forcefully in his friendly quarrel with Leo Strauss. Commenting on a theme that Gadamer shares with Strauss—the importance of the concept of friendship in Aristotle's ethics for enabling us to recognize the limitations of modern ethics—he asks,

Does this insight emerge because we "read" the classics with an eye that is trained by historical science, reconstructing their meaning, as it were, and then considering it possible, trusting that they are right? Or do we see truth in them because we are thinking ourselves as we try to understand them, i.e., because what they say seems true to us when we consider the corresponding modern theories that are invoked? (*TM,* p. 485; *WM,* p. 507)

There is no ambiguity in the answers that Gadamer gives to these questions. He emphasizes *our* thinking, understanding, and argumentation. But then this casts the entire question of truth in a very different light. When it comes to the validation of claims to truth, then the essential issue concerns the reasons and arguments that we can give to support such claims—reasons and arguments that are of course fallible and that are anticipatory, in the sense that they can be challenged and criticized by future argumentation. In effect, I am suggesting that Gadamer is appealing to a concept of truth that (pragmatically speaking) amounts to what can be argumentatively validated by the community of interpreters who open themselves to what tradition "says to us."[53] This does not mean that there is some transcendental or ahistorical perspective from which we can evaluate competing claims to truth. We judge and evaluate such claims by the standards and practices that have been hammered out in the course of history.

Gadamer typically links truth (*Wahrheit*) with the thing (*die Sache*) itself. He tells us, "I repeat again what I have often insisted upon: every hermeneutical understanding begins and ends with the 'thing itself'."[54] In appealing to the thing itself, Gadamer does *not* mean Kant's *Ding-an-sich*. Rather he plays on the implications of Aristotle's assertion, in the *Ethics*, that the appropriate form of knowledge and reasoning is conditioned by the subject matter; on the way in which Hegel, in the *Phenomenology of Spirit*, is always directing us to *die Sache* in order to reveal the dialectical movement of consciousness; and on the significance of the call for the "return to the things themselves" in Husserl and the transformation of this demand in Heidegger's "hermeneutics of facticity." But this appeal to *die Sache* is not sufficient to clarify the concept (*Begriff*) of truth, since the question can always be asked, When do we have a true understanding of the thing (*die Sache*) itself? Gadamer implicitly recognizes that this is always a proper question when he says that our anticipatory interpretations "may not conform to what the thing is."[55] The crucial point as it pertains to truth is that however prominent the thing itself may be in testing our interpretations, a *true* understanding of the thing itself must be *warranted by appropriate forms of argumentation* that are intended to show that we have properly grasped what the thing itself says.[56]

The point that I am making about the concept of truth that is implicit in Gadamer's writings is closely related to the allied concept of criticism. Gadamer says,

It is a grave misunderstanding to assume that emphasis on the essential factor of tradition which enters into all understanding implies an uncritical acceptance of tradition and sociopolitical conservatism. . . . In truth the confrontation of our historic tradition is always a critical challenge of this tradition. . . . Every experience is such a confrontation.[57]

Here too there are echoes of Hegel, for, like Hegel, Gadamer thinks that experience—*Erfahrung*—always involves an element of negativity, of "determinate negation" (see *TM*, pp. 310–25; *WM*, pp. 329–44). But even if we read this passage in the light of a full understanding of Gadamer's approach to tradition, there is a problem here that Gadamer does not squarely confront. All criticism appeals to some principles, standards, or criteria. Gadamer is extremely incisive in exposing the fallacy of thinking that such principles, standards, or criteria can be removed from our own historicity and in showing that there is an essential openness and indeterminacy about them. (This parallels Kuhn's effort to elucidate the criteria for evaluating competing scientific theories.) But even if we grant Gadamer everything that he wants to say about human finitude rooted in historicity, this does not lessen the burden of answering the question of what is and what ought to be the basis for the critical evaluation of the problems of modernity. One can be sympathetic with Gadamer's critique of objectivism, foundationalism, the search for some Archimedean point that somehow stands outside of our historical situation. But if we press the theme of application and appropriation to our historical situation, then we must still address the question, What is the basis for our critical judgments? When Gadamer tells us that the "concept of 'praxis' which was developed in the last two centuries is an awful deformation of what practice really is" or when he speaks of "the peculiar falsehood of modern consciousness[,] the idolatry of scientific method[,] and the anonymous authority of the sciences," he is himself appealing to critical standards and norms that demand rational justification and argumentation. It is not *sufficient* to give a justification that directs us to tradition. What is required is a form of argumentation that seeks to warrant what is valid in this tradition.

We can also approach the question of the inadequacies of Gadamer's conception of truth and criticism from a slightly different perspective. Gadamer frequently presents his own thinking as a corrective to the onesidedness and excesses of the scientism that is so pervasive in contemporary thought, which he traces back to the Cartesian and Enlightenment legacies. It is certainly true that Gadamer does present a strong apologia for the centrality and legitimacy of the concepts of prejudgment, authority, and tradition. But we can ask, in a Gadamerian fashion, Isn't there also a claim to truth in the Enlightenment tradition that needs to be recovered and honored?[58] We do a grave injustice to the Enlightenment if we think that it was simply an "epistemological" movement and fail to recognize that any adequate hermeneutical understanding of the Enlightenment needs to recognize its social and political roots. Thus, for example, we can grant that true authority is not blind obedience, but rather that authority is based on knowledge and recognition. But as the Enlightenment thinkers knew, authority always presents itself as possessing superior knowledge; that is the basis for its claim to legitimacy. Persons in authority do not tell us to obey blindly, but to obey or follow them because they have superior judgment and insight. The real political and practical problem is to be able to critically evaluate when such claims are legitimate and when they are not. Or, if we use the language of Gadamer, the practical issue is to be able to distinguish rightful authority (which is based on knowledge and recognition) from pseudo versions of it that falsely claim to be based on superior knowledge. Gadamer's philosophic hermeneutics does not include a detailed understanding of how power as domination (*Herrschaft*)—the type of domination that deforms *praxis*—operates in the modern world.

At times Gadamer seems to suggest that in the contemporary world the threat and danger for *praxis* comes from *technē*. But such a judgment would be profoundly misleading. Even if we appeal to Plato and Aristotle, they never would draw such a conclusion. And despite contemporary transformations of the meaning and scope of the practical and the technical, the point that we need to be aware of is this: the danger for contemporary *praxis* is not *technē*, but domination (*Herrschaft*).

A philosophic perspective such as philosophic hermeneutics can be judged not only by what it says and what comes into sharp focus but also by what is left unsaid and relegated to the fringes of its horizon. Gadamer's philosophic hermeneutics is virtually silent on the complex issues concerning domination and power. But as Nietzsche, Marx, Freud, Weber, the Frankfurt thinkers, and Foucault have taught us, no intellectual orientation that seeks to illuminate concrete *praxis* in the contemporary world can be judged adequate if it fails to confront questions concerning the character, dynamics, and tactics of power and domination.

These critical remarks about truth, criticism, and power point to some of the difficulties and lacunae in Gadamer's appropriation of *phronēsis*, that distinctive "intellectual virtue" that is required for "ethical know-how" which mediates and codetermines the universal and the particular. Let us examine *phronēsis* carefully, concentrating on the "universal" element that is mediated. Gadamer's meaning is illustrated by his interpretation of the role of natural law in Aristotle. In the realm of *praxis,* natural law is not to be thought of as a law that is eternal, immutable, and fully determinate. Gadamer tells us, "According to Aristotle, the idea of an immutable natural law applies only to the divine world, and he declares that with us humans natural law is in the last analysis just as inconstant as positive law."[59] While natural law is not to be reduced to or confused with positive law, natural law always requires interpretation and specification in concrete, particular situations of *praxis.* Finding justice in a concrete situation demands perfecting law with equity (*epieikeia*): "It follows, then, according to Aristotle that the idea of natural law serves only a critical function. Nothing in the idea authorizes us to use it dogmatically by attributing the inviolability of natural law to particular and concrete juridical contents."[60] The claim that Gadamer makes about Aristotle's understanding of natural law (the universal element) as something that is essentially open to interpretation and that is only specified when mediated in a concrete ethical situation that demands choice and decision is paradigmatic, for Gadamer, of the application of all ethical principles and norms. But as Aristotle stresses, and Gadamer realizes, *phronēsis* presupposes the existence of *nomoi* (funded laws) in the *polis* or community. This is what keeps *phronēsis* from degenerating into the mere cleverness or calculation that characterizes the *deinos* (the clever person).[61] Given a community in which there is a living, shared acceptance of ethical principles and norms, then *phronēsis* as the mediation of such universals in particular situations makes good sense.

The problem for us today, the chief characteristic of our hermeneutical situation, is that we are in a state of great confusion and uncertainty (some might even say chaos) about what norms or "universals" ought to govern our practical lives. Gadamer realizes— but I do not think he squarely faces the issues that it raises—that we are living in a time when the very conditions required for the exercise of *phronēsis*—the shared acceptance and stability of universal principles and laws—are themselves threatened (or do not exist). Of course, Gadamer is right when he insists that no matter how corrupt or deformed a society may be, there can always be *phronēsis.* There can always be those individuals who exemplify the virtues of the *phronimos.* That is a lesson we can learn from Socrates, Plato, and Aristotle. And it is also true that in the best of *polei* there will always be occasions when *phronēsis* degenerates into instrumental or even vicious cleverness. But to insist that these are always real possibilities in any society, no matter how just or unjust the society may be, is not yet to confront a crucial question—the question of what material, social, and political conditions need to be concretely realized in order to encourage the flourishing of *phronēsis* in all citizens.

Furthermore, Gadamer does not adequately clarify the type of discourse that is appropriate when questions about the validity of basic norms (universals) are raised. How is such recognition and agreement to be achieved? When there is serious disagreement about what norms ought to be binding, should all participants be able to have a say? When pressed about these questions, Gadamer frequently deals with a different issue. He tells us that such universals are inherited from tradition, that they are essentially open, that their meaning can be specified only in application to concrete, practical situations. But this does not clarify the issue of what we are to do in a situation in which there is confusion or conflict about which norms or universals are appropriate, or how we are to evaluate a situation in which we question the validity of such norms.

If we follow out the logic of Gadamer's own line of thinking, if we are really concerned with the "sense of what is feasible, what is possible, what is correct, here and now," then this demands that we turn our attention to the question of how we can nurture the type of communities required for the flourishing of *phronēsis*. At the heart of Gadamer's thinking about *praxis* is a paradox. On the one hand, he acutely analyzes the deformation of *praxis* in the contemporary world, and yet on the other hand he seems to suggest, regardless of the type of community in which we live, that *phronēsis* is always a real possibility. Ironically, there is something almost *unhistorical* in the way in which Gadamer appropriates *phronēsis*. Except for some occasional remarks, we do not find any detailed systematic analysis of social structure and causes of the deformation of *praxis* in contemporary society. Insufficient attention is paid to the historical differences that would illuminate precisely how *praxis* and *phronēsis* are threatened and undermined in the contemporary world. Since Aristotle clearly saw the continuity and interplay of ethics and politics, one would think that this is a movement necessitated by Gadamer's own appropriation of *phronēsis*. But although Gadamer acknowledges this to-and-fro movement, he stops short of facing the issues of what is to be done when the *polis* or community itself is "corrupt"—when there is a breakdown of its *nomoi* and of a rational discourse about the norms that ought to govern our practical lives.[62]

In defense of Gadamer, one can see why he stops short of confronting the practical issues of our historical hermeneutical situ-

ation. We can read his philosophic hermeneutics as a meditation on
the meaning of human finitude, as a constant warning against the
excesses of what he calls "planning reason," a caution that philosophy must give up the idea of an "infinite intellect." "The role of
prophet, of Cassandra, of preacher" does not suit the philosopher.
Gadamer, like Heidegger, is deeply skeptical about the human *will*
and about the belief that we can make or engineer communities in
which there are living, shared, universal principles. The claims of
philosophic hermeneutics are at once bold and modest. They are bold
insofar as hermeneutics has the task of defending practical and political reason against the various attacks on it in the contemporary
world and of eliciting the sense of questioning that can make us
aware of our ignorance. But philosophic hermeneutics—or any form
of philosophy—cannot solve the problems of society or politics. It is
dangerous to submit to the temptation of playing the prophet. This
is the way to dogmatism—and even terror. Even if one accepts Gadamer's cautions about prophesy and dogmatism, though, we are still
confronted with a practical task, one to which Gadamer's own investigations lead us: to foster the type of dialogical communities in
which *phronēsis* becomes a living reality and where citizens can
actually assume what Gadamer tells us is their "noblest task"—
"decision-making according to one's own responsibility—instead of
conceding that task to the expert."

There is another significant gap in Gadamer's fusion of hermeneutics and *praxis*. This is not just an innocent omission but a glar-
ing substantive deficiency, if one is concerned about contemporary
practical and political life. Consider again some of Gadamer's reiterated critical judgments about our contemporary historical situation. He tells us that the contempory understanding of practical
reason as "technical control" has degraded the concept of *praxis*. But
if this is true—and I certainly agree that it is—then one wants to
know what is it about modern societies that has *caused* this to
happen. Gadamer speaks of the dangerous role of experts and tech-
nicians in modern society when they are invested with "exaggerated
authority." Again, while I think he is right in his judgment, his
comments raise the problem of how we are to account for this
phenomenon and determine its social consequences. He declares, as
we have seen, that in "modern technological society, public opinion
itself has in a new and really decisive way become the object of very
complicated techniques—and this . . . is the main problem facing
our civilization." But if this phenomenon is "new and really deci-

sive," then again we need some explanation of how this "new" state of affairs has come about.

Trying to precisely formulate and answer such questions is not just a matter of idle theoretical curiosity; it is of the utmost practical importance. Without some sort of theoretical understanding and explanation of the structure and dynamics of modern technological society, there is always the real danger that *praxis* will be ineffectual, merely abstract. Let us not forget that *praxis* requires choice, deliberation, and decision about what is to be done in concrete situations. Informed action requires us to try to understand and explain the salient characteristics of the situations we confront. I do not want to suggest that there is an easy way of answering such questions. We know how much disagreement exists about what is a proper way of trying to give answers—or even about what counts as a satisfactory formulation of questions. But if we are genuinely concerned with *praxis*, we cannot avoid struggling with these complex issues.

One might again seek to come to Gadamer's defense by arguing that I am placing an illegitimate demand upon him. After all, Gadamer explicitly tells us that his first and last concern is philosophy. He is not doing, nor does he claim to be doing, social scientific analysis; this is simply not Gadamer's field of inquiry. The chief task for philosophic hermeneutics is to illuminate what happens when we understand—and this is essentially a philosophic question. But such a line of defense is inadequate, and a bit too facile. Why? Because Gadamer *does* claim to illuminate the essential character of the *Geisteswissenschaften* (although not to provide a methodological treatise on them).

It is here that the disparity between the continental dichotomy of the *Naturwissenschaften* and the *Geisteswissenschaften*, and the Anglo-American trichotomy of natural science, social science, and humanities, comes into sharp relief. There is a fundamental unresolved ambiguity in Gadamer's philosophy concerning the social sciences. However much one recognizes the importance of the hermeneutical dimension of the social sciences, one must also forthrightly confront those aspects of these disciplines that seek to develop *theoretical* and *causal explanations* of social phenomena. Sometimes—and Gadamer's remarks about the social sciences are very sparse—he writes as though they are like underdeveloped natural sciences, implying that it is essential for us to realize their "limited relevance," because they never tell us how they are to be applied. *Phronēsis* is always required to apply the results of the social sciences. But at other times he writes as if all the social sciences, when properly understood, are to be assimilated to practical philosophy as a model of the human sciences.

What is obscured by this indecisiveness can be directly related to the question of the dialectical interplay between *phronēsis* and *technē*. Once we are clear about the categorial distinction between these concepts, then we can ask, Is there any type of contemporary social knowledge that can help us to understand what are the available *techniques* that can inform our *praxis*? I do not find any evidence in Gadamer to show that he faces the complex issues raised by this question. Again, we can even appeal to the Greeks in order to point out that both for them and for us *technē* without *phronēsis* is blind, while *phronēsis* without *technē* is empty.

The major point of this immanent critique of philosophic hermeneutics—that it leads us to questions and practical tasks that take us beyond hermeneutics—can be approached in still another way. Thus far I have been concentrating on Gadamer's appropriation of the "truth" in Aristotle's understanding of *praxis* and *phronēsis*, but a full-scale analysis of Gadamer's philosophic hermeneutics would require seeing how it represents an appropriation and interweaving of themes drawn from Aristotle, Plato, and Hegel—the three philosophers who, in addition to Heidegger, have had the most profound influence on Gadamer. I want to consider two of the most important themes that Gadamer appropriates from Plato and Hegel: the centrality of *dialogue* and *conversation*, and the meaning of *freedom*.

Gadamer's first book dealt with Plato, and throughout his long and productive philosophic career he has returned again and again to the interpretation and appropriation of Plato's texts. In all his work, Gadamer has been drawn to what we can learn from Plato about the meaning of dialogue, and he shows in his detailed studies how illuminating Plato's texts become when we read them as dialogues.[63] But the notion of dialogue has been present from the very beginning of Gadamer's discussion of play as the "clue to ontological explanation."

When one enters into a dialogue with another person and then is carried further by the dialogue, it is no longer the will of the individual person, holding itself back or exposing itself, that is determinative. Rather, the law of the subject matter [*die Sache*] is at issue in the dialogue and elicits statement and counterstatement, and in the end plays them into each other.

A conversation or a dialogue is

a process of two people understanding each other. Thus it is characteristic of every true conversation that each opens himself to the other person, truly accepts his point of view as worthy of consideration and gets inside the other to such an extent that he understands not a particular individual, but what he says. The thing that has to be grasped is the objective rightness or otherwise of his opinion, so that they can agree with each other on the subject [*das sachliche Recht seiner Meinung damit wir in der Sache mitein-ander einig werden Können*]. (*TM*, p. 347; *WM*, p. 363)

In a genuine dialogue or conversation, what is to be understood [*die Sache*] guides the movement of the dialogue. The concept of dialogue is fundamental for grasping what is distinctive about hermeneutical understanding.

Gadamer is, of course, aware of the differences between the dialogue that we have with texts and tradition and that which occurs with other persons. "Texts are 'permanently fixed expressions of life' which have to be understood, and that means that one partner in the hermeneutical conversation, the text [,] is expressed only through the other partner, the interpreter" (*TM*, p. 349; *WM*, p. 365).[64] The conversation or dialogue that Gadamer takes to be the quintessence of hermeneutical understanding always evokes the memory of a living conversation or dialogue between persons. But Gadamer, in his analysis of dialogue and conversation, stresses not only the common bond and the genuine novelty that a turn in a conversation may take but the mutuality, the respect required, the genuine seeking to listen to and understand what the other is saying, the openness to risk and test our own opinions through such an encounter. In Gadamer's distinctive understanding of practical philosophy, he blends this concept of dialogue, which he finds illustrated in the Platonic Dialogues, with his understanding of *phronēsis*.[65] But here, too, there are strong practical and political implications that Gadamer fails to pursue. For Gadamer's entire corpus can be read as showing us that what we truly are, what is most characteristic of our humanity is that we are dialogical or conversational beings in whom "language is a reality." According to Gadamer's reading of the history of philosophy, this idea can be found at the very beginning of Western philosophy and is the most important lesson to be learned from this philosophic tradition in our own time.

But if we are really to appropriate this central idea to our historical situation, it will point us toward important practical and political tasks. It would be a gross distortion to imagine that we might conceive of the entire political realm organized on the principle of dialogue or conversation, considering the fragile conditions that are required for genuine dialogue and conversation. Nevertheless, if we think out what is required for such a dialogue based on mutual understanding, respect, a willingness to listen and risk one's opinions and prejudices, a mutual seeking of the correctness of what is said, we will have defined a powerful regulative ideal that can orient our practical and political lives. If the quintessence of what we are is to be dialogical—and if this is not just the privilege of the *few*—then whatever the limitations of the practical realization of this ideal, it nevertheless can and should give practical orientation to our lives. We must ask what it is that blocks and prevents such dialogue, and what is to be done, "what is feasible, what is possible, what is correct, here and now" to make such genuine dialogue a concrete reality.

What Gadamer appropriates from Hegel is as significant as what he rejects. As we have seen, experience (*Erfahrung*), the movement from certainty (*Gewissheit*) to truth (*Wahrheit*), the centrality of *die Sache selbst* in leading and guiding us, the way in which self-understanding is achieved only in and through the dialectical encounter with the "other," the "recognition" theme that is so central for understanding the movement of Hegel's *Phenomenology of Spirit*, the play of identity and difference, the speculative character of language—all are ideas that have their resonances in Gadamer's philosophic hermeneutics. What Gadamer rejects in Hegel and criticizes is the claim to finality, the idea that humans can achieve the stance of the "infinite intellect," that there is a "true infinity" that completes the process of experience, that there is or can be "absolute knowledge" or *Wissenschaft* that overcomes the essential openness and anticipatory quality of *all* experience. But here, where I am seeking to draw out the practical consequences of what Gadamer is saying, I want to single out his appropriation from Hegel of the principle of freedom—a freedom that is realized only when there is authentic mutual "recognition" among individuals.

Many critics (and defenders) of Gadamer stress the conservative implications of philosophic hermeneutics. Certainly Gadamer seeks to conserve the "truth" that speaks to us through tradition, although, as we have seen, he strongly denies that focusing on the essential factor of tradition implies uncritical acceptance of tradition, or "sociopolitical conservatism." But the critics have neglected the latent radical strain implicit in Gadamer's understanding of hermeneutics as practical philosophy. This radical strain is indicated in his emphasis—which has become more and more dominant in recent years—on freedom and solidarity that embrace all of humanity.

For there is no higher principle of reason than that of freedom. Thus the opinion of Hegel and thus our own opinion as well. No higher principle is thinkable than that of the freedom of all, and we understand actual history from the perspective of this principle: as the ever-to-be-renewed and the never-ending struggle for this freedom.[66]

In a passage that echoes the Frankfurt School's radical interpretation of Hegel, Gadamer writes:

The principle that all are free never again can be shaken. But does this mean that on account of this, history has come to an end? Are all human beings actually free? Has not history since then been a matter of just this, that the historical conduct of man has to translate the principle of freedom into reality? Obviously this points to the unending march of world history into the openness of its future tasks and gives no becalming assurance that everything is already in order.[67]

What Gadamer tells us about freedom is complemented by what he says about solidarity. His understanding of solidarity also goes back to his interpretation of Greek philosophy and the primacy of the principle of friendship in Greek ethics and politics. We recall that when Gadamer examines Aristotle's analysis of the distinction between *phronēsis* and *technē*, he notes that the variant of *phronēsis* which is called *synēsis* requires friendship and solidarity.

Once again we discover that the person with understanding [*synēsis*] does not know and judge as one who stands apart and unaffected; but rather, as one united by a specific bond with the other, he thinks with the other and undergoes the situation with him. (*TM*, p. 288; *WM*, p. 306)

This theme, too, which Gadamer appropriates from Greek philosophy, is universalized. "Genuine solidarity, authentic community, should be realized."[68] In summarizing his answer to the question "What is practice?" he writes:

Practice is conducting oneself and acting in solidarity. Solidarity, however, is the decisive condition and basis of all social reason. There is a saying of Heraclitus, the "weeping" philosopher: The *logos* is common to all, but people behave as if each had a private reason. Does this have to remain this way?[69]

One of the reasons why many modern thinkers have been so suspicious of *phronēsis*, and more generally of the tradition of practical philosophy that was shaped by Aristotle, is because of the elitist connotations of this "intellectual virtue." Aristotle himself did not think of it as a virtue that could be ascribed to every human being but only to those gifted individuals who had been properly educated. And it cannot be denied that many of those who have been drawn to this tradition in the modern age, especially insofar as they have opposed what they take to be the excesses and abstractness of the Enlightenment conception of reason, have not only been critical of political reform and revolution but have been attracted to the elitist quality of *phronēsis*. But Gadamer softens this elitist aura by blending his discussion of *phronēsis* with his analysis of a type of dialogue and conversation that presupposes mutual respect, recognition, and understanding. When all of this is integrated with the Hegelian "truth"—"the principle that *all* are free never again can be shaken"— then the radicalization of *phronēsis* and *praxis* becomes manifest. There is an implicit *telos* here, not in the sense of what will work itself out in the course of history, but rather in the sense of what ought to be concretely realized.

PHILOSOPHIC HERMENEUTICS AND THE CARTESIAN ANXIETY

Earlier I have suggested that if we are to exorcise the Cartesian Anxiety by moving beyond objectivism and relativism, then we need to find an alternative way of thinking and of understanding our being-in-the-world. We are now in a position to see that the whole of Gadamer's project—and all of the bypaths that he has followed—can be interpreted as being addressed to this issue. For the direction of his thinking that is initially concerned with the analysis of works of art, texts, and tradition has universalistic consequences. From the introduction of the concept of play, with its intrinsic to-and-fro movement and buoyancy, to his analysis of dialogue and conversation where "the law of the subject matter [*die Sache*] is at issue in the dialogue and elicits statement and counterstatement, and in the end plays them into each other," all of the themes in Gadamer's philosophic hermeneutics contribute to the movement beyond objectivism and relativism. Gadamer is not simply attempting to reveal what happens when we "understand" in some limited and parochial sense of understanding. If we are truly dialogical beings—always in conversation, always in the process of understanding—then the dynamics of the play of understanding underlie and pervade all human activities. Gadamer deplores the "aesthetic consciousness" (which might just as well be called "subjectivism," or what MacIntyre calls "emotivism" and which leads to relativism) that has become preva-

lent in the modern period. He finds the same deficiencies and inadequacies in that form of "historical consciousness" which thinks of
itself as standing over and against historical "objects." His positive
analysis of prejudgments, of the way in which they both enable us to
understand and are also risked and tested in all genuine encounters
and experience, also helps to contribute to the movement beyond
objectivism and relativism. We find variations on the same theme in
Gadamer's analysis of *praxis* and *phronēsis*. In a variety of subtle
ways Gadamer shows us what is wrong with that way of thinking
that dichotomizes the world into "objects" which exist *an sich* and
"subjects" that are detached from and stand over against them. We
do not comprehend what the things themselves "say" unless we
realize that their meaning transcends them and comes into being
through the happening or event of understanding. And we do not
understand ourselves as "subjects" unless we understand how we are
always being shaped by effective-history and tradition. We are always
in medias res: there are no absolute beginnings or endings. Experience is always anticipatory and open. "The truth of experience always
contains an orientation towards new experience. . . . The dialectic of
experience has its own fulfillment not in definitive knowledge, but
in that openness to experience that is encouraged by experience itself"
(*TM*, p. 319; *WM*, p. 337). Overcoming the Cartesian Anxiety is
learning to live without the idea of the "infinite intellect," finality,
and absolute knowledge. The approach that pervades so much of
Gadamer's thinking and helps to give it unified perspective, his practical-moral orientation, is directed toward reminding us, and calling
us back to, an understanding of what it means to be finite historical
beings who are always "on the way" and who must assume personal
responsibility for our decisions and choices.

While Gadamer's sustained and multifaceted critique of objectivism is apparent, it may seem more questionable whether he escapes
from the clutches of relativism. But Gadamer's philosophic hermeneutics is just as critical of the varieties of relativism as it is of
objectivism. Indeed, insofar as Gadamer begins his analysis in *Truth
and Method* with a critique of aesthetic consciousness and historicism, one might say that developing a critique of relativism is his
primary concern. "Aesthetic consciousness," as we have seen, does
lead to relativism—not only in the realm of the aesthetic but in all
domains of human life. Relativism ultimately makes sense (and gains
its plausibility) as the dialectical antithesis to objectivism. If we see
through objectivism, if we expose what is wrong with this way of

thinking, then we are at the same time questioning the very intelligibility of relativism.

But we do not have to leave matters at this abstract level of analysis. We can appreciate how Gadamer's reflections on language, horizons, and historicity contribute to undermining relativism. Understanding, he says, is limited, but not closed; it is essentially open to appropriating what is alien. Gadamer, no less than Popper, is sharply critical of the Myth of the Framework, the myth that we forever are enclosed in our own horizons, our own paradigms, our own culture. "Just as the individual is never simply an individual, because he is always involved with others, so too the closed horizon that is supposed to enclose a culture is an abstraction. The historical movement of human life consists in the fact that it is never utterly bound to any one standpoint, and hence can never have a truly closed horizon" (*TM*, p. 271; *WM*, p. 288). Gadamer helps us to understand the "truth" of the incommensurability thesis and to reject what is false about it. He shows that insofar as the appeal to incommensurability has been used (or misused) to justify the Myth of the Framework or the notion that there is no way of comparing and communicating with alien horizons and forms of life, it is to be rejected as false. But insofar as it is used to point to the openness of all experience and language and to describe our situation as that of being constantly challenged to understand what is alien, and thereby to risk our prejudices, the incommensurability thesis, for Gadamer, is an idea that is basic for an understanding of our being-in-the-world.

Gadamer also exposes another feature of relativism. The varieties of relativism constantly flirt with the suggestion that what we take to be real, or true, or right is arbitrary, as if we could somehow simply decide by an act of will what is real, true, and right. But historicity is not to be confused with arbitrariness. Gadamer reminds us that we belong to tradition, history, and language before they belong to us. We cannot escape from the dynamic power of effective-history, which is always shaping what we are becoming. We become fools of history if we think that by an act of will we can escape the prejudgments, practices, and traditions that are constitutive of what we are, and that in Rorty's phrase have been "hammered out" in the course of history. But we are also always in the process of modifying and shaping what we are becoming.

But even when we understand how philosophic hermeneutics contributes to the movement beyond objectivism and relativism and provides concrete exemplification of what such a movement means, it does not entirely succeed in charting the course beyond objectivism and relativism. I have tried to show that many of the problems that Gadamer leaves unsolved are related to the ambiguities he allows concerning the meaning of truth, and specifically concerning the validation of the "claims to truth" that tradition makes upon us. And here one must frankly admit that there is a danger of lapsing into relativism. I have argued Gadamer is really committed to a communicative understanding of truth, believing that "claims to truth" always implicitly demand argumentation to warrant them, but he has failed to make this view fully explicit. He also fails to notice how this ambiguity transforms much of the rest of what he says. For although all claims to truth are fallible and open to criticism, they still require validation—validation that can be realized only through offering the best reasons and arguments that can be given in support of them—reasons and arguments that are themselves embedded in the practices that have been developed in the course of history. We never escape from the obligation of seeking to validate claims to truth through argumentation and opening ourselves to the criticism of others.

The ambiguity that Gadamer allows concerning the meaning and validation of claims to truth has consequences for the distinction and contrast between Truth and Method. Typically, when dealing with hermeneutical understanding, Gadamer speaks of it as an "entirely different type of knowledge and truth" from that which is yielded by Method and science. But he has never developed a full-scale analysis of the type of knowledge and truth that he takes to be characteristic of Method and the natural sciences. It is never quite clear, then, what is *common* to these *different* forms of knowledge and truth. And there are conflicting tendencies in what Gadamer does say. At times, he suggests that these two types of knowledge and truth are compatible as long as we are aware of the limits and proper domain of science. It is not science that is the main target of Gadamer's criticism, but scientism. But Gadamer often seems to suggest that Method (and science) is never sufficient to reveal Truth. Given the strong claims that Gadamer makes about the universality of hermeneutics, there is something misleading about this contrast. For if understanding underlies all human inquiry and knowledge, then what Gadamer labels Method must itself be hermeneutical. The appropriate contrast would then be not between Truth and Method but between different types or dimensions of hermeneutical practice. Gadamer tends to rely on an image of science which the postempiricist philosophy and history of science have called into question. In fairness to Gadamer, it should be noted that he completed his major study of hermeneutics before the emergence of the postempiricist philosophy and history of science. There is something right about understanding the importance of the mathematization of the physical world, the search for invariant laws, the centrality of the hypothetical-deductive form of explanation in the sciences, and the central role that prediction plays in science. But as we have seen, all this needs to be qualified by the hermeneutical dimension of the sciences. Method is more like hermeneutical understanding than Gadamer frequently acknowledges, and when it comes to validating competing understandings and interpretations we are confronted with the type of critical problems that are so fundamental for understanding scientific inquiry. Gadamer speaks of his emphasis on tradition and the assimilation of what is past and handed down as a corrective to those tendencies in modern thought that neglect or are insensitive to tradition and effective-history. But as we think through this "corrective," we come back to the need to integrate the "truth" of the Cartesian and Enlightenment traditions that Gadamer is criticizing—the demand for intersubjective and public criteria for the evaluation of all claims to truth by the community of interpreters.

All of these tensions and problems come into sharp focus in Gadamer's elucidation of *praxis* and *phronēsis*. He has opened us to many questions that he does not adequately answer. If we pursue what he means by truth and criticism, if we turn our attention to the status of the shared principles and universals required for the exercise of *phronēsis*, or to examining what type of communities are required for all individuals to be able to assume the "noblest task of the citizen—making decisions according to one's responsibility"— or to the legitimate causal questions that need to be confronted in seeking to understand and explain the dynamics, conflicts, and contradictions of contemporary society or to the practical implications of what he has to say about dialogue, conversation, freedom, and solidarity, then we are led beyond philosophic hermeneutics. These questions lead us—with a deepened understanding of human finitude that helps us to exorcise the Cartesian Anxiety—to the task of further clarifying what *praxis* means in our historical situation and to the practical tasks of concretely realizing what Gadamer so nobly defends as being central to our humanity.

PART FOUR

PRAXIS,
PRACTICAL DISCOURSE,
AND JUDGMENT

A T this stage of our inquiry, we have opened up the play—the to-and-fro movement—of science, hermeneutics, and *praxis*. In exploring the new image of science that has been developing in the postempiricist philosophy and history of science, we have witnessed the recovery of the hermeneutical dimension of science in both the natural and the social sciences. In the philosophy of the natural sciences, this development has been characterized as having begun with an obsession with the meaning and reference of single terms (logically proper names and ostensive definition), moved to the search for a rigorous criterion for discriminating empirically meaningful sentences or propositions, shifted to the evaluation of competing conceptual schemes, and finally turned to the realization that science must be understood as a historically dynamic process in which there are conflicting and competing paradigm theories, research programs, and research traditions. In order to gain a fruitful perspective on the rationality of science itself, it is necessary to see that reasons and arguments employed by the community of scientists are grounded in social practices and that there is an essential openness in the very criteria and norms that guide scientific activity. There has been a growing awareness of the vital role that interpretation plays at every stage of scientific activity and a questioning of any permanent division between observation and theory. The distinction between the relevant facts and observations and our theoretical explanation of these is a changing and a pragmatic one; what are taken to be the facts themselves are shaped by our preunderstandings and theoretical interpretations. We have come to appreciate the extent to which scientific theories are underdetermined by the "facts" and how this allows for alternative and competing theoretical explanations. We have seen the error of thinking that there is or can be some calculus or algorithmic decision procedure for evaluating scientific hypotheses and theories. Although much of the polemic in the field of the philosophy and history of science is still influenced by the dichotomy of objectivism and relativism, this dichotomy obscures the underlying coherence and the common ground shared by the participants in the discussion. And central to this new understanding is a dialogical model of rationality that stresses the practical, *communal* character of this rationality in which there is choice, deliberation, interpretation, judicious weighing and application of "universal criteria," and even rational disagreement about which criteria are relevant and most important. It is an illusion to think that before the fact we always know (in principle) what will count as a decisive refutation of a proposed theory or that the epistemologist can discover fixed, permanent rules that are to be used to resolve differences. Various theories of "instant rationality" fail to capture what is distinctive about science as a rational activity. Yet alternative paradigms, theories, and research programs can be warranted by communal rational argumentation. What is to count as evidence and reasons to support a proposed theory can be rationally contested— even what is to count as proper criticism. Hunches, intuitions, guesses all have a role to play in scientific inquiry, but the scientist never escapes the obligation to support his or her judgments with the best possible reasons and arguments. Communal decisions and choices are not arbitrary or merely subjective. There may be losses and gains in the replacement of one scientific tradition by another, but science does progress. The new understanding of science does not call into question scientific progress and the growth of scientific knowledge but rather faulty epistemological doctrines that claim that progress can be measured by an appeal to a permanent ahistorical matrix or a neutral descriptive language. The "truth" of the incommensurability thesis does not support the type of relativism suggested by the

Myth of the Framework, according to which we are prisoners trapped in closed linguistic frameworks. Rather it enables us to become more sensitive to the challenges to be confronted in the comparison and evaluation of different paradigms and theoretical orientations.

We have seen, too, how many parallels there are between the rationality debates in the natural sciences and the social sciences. We have noted that the hermeneutical dimension is even more important in the social disciplines than in the natural sciences, since the social disciplines are concerned with human beings who are always engaged in the social construction and deconstruction of their world. While such a difference presents us with a variety of problems in the understanding of human beings, it is not *sufficient* to justify our concluding that there is a logical gap or a conceptual dichotomy between the natural and social disciplines. A false picture is suggested when we think that our task is to leap out of our own linguistic horizon, bracket all our preunderstandings, and enter into a radically different world. Rather the task is always to find the resources within our own horizon, linguistic practices, and experience that can enable us to understand what confronts us as alien. And such understanding requires a dialectical play between our own preunderstandings and the forms of life that we are seeking to understand. It is in this way that we can risk and test our own prejudices, and we can not only come to understand what is "other" than us but also better understand ourselves.

Underlying the recovery of the hermeneutical dimension of the sciences is a practical-moral concern, one which seeks to root out the various forms of scientism and positivism that are still so prevalent and to open a space for the concept of "learning from" what is different and alien, and for reclaiming the integrity of the concept of practical wisdom.

The recovery of the hermeneutical dimension of the sciences has led to an encounter with philosophic hermeneutics itself, especially as it has been elaborated by Gadamer. Ever since the nineteenth century, whenever an appeal has been made to hermeneutics to clarify what is distinctive about the *Geisteswissenschaften*, there has been a tendency to contrast the *Geisteswissenschaften* with the *Naturwissenschaften*—to "locate" some fixed principle of demarcation. But much of this discussion and many of the typical contrasts between the *Naturwissenschaften* and the *Geisteswissenschaften* have been based on a false and discredited epistemological understanding of the natural sciences. There are continuities and differences among these various disciplines, and these continuities and differences are shifting and pragmatic. Whereas an earlier stage of inquiry was directed to the search for some fixed and rigorous principle of demarcation—between science and nonscience, or between the natural and the social sciences, or between *Naturwissenschaften* and *Geisteswissenschaften*, this global strategy has now been replaced by the highlighting of changing pragmatic differences.

We have seen, too, how in the twentieth century there has been a significant shift in the very understanding of hermeneutics. Hermeneutics is now claimed to be ontological and universal. In Gadamer's investigations of the role of prejudgments and prejudices in all understanding and knowing, in his restoration of the centrality of the concept of tradition as always effectively shaping what we are in the process of becoming, in his attempt to situate rationality itself within the context of developing, living traditions, we have pursued themes that are implicit in the recovery of the hermeneutical dimension of the natural and social sciences. But the movement or play here is not simply in one direction. Gadamer, we have seen, is at his weakest in clarifying the role of argumentation in the validation of all claims to truth and in elucidating the nature of criticism in hermeneutical interpretation. His contrast between Method and Truth is overdrawn. This dichotomy obscures the continuity between the *Naturwissenschaften* and the *Geisteswissenschaften.* The judgmental character of evaluating competing scientific theories and paradigms is more like the judgmental character of evaluating rival hermeneutical interpretations than Gadamer makes explicit. And just as it is essential to focus attention on the effective criteria for evaluating rival theories and research traditions in science, there is an analogous problem when it comes to testing and evaluating rival interpretations of texts, works of art, and traditions.

The outstanding theme in Gadamer's philosophic hermeneutics is his fusion of hermeneutics and *praxis,* and the claim that understanding itself is a form of practical reasoning and practical knowledge—a form of *phronēsis.* Initially Gadamer's appeal to *phronēsis* was introduced to clarify the moment of application or appropriation that is involved in all understanding. But in arguing that hermeneutics itself is the heir to the older tradition of practical philosophy, Gadamer has sought to show how the appropriation of the classical concepts of *praxis* and *phronēsis* enables us to gain a critical perspective on our own historical situation, in which there is the constant threat and danger of the domination of society by technology based on science, a false idolatry of the expert, a manipulation of public opinion by powerful techniques, a loss of moral and political orientation, and an undermining of the type of practical and political reason required for citizens to make responsible decisions. I have tried to show how the various paths that Gadamer pursues all contribute to an understanding of our being-in-the-world as dialogical, and how they contribute to the movement beyond objectivism and relativism. But at the same time I have sought to expose some of the deficiencies and tensions in his own appropriation of *praxis* and *phronēsis* and to reveal the radical thrust of his own thinking, one which points to the goal of nurturing the type of dialogical communities in which *phronēsis* can be practiced and where the freedom of all human beings is concretely realized.

In this part, I want to explore further the issues that arise in addressing our historical situation and in understanding the meaning of *praxis, phronēsis,* and such related concepts as practical discourse and judgment. And I want to do this by considering the contributions to this conversation by two thinkers who at once have a great deal in common with Gadamer but who also give strikingly different emphases than Gadamer does to the significance of *praxis:* Jürgen Habermas and Hannah Arendt. By playing off the strengths and weaknesses of these thinkers against each other, we can enrich our understanding of *praxis* and of the tasks that confront us in our historical situation. I also want to test the projects of Gadamer and Habermas against the type of deconstructive criticism that has become so fashionable today. By pressing the objections of Richard Rorty, I hope to show that despite what at first might appear to be a devastating critique, Rorty helps to bring out the most essential insights in the respective visions of Gadamer and Habermas. Throughout this part, then, my primary objective is to bring forth the ground that is shared which helps to make sense of the differences among these thinkers. It is this common ground that is most relevant to us and that enables us to grasp what might be called the modern (or postmodern) paradox concerning the prospects of human *praxis*—that the type of solidarity, communicative interaction, dialogue, and judgment required for the concrete realization of *praxis* already presupposes incipient forms of the community life that such *praxis* seeks to foster. Finally, we will see the sense in which the movement beyond objectivism and relativism is itself a practical task.

A HISTORICAL INTERLUDE

Before exploring some of the family resemblances and convergences in Gadamer, Habermas, Rorty, and Arendt with regard to the question of *praxis* and *phronēsis,* I want to do justice to the striking and consequential differences among them. These differences can be explored from two interrelated perspectives: by sketching the different philosophic and intellectual traditions and experiences that have effectively shaped their thinking, and by outlining the different problematics that provide the focus for their work. It is because these differences initially appear to be so sharp that the convergence that I want to show becomes so significant. I do not want to claim that they are all really saying the "same thing," or even that there is some grand synthesis in which their conflicting viewpoints can be integrated. In the end there are important conflicts among them. Yet their views do complement each other, and they can be interpreted as contributing to a common discourse. Most of the major trends of twentieth-century philosophy are represented in their work. So if there really is a commonality—a commonality reflected in the emergence of a shared universe of discourse and concern—this shows a way of bringing together highly divergent viewpoints. I will begin by placing each of them in his or her distinctive intellectual milieu, and then show how their personal experience has affected the problems that they have chosen to place in the foreground of their work.

We have already seen that much of Gadamer's understanding of philosophic hermeneutics has been determined by his appropriation of Greek philosophy (especially Plato and Aristotle) and Hegel, and by his ongoing dialogue with Heidegger, and that his appropriation has been critical and transformative—that what he takes from each of these philosophers is as important as what he decisively rejects. Gadamer himself frequently claims that his point of departure—the tradition within which he places himself—is German Romanticism. It is almost as if Gadamer set himself the task of rethinking the "claim to truth" implicit in this tradition in a manner that would avoid the paradoxes of nineteenth-century historicism and relativism. Despite his interest in ethics and politics (where the model is always Greek *ethos* and *politikē,* rather than contemporary social scientific analyses of society and politics), as we have seen, his abiding concern has been to understand understanding itself, especially as it pertains to works of art, literary texts, and history.

The formative intellectual period in Gadamer's career was the first quarter of the twentieth century. We can detect a strong continuity between Gadamer's early interests and those that emerged in Germany in the latter part of the nineteenth century and the first decades of the twentieth: the Romantic tradition; the growth of historical consciousness; hermeneutics; the *Geisteswissenschaften*, understood as moral disciplines; and the origins of phenomenology in the pioneering work of Husserl. Gadamer has also noted how important Kierkegaard was for him, as well as the cultural ambience that surrounded the Stefan George circle. Consequently there is a strong historical continuity between Gadamer's formative intellectual development and nineteenth-century German philosophy. We can see this vividly when we recall the development of German thought from Schleiermacher to Dilthey, Husserl, and Heidegger, with each successive thinker defining his own beginning point in relation to (or opposition to) his predecessor.[1]

To appreciate the differences between Gadamer and Habermas, it is essential to realize how much more separates these two German philosophers than approximately thirty years difference in age. For the world in which Habermas grew up and came to intellectual maturity, which coincides with the rise and fall of Nazi Germany, was virtually a totally different world than the one in which Gadamer grew up. Whereas Gadamer's primary experience has been one of historical continuity, the primary formative experience for Habermas was that of discontinuity—the trauma of almost a total break in tradition. Many commentators on Habermas tend to ignore or downplay the specific historical circumstances that had a decisive influence on him during the decades of the 1940s through the 1960s: the collapse of Nazi Germany, the discovery by Germans only after the war of the immensities of the horrors of this era, and the hope of making a new beginning. Yet we fail to adequately understand even Habermas's most theoretical work if this context is ignored. What impressed Habermas, as a young student, was the failure of twentieth-century German culture to provide a serious counterthrust to the rise of Nazi ideology. This has always colored his wariness about the influence and effects of Heidegger's teachings, even though Habermas acknowledges Heidegger's distinctive philosophic genius. Even the tendency to place Habermas in the tradition of the Frankfurt School is something of a historical fiction. One is tempted to say that the "Frankfurt School" is an invention that came into being only after the Second World War, when Horkheimer and Adorno returned to Germany to refound the Institute for Social Research in Frankfurt. Although he was an assistant to Adorno, Habermas only gradually became aware of the early work of the institute. Only in the 1960s did he discover for himself the full dimensions of the highly creative work that was done in exile in New York by members of the Institute for Social Research.

As Habermas reported in a recent interview, during his student years he "theoretically lived" in the 1920s:

> I had read Lukács. Inspired by the young Hegelians, I looked at the transition from Kant to "objective" idealism with great interest. Alongside all this were my very strong everyday political interests. I had read *History and Class Consciousness* both with fascination and regret that it belonged to the past. Then I read *The Dialectic of Enlightenment* and the first things published by Adorno after the war. That gave me the courage to read Marx systematically and not simply historically. Critical Theory, a Frankfurt School—there was no such thing at the time. Reading Adorno had given me the courage to take up systematically what Lukács and Korsch represented historically: the theory of reification as a theory of rationalization, in Max Weber's sense. Already at that time, my problem was a theory of modernism, a theory of the pathology of modernism, from the viewpoint of the realization—the deformed realization—of reason in history.[2]

Habermas began his intellectual career, then, with the attempt to rediscover, reconstruct, and rethink the development of German thought that runs from Kant through Fichte, Schelling, Hegel, to Marx. While always critical of the varieties of Marxist orthodoxies and concerned to root out the origins of these orthodoxies in Marx himself, Habermas thinks of himself as working in a Hegelian–Marxist tradition, where the project now is to radically reconstruct what is living in this tradition, to boldly and honestly reject what no longer can be warranted, and to meet the new cultural, scientific, social, and political challenges of the contemporary world. In addition to the tradition of German thought from Kant to Marx, Habermas has also sought to reappropriate the sociological tradition that includes Weber, Durkheim, and Parsons. The break in tradition that Habermas experienced was profoundly traumatic, but it also had a liberating intellectual effect. It provided an opportunity for a fresh and open encounter with other intellectual orientations and scientific developments, including Anglo-American linguistic and analytic philosophy, contemporary linguistics, psychoanalysis, theories of cognitive and moral development, and varieties of new approaches in the range of the social disciplines. One primary and deep influence on Habermas has been American pragmatism, especially as represented by Peirce, Dewey, and Mead. Habermas is one of the few German thinkers to take American pragmatism seriously and to study it without the blinding prejudices characteristic of so many continental thinkers. It is, perhaps, ironic that Habermas's grasp and appropriation of pragmatism is far more incisive than that of many contemporary professional American philosophers.

Hannah Arendt was always an intellectual maverick and took pride in thinking of herself as an independent thinker who did not belong to any school of thought or subscribe to any "ism." But we must not forget how deeply she was affected by the charismatic influence of the young Heidegger, when in 1924, as a precocious Jewish woman of eighteen, she went to study with Heidegger at Marburg. (In 1924 Heidegger was thirty-five and Gadamer, who was also at Marburg, was twenty-four.) After leaving Marburg in order to spend a semester studying with Husserl, Arendt went to Heidelberg, where she became the student of Jaspers. During these years at Heidelberg (1925–29) Jaspers, with whom Arendt became a lifelong friend, helped to encourage Arendt's abiding interest in Kant. In these early days Arendt had little direct interest in politics and even less interest in theoretical issues of politics. If the events of the twentieth century had been different, Arendt might well have pursued a distinguished academic career in the relatively insular world of the German university. But Arendt, who always claimed that her thinking was grounded in her experiences, witnessed the horrors and traumas of twentieth-century Europe. She experienced the rise of anti-semitism, facism, and totalitarianism. She directly experienced her own break with tradition. She began to formulate the project of trying to comprehend the darkness of our times. Whether probing the origins of totalitarianism, the Eichmann trial, or new political movements, she was always seeking to develop distinctions, categories, and a mode of thinking that would shed some light on what appeared almost incomprehensible.[3]

Richard Rorty, the one native American among these four thinkers, is a contemporary of Habermas. Whereas an explicit interest in understanding *praxis* has been focal for the other three, this has not been true for Rorty. He was a student of philosophy at the University of Chicago and Yale University during the late 1940s and early 1950s, a time when the leading philosophic orthodoxies in America were logical empiricism and so-called ordinary language philosophy. While these movements were spreading and conquering many graduate philosophy departments, both Chicago and Yale were bastions of resistance.

So, even at a later stage of Rorty's development, when he was deeply influenced by the work of Sellars and Quine, Rorty's own early intellectual formation provided something of a critical edge in assessing the various strains in analytic philosophy. His first published article, "Pragmatism, Categories, and Language" (1961), already introduced themes that were to pervade his work: the American pragmatic tradition, and the therapeutic power of the later Wittgenstein. During the 1960s and early 1970s Rorty wrote a number of important papers on the problems that most preoccupied the Anglo-American community of professional philosophers. But a close reading of his papers also reveals that something else was going on. At the same time that Rorty was arguing in a style that had become canonical for analytic philosophers, he also seemed to be raising deeply disturbing questions about some of the unstated presuppositions and unquestioned assumptions of these philosophers. What had at first seemed to be merely hesitations and reservations emerged, in *Philosophy and the Mirror of Nature* in 1979, as a comprehensive critique of not only analytic philosophy but the entire "Cartesian-Lockean-Kantian tradition." And, in marshalling a variety of rhetorical devices and alternative philosophic languages to carry out his therapeutic critique, Rorty exhibited an affinity with the type of deconstructive strategies that have become so fashionable in French poststructuralism. In his most recent work he champions a new form of pragmatism derived from his reading and appropriation of James and Dewey. But throughout Rorty's philosophic development, and despite subtle changes in his thought, one concern runs through all his writing: his fascination with the issues of metaphilosophy, with seeking to unmask the pretensions of various forms of philosophic discourse and to clarify what role philosophy might yet play in contemporary cultural life.

I have presented these brief sketches of the contexts in which Gadamer, Habermas, Arendt, and Rorty have developed their distinctive philosophic perspectives primarily because it helps to focus attention on the key problems and themes in their work. Gadamer fits directly into the tradition of humanistic thought that traces its origins back to Greek philosophy and that was rejuvenated, and flourished, in nineteenth-century Germany. His entire philosophic project can be characterized as an apologia for humanistic learning. Gadamer, throughout his long career, has sought to show that the humanistic tradition, properly understood, is an essential corrective to the scientism and obsession with instrumental technical thinking that is dominant today. According to Gadamer, authentic understanding grounded in tradition and rightful authority yields a distinctive type of practical knowledge and practical truth.

Habermas, who discovered that hermeneutics not only helps to highlight the limitations of positivist modes of thought but that there is also an essential hermeneutic dimension in all social knowledge, has been primarily concerned with the question of the foundation of a critical theory of society. From his perspective, neither the critique of ideology, as developed in Marx, nor the critical theory of the older Frankfurt thinkers is sufficient to provide a satisfactory answer to this foundational question. Habermas gradually came to realize more and more clearly the need to elaborate a comprehensive theory of rationality. While aware of the immensity and complexity of this research program, he has argued that the task is unavoidable if we are to rationally ground a critical theory of society. Another way of characterizing Habermas's project is to say that while fully aware of the dark side of the dialectic of the Enlightenment, he has sought to show that there is still a way of redeeming, reconstructing, and rationally defending the emancipatory aspirations of the Enlightenment—emancipatory aspirations that call for autonomy and concrete freedom embracing all of humanity.

Arendt's chief intellectual concern became the attempt to recover what is distinctive about the *vita activa,* and especially the highest form of human activity—what she calls action *(praxis).* To her this was not just an intellectual problem but the most vital issue of modern times. She felt that professional thinkers from Plato on had tended to distort the nature of action and politics, and that in the modern world a catastrophic reversal within the *vita activa* had taken place, resulting in the victory of a fabricating and laboring mentality. Even her approach to the study of totalitarianism was influenced by this understanding of action, for totalitarianism, she thought, was something distinctively "new" that had emerged only in the twentieth century which sought to destroy the very plurality that she took to be the condition for action and politics.

Rorty's central question has been the question of the nature of philosophy itself. Perhaps it is true that the whole history of philosophy, when examined closely, has been a history of crises for philosophy. But in no other age has there been such deep and radical questioning about what philosophy is; what it can be; what, if anything, it contributes to human culutre. All of Rorty's writings revolve about this question.

In the *Spiel*—the interplay—of contrasting and comparing Gadamer, Habermas, Rorty, and Arendt, I will be employing a notion that runs through all of their work. I want to show how they can be read as different voices in a coherent conversation. After bringing out their strengths and weaknesses and showing some of the ways in which they complement each other, I want to reflect on the common themes that emerge by speaking more directly in my own voice.

PRACTICAL DISCOURSE: HABERMAS

The perspective that is most illuminating for understanding the significant differences between Gadamer and Habermas is one that begins with examining how much they share in the "application" theme. Already in Habermas's initial critical review of *Truth and Method*, he declared, "I find Gadamer's real achievement in the demonstration that hermeneutical understanding is linked with transcendental necessity to the articulation of an action-orienting self-understanding."[4] It is instructive to see how this perspective is worked out and transformed in Habermas's own attempt to develop a comprehensive theory of communicative action and rationality. For Habermas, no less than for Gadamer, we cannot completely escape from our horizon in seeking to understand what is alien. This has central significance for the entire theory of rationality. Habermas argues that it is an illusion to think that we can assume the position of disinterested observers by bracketing all our preunderstandings, when it comes to understanding other forms of life, horizons, and what purport to be other standards of rationality. If we want to describe other forms of life or earlier stages of our own social development, then we can only do this by adopting the "performative attitude" of one who participates in a process of mutual understanding.

It is important to distinguish the different roles that evaluation plays in this process. Habermas's main point is that "classifying" or "describing" speech acts presupposes that we understand the types of validity claim that they make. An interpreter must have the ability to make clear to himself or herself the implicit reasons that enable participants to take the positions that they do take. In order to *understand* an expression, the interpreter must bring to mind the reasons with which the actor would, under suitable circumstances, defend its validity. Consequently, the interpreter is drawn into the process of assessing validity claims. But this process of determining that a validity claim has been made (which requires virtual participation by the interpreter) does not yet involve making an evaluative judgment about the soundness of the validity claim.

Habermas's point can be illustrated by appealing again to the familiar example of Zande witchcraft. We could not even begin to understand Zande witchcraft unless we had the ability to discriminate what the Azande consider to be reasons for acting in one way or another. To do this requires a preunderstanding on our part of what it means to make a validity claim and the ability to identify those situations in which one is made. This is the sense in which understanding what the Azande are saying and doing requires identifying validity claims. But it is a different (although related question) to evaluate whether the reasons given by the Azande are good or bad reasons, and even here we need to make an important distinction. Understanding the practice of Zande witchcraft requires that we be able to discriminate what the Azande themselves consider good and bad reasons. (Presumably the Azande themselves can make mistakes.) This judgment can also be distinguished from a judgment as to whether (and in what sense) the type of reasons that the Azande give are adequate or inadequate. Habermas is, of course, aware of the ever-present danger of ethnocentricism, of unreflectively imposing alien standards of judgment and thereby missing the point or meaning of a practice. But Habermas's primary thesis is that it is an illusion to think that we can escape from this danger by imagining that we can describe alien linguistic practices without determining the validity claims that are implicitly made in speech acts. For Habermas, this is a condition for all understanding, whether it is the understanding that arises among participants in communicative action or that of the social scientist who seeks to understand alien linguistic practices.[5]

The theme of our historicity, in which we are always critically appropriating what we seek to understand, is no less fundamental for Habermas than it is for Gadamer. But for Habermas the primary problem becomes one of how we can reconcile this "performative participation" with the type of intersubjective understanding that makes the claim to objectivity. When Habermas seeks to develop a comprehensive theory of communicative action or a universal pragmatics, he is not claiming that we do this *sub specie aeternitatis* or that we assume the position of an "infinite intellect." Rather he is claiming that within the horizon of our hermeneutical situation, we can seek to elucidate the "unavoidable" universal conditions of communicative action, discourse, and rationality. We aspire to universality, recognizing that any such claim is eminently fallible. If we were to translate Habermas's project into Gadamerian terms, we might imagine Habermas saying to Gadamer: "You yourself have argued that all understanding involves application or appropriation, and furthermore you stress the openness of language, which is the medium of understanding. How are we to account for the fact that we can in principle always understand that which initially strikes us as alien in other horizons and other forms of life? What is it about the very character of language that enables us to grasp the possibility of the dialogue, conversation, and questioning that you have so penentratingly elucidated? What are the practical consequences of the claims that we are essentially dialogical beings, that 'no higher principle is thinkable than the freedom of all,' and that practice itself is based upon solidarity?"

Now it may seem as though I am suggesting that if we press Gadamer's insights and claims we are led to the very issues that are central for Habermas. I do think this is true, but it needs to be carefully qualified, because it might suggest a misleading asymmetry, with an immanent critique of Gadamer leading inevitably to Habermas's project. So I want to emphasize that the critique can also be reversed, that we can use Gadamer to highlight some of the problems that stand at the heart of Habermas's work. A hermeneutical perspective derived from Gadamer can sharpen our perception of the strengths and weaknesses of Habermas's project, especially his theory of communicative action and its relation to his thesis about the redemption of universal normative validity claims through practical discourse. For Habermas argues that corresponding to *theoretical discourse,* in which we seek to validate claims to *theoretical truth,* there is a cognitive form of *practical discourse* in which we seek argumentatively to redeem claims to *normative validity or rightness.* What kind of theory or intellectual endeavor is a theory of communicative action, and how is it to be validated or warranted? Habermas, I will be arguing, speaks with two voices, which might be called the "transcendental" and the "pragmatic." Alternatively, I can clarify what I mean by employing a distinction which Charles Taylor makes in his book on Hegel between "strict dialectics" and "interpretative or hermeneutical dialectics." Taylor distinguishes two ways in which a dialectical argument can command our assent. "There are strict dialectics, whose starting point is or can reasonably claim to be undeniable. And then there are interpretative or hermeneutical dialectics, which convince us by the overall plausibility of the interpretation they give."[6] This is a most un-Hegelian type of distinction, because Hegel's claim to truth, system, *Wissenschaft* depends ultimately on the validity of "strict dialectics." Yet I agree with Taylor that Hegel's most enduring and valuable contributions are revealed through his interpretative or hermeneutical dialectics. But how is this distinction relevant to Habermas?

At times, Habermas slips into the language of strict dialectics or strict transcendental argument. This is apparent in his original discrimination of the three "quasi-transcendental" cognitive interests—the technical, the practical, and the emancipatory—and is also evident in some of his initial attempts to argue that four different types of validity claims are implicitly raised in communicative action.

Habermas's frequent use of expressions like "what must be presupposed," what is "unavoidable," what is "necessary" easily lead one to think that he is advancing a transcendental argument in the tradition of Kant, even when he stresses his differences with Kant. But in the years since the publication of *Knowledge and Human Interests*, Habermas has qualified his project to disassociate himself from this strong transcendental strain—and with good reason. Not only have powerful objections been pressed against the possibility of strong transcendental arguments or strict dialectics, but Habermas himself has seen more clearly that a theory of communicative action is not intended to be a transcendental, a priori theory, but an empirical, scientific theory. In stating his reasons for abandoning the expression "transcendental," Habermas tells us that "adopting the expression *transcendental* could conceal the break with apriorism that has been made in the meantime. Kant had to separate empirical from transcendental analysis sharply."[7] It is just this dichotomy that a reconstructive theory of communicative action is intended to overcome. This is why Habermas now prefers to speak about the logic of *reconstruction* or *reconstructive analysis* and to argue that within the domain of scientific theories we must distinguish empirical-analytical theories, which are essentially hypothetical-deductive theories, from reconstructive theories, the latter type illustrated by the theories of Chomsky, Piaget, and Kohlberg, who seek to elucidate universal conditions and rules that are implicit in linguistic competence and in cognitive or moral development.[8] A theory of communicative action is intended to be a scientific reconstructive theory of this type—one directed toward uncovering the universal conditions that are presupposed in all communicative action. But before questioning the adequacy of Habermas's conception of reconstructive analysis and the extent to which it is successful in overcoming the Kantian distinction between the *a posteriori* and the *a priori*, we need to provide a sketch of this theory, and examine some of the essential claims that he makes about practical discourse.

Communicative action is the type of social interaction that is *oriented toward reaching understanding*. Communicative action, according to Habermas, must be carefully distinguished from nonsocial *instrumental* action and *social strategic* action, both of which are oriented toward success.[9] Although the class of communicative actions is broader than speech acts, Habermas focuses his attention on those communicative actions that are exhibited in speech. "The goal of coming to an understanding [*Verständigung*] is to bring about an agreement [*Einverständnis*] that terminates in the intersubjective mutuality of reciprocal understanding, shared knowledge, mutual trust, and accord with one another. Agreement is based on recognition of the corresponding validity claims of comprehensibility, truth, truthfulness and rightness."[10] According to Habermas, anyone acting communicatively must, in the performing of a speech action, raise universal validity claims and suppose that they can be vindicated or redeemed *(Einlösen)*. While all speech presupposes a background consensus which is typically taken for granted, this consensus can break down or be challenged. When such a break or challenge takes place, then *discourse* becomes relevant. Discourse consists of the type of elucidation and argumentation in which we suspend immediate action and in which participants seek to redeem the validity claims that have been challenged. "Discourse" is a term of art, a construct, an "ideal type" introduced to highlight the type of speech that is relevant for argumentative redemption of validity claims. Habermas realizes that it rarely exists in its pure form and that, empirically, "breaks" in communicative action are typically resolved by a variety of nondiscursive strategies.

If we simplify the situation, and think of a communicative interaction between two individuals, we can grasp what Habermas means by the four types of validity claims. For I may not understand what my interlocutor is saying, in the sense that I do not find the utterance comprehensible or intelligible. Then the task is to seek to come to a mutual agreement so that the utterance becomes comprehensible. In the context of ordinary speech actions, this may be easily resolved, but in complex cases it may require sophisticated hermeneutical skills. Or while I may find that the utterance is comprehensible, I may question whether what is being said or implied is true. In this case, what is required is a theoretical discourse that seeks to ascertain the truth of the statements made or implied. Or I may suspect that my interlocutor is lying, insincere, trying to deceive me, or is self-deceived. Then the question becomes one of determining the truthfulness of what is said. Finally, I may question the appropriateness or rightness of what is uttered, its implied claim to normative validity. In this case what is required is a *practical discourse* that seeks to redeem the normative validity claim. Habermas is not primarily interested in empirical pragmatics that elucidate the complex ways in which breaks in everyday communication are negotiated and resolved. Rather he wants to outline a research program for a universal pragmatics that aspires to identify and reconstruct the universal conditions of possible understanding.

While there are many controversial details in the development of such a universal pragmatics, perhaps the most controversial, and certainly the most relevant for our inquiry, are the claims that Habermas makes about *practical discourse*—the type of discourse relevant to the redemption of universal normative validity claims. Against Weber, and against all forms of emotivist and decisionist understanding of norms, Habermas argues that there is a type of argumentation and rationality that is appropriate for the redemption of universal normative validity claims. And his essential thesis is even stronger: he asserts that the "expectation of discursive redemption of normative validity claims is already contained in the structure of intersubjectivity."[11]

In taking up a practical discourse, we unavoidably suppose an ideal speech situation that, on the strength of its formal properties, allows consensus only through *generalizable* interests. A cognitivist linguistic ethics *[Sprachethik]* has no need of principles. It is based only on fundamental norms of rational speech that we must always presuppose if we discourse at all. This, if you will, transcendental character of ordinary language ... can ... be reconstructed in the framework of a universal pragmatic.[12]

We can grasp Habermas's point by relating his theory of communicative action to his quarrel with Weber and Marx.[13] Although both contributed to an understanding of communicative action, Habermas thinks that both failed to adequately distinguish between two categorically different forms of action and action systems, and their corresponding forms of rationality. Consequently, both failed to perceive the complex ways in which these two types of action (purposive-rational and communicative) are interrelated.

Purposive-rational actions can be regarded under two different aspects—the empirical efficiency of technical means and the consistency of choice between suitable means. Actions and action systems can be rationalized in both respects. The rationality of means requires technically utilizable, empirical knowledge; the rationality of decisions requires the explication and inner consistency of value systems and decision maxims, as well as the correct derivation of acts of choice.[14]

But purposive-rational actions and the ways in which they can be rationalized must be sharply distinguished from communicative actions and their rationalizaton.

Communicative action can be rationalized neither under the technical aspect of the means selected nor under the strategic aspect of the selection of means but only under the moral-practical aspect of the responsibility of the acting subject and the justifiability of the action norm. Whereas the rationalization of purposive-rational action depends on the accumulation of true (empirically or analytically true) knowledge, the rationalizable aspect of communicative action has nothing to do with propositional truth, but it has everything to do with the truthfulness of intentional expressions and with the rightness of norms.

Rationalization here means extirpating those relations of force that are inconspicuously set in the very structures of communication and that prevent conscious settlement of conflicts, and consensual regulation of conflicts, by means of intrapsychic as well as interpersonal communicative barriers. Rationalization means overcoming such systematically distorted communication in which the action-supporting consensus concerning the reciprocally raised validity claims—especially consensus concerning the truthfulness of intentional expressions and the rightness of underlying norms—can be sustained in appearance only, that is, counterfactually.[15]

For Habermas the type of rationality and rationalization process appropriate for communicative action at once provides a *telos* (a formal-procedural one) for orienting our *praxis* and a standard—or at least a necessary condition—for evaluating the degree to which a substantive form of life satisfies this *telos*, one which is "always already" implicit in communicative action.

In part III I argued that there is a radical strain in Gadamer's understanding of *praxis* as he moves from *phronēsis* to dialogue, to the principle of freedom that embraces all of humanity. Now we can see how Habermas's understanding of communicative action makes this radical strain fully explicit. For although Habermas himself recognizes the integrity of the type of practical reasoning that is exhibited in *phronēsis*, he is rightly critical of a neo-Aristotelianism that fails to appreciate that in Aristotle *phronēsis* is to be understood in the context of Aristotle's metaphysics and ontology and presupposes a dubious "metaphysical biology."[16]

There are four primary reasons why Habermas, who himself systematically employs the categorial distinction between the practical *(praxis)* and the technical *(technē)*, is so skeptical and wary of the attempts to appropriate Aristotle's definition of these concepts—and also wary of the resulting neo-Aristotelianism. Basically I think Habermas is right, for each of these reasons. The first reason is primarily philosophic. Aristotle's ethics and politics are intricately intertwined with his metaphysics, cosmology, analysis of scientific knowledge *(epistēmē)*, physics, psychology, and biology. This is at once the source of the systematic power of the *Ethics* and the *Politics* and what is so problematic for any contemporary appropriation of Aristotle. There is scarcely a claim that Aristotle makes in his *Ethics* or *Politics* that does not at once presuppose and draw upon doctrines that are embedded in other parts of Aristotle's corpus. One cannot simply extract a core of ethical and political claims, as many neo-Aristotelians are tempted to do, without squarely confronting questions about whether Aristotle's metaphysics, cosmology, and psychology are still valid for us today. As Habermas points out,

The ethics and politics of Aristotle are unthinkable without the connection to physics and metaphysics, in which the basic concepts of form, substance, act, potency, final cause, and so forth are developed. . . . Today it is no longer easy to render the approach of this metaphysical mode of thought plausible. It is no wonder that the neo-Aristotelian writings do not contain systematic doctrines, but are works of high interpretive art that suggest the truth of classical texts through interpretation, rather than by grounding it.[17]

The second reason is primarily political. The fact is that many of those who have appealed to Aristotle's ethics and politics and have endorsed some form of neo-Aristotelianism in the contemporary world have done so to buttress a dubious neo-conservatism—to give it intellectual respectability. This conjunction of neo-Aristotelianism and bourgeois conservative thought has been more evident in German thought than in other varieties of conservatism, but it arouses a legitimate suspicion about the use of Aristotle to justify an ideological position. More generally, neo-Aristotelians tend to use Aristotle as a weapon in the battle against the legacy of the Enlightenment.[18]

The third reason emerges from a blending of the first two considerations and helps to set the context within which Habermas places himself and what he regards as the primary problematic of our time. Habermas is well aware of the "dialectic of the Enlightenment" and of the dark side of the Enlightenment legacy. He knows that the rise of positivism, scientism, the disenchantment of the world, relativism, emotivism, and the triumph of instrumental reason all have their origins in the systematic ambiguities of the Enlightenment tradition. But at the same time he realizes that we need to preserve the truth implicit in this tradition and reconstruct its emancipatory potential. What is needed is a genuine dialectical synthesis of the ancients and the moderns, not turning one's back on modernity as many neo-Aristotelians are tempted to do.

We may pose the basic issue as Habermas did in his early work when he asked,

How can the promise of [classical] practical politics—namely, of providing practical orientation about what is right and just in a given situation—be redeemed without relinquishing, on the one hand, the rigor of scientific knowledge, which modern social philosophy demands in contrast to the practical philosophy of classicism? And on the other, how can the promise of social philosophy to furnish an analysis of the inter-relationships of social life, be redeemed without relinquishing the practical orientation of classical politics?[19]

Habermas's entire intellectual project, as well as his distrust of the vogue of neo-Aristotelianism, can be viewed as an attempt to answer these basic questions systematically.

The fourth reason subsumes the first three considerations. The primary problem today, if we are concerned with *praxis* in the contemporary world, is to gain some clarity about the critical standards for guiding *praxis* and about how such standards are to be rationally warranted. This does not mean proposing a set of blueprints for action, but it does require developing a comprehensive theory of rationality. This is what Habermas means when he speaks of the *foundations* of a critical theory of society. And for all the virtues of Aristotle and lessons that we can learn from him and his texts, neo-Aristotelianism is not sufficient to answer this central critical issue.

Gadamer, as we have seen, softens the elitist connotations of *phronēsis* by integrating it with his understanding of dialogue. But in his analysis of dialogue, Gadamer emphasizes the type of mutuality, sharing, respect, and equality required for a genuine dialogue, and the principle of dialogue is universalized when Gadamer endorses the principle of freedom that encompasses all of humanity. Habermas agrees with all of this, but what he emphasizes is that there are structural societal barriers that systematically distort such dialogue and communication. This is why Habermas thinks it is not sufficient simply to concentrate on the universality of the linguistic medium but that we must also be aware of the forms of purposive-rational action and power that affect social interactions. If the possibility of the argumentative redemption of normative validity claims is to be more than an empty "ought," and if it is to be concretely embodied in social practices, this requires a transformation of the material conditions that block and distort communication. Such discourse extends to the validation of those very universals or norms that Gadamer sees as handed down in tradition. Whatever role authority may play, it is not sufficient when challenges are made to the validity of such universal norms. The norms can only be validated by the *participants* in a practical discourse.

For Habermas (as for Gadamer), the principle of unconstrained dialogue and communication is not an arbitrary ideal or a norm that we "choose"; it is grounded in the very character of our linguistic intersubjectivity. Habermas keeps drawing us back to what he claims is "always already" implicit in our pretheoretical ordinary forms of communication, no matter how distorted they may in fact be. For Habermas, this is the most fundamental insight of the tradition of German thought from Kant to Marx, but we can also see that there is something essentially Socratic about it. For he tells us:

In practical discourse we thematize one of the validity claims that underlie speech as its *validity basis*. In action oriented to reaching understanding, validity claims are "always already" implicitly raised. These universal claims . . . are set in the general structures of possible communication. In these validity claims communication theory can locate a gentle but obstinate, a never silent although seldom redeemed claim to reason, a claim that must be recognized de facto whenever and wherever there is to be consensual action.[20]

He strikes the same chord in a recent reply to his critics:

Marx wanted to capture the embodiments of unreason. In the same sense, we are also concerned today with the analysis of power constellations that suppress an intention intrinsic to the rationality of purposive action and linguistic understanding—the claim to reason announced in the teleological and intersubjective structures of social reproduction themselves—and that allow it to take effect only in a distorted manner. Again and again this claim is silenced; and yet in fantasies and deeds it develops a stubbornly transcending power, because it is renewed with each act of unconstrained understanding, with each moment of living together in solidarity, of successful individuation, and of saving emancipation.[21]

Habermas's fundamental thesis about "communicative reason" is at once bold and modest. It is bold insofar as he argues that communicative reason is anticipated and presupposed in "the general structures of possible communication" and in the "structures of social reproduction themselves," and that although it is silenced again and again, it nevertheless develops a "stubbornly transcending power." But such a communicative reason only conceptualizes a *procedural rationality*; it is not sufficient to judge or dictate a substantial form of social life.

This perspective comprises *only* formal determinations of the communicative infrastructure of *possible* forms of life and life histories; it does not extend to the concrete shape of an exemplary life-form or a paradigmatic life history. Actual forms of life and life-histories are embedded in unique traditions.[22]

This point, which Habermas clarifies in his most recent writings, is important, because many of his critics (and defenders) have misread his theory of communicative action as laying out a blueprint of an ideal society or form of life, as if communication theory could determine what ought to be the good life. But this reading of Habermas (for which he is in part responsible) seriously misunderstands his primary point: that in the genuine plurality of forms of life rooted in their unique traditions, we can detect a gentle but obstinate, although seldom redeemed, claim to reason, a claim to reason that points to the possibility of the argumentative redemption of validity claims through mutual dialogue and discourse.[23]

However sympathetic one may be to the basic intuition that underlies Habermas's theory of communicative action, there are still difficult issues to be faced about how this intuition is to be explicated and warranted. There is still a crucial ambiguity concerning the theory of communicative action as a "reconstructive" scientific theory. Even if we accept the distinction between empirical-analytic and reconstructive scientific theories, how are we to understand this distinction? Habermas insists—and this is vital for his entire project— that the distinction is one of alternative types of research programs within the domain of scientific discourse. Questions about empirical evidence, confirmation, and falsification (when properly formulated) are just as necessary for validating reconstructive hypotheses and theories as they are for validating hypotheses and theories in the empirical-analytic disciplines. If we turn to the critical literature about those reconstructive theories that Habermas takes to be paradigmatic, we find extensive discussions of whether empirical or experimental evidence does or does not support the hypotheses advanced by Chomsky, Piaget, and Kohlberg. From a methodological perspective, it is still an open question whether reconstructive research programs or empirical-analytic programs will prove more fruitful scientifically. I agree with Habermas that there are no good reasons to rule out the viability of scientific reconstructive theories. But there are also no good reasons to rule out the possibility that such analyses and theories might be replaced or displaced by new, sophisticated empirical-analytic theories. The important point here is that insofar as we seek to advance scientific knowledge, it is methodologically prudent to be open to different types of research programs. Habermas can draw support from the postempiricist philosophy of science, which holds that it is vital to keep ourselves open to alternative research programs, especially in the early stages of the development of a new program. I am emphasizing what Habermas himself does when he argues that a theory of communicative action and a universal pragmatics are *scientific* theories. But when we turn to the details of the theory of communicative action and to some of the strong claims that Habermas makes about practical discourse and the rational norms of speech, the scientific status of such a theory becomes extremely dubious. Presumably when questions about universal normative validity claims are raised, no matter how these questions and potential conflicts are resolved, the participants are "unavoidably" committed to the idea that such claims can be argumentatively redeemed in a practical discourse. But it is not clear in what sense this is unavoidable or that it is a "necessary presupposition." Certainly someone who denies it is not involved in a logical contradiction, nor is it clear in what sense, if any, there is an existential or pragmatic contradiction.

Sometimes it seems that Habermas is defining practical discourse so that while it is always possible to opt out of such discourse, once we commit ourselves to it then we are already committed to the possible argumentative redemption of universal normative validity claims. But Habermas has not established that such a commitment is built into the very nature of communicative action or that such a commitment is unavoidable. It is not helpful to say, as he does, that however counterfactual the ideal speech situation may be, it is *anticipated* and *presupposed* in every act of communication. There is, of course, nothing objectionable about the appeal to counterfactuals in scientific theories; establishing them is just as important for empirical-analytic theories as it is for reconstructive theories. But there is something very peculiar about Habermas's counterfactual, for it is not clear what type of scientific evidence would even be relevant to supporting or refuting such a claim. In this context the Popperian demand for refutability or falsifiability is perfectly appropriate. If we are dealing with a scientific theory, one wants to know what could possibly count as a refutation of the theory. Such a refutation may be contestable, but it must at least be conceivable. What evidence or arguments would even be relevant to refute the counterfactual claim that despite all signs to the contrary every speaker who engages in communicative action is committed to the presupposition of the discursive redemption of universal normative validity claims? It even begins to look as though when Habermas argues for what is presupposed and anticipated in communicative action or when he deals with the highest stages of moral or social development, his own arguments have more of the flavor of those transcendental arguments that are supposed to be overcome by reconstructive analysis.[24]

One can also criticize Habermas from the opposite point of view. If a theory of communicative action and a universal pragmatics are supposed to be scientific theories that are hypothetical, fallible, and refutable, then what would be the consequences if such a theory were in fact refuted or falsified? Does this mean that the basic issue of the type of communicative or linguistic ethics that Habermas defends and the decisionism and relativism that he opposes is to be construed as a *scientific* issue that is to be decided by the fate of rival research programs? It is hard to see how Habermas can avoid such a consequence. Habermas gets himself entangled in these and related *aporias* the more he insists on the scientific status of the theory of communicative action and a universal pragmatics. Habermas still seems to be haunted by the dichotomy of objectivism and relativism. Like Gadamer he has been a forceful critic of those forms of objectivism that are characteristic of scientism and positivism. And he does think of himself as battling the variety of forms of relativism and historicism that are so popular today. But the very way in which he poses the basic issues seems to leave us with only two alternatives: *either* there is a communicative ethics grounded in the very structures of intersubjectivity and social reproduction, *or* there is no escape from relativism, decisionism, and emotivism. Despite his manifest break with Kantian tradition of transcendental argument, he nevertheless leads us to think that a new reconstructive science of communicative action can establish what Kant and his philosophic successors failed to establish—a solid ground for a communicative ethics. When Habermas is read in this way, a way in which he frequently presents himself, then we come dangerously close to seeing his work as another failed transcendental argument that only feeds into relativism and decisionism.

I suggested that there is an alternative reading of Habermas when I referred to his pragmatic voice and his interpretative dialectics. The fascinating and confusing thing about Habermas's work is the way in which these two voices are superimposed on each other. To explain what I mean about this other voice in Habermas, this other way of reading him, let me cite a passage from Thomas McCarthy's judicious study of Habermas. He begins his book by telling us:

His contributions to philosophy and psychology, political science and sociology, the history of ideas and social theory are distinguished not only by their scope but by the unity of perspective that informs them. The unity derives from a vision of mankind, our history and our prospects, that is rooted in the tradition of German thought from Kant to Marx, a vision that draws its power as much from the moral-political intention that animates it as from the systematic form from which it is articulated.[25]

I think McCarthy is right when he calls attention to the "moral-political intention" that animates Habermas's multifaceted investigations and says that their unity derives from a "vision of mankind, our history and its prospects." The reading of Habermas that I want to bring out and endorse is the one that underscores this aspect of his thinking—that sees his work not as another failed attempt of strict dialectics or transcendental argument—or even as proposing a "new" scientific research program. Rather, it is a perspective that sees his project as really one of interpretative or hermeneutical dialectics which seeks to command our assent "by the overall plausibility of the interpretation that [it gives]."[26] Whether we focus on Habermas's early discussion of the relation of theory and *praxis*, his elucidation of the three primary cognitive interests, his analysis of legitimacy and legitimation crises, or his more recent attempts to develop a theory of communicative action and a theory of social development, these investigations can be viewed as stages in the systematic articulation and defense of a "vision of mankind, our history and our prospects." The interpretations that Habermas develops in these interrelated contexts are animated by a unifying "moral-political intention," the desire to show that there is a *telos* immanent in our communicative action that is oriented to mutual understanding. This is not to be understood as a *telos* that represents the inevitable march of world history or the necessary unfolding of a progressive form of social evolution, but rather as "a gentle but obstinate, a never silent although seldom redeemed claim to reason," a claim to reason that "although silenced again and again, nevertheless develops a stubbornly transcending power." It is a *telos* that directs us to overcoming systematicaly distorted communication. It can orient our collective *praxis* in which we seek to approximate the ideal of reciprocal dialogue and discourse, and in which the respect, autonomy, solidarity, and opportunity required for the discursive redemption of universal normative validity claims are not mere abstract "oughts" but are to be embodied in our social practices and institutions.

To argue, as I have been doing, for a reading of Habermas that calls attention to his pragmatic voice and his practice of interpretative dialectics is not yet to make a judgment about how plausible his interpretations really are. I do not think that there is any simple way

of doing this, for it requires that we actually work through his interpretations and show precisely what their strengths and weaknesses
are. Here too there is a lesson to be learned from Gadamer. It is all
too frequently assumed that if we cannot come up with universal,
fixed criteria to evaluate the plausibility of competing interpretations, this means that we have no rational basis for distinguishing
the better from the worse, the more plausible from the less plausible
interpretations—whether these be the interpretations of texts, actions,
or historical epochs. But Gadamer's analysis of understanding and
the hermeneutical circle shows us that we can and do make comparative judgments in concrete cases and that we can support them with
the appeal to reasons and argumentation.

The reading of Habermas that I am advocating can be stated in a
different manner which shows how he contributes to the movement
beyond objectivism and relativism. Returning to Gadamer, we
remember how Gadamer is always reminding us of the inescapabil-
ity of understanding and interpreting from our own historical hermeneutical situation. We know, of course, that there are always dangers
and risks in doing this. We can be guilty of ethnocentrism, of subtly
rewriting history from a Whiggish perspective, of being insuffi-
ciently self-critical of "our standards of rationality." But as Hegel
tells us, sometimes we need to be mistrustful of the very fear of
falling into error. We can flirt with that form of relativism that imag-
ines that it can bracket all preunderstandings and all prejudgments
and simply "describe" the relativity of the plurality of forms of life.
Both Gadamer and Habermas see through the speciousness of these
flights from our historical situation. Both, although in different ways,
have argued that we can take our historical situation and our existing
social practices seriously and at the same time develop a critical
perspective on them that is informed by an understanding of our
history and oriented to an open future.

But this commonness between them points to a double irony.
For I am claiming that we can employ Gadamer's analysis of what
constitutes hermeneutic understanding to get a clearer grasp of what
Habermas is actually doing (as distinguished from what he sometimes says he is doing); and I am also claiming, although I cannot
adequately substantiate it here, that Habermas elaborates a more
comprehensive, penetrating, and plausible interpretation of our
historical situation than does Gadamer. There is even a further twist
here. Gadamer's own interpretation of the problems of modern society, and what I have called the radical thrust of his thinking, can be

used to support the interpretation and vision that Habermas has developed.

RORTY'S METACRITIQUE

But now we must ask, Can the visions projected by Gadamer and Habermas, and their respective understandings of our history and our prospects, withstand the deconstructive critiques of modernity? As we have seen, despite their own critiques of modernity and of the excesses, naiveté, and even the dark side of the Enlightenment legacy, both seek to recover and preserve the "truth" of this legacy. That might seem to be more evident in Habermas than in Gadamer, especially in light of Gadamer's critique of the Enlightenment's prejudice against prejudice. But this should not obscure the fact that there is something vital from this legacy that Gadamer also wants to preserve. We can see this in his strong endorsement of the idea that "the principle of freedom is unimpugnable and irrevocable. It is no longer possible for anyone still to affirm the unfreedom of humanity. The principle that all are free can never again be shaken." For this is the most basic principle of the Enlightenment legacy—a principle affirmed by Kant, taken up by Hegel, and just as fundamental for Marx. To bring out what is most vital in the visions of Gadamer and Habermas, I want to test them against the type of criticisms advanced by one of the most astute deconstructive critics of our time, Richard Rorty. I want to show that when we press the types of criticisms suggested and developed by Rorty, they actually help us to grasp what is most essential about these visions.

There is dazzling quality in Rorty's deconstructions of what he takes to be the misguided pretensions of philosophic discourse. He is certainly sympathetic with Habermas's plea for "undistorted communication," but scornful of what happens when "Habermas goes transcendental and offers principles."[27] By constantly leading us to think that what we really need is some sort of *theory* on which to ground our communication and conversation, Habermas, Rorty thinks, is making the same sorts of mistakes that philosophers have always made in their desperate (and failed) attempts to discover permanent foundations and basic constraints. Habermas is a victim of the illusion that has haunted modern thinkers—that they must dignify the contingent social practices that have been worked out in the course of history with something that pretends to be more solid and substantial. Underlying Habermas's "new" reconstructive theory of communicative action, Rorty asserts, is nothing more and nothing less than a "moral-political vision." A perhaps even more misguided feature of Habermas's constant appeal to rational consensus and the redemption of validity claims through discursive argumentation is that it turns out to be retrogressive. When this is unmasked, it turns out to be only another version of what has been the basis for modern epistemology—the assumption that "all contributions to a given discourse are commensurable." "Hermeneutics," in Rorty's view, is "largely a struggle against this assumption." If Rorty is right about what characterizes the conversation of the West, then we should not deceive ourselves into thinking that there are any limitations or hidden constraints on the invention of new vocabularies or new forms of "abnormal discourse." The appeal to something like a rational consensus has always been used to block, stifle, or rule out revolutionary turns in the conversation. To speak of the argumentative redemption of validity claims through an appropriate type of discourse is either potentially stifling or sheer bluff. It becomes either a glorification and reification of existing, normal, contingent social practices or a pious and vacuous generality. We do not have the slightest idea, before the fact, of what rules or procedures of argumentation (if any) will be applicable to new, abnormal forms of discourse. Habermas, in Rorty's view, fails to realize that he is just giving expression to the old positivist hope that we can once and for all (in principle) decide what is to count as legitimate and illegitimate (or meaningless) discourse.

Rorty's major complaint against Habermas can be found in still another form in Rorty's apologia for pragmatism (shaped more by his reading of Dewey and James than by Peirce and Mead). The heart of this pragmatism is a defense of the Socratic virtues: "willingness to talk, to listen to other people, to weigh the consequences of our actions upon other people."[28] But according to Rorty, "These are *simply* moral virtues," and there is no metaphysical or epistemological guarantee of success. *"We do not even know what 'success' would mean except simply 'continuance' "* of the conversation which is *"merely* our project, the European intellectual's form of life."[29] Nietzsche, he points out, helped us to see that there is no "metaphysical comfort" to be found that grounds or secures these virtues, and we must resist the illusion that we can find some comfort. The antipragmatist (and in this respect Rorty would see Habermas as an antipragmatist) thinks that "loyalty to our fellow-humans presupposes that there is something permanent and unhistorical which explains *why* we should continue to converse in the manner of

Socrates, something which guarantees convergence to agreement."[30] As Rorty tells us,

For the traditional, Platonic or Kantian, philosopher [and he would include Habermas in this tradition] . . . the possibility of *grounding* the European form of life—of showing it to be more than European, more than a contingent human project—seems the central task of philosophy [or of a reconstructive science of communicative action].[31]

And while Rorty concedes that he has not presented an "argument" for pragmatism or answered the criticism that "the Socratic virtues cannot, as a practical matter, be defended save by Platonic means, that without some sort of metaphysical comfort nobody will be able *not* to sin against Socrates,"[32] he leaves little doubt that no one from Plato on has come close to "grounding" these virtues. So, what has been Habermas's preoccupation ever since the publication of *Knowledge and Human Interests* (and seems to have been his project from his earliest writings)—to show that we can ground these virtues and a critical theory in the very nature of human intersubjectivity—is, according to Rorty, only another version of the old Platonic urge "to escape from conversation to something atemporal which lies in the background of all possible conversations."[33]

As for Gadamer, despite Rorty's appropriation of the term "hermeneutics" from Gadamer and his sympathy with Gadamer's suspicion about a hermeneutical method, Rorty, if he were to comment on Gadamer, would be no less sharply critical of him than he is of Habermas.[34] He would find all the talk of "an entirely different notion of truth and knowledge" that is revealed through hermeneutical understanding to be a form of mystification. Despite Gadamer's incisive critiques of epistemology and the Cartesian legacy, Gadamer unwittingly is a victim of the very Cartesian legacy that he is reacting against. For Gadamer is constantly playing on the idea that it is really philosophic hermeneutics (and not epistemology, science, or method) that can achieve what philosophy has always promised us— some more profound access to truth than is available to us by the normal procedures of science. Gadamer fits right into the tradition of metaphysical idealism, whose principal legacy is "the ability of the literary culture to stand apart from science, to assert its spiritual superiority to science, to claim to embody what is most important for human beings."[35] The trouble with Gadamer is that he is only a "half-hearted pragmatist" or a "weak textualist."

The weak textualist—the decoder—is just one more victim of realism, of the "metaphysics of presence." He thinks that if he stays within the boundaries of a text, takes it apart, and shows how it works, then he will have "escaped the sovereignty of the signifier," broken with the myth of language as a mirror of reality, and so on. But in fact he is just doing his best to imitate science—he wants a *method* of criticism, and he wants everybody to agree that he has cracked the code.[36]

So again, despite Gadamer's repeated protestations that the essential question of hermeneutics is not a question of method at all but rather of what *happens* whenever we understand, in Rorty's view, Gadamer fails to perceive the consequences of what he is saying. He too wants the "comforts of consensus," even if it is only the comforts of consensus of those interpreters who have the proper *Bildung*.

I have put Rorty's critique in the strongest and most vivid way because it dramatizes the issues involved in the critiques of modernity. From Rorty's perspective, the trouble with Gadamer and Habermas is that they are not sufficiently radical in exposing the illusions and pretensions of philosophy (or of some appropriate successor discipline). They still cling to the hope that philosophy or its true successor can be a foundational discipline of culture. Rorty's strong criticisms would no doubt be matched by an equally strong rebuttal. Both Gadamer and Habermas would see Rorty as expressing a new, sophisticated version of a very old form of relativism—the type of relativism that they have both sought to defeat. And if they wanted to get really nasty, they might accuse Rorty of failing to perceive the consequences of what he is saying. They might draw on their respective appropriations of Hegel to accuse Rorty of failing to see how easily a playful relativism that seems so innocent in "civilized" conversation can turn into its opposite in the practical realm—how the restless *esprit* of unrestrained negativity can become a potent force for unrestrained destruction. Rorty's techniques of deconstruction can be turned against him. When decoded, his celebration of relativism is perhaps more honestly revealed by Feyerabend:

Reason is no longer an agency that directs other traditions, it is a tradition in its own right with as much (or as little) claim to the centre of the stage as any other tradition. Being a tradition it is neither good nor bad, it simply is. The same applies to all traditions—they become good or bad (rational/irrational; pious/impious; advanced/"primitive"; humanitarian/vicious; etc.) only when looked at from the point of view of some other tradition. "Objectively" there is not much to choose between anti-semitism and humanitarianism. But racism will appear vicious to a humanitarian while humanitarianism will appear vapid to a racist. *Relativism* (in the old and simple sense of Protagoras) gives an adequate account of the situation which thus emerges.[37]

Rorty, although at times identifying himself with relativists, seeks to deflate the issue.

"Relativism" is the view that every belief on a certain topic, or perhaps about *any* topic, is as good as every other. No one holds this view. Except for the occasional cooperative freshman, one cannot find anybody who says that two incompatible opinions on an important topic are equally good. The philosophers who get *called* "relativists" are those who say that the grounds for choosing between opinions are less algorithmic than had been thought. . . . So the real issue is not between people who think one view is as good as another and people who do not. It is between those who think our culture, or purpose, or intuitions cannot be supported except conversationally, and people who still hope for other sorts of support.[38]

It might seem that there is no way of reducing the striking difference between Rorty, on the one hand, and Gadamer and Habermas on the other. One might even be inclined to say that both Gadamer and Habermas are still representatives of modernity, at least insofar as they believe that philosophy or some successor discipline like philosophic hermeneutics or universal pragmatics can still provide the type of support or surrogate for the metaphysical and epistemological comfort that has obsessed philosophers, even when all the concessions are made to human finitude, historicity, and fallibility— while Rorty is a "postmodern" thinker who seeks to root out the last vestiges of the "metaphysics of presence." Or, using Rorty's terminology, we might say that Gadamer and Habermas are "weak textualists," while Rorty sides with the "strong textualists" who try to live without "metaphysical comfort." The strong textualist

recognizes what Nietzsche and James recognized, that the idea of *method* presupposes that of a *privileged vocabulary*, the vocabulary which gets to the essence of the object, one which expresses the properties which it has in itself as opposed to those which [are] read into it. Nietzsche and James said that the notion of such a vocabulary was a myth—that even in science, not to mention philosophy, we simply cast around for a vocabulary which lets us get what we want.[39]

But is this the last word? Are we simply faced with an irreconcilable and incommensurable opposition? I think not, and I now want to show that when we scrutinize what Rorty is saying, we will see that his differences with Habermas and Gadamer are not quite what they initially appear to be.

In order to decode what Rorty is saying, let me introduce a rough but helpful distinction between Rorty's metacritique and his "rhetorical" defense of pragmatism. Thus far I have mainly presented the metacritique. But there is also a subtext in his writings. Rorty has attempted to block any suggestion that he is laying the foundations for a new type of philosophy or a new constructive program for philosophy. His deliberate use of such vague distinctions as the "normal" and the "abnormal," the "familiar" and the "unfamiliar," or even between "systematic" and "edifying" philosophy are rhetorical devices employed to cure us of the expectation that philosophy must be "constructive," must be conceived of as a form of inquiry that provides us with foundations. Still, one wants to know, Where does Rorty really stand? What is the basis for his metacritique? Is he an "epistemological behaviorist," a "holist," a "pragmatist"? Aren't these substantive philosophic positions that need to be defended? Rorty is acutely aware that these are types of questions that will be raised about his metacritique. Every time we think we can really pin him down, he nimbly dances to another place and introduces a new set of distinctions.[40]

"Epistemological behaviorism" and "holism," he says, are not to be taken as labels for a new philosophic "position," but rather as expressions that are intended to call epistemology and the project of modern philosophy into question. He even tells us that "pragmatism is, to speak oxymoronically, postphilosophical philosophy."[41] One of the persistent aspirations of thinkers since Hegel—including Kierkegaard, Nietzsche, Marx, Freud, Heidegger, Wittgenstein, Foucault, and Derrida—has been to "end" philosophy (and the meaning of the "end of philosophy" has been played out in its many variations). Rorty places himself in this tradition, with still a further ironical twist on the meaning of the "end of philosophy."[42] This also helps to make sense of what might be called the *crypto-positivism* that he ironically employs for rhetorical shock value. He is employing this ironic mode, for example, when he asserts that "physicalism is probably right in saying that we shall someday be able, 'in principle,' to predict every movement of a person's body (including those of his larynx and his writing hand) by reference to microstructures within his body,"[43] or when he says about Hegel that "under cover of Kant's invention, a new superscience called 'philosophy,' Hegel invented a literary genre which lacked any trace of argumentation."[44] After all, these are just the type of claims that positivists have always made. I do not want to suggest that Rorty does not mean what he is saying. He means precisely what he is saying, but the irony becomes apparent when we realize that whereas positivists have made these sorts of statements against a background of regarding the "tough-minded" natural scientist as the cultural hero, Rorty sympathizes with those strong textualists who, without denigrating science, seek to replace the scientist with the poet and the literary critic as the new cultural heroes. Rorty wants to show us how little has been said, when (to use a positivist turn of phrase) we have extracted the "cognitive content" of the positivist's assertions. Science is nothing more nor less than a very effective vocabulary for coping, one which is likely to win out over philosophy or any other cultural discipline when it comes to matters of prediction or following relatively clear patterns of argumentation. The point is not to get trapped into thinking that science is the only vocabulary available to us or that it limits the possibility of inventing new vocabularies, or that philosophy or any other cultural discipline ought to be able to beat science at its own game.

But let me turn directly to what I have called Rorty's subtext, his rhetorical apologia for pragmatism. I call it "rhetorical" because Rorty does not want to claim that one can *argue* for pragmatism, if we mean by argumentation what goes on in science or what positivists sought to reify as the standards for all genuine argumentation. The content of Rorty's pragmatism, as I have mentioned, is the defense of the Socratic virtues, "the willingness to talk, to listen to other people, to weigh the consequences of our actions upon other people." It means taking conversation seriously (and playfully), without thinking that the only type of conversation that is important is the type that aspires to put an end to conversation by reaching some sort of "rational consensus," or that all conversation is to be construed as a disguised form of inquiry about the "truth." It means not being fooled into thinking that there is or must be something more fundamental than the contingent social practices that have been worked out in the course of history, that we can find some sort of foundation or metaphysical comfort for our human projects. It means resisting the "urge to substitute *theoria* for *phronēsis*," and realizing that there are no constraints on inquiry save conversational ones, and even these "cannot be anticipated." It means turning away from the obsession "to get things right" and turning our attention to coping with the contingencies of human life. One of the possible consequences of this type of pragmatism might be a "renewed sense of community."

Our identification with our community—our society, our political tradition, our intellectual heritage—is heightened when we see this community as *ours* rather than *nature's*, *shaped* rather than *found*, one among many which men have made. In the end, the pragmatists tell us, what matters is our loyalty to other human beings clinging together against the dark, not our hope of getting things right."[45]

It would be a mistake to think that such a reflection of human finitude entails an acceptance of the status quo. The critical impulse in Rorty is no less strong than it is in Habermas and even Gadamer. Rorty is constantly criticizing what he takes to be prevailing illusions and self-deceptions, and he provides a hint of how our lives might be changed. A profound practical-moral vision animates his work. Rorty's deepest sympathies, as well as his tentativeness, are expressed when he distinguishes between two types of "strong textualists":

Pragmatism appears in James and Bloom as an identification with the struggles of finite men. In Foucault and Nietzsche, it appears as contempt for one's own finitude, as a search for some mighty force to which one can yield up one's identity. . . . I have no wish to defend Foucault's inhumanism, and every wish to praise Bloom's sense of our common human lot. But I do not know how to back up this preference with argument, or even with a precise account of the relevant differences. To do so I think, would involve a full scale discussion of the possibility of combining private fulfillment, self-realization, with public morality, a concern for justice.[46]

Now if we "bracket" Rorty's metacritique and pay close attention to his own "preference" or "vision," and then compare that vision with those of Gadamer and Habermas, we see something remarkable. There is a significant overlap; there is common ground here. We can even find suitable translations for what Rorty is saying in Gadamerian and Habermasian terms. Rorty, too, believes that all understanding involves application or appropriation, but for him this means we must honestly accept the radical contingency of the social practices that define what we are, that our task is to cope with these and to keep open the possibility of dialogue and conversation. To say that these social practices are radically contingent does not mean that they are arbitrary, if by this we mean that we can somehow leap out of our historical situation and blithely accept other social practices. There is an effective-history that is always shaping what we are in the process of becoming. Rorty is calling for a clear recognition of what constitutes our historicity and finitude and for giving up the false metaphysical or epistemological comfort of believing that these practices are grounded on something more fundamental. We must appreciate the extent to which our sense of community is threatened not only by material conditions but by the faulty epistemological doctrines that fill our heads. The *moral* task of the philosopher or the cultural critic is to defend the openness of human conversation against all those temptations and real threats that seek closure. And for Rorty, too, this theme is universalized, in the sense that he is concerned not only with the European intellectuals' form of life but with extending conversation and dialogue to all of humanity.

Even Rorty's pragmatism has undergone a subtle shift in the course of his intellectual development. His first published article (1961) was a defense of Peirce and an attempt to show the family resemblances between Peirce and the investigations of the later Wittgenstein.[47] In *Philosophy and the Mirror of Nature* (1979), Dewey, as the critic of foundationalism, replaces Peirce as the hero of pragmatism. And in some of Rorty's most recent writings, he champions James's humanistic pragmatism. The line of development here is that of an increasing break with the Kantian epistemological tradition. There is a certain tension in Rorty's appropriation of the pragmatic tradition. For Peirce, Dewey, and even James, the scientist was still the culture hero. They sought to imbue philosophy with what they took to be the openness of the scientific experimental spirit. But unlike them, Rorty's affinities are with what he calls "literary culture." The narrative that he tells is one where representatives of "literary culture" such as Bloom and Derrida replace professional philosophers as the dominant cultural voices in the present conversation of mankind. Dewey is one of Rorty's heroes, but Rorty does not really follow Dewey in his sociopolitical critiques of the "problems of men." But although Rorty himself has not practiced the type of sociopolitical critique that was so important for Dewey, he expresses sympathy with it. Rorty also defends the democratic virtues that Dewey valued so highy.[48]

There is an important difference between Rorty and Habermas, one that also reveals their common ground. For Rorty's descriptions of what characterize the social practices of our time are rather "thin" when compared with the "thick" descriptions of Habermas. If, as Rorty tells us, the legacy of the pragmatists is to call for a change of orientation on how we can best cope with "the problems of men," how to live our lives so that we can "combine private fulfillment, self-realization with public morality, a concern with justice," this demands a critical analysis of those practices that characterize our lives and of the conflicts embedded in them. This change of orientation also requires us to undertake the practical endeavor of achieving what Dewey once characterized as the primary task of democracy, "the creation of a freer and more humane experience in which all contribute."[49] I indicated earlier that we can use Rorty to sharpen our understanding of Gadamer's and Habermas's projects. In Rorty's terms, the importance of these writers is to be found in their "vision of mankind, our history, and our prospects." Their interpretative dialectics can best be appreciated as contributing to an elucidation of our human project, and their "moral-political visions" highlight the need for the concrete realization and universalization of the very Socratic virtues that Rorty himself defends.

I do not want to suggest that there is some grand synthesis in which we can integrate the conflicting claims of Gadamer, Habermas, and Rorty. We need to listen carefully to their different voices. Gadamer underscores the need to be sensitive to understanding ourselves and our hermeneutical situation with regard to the traditions that are always effectively shaping what we are in the process of becoming. Habermas emphasizes the project of reconstruction and critique that points to the *telos* that should guide our *praxis*. Rorty warns that we must resist the temptation of thinking that our project can be supported by some sort of theory that provides it with a permanent ahistorical foundation. But all three are concerned to show us what is vital to the human project and to give a sense of what dialogue, conversation, questioning, solidarity, and community mean. All three stress the multiple ways in which these are threatened in the contemporary world. Their critiques of modernity do not lead to a total rejection of it; they are dialectical in seeking to reclaim the "truth" that is implicit in it. They do not subscribe to the myth of the necessary march of world history toward the realization of freedom. All three resist the seductive temptation of thinking that "only a god can save us now" or that there is "some mighty inhuman force to which one can yield up one's identity."

What Gadamer seeks to elucidate through his appropriation and blending of the classical meaning of *praxis, phronēsis,* and dialogue with the modern principle of freedom that embraces all of humanity; what Habermas probes through his theory of communicative action and the claim to reason which "develops a stubbornly transcending power, because it is renewed with each act of unconstrained understanding, with each moment of living together in solidarity"; what vitally interests Rorty in his defense of pragmatism and the Socratic virtues—is approached in still another way in Hannah Arendt's analysis of action (*praxis*) and her discussion of the type of public space that comes into being in between individuals when they act together.

An awareness of the areas in which Arendt shares the vision that we have been trying to capture, and also of those in which her view is very different, can further our understanding of a *praxis* that is relevant to our historical situation. Arendt's reflections on opinion and judgment, in the context of her analysis of action—the "highest form of human activity"—at once contributes to, textures, and qualifies this common vision.

JUDGMENT: ARENDT

In order to appreciate the distinctive force of Arendt's understanding of opinion and judgment and to understand how it is related to Gadamer's analysis of *phronēsis* and Habermas's analysis of practical discourse, we need first to examine how these concepts are treated in her analysis of the *vita activa* and, in particular, in her discussion of the form of human activity which she calls "action," which she sharply and categorically distinguishes from "work" and "labor."[50] The concepts of action, politics, public space, speech, plurality, freedom, equality or isonomy, and power are all interwoven for Arendt into an integrated whole. In order to explicate what she means by action and politics, let me start by reflecting on what Arendt would consider a truism—a truism that has all sorts of ramifications once these are teased out. She tells us, almost casually, that "debate constitutes the very essence of political life."[51] Note that in what initially appears to be an innocuous remark, she does not say that the essence of politics is domination, or the control of the "legitimate" means of violence, or that it consists of the ways in which individuals, groups, or classes seek to impose their interests on other individuals, groups, and classes. The essence of politics is debate, and we will see that this has a special meaning for Arendt.

Debate itself is a form of action, and "action" is the term that Arendt uses to designate what she takes to be the highest form of the *vita activa*. Action is not to be confused with or reduced to labor or work. *Labor* is the human activity grounded in biological necessity—the necessity to sustain and reproduce life. Labor must be distinguished from *work* or fabrication, which has as its end the fabrication of products and artificial objects that make up and constitute a human world.[52] A human being is both an *animal laborans* and a *homo faber*. Both forms of activity are grounded in the human condition, but neither of these forms of activity is to be confused with action. And action itself is intimately related to speech.

Action and speech are so closely related because the primordial and specifically human act must at the same time contain the answer to the question asked of every newcomer: "Who are you?" This disclosure of who somebody is, is implicit in both his words and his deeds. . . . Without the accompaniment of speech, at any rate, action would not only lose its revelatory character, but, and by the same token, it would lose its subject, as it were; not acting men but performing robots would achieve what, humanly speaking, would remain incomprehensible. Speechless action would no longer be action because there would no longer be an actor, and the actor, the doer of deeds, is possible only if he is at the same time the speaker of words.[53]

A number of consequences follow from this rich passage about the close relationship between action and speech. The most important is that human plurality is the basic condition of action and speech. By *plurality*, Arendt does not merely mean that there is "otherness," that there are individuals who oppose or thwart my desires, passions, interests, and ambitions. Rather it means that there is a unique distinctiveness about each and every individual, rooted in human *natality*, the capacity to begin, to initiate, to act. Plurality is not so much a permanent state of being as an achievement realized only when individuals act. "To act, in its most general sense, means to take an initiative, to begin . . . to set something into motion."[54] A life without speech and without action . . . is literally dead to the world; it has ceased to be a human life because it is no longer lived among men."[55] Human plurality is the basic condition of action and speech because action and speech take place *in between* men in their singularity and plurality. Action then is, intrinsically, political activity requiring the existence of that public space or *polis* within which individuals can encounter others and reveal who they are.

Given this account of action and speech as basically intersubjective communal activities which require a public space *in between* individuals, we can detect further important consequences for understanding action and politics. Equality or isonomy among citizens is also a condition for politics as debate. Equality is not a natural condition of men, not an attribute or right with which men have been endowed by their creator. Drawing on her interpretation of the Greek *polis*, Arendt writes:

Isonomy guaranteed ἰσότης, equality, but not because all men were born or created equal, but, on the contrary, because men were by nature (φύσει) not equal, and needed an artificial institution, the polis, which by virtue of its νόμος would make them equal. Equality existed only in this specifically political realm, where men met one another as citizens and not as private persons. . . . The equality of the Greek polis, its isonomy, was an attribute of the polis and not of men, who received their equality by virtue of citizenship, not by virtue of birth.[56]

Returning to the gloss on the truism that "debate is the very essence of politics," we can see more clearly why Arendt does not think of politics as involving rulership, where one person, group, or class dominates others. Rather it involves "no rule," the mutual and joint action grounded in human plurality and the isonomy of citizenship where individuals debate and seek to persuade each other. Persuasion is not manipulation of others by image making. Persuasion involves free and open debate among equals in which they mutually seek to clarify, test, and purify opinions.

We can further our understanding of what Arendt means by action by examining how she integrates the concepts of freedom and power. Referring to the *philosophes* of the Enlightenment, whose importance, she says, lies in their shrewd insight into the *public* character of freedom, Arendt tells us:

> Their public freedom was not an inner realm into which men might escape at will from the pressures of the world, nor was it the *liberum arbitrium* which makes the will choose between alternatives. Freedom for them could exist only in public; it was a tangible, worldly reality, something created by men to be enjoyed by men rather than a gift or a capacity, it was the man-made public space or market-place which antiquity had known as the area where freedom appears and becomes visible to all.[57]

Freedom, according to Arendt, must be sharply distinguished from *liberation*. For liberation is always liberation *from* something, whether it is liberation from the hardships and necessities of life or liberation from oppressive rulers. But freedom does not have this negative connotation. It is the positive achievement of human action and exists only as long as that public space exists in which individuals debate together and participate with each other in determining public affairs. The distinction between freedom and liberation takes on enormous significance for Arendt. It is the key to her interpretation of history since the French and American revolutions. She argues that the conceptual and practical confusions between freedom and liberation, between political freedom and the social question of poverty have had disastrous consequences. In what might seem to be a harsh, but for Arendt only a realistic judgment, she declares, "Nothing, we might say today, could be more obsolete than to attempt to liberate mankind from poverty by political means; nothing could be more futile and more dangerous."[58] The key term here is "political." For Arendt the problem of poverty is a social problem, not a political issue. She certainly thinks individuals ought to be liberated from poverty, and that this indeed is the primary social question. Never-theless she argues that it is illusory and dangerous to think that this social question can be solved by political means.

To complete this sketch of Arendt's conception of action (which sets the context for her analysis of opinion and judgment), let us see how *power* fits into this network of concepts. We want to observe not only how her concept of power differs from many other views, but why it does. A full-scale analysis would require examining the ways in which she distinguishes among *power, authority, force, strength,* and *violence*—violence being the furthest removed from politics but always ready to destroy the fragile public space required for politics.[59] Power is not a fixed quantum that is distributed unevenly among human individuals. Power is created through participation.

In distinction to strength, which is the gift and the possession of every man in his isolation against all other men, power comes into being only if and when men join themselves together for the purpose of action, and it will disappear when for whatever reason, they disperse and desert one another. Hence, binding and promising, combining and covenanting are the means by which power is kept in existence; where and when men succeed in keeping intact the power which sprang up between them during the course of any particular act or deed, they are already in the process of foundation, of constituting a stable worldly structure to house, as it were, their combined power of action.[60]

So power, too—like freedom, equality, speech, and action—is essen-tially intersubjective and communicative; it comes into existence only in the mutual creation of a public space in between individuals.

Before turning to the question of how Arendt's concepts of opin-ion and judgment fit into her analysis of action, let me address an often-repeated criticism of her concept of action that I think is wide of the mark. It is frequently argued that this understanding of action and politics is nothing but an idealized and romanticized image of the Greek *polis*, an image that does not even correspond to the real-ities of Greek life. And it is furthermore argued that whatever the merits of these concepts of action and politics, they seem to be completely irrelevant to the harsh realities and complexities of the politics of the modern state. I think it is false to suggest that Arendt was primarily interested in a "golden era" of the Greek city-state that many have argued never really existed. There is nothing nostal-gic or sentimental about her thinking—though, as we shall see, there is a utopian element to it. On the contrary, her primary intention is to reclaim what she takes to be a *permanent* human possibility, one that is rooted in the human capacity to begin, to initiate, to act together, and which she claims has been exemplified in historical phenomena as diverse as the Greek *polis*, the American revolution, the Paris Commune, the original Russian soviets, the citizens councils formed in the Hungarian Revolution in 1956, and the beginnings of the civil rights movement and the anti–Vietnam War movement in the United States. Indeed, in *On Revolution* she argues that in the modern age it is only in the wake of revolutions that there have been the brief and fragile manifestations of this form of politics, which she takes to be the quintessence of "the revolutionary spirit." This is the "lost treasure" that she seeks to reclaim. She can more easily be faulted for being ahistorical in her understanding of politics. For the essence of politics is always the same, wherever and whenever it spontaneously arises.

This characteristic of her *thinking* what we are doing, where it becomes manifest that she seeks to think in the gap between the past and the future[61] and to recover what is still a permanent human possibility, helps to make sense of another leitmotif that pervades her work. In almost everything that Arendt wrote she was carrying on a battle against all forms of totalizing and necessaritarian arguments, whether they have their roots in Hegelian, Marxist, Weberian, or the new, cooler, technocratic modes of thought.[62] The belief that there is an underlying logic to history that is ruthlessly working itself out behind the backs of men, a logic of history that according to some must lead to progress and the eventual triumph of freedom and according to others must inevitably result in total disaster, is not only false; it is one of the most virulent and dangerous diseases of the modern age. Her attacks on these doctrines have been sharp and multifaceted, in keeping with her central vision that ultimately such doctrines negate what is most distinctive about human individuals—their natality and plurality.

The story that she tells in *The Human Condition* is one of a double reversal, the first of which took place when the *vita activa* was taken to have precedence over the *vita contemplativa*, and the second of which occurred within the *vita activa*, when, in the modern age, the traditional hierarchy of action, work, and labor was inverted. But even *The Human Condition* ends on an ambiguous note when she says, "Needless to say, this does not mean that modern man has lost his capacities or is on the point of losing them."[63] This ambiguity, Arendt thought, is rooted in our contemporary situation. Action may be suppressed, repressed, forgotten, and defeated, but it can never be eliminated as long as there are human beings with their capacity to begin, to act together. Her concept of action is best seen as a critical concept. There is a utopian strain in her thinking, but it is utopian in the sense characterized by Gadamer when he says, "Utopia is not the projection of aims for action. Rather the characteristic element of utopia is that it does not lead precisely to the moment of action, the 'setting one's hand to a job here and now'. . . . It is not primarily a project of action but a critique of the present."[64]

It is difficult to classify Arendt's position with traditional labels, and throughout her life she was consistently attacked by those who identified themselves with both the political right and the left. She took herself to be an independent thinker. Against conservatives and neoconservatives she consistently maintained that in the modern age it is only with the "revolutionary spirit"—which was not anticipated by professional revolutionaries, and quickly defeated—that public freedom has made its brief appearances. But against radicals she consistently maintained that politics is only for the few, and that it must be sharply distinguished from "the social question." She read Marx not as the great champion of public and political freedom but as the theoretician who sought to put an end to politics, to replace it with the administration of society—in short, as a thinker who gave expression to the triumph of a laboring mentality over that of fabrication and action. She even claimed that the tradition of political philosophy came to an end with Marx.[65]

But, as in Gadamer, there is also a radical impetus to her thinking that became increasingly evident over the years. It came into prominence in the 1960s in *On Revolution* and in her book of essays, *Crises of the Republic*, in which she turned to the question of a new concept of the state—a council system—in which the type of power, public freedom, and participation characteristic of her vision of politics might be "housed."

Although I am not primarily concerned here with the development of Arendt's thought, it is important to note a subtle but important shift of emphasis in her understanding of action in the course of her writings. In *The Human Condition*, when she first introduces her analysis of action, she emphasizes the revelatory quality of speech and action, the disclosure of who the agent is in his or her deeds and words, and tells us that "action needs for its full appearance the shining brightness we once called glory, and which is possible only in the public realm."[66] But while these themes are still present in her discussion of action in *On Revolution* and *Crises of the Republic*, in the latter books one finds a much greater stress on *mutual* debate, isonomy, persuasion among equals, public happiness, and public freedom, the features characteristic of action and authentic politics.

This new form of government is the council system, which, as we know, has perished every time and everywhere, destroyed either directly by the bureaucracy of the nation-states or by the party machines. Whether this system is a pure utopia—in any case it would be a people's utopia, not the utopia of theoreticians and ideologies—I cannot say. It seems to me, however, the single alternative that has ever appeared in history, and has reappeared time and again. Spontaneous organization of council systems occurred in all revolutions, in the French Revolution, with Jefferson in the American Revolution, in the Parisian commune, in the Russian revolutions, in the wake of the revolutions in Germany and Austria at the end of World War I, finally in the Hungarian Revolution. What is more, they never came into being as a result of a conscious revolutionary tradition or theory, but entirely spontaneously, each time as though there had never been anything of the sort before. Hence the council system seems to correspond to and to spring from the very experience of political action.[67]

She never developed the idea of this council system in detail, and she was skeptical about the prospect of its being realized; like her concept of action, it serves primarily as a critical concept for judging the present. She did not think that every person must or should participate in such councils; politics is ony for the few, but the radical implications of her understanding of politics and action become clear when she says,

Not everyone wants to or has to concern himself with public affairs. In this fashion a self-selective process is possible that would draw together a true political elite in a country. Anyone who is not interested in public affairs will simply have to be satisfied with their being decided without him. *But each person must be given the opportunity.*[68] (italics added)

I do not think that Arendt ever fully pursued the consequences of what she says here—that each person must be given the opportunity to participate in politics. If she had done this, it would have required a major revision of her fundamental concepts and distinctions. For this passage indicates that the "social" and the "political" are much more intimately interrelated than Arendt at times leads us to think. There may be empirical limits to solving the social question of poverty, but no serious political program in the contemporary world can avoid confronting the question. Why? Because authentic politics requires that each person have the opportunity to participate in politics, and this at the very least means that each person must have the material means of life needed to permit him or her to participate in politics.[69] Indeed, much more is required. To participate in the type of politics that Arendt describes requires a high level of education and culture. So if the opportunity to participate in politics is to be more than an empty "legal" right, then the social conditions that are necessary for such participation must be concretely realized. This *telos* or regulative ideal is implicit in Arendt's own claim that no person (in principle) is to be excluded from public freedom. Furthermore, it is not just that certain necessary material conditions must be satisfied in order for politics to become manifest, but that the testing ground for politics in the modern and contemporary world has been in struggles for *social liberation*. Arendt knows this, but fails to emphasize it. Consider again some of the exemplary moments of politics which she says have manifested the "revolutionary spirit": the Paris Commune, the original Russian soviets; the councils formed in the wake of the Hungarian revolution. No account of these movements is adequate that fails to consider how they originated out of the demand for social liberation.[70]

Arendt never fully appreciated a lesson that she might have learned from Marx. Marx realized, more profoundly than any other modern thinker, that the type of politics and action portrayed by Arendt is always in danger of becoming hypocritical and repressive unless one addresses the "social question" in its full complexity. Consequently, if one pursues the ideas that are implicit in her understanding of *praxis*, one is led to a far more radical understanding of action and politics than Arendt frequently acknowledges.[71]

There is another awkward and potentially disastrous consequence of Arendt's categorial dichotomy of the "social" and the "political." Like Gadamer and Habermas, Arendt was battling the modern mentality that gives a false authority to the rule of experts, social engineers, and technocrats. But the rigorous distinction between the "social" and the "political" that she makes has the consequence of endorsing the self-understanding of experts who claim special authority in "solving" social problems. Most of the major political questions of the day are classified by Arendt as social problems— problems of racism, economic well-being, housing, energy, even ecology. But as social problems they involve technical questions of administration and distribution of resources. According to her distinctions, they are problems to be "solved" by social experts.[72] At times Arendt does show awareness that problems may have political and social dimensions.[73] But she never explains clearly how one is to make this distinction in concrete situations of conflict.

This fundamental confusion in Arendt can be related to her appropriation and use of the concepts of *praxis* and *technē*. Although Arendt insists that both *praxis* (action) and *technē* (fabrication or making) are grounded in the human condition, her rhetoric frequently suggests that the threat to *praxis* in the modern age comes from *technē* and a laboring mentality. But the criticism of Gadamer that I suggested earlier is also applicable to Arendt: the danger for *praxis* does not come from *technē*, but from *domination*.[74]

In analyzing Arendt's understanding of action and politics, I have already anticipated the central role that opinion and judgment play for her.[75] Arendt, who was a great lover of distinctions, distinguishes between *truth* and *opinion*, and also between *interest* and *opinion*. There has always been a battle, she says, between truth (*alētheia*) and opinion (*doxa*). But the procedures, standards, and means of establishing the validity of claims to truth are different from those appropriate to opinion, whether it be the sort of "rational truth" that has inspired pure philosophers or the empirical truth of "fact gatherers."[76] This is not to deny the relevance of truth and facts for the formation of opinion but to stress that the relevance of truth for the formation of opinion is no warrant for identifying truth and opinion. There have always been those who have sought to impose the standards appropriate to truth, and the peculiar element of coercion that truth carries, on the realm of politics, typically with disastrous results. To impose these standards on politics is in effect to destroy politics and action, with its essential and nonreducible plurality and variability of opinions. Arendt thought that the main tradition of political philosophy was not so much concerned with doing justice to what is distinctive about action and politics but with judging politics by the alien standards of truth. In ancient times the battle between truth and opinion was articulated in terms of the contest between a rational or philosophic truth and opinion. However, in the contemporary world, where there is so much skepticism about the very possibility of rational or philosophic truth, there has been a new twist in this battle. There is a tendency, exhibited not only in totalitarian regimes but in those forms of government obsessed with image making, that seeks to deny or transform the coerciveness of factual truth by blurring the distinction between facts and opinions. There is a tendency to try to destroy factual truths by treating them as if they were faulty opinions.

Opinions, however, are the very stuff of politics. Individuals do not simply "have" opinions, they *form* opinions. In this respect the political thinking required for the formation of opinions is representative thinking.

I form an opinion by considering a given issue from different viewpoints, by making present to my mind the standpoints of those who are absent; that is, I represent them. . . . The more people's standpoints I have present in my mind while I am pondering a given issue, and the better I can imagine how I would feel and think if I were in their place, the stronger will be my capacity for representative thinking and the more valid my final conclusions, my opinion.[77]

The formation of opinions is not a private activity performed by a solitary thinker. Opinions can be tested and enlarged only where there is a genuine encounter with differing opinions, whether this be an actual encounter or one achieved through imagination and "representative thinking." There is no test for the adequacy of an opinion, no authority for judging it, other than the force of the better public argument. The formation of opinions therefore requires a political community of equals and a willingness to submit opinions to public exposure and debate.

Opinion must not only be distinguished from truth; it must also be distinguished from interest.

Interest and opinion are entirely different political phenomena. Politically, interests are relevant only as group interests, and for the purification of such group interests it seems to suffice that they are represented in such a way that their partial character is safe-guarded under all conditions, even under the condition that the interest of one group happens to be the interest of the majority. Opinions, on the contrary, never belong to groups but exclusively to individuals, who "exert their reason cooly and freely," and no multitude, be it the multitude of a part or of the whole of society, will ever be capable of forming an opinion. Opinions will rise wherever men communicate freely with one another and have the right to make their views public; but these views in their endless variety seem to stand also in need of purification and representation.[78]

The stress on communication, testing, and purification of opinions in a public arena enables us to see how *judging* is involved in the formation of opinions. "Judging is one, if not the most, important activity in which this sharing-the-world-with-others comes to pass."[79] Although Arendt recognizes the affinity between what she means by judging and the Greek concept of *phronēsis*, she draws her inspiration from a highly original (and controversial) interpretation of Kant's *Critique of Judgment*.[80] She even claims that of all philosophers, only Kant provides us with insight about the distinctiveness of judgment, and that "what . . . is quite new and even startlingly new in Kant's propositions in the *Critique of Judgment* is that he discovered this phenomenon in all its grandeur precisely when he was examining the phenomenon of taste."[81]

Leaving aside the scholarly question of how faithful or accurate her interpretation of Kant is, let me focus on what she thinks that Kant "discovered." Arendt makes the striking claim that it is in the first part of the *Critique of Judgment*, where Kant deals with aesthetic judgments (which are frequently thought to be the furthest removed from politics), that we find his "unwritten political philosophy." What she has in mind is Kant's analysis of "reflective judgment," the mode of judging particulars that does not subsume particulars under general rules but ascends "from particular to universal." Such judging requires an "enlarged mentality" (*eine erweiterte Dekungsart*) that enables one to "think in the place of everybody else." "The judging person, as Kant says quite beautifully, can only 'woo the consent of everyone else' in the hope of coming to an agreement with him eventually."[82] This wooing itself is a form of rational persuasion that is characteristic of politics. What fascinated Arendt about Kant's insight into reflective judgment is that he was able to define the "specific validity" of judgment, which is not to be identified with the "universal validity" of cognition. Judgment's claim to validity can never extend further than the others in whose place the judging person has put himself or herself in the process of making a judgment. "Judgment, Kant says, is valid 'for every single judging person' but the emphasis in the sentence is on 'judging'; it is not valid for those who do not judge or for those who are not members of the public realm where the objects of judgment appear."[83]

Kant was particularly incisive in basing judgment on taste, taste which is a discriminatory sense and is not to be identified with "private feelings." On the contrary, taste is a kind of *sensus communis:* it is a "community sense," the sense that fits us into human community. What Arendt is struggling to discriminate and isolate for us is a mode of thinking that is neither to be identified with the expression of private feelings nor to be confused with the type of universality characteristic of "cognitive reason." It is a mode of thinking that is capable of dealing with the particular in its particularity but which nevertheless makes the claim to communal validity. When one judges, one judges as a member of a human community. The condition *sine qua non* for such judgment is an "enlarged mentality" achieved through imagination and "representative thinking."[84] This is the mode of thinking that is essential for politics—

the debate, opinion formation, persuasion, and argumentation that are characteristic of action. And what is important for this mode of thinking is to be able to discriminate those particulars that have *exemplary validity.* We might even say that Arendt herself, in singling out, emphasizing, and reclaiming those brief moments in history when action, politics, and public freedom have appeared, is exercising her own faculty of judgment.[85] She seeks to call attention to those particular instances that have exemplary validity for understanding *praxis.*

Arendt realizes that in approaching the analysis of reflective judgment, Kant was primarily concerned with the disinterested judgment of the "pure" spectator, not with that of the participant in human affairs. In this respect there is a tension in her own thinking when she compares judging with *phronēsis* and says that the "wooing" or persuading characteristic of judging "corresponds closely to what the Greeks called, πειθειν, the convincing and persuading speech which they regarded as the typically political form of people talking with one another."[86] But Arendt seeks to reconcile the different perspectives of the actor and the spectator by declaring that the "critic or spectator sits in every actor and fabricator; without this critical, judging faculty the doer or maker would be so isolated from the spectator that he would not even be perceived."[87] Many of the essential characteristics of Arendt's understanding of judgment are summed up in the following passage:

The power of judgment rests on a potential agreement with others, and the thinking process which is active in judging something is not, like the thought process of pure reasoning, a dialogue between me and myself, but finds itself always and primarily, even if I am quite alone in making up my mind, in an anticipated communication with others with whom I know I must finally come to some agreement. From this potential agreement judgment derives its specific validity. This means, on the one hand, that such judgment must liberate itself from the "subjective private conditions," that is, from the idiosyncrasies which naturally determine the outlook of each individual in his privacy and are legitimate as long as they are only privately held opinions, but which are not fit to enter the market place, and lack all validity in the public realm. And this enlarged way of thinking, which as judgment knows how to transcend its own individual limitations, on the other hand, cannot function in strict isolation or solitude; it needs the presence of others "in whose place" it must think, whose perspectives it must take into consideration, and without whom it never has the opportunity to operate at all.[88]

We are now ready to compare Arendt's analysis of action, speech, public space, judgment, and the type of wooing and persuading that are essential for politics with the views of Gadamer and Habermas.

Such a comparison brings their similarities and differences into sharp relief. For all three there is an attempt to reclaim *praxis* from assimilation to *technē*.

Like Gadamer, Arendt sees that the essential feature of the type of reasoning appropriate to *praxis* is the ability to do justice to particular situations in their particularity. She is just as skeptical as he is of any model of practical reasoning that identifies it with the subsumption of particulars to general rules or universals. This is what draws her to Kant's analysis of reflective judgment, which Kant contrasted with the type of subsumption of particulars characteristic of determinative judgment.[89] Like Gadamer, she seeks to show the importance of taste as a communal civic sense, a *sensus communis* that is basic for aesthetics, understanding, and politics. Her analysis of judgment as an intrinsically political mode of thinking is also motivated by the desire to show how this mode of thinking escapes the dichotomy of objectivism and relativism. Judgment is not the expression of private feelings or idiosyncratic subjective preferences. Neither is it to be identified with the type of universality that she takes to be characteristic of "cognitive reason." Judgment is communal and intersubjective; it always implicitly appeals to and requires testing against the opinions of other judging persons. It is not a faculty of Man in his universality, but of human individuals in their particularity and plurality.

Many of the most significant differences between Gadamer and Arendt can be related to the different roles that the interpretation of Aristotle and Kant play in their thinking. When Gadamer wants to show us "what practice really means," he turns to Aristotle's analysis of *phronēsis*. But although Arendt was deeply influenced by Aristotle, it is Kant—the Kant of the *Critique of Judgment*—who is the source of her analysis of judgment. Ironically, Gadamer sees the *Critique of Judgment* as the decisive text for encouraging the rise of "aesthetic consciousness" and the modern subjectivism that he deplores, while Arendt interprets the *Critique of Judgment* as pointing to a way beyond this modern subjectivism.

This difference is consequential for their differing understandings of action and politics. When Gadamer asserts the crucial role of dialogue, conversation, and questioning, he does so, as we have seen, primarily in the context of a dialogue with works of art, texts, and tradition—which he then extends to the practical and political sphere. But when he makes this subtle shift, the very meaning and weight of these key concepts undergo an important shift of emphasis. A dialogue or conversation among individuals (as Gadamer acknowledges) must be based on mutual respect, equality, a willingness to listen and to risk one's prejudices and opinions. Arendt's analysis of action helps to bring into sharp focus the radical implications of Gadamer's analysis.

This even has consequences for their differing understandings of authority. Arendt agrees with Gadamer that authority "precludes the use of external means of coercion; where force is used authority itself has failed." But she also goes on to say that

> authority, on the other hand, is incompatible with persuasion, which presupposes equality and works through a process of argumentation. Where arguments are used, authority is left in abeyance. Against the egalitarian order of persuasion stands the authoritarian order, which is always hierarchical. If authority is to be defined at all, then, it must be in contradistinction to both coercion by force and persuasion through arguments.[90]

In this respect, then, Arendt is much closer to Habermas and the types of criticisms he presses against Gadamer.

The differences between Arendt and Gadamer stand out especially clearly when we realize that whereas for Gadamer the key concept is tradition, for Arendt it is revolution—or more specifically the "revolutionary spirit" which attempts to found public freedom.[91] While she realizes that the revolutionary spirit always appeals to tradition, what is most important for her is its spontaneous quality, rooted in human natality. And it is with the appearance of this revolutionary spirit in the modern age that we find those experiences that have "exemplary validity" for the type of debate, mutual participation, and persuasion that Gadamer himself makes so essential for political reason. Both see the principle of public freedom as being fundamental for the modern project. But whereas this theme is barely developed in Gadamer, it becomes the major motif in Arendt's analysis of *praxis*.

Comparing Habermas with Arendt also enriches our understanding of *praxis* and the mode of thinking appropriate to it. What Arendt calls "judgment" and Habermas "practical discourse" must be understood within the context of communicative action that is oriented to mutual understanding. Both writers stress the categorical difference between this type of activity and instrumental or strategic activity. For both, too, there is a sharp distinction to be made between "subjective private feelings" and those "generalizable interests," or communal opinions, that are tested and purified through public debate.[92] I have noted that for Arendt judgment must liberate itself from "subjective private conditions" and the idiosyncrasies that determine the outlook of each individual in his or her privacy. This point is echoed by Habermas when he says,

The limits of a decisionistic treatment of practical questions are overcome as soon as argumentation is expected to test the generaliz*ability* of interests, instead of being resigned to an impenetrable pluralism of apparently ultimate value orientations. . . . It is not the fact of this pluralism that is here disputed, but the assertion that it is impossible to separate by argumentation generalizable interests from those that are and remain particular.[93]

Arendt's underscoring of equality, isonomy, and "no rule" is paralleled by Habermas's insistence on the symmetry of roles in a genuine practical discourse and by his demand for uncoerced communication that is free from systematic distortion and "structural violence." For both, the power of judgment rests upon a potential agreement with others, an anticipated communication with others with whom I know I must finally come to agreement.

The concepts of validity and argumentation are as important to Arendt's analysis of judgment as they are to Habermas's analysis of practical discourse. And there is even similarity in what these writers mean by "validity" in this context. The only test for communal validity, both hold, is the argumentation of the participants or the judging persons in a discourse or debate.

But these similarities also point to an important and consequential difference between Arendt and Habermas. Neither identifies theoretical discourse that seeks to validate claims to truth with practical discourse or judgment. But whereas Habermas stresses the similarities between theoretical and practical discourse, Arendt stresses the differences. This is the point of her sharp contrast between opinion and truth, and of her claim that judgment is not cognition. She consistently claims that truth "coerces" and "compels," that it is completely foreign to the wooing and persuasion of judgment. Her intention is to defend opinion and judgment against the tyrannical tendencies of "professional truth-tellers." Her frequent characterizations of truth as coercive, compelling, and tyrannical is not accidental. The Platonic tendency to denigrate the realm of opinion, to judge and condemn it for the failure to live up to the standards of truth, is essentially antipolitical. But Arendt seems to be oblivious to what we have learned from the postempiricist philosophy of science—that judgment has an essential role to play in science itself. What is worse, in stressing the gap between opinion and truth she tends to underestimate the importance of a concept that is most essential for her own understanding of judgment—argumentation.

Argumentation does not make any sense unless there is some common acceptance of what is to count in support of, or against, an opinion. Without the possibility of a potential agreement that can be backed by reasons, argumentation, as the positivists and emotivists have claimed, is "pseudo argumentation." Arendt failed to realize that in exaggerating the differences between truth and opinion and between the validity tests for each of them, she was leading us down the slippery slope of "noncognitivism," where all argumentation about practical affairs is "pseudo argumentation."

In this respect, Habermas serves as an important corrective to Arendt. By showing that the implicit claim to validity is just as essential for practical discourse as it is for theoretical discourse, he reveals the importance of argumentation for both forms of discourse.[94] He even helps to make sense of Arendt's own thesis that the power of judgment rests on a potential agreement with others and that the specific validity of such judgment depends on an anticipated communication with others with whom I know I must finally come to some agreement.

But Arendt also serves as a corrective to Habermas. For while Habermas acknowledges the nonreducible plurality of opinions that is characteristic of politics and action, he is not always as sensitive to the consequences of this plurality as Arendt is. This difference between them can be related to the different problematics that constitute the major focus for each of them. It is decisionism, emotivism, and relativism that Habermas seeks to challenge in his theory of communicative action and practical discourse. He carries out his analysis at a level of abstraction that is intended to isolate the "formal-pragmatic" universals of the norms of rational speech. Arendt also rejects the varieties of relativism when she discusses judgment, but she is much more wary of the invidious ways in which action and politics are threatened when we fail to acknowledge the irreducible plurality and variability of opinions that are to be tested, purified, and validated through reciprocal argumentation.

Consequently, to use the dichotomy of the cognitive and the noncognitive to characterize the difference between Habermas and Arendt is misleading, despite the fact that Habermas insists that practical discourse is "cognitive" while Arendt emphatically declares that judgment is "not cognition," for they are using the term "cognitive" in different ways. When Habermas claims that practical discourse is cognitive, his major point is that such discourse presupposes and involves *rational argumentation.* But this is precisely the point that Arendt wants to make about judgment, insisting, however, that such rational argumentation always presupposes the plurality of opinions that are tested and purified in communal debate. Paradoxically, despite Arendt's understanding of the coercive power of "truth" and of what she takes to be cognition proper, she thinks argumentation (as debate) is irrelevant to truth and cognition. But this tells us more about her peculiar (and inadequate) conception of truth and cognition than it does about her positive analysis of judgment, which always presupposes intersubjective and communal argumentation.[95]

BEYOND OBJECTIVISM AND RELATIVISM: THE PRACTICAL TASK

Throughout my discussion of Gadamer, Habermas, Rorty, and Arendt, I have sought to elicit the common concerns that they share, without denying the important differences among them. In all of them we have felt a current that keeps drawing us to the central themes of dialogue, conversation, undistorted communication, communal judgment, and the type of rational wooing that can take place when individuals confront each other as equals and participants. We have been made aware of the practical and political consequences of these concepts—for as we explore their implications, they draw us toward the goal of cultivating the types of dialogical communities in which *phronēsis*, judgment, and practical discourse become concretely embodied in our everyday practices.

Such a vision is not antithetical to an appreciation of the depth and pervasiveness of conflict—of the *agōn*—which characterizes our theoretical and practical lives. On the contrary, this vision is a response to the irreducibility of conflict grounded in human plurality. But plurality does not mean that we are limited to being separate individuals with irreducible subjective interests. Rather it means that we seek to discover some common ground to reconcile differences through debate, conversation, and dialogue. The role of conflict in democratic politics has been eloquently and succinctly stated by Pitkin and Shumer:

Democratic politics is an encounter among people with differing interests, perspectives, and opinions—an encounter in which they reconsider and mutually revise opinions and interests, both individual and common. It happens always in a context of conflict, imperfect knowledge, and uncertainty, but where community action is necessary. The resolutions achieved are always more or less temporary, subject to reconsideration, and rarely unanimous. What matters is not unanimity but discourse. The substantive common interest is only discovered or created in democratic political strug-gle, and it remains contested as much as shared. Far from being inimical to democracy, conflict—handled in democratic ways, with openness and persuasion—is what makes democracy work, what makes for the mutual revision of opinions and interest.[96]

In comparing these four philosophers, I have been using their work to develop a complex argument. Peirce, in characterizing philo-sophic argumentation, tells us that philosophy ought "to trust rather to the multitude and variety of its arguments than to the conclusive-ness of any one. Its reasoning should not form a chain which is no stronger than its weakest link, but a cable whose fibers may be ever so slender, provided they are sufficiently numerous and intimately connected."[97] Suppose we take Peirce's metaphor of the cable and its fibers seriously and apply it to these four thinkers. Concerning Gada-mer, we can say that his philosophic project has been concerned to offer us a reading of philosophy which shows that what is most distinctive about our being-in-the-world is that we are dialogical beings. Gadamer's reflections on the speculative character of language provide a rich phenomenological understanding of what dialogue, conversation, and questioning mean. I have argued (sometimes against Gadamer) that if we draw out the meaning of what he says and appropriate it for an understanding of *praxis* today, we are compelled to recognize the radical tendency implicit in his work.

Indeed, this is the point where a rapprochement can be made with Habermas, and where his independent line of research can be woven into a cable that is stronger than its individual fibers. Haber-mas does not really disagree with what Gadamer means by dialogue, conversation, and questioning, but is rather (as Marx did in a differ-ent time) constantly drawing our attention to those systemic features of contemporary society that inhibit, distort, or prevent such dialogue from being concretely embodied in our everyday practices.

When we unmask or decode Rorty's quasi-positivist and quasi-existentalist rhetoric and explore his neopragmatism, we find further support for a vision of community life in which there is genuine participation. Habermas may be too "foundational" for Rorty, and Gadamer too wedded to traditional philosophy. But if we apply the pragmatic principle to Rorty's own neopragmatism, we can ask, What is the difference that makes a difference for the vision of community life that Rorty outlines and the visions embedded in Gadamer's and Habermas's projects?

Arendt vividly and concretely describes and reclaims the mean-ing of *praxis*. She graphically reminds us that it is a permanent human possibility that still has the power to orient our communal action. Despite the many tensions, conflicts, and contradictions in her writings, her exercises in political thinking illuminate the distinctive fragile character of *praxis* as communal action among equals in which public freedom becomes tangible.

While doing justice to their different problems, emphases, and voices, we can now see that we are not confronted with a babble of "incommensurable" languages but a coherent, powerful conversation that has direction. Each contributes to exorcising the Cartesian Anxiety and to the movement beyond objectivism and relativism—not only in our theoretical endeavors but in conducting our practical lives.

But there is also something problematic and paradoxical about this common vision. We can see this paradox emerging in different ways. When Gadamer tells us that practice is conducting oneself, and acting, in solidarity, that *phronēsis* requires a type of community in which there is an *ethos* and the shared acceptance of *nomoi*, that practical and political reason can be realized and transmitted only through dialogue, he *presupposes*, at least in an incipient form, the existence of the very sense of community that such practical and political reason is intended to develop. Gadamer is always scanning the horizon in search of "the rediscovery of solidarities that could enter into the future society of humanity."[98] For all his critique of the ways in which practice has degenerated into technique in the modern age, Gadamer does not think that we have yet arrived at that "cosmic night" in which science expands into a total technocracy. He is always seeking to show us that no matter how fragmented and distorted, there are still solidarities that constitute our social being and that provide a basis for hope of the revitalization of *phronēsis* and *praxis*. Arendt too, however much she stresses the unpredictability, spontaneity, the "miraculous" quality of the appearance of action and public, tangible freedom, is acutely aware that such action presupposes a prior sense of community. When she turns to describing those moments in history when such public freedom has become manifest, she stresses the communal experiences that individuals share and that bind them together. For unless individuals already have had the experience of confronting each other as equals and share a sense of what public freedom means, they will not be able to act together. When Rorty says that "our identification with our community—our society, our political tradition, our intellectual heritage—is heightened when we see this community as *ours* rather than *nature's*, *shaped* rather than *found*," when he calls for "renewed sense of community" and speaks of the need for "a vital sense of human solidarity," he too presupposes that we already have a sense of such community and solidarity. Even Habermas, who is most concerned with reconstruction and critique, keeps emphasizing that the anticipation of undistorted communication and the reciprocal redemption of normative validity claims is "renewed with each act of unconstrained understanding, with each moment of living together in solidarity, of successful individuation, and of saving emancipation." He is not projecting some ideal that is divorced from our everyday practices but is seeking to remind us of what is always already implicit in our everyday forms of communicative action.

Each of these thinkers points, in different ways, to the conclusion that the shared understandings and experience, intersubjective practices, sense of affinity, solidarity, and those tacit affective ties that bind individuals together into a community must already exist. A community or a *polis* is not something that can be made or engineered by some form of *technē* or by the administration of society. There is something of a circle here, comparable to the hermeneutical circle. The coming into being of a type of public life that can strengthen solidarity, public freedom, a willingness to talk and to listen, mutual debate, and a commitment to rational persuasion presupposes the incipient forms of such communal life.

But what, then, is to be done in a situation in which there is a breakdown of such communities, and where the very conditions of social life have the consequences of furthering such a breakdown? More poignantly, what is to be done when we realize how much of humanity has been systematically excluded and prevented from participating in such dialogical communities?

We know what has been a typical modern response to this situation: the idea that we can make, engineer, impose our collective will to form such communities. But this is precisely what cannot be done, and the attempts to do so have been disastrous. Such failures occur when we restrict ourselves to the horizon of technical reason, to the mentality of fabrication, or confine ourselves to the perspective of purposive-rational action.

The thinker who most acutely grasped the full dimensions of this paradox—that the coming into being of community already presupposes an experienced sense of community—was Hegel, who saw it as the paradox of the modern age. Few thinkers have had a more profound sense of the meaning of communal life—what he called *Sittlichkeit*—than Hegel. He celebrated what he took to be the exemplar of this ideal—the Hellenic ideal—but he knew very well that there was no possibility of a return to this form of "immediacy." Hegel also saw that the various attempts of modern man to impose his will in order to create a new, mediated form of universal community have resulted in a series of grotesque failures—what Judith Shklar aptly calls the "moral failures of asocial man."[99] Whether there can be an overcoming (*Aufhebung*) of this situation—the emergence of a form of community life that does justice to particularity and universality—is an issue that is clouded in ambiguity in Hegel.

Hegel's official position is that a new stage of "objective spirit" is about to be realized, one in which freedom is embodied in a universal community that is in the process of being actualized. But Hegel, more trenchantly than many subsequent thinkers, is constantly showing us the obstacles, conflicts, and contradictions that stand in the way of a new, mediated form of *Sittlichkeit*. It is never quite clear whether Hegel's narrative is that of a divine comedy, where all alienation and self-estrangement are superseded in a grand *Aufhebung*, or of a human tragedy in which we are haunted by the image of a new form of *Sittlichkeit* and human community but where there is only the "highway of despair." Charles Taylor draws out the consequences of Hegel's ambivalent reflections for modern democracy when he says:

Thus Hegel's dilemma for modern democracy, put at its simplest, is this: The modern ideology of equality and of total participation leads to a homogenization of society. This shakes men loose from their traditional communities, but cannot replace them as a focus of identity. Or rather, it can only replace them as such a focus under the impetus of militant nationalism or some totalitarian ideology which would depreciate or even crush diversity and individuality.

. . . .

One of the great needs of the modern democratic polity is to recover a sense of significant differentiation, so that partial communities, be they geographical, or cultural, or occupational, can become again important centres of concern and activity for their members in a way which connects them to the whole.[100]

But where does this leave us today in confronting our historical situation? I think Habermas is right when he declares that our situation is one in which "*both revolutionary self-confidence and theoretical self-certainty are gone.*"[101] But like Gadamer, Habermas, Rorty, and Arendt, I want to stress the danger of the type of "totalizing" critique that seduces us into thinking that the forces at work in contemporary society are so powerful and devious that there is no possibility of achieving a communal life based on undistorted communication, dialogue, communal judgment, and rational persuasion. What we desperately need today is to learn to think and act more like the fox than the hedgehog—to seize upon those experiences and struggles in which there are still the glimmerings of solidarity and the promise of dialogical communities in which there can be genuine mutual participation and where reciprocal wooing and persuasion can prevail. For what is characteristic of our contemporary situation is not just the playing out of powerful forces that are always beyond our control, or the spread of disciplinary techniques that always elude our grasp, but a paradoxical situation where power creates counter-power (resistance) and reveals the vulnerability of power, where the very forces that undermine and inhibit communal life also create new, and frequently unpredictable, forms of solidarity.

Gadamer, Habermas, Rorty, and Arendt all help us to think about our situation, our history, and our prospects. Gadamer is constantly directing us to a critical appropriation of the traditions that have shaped us, but he is motivated by the practical-moral intention of searching for ways in which we can "here and now" foster a "reawakening consciousness of solidarity of a humanity that slowly begins to know itself as humanity, for this means knowing that it has to solve the problems of life on this planet." Arendt, who was so preoccupied with trying to comprehend the darkness of our times, seeks to reclaim the "lost treasure" of the revolutionary spirit of public freedom, to remind us of the spontaneity and the "miraculous" quality of action, how it can make its appearance against all odds. Habermas shows how deeply embedded the claim to communicative reason is in our everyday forms of social life and reproduction, how it develops a stubbornly transcending power even when it is violated and silenced again and again. Without suggesting or supplying any blueprints for action, he directs us toward the tasks in which we seek to overcome systematically distorted communication and to develop the types of communities in which we can reason and discourse together. And although he is sensitive to the plurality of forms of life and life histories rooted in different traditions, he is always reminding us that the ideal of unconstrained communication is a universal ideal that embraces all of humanity. And Rorty's advocacy of a type of pragmatism that changes our orientation for coping with human problems is also directed to cultivating the types of communities in which human solidarity and the "Socratic virtues" are concretely embodied in social practices; this is what Rorty himself calls "social hope."

Even in critics of modernity and the Enlightenment legacy like MacIntyre and Foucault, a similar theme emerges. Despite MacIntyre's claim that the Enlightenment project has been a failure—and indeed that it had to fail—he himself appropriates the most vital theme of this project. He tells us that "what matters at this stage is the construction of local forms of community within which civility and the intellectual and moral life can be sustained."[102] But despite MacIntyre's rightful skepticism about the very idea of a single universal community embracing all of mankind, it is clear that he thinks that no one can or should be excluded from such new forms of community life. In spite of his defense of Aristotle and the tradition of the moral virtues, he rejects the idea that such a communal life is in principle limited to the few. Consequently, there is a universalistic thrust to his own analysis. And like Foucault, with all his explicit scorn for modern humanism and his skepticism about any form of normative discourse, MacIntyre is constantly pointing us in the direction of a politics of everyday life in which individuals act together to form new specific and local forms of community.

In the face of the multifaceted critiques of modernity, no one needs to be reminded of how fragile such communities are, how easily they are coopted and perverted. But at a time when the threat of total annihilation no longer seems to be an abstract possibility but the most imminent and real potentiality, it becomes all the more imperative to try again and again to foster and nurture those forms of communal life in which dialogue, conversation, *phronēsis*, practical discourse, and judgment are concretely embodied in our everyday practices. This is the *telos* that is common to the visions of Gadamer, Habermas, Rorty, and Arendt. This is the practical significance of Gadamer's understanding of human finitude and of his revelation that what is most essential to our being-in-the-world is that we are dialogical. This is the end to which Habermas directs us in his analysis of the rationalization of communicative action. This is the hope that Arendt seeks to reclaim in her exploration of the meaning of action. Finally, this is the "cash value" of what Rorty means when he says he calls for a "renewed sense of community."

I began this study by speaking of the need to exorcise the Cartesian Anxiety, and characterized the present turn in the "conversation of mankind" as an effort to move beyond objectivism and relativism. Initially this appeared to be primarily a theoretical problem involving the oppositions that have shaped so much of modern thinking. But as I have pursued these themes in the current understanding of science, hermeneutics, and *praxis,* what has become manifest is that the movement beyond objectivism and relativism is not just a theoretical problem but a practical task.

At the beginning of this study, when I raised the question "Why is it that in our time the battle between objectivists and relativists has become so dominant and obsessive?", I suggested that a primary reason is the growing sense that there may be nothing—not God, Philosophy, Science, or Poetry—that satisfies our longing for ultimate foundations, for a fixed Archimedean point upon which we can secure our thought and action. But as we have pursued contemporary reflections on science, hermeneutics, and *praxis,* we have witnessed a deep questioning of this dichotomy in coming to an understanding of our human situation. In each of these interrelated contexts, we have been following the attempts to open a way of thinking that challenges this dichotomy and to show how we might recover a sense of practical rationality. We have seen how the questioning of the Either/Or of objectivism or relativism and the attempt to exorcise the Cartesian Anxiety are motivated by a practical-moral concern. We have seen that the various pathways lead to a recognition of the autonomy and fragility of *phronēsis,* practical discourse, and judgment, and that all of these presuppose the existence of a sense of community and solidarity. But in addition to the attempt to recover and reclaim the autonomy of practical rationality and show its relevance to all domains of culture, we realize that today the type of dialogical communities that are required for its flourishing are being distorted, undermined, and systematically blocked from coming into existence. When Aristotle sought to clarify what he meant by *phronēsis* and the *phronimos,* he could still call upon the vivid memory of Pericles as the concrete exemplar of the individual who possessed the faculty of discriminating what was good for himself and for the *polis.* But today, when we seek for concrete exemplars of the types of dialogical communities in which practical rationality flourishes, we are at a much greater loss. Yet we can recognize how deeply rooted this frustrated aspiration is in human life. Gadamer, Habermas, Rorty, and Arendt all help us see this and show how vital it is in understanding our own humanity and our solidarity with our fellow human beings.

Marx's second thesis on Feuerbach, especially his claim that "man must prove the truth, that is, the reality and power, the this-sidedness of his thinking in *practice,*" is a fitting conclusion to this study.[103] We can no longer share Marx's theoretical certainty or revolutionary self-confidence. There is no guarantee, there is no necessity, no "logic of history" that must inevitably lead to dialogical communities that embrace all of humanity and in which reciprocal judgment, practical discourse, and rational persuasion flourish. If anything, we have or should have learned how much the contemporary world conspires against it and undermines it. And yet it is still a *telos*, a *telos* deeply rooted in our human project. As Marx cautions us, it is not sufficient to try to come up with some new variations of arguments that will show, once and for all, what is wrong with objectivism and relativism, or even to open up a way of thinking that can move us beyond objectivism and relativism; such a movement gains "reality and power" only if we dedicate ourselves to the practical task of furthering the type of solidarity, participation, and mutual recognition that is founded in dialogical communities.

NOTES

PREFACE

1. Richard J. Bernstein, *Praxis and Action* (Philadelphia: University of Pennsylvania Press, 1971), p. 5.
2. Richard J. Bernstein, *The Restructuring of Social and Political Theory* (New York: Harcourt Brace Jovanovich, 1976), p. xiii.
3. Ludwig Wittgenstein, *Culture and Value* (Oxford: Basil Blackwell, 1980), p. 27e.

PART ONE: BEYOND OBJECTIVISM AND RELATIVISM: AN OVERVIEW

1. For a critical discussion of the "realist reaction," or what Richard Rorty calls the "anti-pragmatist backlash," see "Pragmatism and Philosophy," Rorty's introduction to his *Consequences of Pragmatism* (Minneapolis: University of Minnesota Press, 1982).
2. See Karl R. Popper, *The Open Society and Its Enemies*, 5th ed. rev. (London: Routledge & Kegan Paul, 1966).
3. See *Science in a Free Society* (London: NLB, 1978).
4. Michael Dummett, "Can Analytical Philosophy Be Systematic, and Ought It To Be?", in his *Truth and Other Enigmas* (London: Gerald Duckworth, 1978), p. 458.
5. Richard Rorty, *Philosophy and the Mirror of Nature* (Princeton: Princeton University Press, 1979), pp. 5–6.
6. See my critical study of Rorty, "Philosophy in the Conversation of Mankind," *Review of Metaphysics* 33 (1980):745–76.
7. Edmund Husserl, *The Crisis of European Sciences and Transcendental Phenomenology*, trans. David Carr (Evanston, Ill.: Northwestern University Press, 1970), pp. 68–69.
8. Ibid., p. 69.
9. Ibid.
10. Ibid., p. 70.
11. Considering the strong contrast that Husserl draws between objectivism and transcendentalism, it may seem facile and perverse to label both of these antitheses as objectivism. Philosophers who have taken the transcendental turn typically think of objectivism as the enemy that is to be defeated. But the primary issue here is not merely verbal; it is substantive. Transcendentalism, as portrayed by Husserl, suppos-

edly represents the "most radical transformation" and fulfillment of "the whole movement of philosophical history in the modern period." Transcendentalism promises "apodictic certainty," a genuine "beginning," a new foundation and Archimedean point for philosophy. It promises a final escape from all forms of historicism and "anthropological relativism." In short, transcendentalism aims to achieve for philosophy what the varieties of objectivism have always claimed to achieve. Transcendental phenomenology is supposed to be the "final form" of philosophy itself.

Heidegger, Derrida, Adorno, and Kolakowski—with different philosophic motivations—have closely scrutinized and exposed this self-understanding of the character and *telos* of transcendental phenomenology. They have all contributed to its deconstruction. They can be interpreted as exposing the objectivist bias that lies at the very core of transcendentalism. See especially Jacques Derrida, *Speech and Phenomena*, trans. David B. Allison (Evanston, Ill.: Northwestern University Press, 1973); Leszek Kolakowski, *Husserl and the Search for Certitude* (New Haven: Yale University Press, 1975); and Theodor W. Adorno, *Against Epistemology*, trans. Willis Domingo (Cambridge, Mass.: M.I.T. Press, 1983).

12. See the several essays on the phenomenological movement in pt. 2 of Hans-Georg Gadamer, *Philosophical Hermeneutics*, trans. and ed. David E. Linge (Berkeley: University of California Press, 1976). See also the references in n. 11.

13. See Steven Lukes, "Relativism: Cognitive and Moral," in his *Essays in Social Theory* (New York: Columbia University Press, 1977), pp. 154–74.

14. See Alasdair MacIntyre's provocative analysis in *After Virtue: A Study in Moral Theory* (Notre Dame, Ind.: University of Notre Dame Press, 1981). MacIntyre argues not only that "the Enlightenment Project of Justifying Morality" has failed, but that it *"had to fail."* He seeks to explain why "to a large degree people now think talk and act *as if* emotivism [or relativism] were true no matter what their avowed theoretical stand-point may be" (p. 21).

15. See the discussion of Max Weber in my *Restructuring of Social and Political Theory* (New York: Harcourt Brace Jovanovitch, 1976), pp. 45–51.

16. For a forceful but controversial analysis of the nihilism implicit in Weber and the modern conception of social science, see Leo Strauss, *Natural Right and History* (Chicago: University of Chicago Press, 1953), chap. 2.

17. *Science in a Free Society*, pp. 8–28.

18. See the following passage by Gadamer:

> However clearly one demonstrates the inner contradictions of all relativist views, it is as Heidegger has said: all these victorious arguments have something about them that suggests they are attempting to bowl one over. However cogent they may seem, they still miss the main point. In making use of them one is proved right, and yet they do not express any superior insight of any value. That the thesis of scepticism or relativism refutes itself to the extent that it claims to be true is an irrefutable argument. But what does it achieve? The reflective argument that proves successful here falls back on the arguer, in that it renders the truthfulness of all reflection suspect. It is not the reality of scepticism or of truth dissolving relativism, but the claim to truth of all formal argument that is affected. (*TM*, pp. 308–9; *WM*, p. 327)

Gadamer has been well served by most of his recent English translators. But the translation of *Wahrheit und Methode* by Garrett Barden and John Cumming (New York: Seabury Press, 1975) is extremely unsatisfactory. Not only are there many mistranslations, but systematic distinctions such as that which Gadamer makes between *Erlebnis* and *Erfahrung* are completely obscured in the English. One could not tell from the English translation that the concept of *die Sache* is central for Gadamer. Even worse, while Gadamer's German style is subtle and graceful, some passages in the English translation are unintelligible. In quoting from the English translation, I have occasionally inserted the original German expression where the English text is especially misleading, and I have given the reference to the German edition for all passages cited from the translation. Readers of German are strongly advised to consult the German text for the sake of accuracy and in order to catch the subtle nuances of Gadamer's German prose. References to the English translation, *Truth and Method* (hereafter cited as *TM*), are followed by German references to *Wahrheit und Methode*, 4th ed. (Tübingen: J. C. B. Mohr [Paul Siebeck], 1975), hereafter cited as *WM*.

19. *Meditations*, vol. 1 of Philosophical Works of Descartes, trans. Elizabeth S. Haldane and G. R. T. Ross (Cambridge, England: Cambridge University Press, 1969), p. 144.

20. Ibid., p. 149.

21. Ibid.

22. Ibid., p. 198–99. In reading the *Meditations* as a spiritual journey, one should also consider Descartes' famous dream. See the interpretation of this dream by Richard Kennington, "Descartes' 'Olympica'," *Social Research* 28 (1961):171–204.

For an illuminating dispute about the meaning and role of madness in the *Meditations*, see Michel Foucault, *Madness and Civilization*, trans. Richard Howard (New York: Pantheon, 1965), and Jacques Derrida, "Cogito and the *History of Madness*," in his *Writing and Difference*, trans. Alan Bass (Chicago: University of Chicago Press, 1978), pp. 31–63.

23. For an analysis of Descartes' metaphors, see Nathan Edelman, "The Mixed Metaphor in Descartes," in his *Eye of the Beholder* (Baltimore: Johns Hopkins Press, 1974), pp. 107–20.

24. See Hiram Caton, *The Origin of Subjectivity* (New Haven: Yale University Press, 1973).

25. Immanuel Kant, *The Critique of Pure Reason*, trans. Norman Kemp Smith (London: Macmillan, 1929), p. 257.

26. Thomas S. Kuhn, "Second Thoughts on Paradigms," in his *Essential Tension: Selected Studies in the Scientific Tradition and Change.* (Chicago: University of Chicago Press, 1977), p. 293.

27. This is the initial characterization of paradigms that Kuhn gives in *The Structure of Scientific Revolutions*, 2d. ed. enl. (Chicago: University of Chicago Press, 1970), p. viii.

28. There is a verbal fluctuation in Kuhn's use of the terms "paradigm" and "theory." A paradigm is not necessarily a theory (although theory may be one component of a paradigm), and not all scientific theories are paradigm theories. See my discussion of this point in *Restructuring of Social and Political Theory*, pp. 93–102. See also Kuhn's *Structure of Scientific Revolutions*, p. 61, where he explicitly states, "but not all theories are paradigm theories." Following Kuhn, I shall use both terms, "paradigm" and "theory." In speaking of theories in the context of the problem of theory-choice, I mean *paradigm theories*.

29. Kuhn, *Structure of Scientific Revolutions*, p. 148.

30. Ibid., p. 135.

31. See the following critics: D. Shapere, "The Structure of Scientific Revolutions," *Philosophical Review* 73 (1964):383–94; I. Scheffler, *Science and Subjectivity* (Indianapolis: Bobbs-Merrill, 1967); and I. Lakatos, "Falsification and the Methodology of Scientific Research Programmes," in *Criticism and the Growth of Knowledge*, ed. I. Lakatos and A. Musgrave (Cambridge, England: Cambridge University Press, 1970), pp. 91–195.

32. Mary Hesse uses the felicitous expression "post empiricist philosophy and history of science" in her article "In Defence of Objectivity." She also gives a lucid and succinct account of the postempiricist analysis. This article has been reprinted in her *Revolutions and Reconstructions in the Philosophy of Science* (Brighton, England: Harvester Press, 1980), pp. 167–86.

33. See especially his "On the Sources of Knowledge and Ignorance," in *Conjectures and Refutations: The Growth of Scientific Knowledge*, 4th ed. rev. (London: Routledge & Kegan Paul, 1972), pp. 3–32.

34. *Structure of Scientific Revolutions*, p. 200.

35. Larry Laudan, *Progress and Its Problems* (London: Routledge & Kegan Paul, 1977), p. 3.

36. Ibid.

37. Peter Winch, "Mr. Louch's Idea of a Social Science," *Inquiry* 7 (1964):203.

38. For a critical discussion of Winch, see my *Restructuring of Social and Political Theory*, pp. 63–74. There is some evidence in *Idea of a Social Science* that Winch is aware of the inadequacies of a logical empiricist conception of natural science. However, the polemical contrast that Winch draws between the social disciplines as interpretive studies and the social sciences conceived of as "primitive" natural sciences is based upon a simplistic conception of natural science—one that comes close to being a caricature.

39. See my discussion of *Verstehen* in *Restructuring of Social and Political Theory*, pp. 38, 136–41.

40. *Idea of a Social Science*, p. 113.

41. "Understanding a Primitive Society" is reprinted in Winch's *Ethics and Action* (London: Routledge & Kegan Paul, 1972), pp. 8–49.

42. See the articles collected in *Rationality*, ed. B. R. Wilson (Oxford: Basil Blackwell, 1970). To see how this debate has developed, see the articles collected in *Rationality and Relativism*, ed. Martin Hollis and Steven Lukes (Oxford: Basil Blackwell, 1982).

43. "Understanding a Primitive Society," p. 42.

44. In some ways Dilthey was far more subtle than Winch, especially in his attempt to show the differences between, and the unity of, the *Naturwissenschaften* and the *Geisteswissenschaften*. See Rudolf A. Makkreel, *Dilthey: Philosopher of the Human Studies* (Princeton: Princeton University Press, 1975).

45. Kuhn, *Essential Tension*, p. xiii.

46. Ibid., p. xv.

47. Ibid., p. xii.

48. Hesse, "In Defence of Objectivity," pp. 170–71. See also her essay "Theory and Observation" for a lucid sorting out of the ways in which observation is and is not "theory-laden" or "theory-impregnated." This essay is reprinted in her *Revolutions and Reconstructions*, pp. 63–110.

In listing the five contrasts that have traditionally been drawn between the natural sciences and the human sciences, Hesse tends to gloss over what has frequently been regarded as the most important and consequential difference. This has to do with the "peculiar" fact that in the human or social disciplines we are typically concerned with human beings who themselves "construct" social reality, or define themselves through symbolic forms, or who engage in "common sense" understandings and interpretations of their world. This is a theme that was stressed by Max Weber in his methodological writings on the social sciences and that has been developed in the phenomenological sociology of Alfred Schutz. It is a key tenet in the sociological tradition of symbolic interactionism and a basic precept in recent ethnomethodology. It has been given a distinctive linguistic interpretation by such writers as Charles Taylor and Peter Winch and is central for Jürgen Habermas's understanding of communicative action. Anthony Giddens has characterized this dimension of the human and social disciples as a "double hermeneutic":

> The theory-laden character of observation-statements in natural sciences entails that the meaning of scientific concepts is tied-in to the meaning of other terms in a theoretical network; moving between theories or paradigms involves hermeneutic tasks. The social sciences, however, imply not only this single level of hermeneutic problems, involved in the theoretical metalanguage, but a "double hermeneutic," because social-scientific theories concern a "pre-interpreted" world of lay meanings. There is a two-way connection between the language of social science and ordinary language. The former cannot ignore the categories used by laymen in the practical organization of social life; but on the other hand, the concepts of social science may also be taken over and applied by laymen as elements of their

conduct. Rather than treating the latter as something to be avoided or minimized as far as possible, as inimical to the pinterests of "prediction," we should understand it as integral to the subject–subject relation involved in the social sciences. [*Studies in Social and Political Theory* [New York: Basic Books, 1977], p. 12.]

Even if one stresses the importance of this double hermeneutic, it is still an open question what consequences we can legitimately draw from it concerning the relation of the natural and the human or social sciences. Some thinkers have mistakenly argued that recognizing this double hermeneutic is *sufficient* to show that there is a conceptual dichotomy between the natural and the social or human sciences. I have explored the significance of the double hermeneutic for understanding the relation of the natural and social or human sciences in *Restructuring of Social and Political Theory.*

49. Hesse, "In Defence of Objectivity," pp. 171–72.

50. Ibid.

51. In the essay "In Defence of Objectivity," Hesse stresses continuities between the natural and the human sciences, but she is also sensitive to important differences. See the introduction and the essays in pt. 3 of her *Revolutions and Reconstructions*, where she elucidates and stresses the importance of the "pragmatic criterion" for characterizing an essential aspect of the natural sciences.

52. "The Problem of Historical Consciousness," in *Interpretive Social Science: A Reader*, ed. Paul Rabinow and William M. Sullivan (Berkeley: University of California Press, 1979), pp. 129–30. "The Problem of Historical Consciousness" is an English translation of lectures that were originally delivered in French in 1957 at the University of Louvain, and which were published in French in 1963.

53. This point of comparison between Winch and Gadamer has been emphasized by Jürgen Habermas, Albrecht Wellmer, and Karl-Otto Apel. See Habermas, "A Review of Gadamer's *Truth and Method*," reprinted in *Understanding and Social Inquiry*, ed. Fred R. Dallmayr and Thomas A. McCarthy (Notre Dame, Ind.: University of Notre Dame Press, 1977), pp. 335–63; Albrecht Wellmer, *Critical Theory of Society*, trans. John Cumming (New York: Herder & Herder, 1971); and Karl-Otto Apel, *Towards a Transformation of Philosophy*, trans. Glyn Adey and David Frisby (London: Routledge & Kegan Paul, 1980).

54. See especially the set of papers published by Peirce in 1868 in the *Journal of Speculative Philosophy*, reprinted in vol. 5 of the *Collected Papers of Charles Sanders Peirce*, ed. Charles Hartshorne and Paul Weiss (Cambridge, Mass.: Harvard University Press, 1931–35).

55. "Problem of Historical Consciousness," p. 124. For a different interpretation of Dilthey, which challenges this claim, see Makkreel, *Dilthey.*

56. See Gadamer's remarks on relativism in *TM*, pp. 209, 308–9; *WM*, pp. 223, 327.

57. Gadamer, "Problem of Historical Consciousness," p. 113. It is instructive to compare this theme in Gadamer, who approaches it from the perspective of hermeneutics, with Hilary Putnam's development of a similar theme from the perspective of the philosophy of science, in *Meaning and the Moral Sciences* (London: Routledge & Kegan Paul, 1978).

58. In addition to *Truth and Method* and "Problem of Historical Consciousness," see how Gadamer treats rationality in "Historical Transformations of Reason," in *Rationality Today*, ed. T. F. Geraets (Ottawa: University of Ottawa Press, 1979), pp. 3–14.

59. For a discussion of the differences among *epistēmē*, *technē*, and *phronēsis*, see *TM*, pp. 278–89; *WM*, pp. 295–307; and "Problem of Historical Consciousness," pp. 135–60.

60. "Problem of Historical Consciousness," p. 107.

61. "Hermeneutics and Social Science," *Cultural Hermeneutics* 2 (1975):312.

62. For a discussion of temporal distance, see *TM*, pp. 258–67; *WM*, pp. 275–83.

63. "Hermeneutics and Social Science," p. 316.

64. The following books in English are helpful for gaining an overall perspective on recent developments in hermeneutics and for following some of the controversies that have been generated: David C. Hoy, *The Critical Circle: Literature and History in Contemporary Hermeneutics* (Berkeley: University of California Press, 1978); Richard Palmer, *Hermeneutics: Interpretation Theory in Schleiermacher, Dilthey, Heidegger, and Gadamer* (Evanston, Ill.: Northwestern University Press, 1969); and Josef Bleicher, *Contemporary Hermeneutics: Hermeneutics as Method, Philosophy and Critique* (London: Routledge & Kegan Paul, 1980).

65. Emilio Betti, *Die Hermeneutik als allgemeine Methodik der Geisteswissenschaften* (Tübingen: J. C. B. Mohr, 1962). See also E. D. Hirsch, Jr., *Validity in Interpretation* (New Haven: Yale University Press, 1967). Hoy and Palmer, in the works cited in n. 64, seek to defend Gadamer against the type of criticisms advanced by Betti and Hirsch. See Gadamer's discussion of Betti in "Supplement I: Hermeneutics and Historicism," in *TM*, pp. 460–91; *WM*, pp. 477–512.

66. Gadamer refers to this event in numerous places. See, for example, "Heidegger and Marburg Theology," in *Philosophical Hermeneutics*, p. 201, and "Hermeneutics and Historicism," in *TM*, p. 489; *Die Idee des Guten zwischen Platon und Aristoteles* (Heidelberg: C. Winter Universitätsverlag, 1978), p. 6.

67. In a perceptive review of Gadamer, Ernst Tugenhat makes a similar point and calls attention to the shift of concern that has taken place in Gadamer's writings since the publication of *Wahrheit und Methode*, a shift that is due in part to Gadamer's serious attempt to engage in dialogue with his critics. See "The Fusion of Horizons," *Times Literary Supplement* (19 May 1978), p. 565.

68. Gadamer himself remarks,

> I have heard with a certain surprise that Habermas should be an introduction to hermeneutics and not that hermeneutics should be an introduction to Habermas. Certainly, that was in his eyes the function which hermeneutics had in the sense that by coming to terms with my own analyses he was able to better clarify the critique of positivism and its lack of ideological reflection. ("Summation," *Cultural Hermeneutics* 2 [1975]:330)

69. See Wellmer, *Critical Theory of Society*, and Apel, *Towards a Transformation of Philosophy*.

70. Several articles in this debate were published in *Hermeneutik und Ideologiekritik* (Frankfurt: Suhrkamp Verlag, 1971). For a helpful overview of this debate, see Jack Mendelson, "The Habermas–Gadamer Debate," *New German Critique* 18 (1979):44–73; Dieter Misgeld, "Critical Theory and Hermeneutics: The Debate between Habermas and Gadamer," in *On Critical Theory*, ed. John O'Neill (New York: Seabury Press, 1976), pp. 164–83; and Martin Jay, "Should Intellectual History Take a Linguistic Turn?: Reflections on the Habermas–Gadamer Debate," in *Modern European Intellectual History*, ed. Dominick LaCapra and Steven L. Kaplan (Ithaca: Cornell University Press, 1982), pp. 86–110. See also Thomas McCarthy's discussion of the debate in *The Critical Theory of Jürgen Habermas* (Cambridge, Mass.: M.I.T. Press, 1978), and Paul Ricoeur, "Hermeneutics and the Critique of Ideology," in *Paul Ricoeur: Hermeneutics and the Human Sciences*, ed. and trans. John B. Thompson (Cambridge, England: Cambridge University Press, 1981), pp. 63–100.

71. See his *Knowledge and Human Interests*, trans. Jeremy J. Shapiro (Boston: Beacon Press, 1971).

72. For a succinct statement of this position, see Habermas's inaugural lecture when he became professor at the University of Frankfurt, reprinted as an appendix to his *Knowledge and Human Interests*, pp. 301–17.

73. In his review of *Truth and Method*, Habermas says: "I find Gadamer's real achievement in the demonstration that hermeneutic understanding is linked with transcendental necessity to the articulation of an action-orienting self-understanding." "A Review of Gadamer's *Truth and Method*," p. 351.

74. For Habermas's critique of "neo-Aristotelianism," see his remarks in "Legi-

timation Problems in the Modern State," in his *Communication and the Evolution of Society*, trans. Thomas McCarthy (Boston: Beacon Press, 1979), pp. 201–5.

75. "Hermeneutics and Social Science," p. 312.

76. "Dogmatism, Reason, and Decision: On Theory and Praxis in Our Scientific Civilization," in his *Theory and Practice*, trans. John Viertel (Boston: Beacon Press, 1973), p. 255.

77. See Hannah Arendt, *The Human Condition* (Chicago: University of Chicago Press, 1958).

78. See Habermas, "Hannah Arendt's Communications Concept of Power," *Social Research* 44 (1977):3–24.

79. See Arendt's discussion of judgment in "The Crisis in Culture: Its Social and Its Political Significance," in her *Between Past and Future* (New York: Viking Press, 1961), pp. 197–226, and the excerpts from her lectures on Kant's political philosophy printed as an appendix to her *Life of the Mind* (New York: Harcourt Brace Jovanovich, 1978). The full text (from which these excerpts have been selected) of Arendt's lectures on Kant has recently been published, together with an excellent interpretive essay. See *Hannah Arendt: Lectures on Kant's Political Philosophy*, ed. with an interpretive essay by Ronald Beiner (Chicago: University of Chicago Press, 1982). Compare these with Gadamer's discussion of *phronēsis* and judgment in *Truth and Method*. The different interpretations by Arendt and Gadamer of Kant's understanding of judgment, especially as it is developed in his *Critique of Judgment*, is not only fascinating in itself but is intimately related to some of the major differences in their philosophic orientations.

80. See Charles Taylor, "Interpretation and the Sciences of Man," reprinted in Rabinow and Sullivan, *Interpretive Social Science*, pp. 25–71; Hannah Pitkin, *Wittgenstein and Justice* (Berkeley: University of California Press, 1972); and Sheldon Wolin, "Political Theory as a Vocation," in *Machiavelli and the Nature of Political Thought*, ed. M. Fleisher (New York: Atheneum, 1972), pp. 23–75.

81. Wolin, "Political Theory as a Vocation," pp. 28, 38.

82. Ibid., pp. 44–45.

83. I am using "inversion" in the sense in which Hegel systematically uses it in his *Phenomenology of Spirit*, where he argues that the thinking and working through of a form of consciousness (*Gestalt des Bewusstsein*) leads us to its dialectical opposite—its inversion. See the discussion of inversion by Gadamer, "Hegel's 'Inverted World'," in his *Hegel's Dialectic*, trans. P. Christopher Smith (New Haven: Yale University Press, 1976), pp. 35–53.

84. This realization is one of the most interesting consequences of Rorty's *Philosophy and the Mirror of Nature*. See my discussion of this in "Philosophy in the Conversation of Mankind." Like Rorty, I think that this is one of the most important and relevant themes in the American pragmatic tradition.

85. For a sampling of the ways in which present-day scholars of Aristotle have struggled with this book, and more generally with Aristotle's understanding of the relation of the practical and theoretical lives, see A. Rorty, ed., *Essays on Aristotle's Ethics* (Berkeley: University of California Press, 1980).

86. Aristotle, *Nicomachean Ethics*, trans. H. Rackham (Cambridge, Mass.: Harvard University Press, 1926), 10.7, 1177a, 16–19.

87. Ibid., 10.8, 1178a, 7–8.

88. The question of the unity of science is not the issue here. Rather it is a question of how one characterizes this unity—or better *continuity*—which seeks to do justice to similarities and differences among the sciences but is skeptical of the various attempts to fix boundaries once and for all. In logical positivism and empiricism, the thesis of the unity of science was intimately related to the program of reductionism and physicalism. From such a perspective, any rival claim to knowledge must satisfy the stringent logical requirements for translation or reduction to an ideal universal physics. In principle there is only one science. In addition to the many internal criticisms of what is meant by "reduction" and whether it is possible, the

entire project loses its credibility as a global one (as distinguished from piecemeal reductions) when we realize that the picture of what science was supposed to be like that was endorsed by positivists is a discredited one. One way of characterizing the inversion that has taken place in the postempiricist philosophy and history of science is to realize that the natural sciences exhibit many of the characteristic features of what were originally taken to be pseudo-sciences (i.e., the human sciences). In this respect the recovery of the hermeneutical dimension of the sciences transforms the question of how the unity of the sciences is to be characterized.

PART TWO: SCIENCE, RATIONALITY, AND INCOMMENSURABILITY

1. William James, *The Works of William James: Pragmatism*, ed. Fredson Bowers and Ignas K. Skrupskelis (Cambridge, Mass.: Harvard University Press, 1975), p. 95.

2. See the references in pt. I, n. 31.

3. See the articles collected in Lakatos and Musgrave, *Criticism and the Growth of Knowledge*, especially John Watkins, "Against 'Normal Science'."

4. See the judicious discussions of Kuhn by Gerald Doppelt, "Kuhn's Epistemological Relativism: An Interpretation and Defense," *Inquiry* 21 (1978):33–86, and Wolfgang Stegmüller, *The Structure and Dynamics of Theories* (New York: Springer-Verlag, 1976).

5. Although S. E. Toulmin, D. Shapere, L. Laudan, and I. Lakatos have all sharply criticized Kuhn, their own contributions to the understanding of science share many of the characteristics and themes found in Kuhn. See the bibliography for references to their works.

6. *Structure of Scientific Revolutions*, pp. 148, 151–52. Unless otherwise noted, all page references to Kuhn refer to this work.

7. See A. J. Ayer, *Language, Truth and Logic* (New York: Dover, 1946); and Charles L. Stevenson, *Ethics and Language* (New Haven: Yale University Press, 1944).

8. See, for example, S. E. Toulmin, "Does the Distinction between Normal and Revolutionary Science Hold Water?", and Kuhn's reply, "Reflections on My Critics," in Lakatos and Musgrave, *Criticism and the Growth of Knowledge*.

9. See, for example, the following passage:
> This is not to suggest that new paradigms triumph ultimately through some mystical aesthetic. On the contrary, very few men desert a tradition for these reasons alone. Often those who do turn out to have been misled. But if a paradigm is ever to triumph it must gain some first supporters, men who will develop it to the point where hardheaded arguments can be produced and multiplied. And even those arguments, when they come, are not individually decisive. Because scientists are reasonable men, one or another argument will ultimately persuade many of them (*Structure of Scientific Revolutions*, p. 158).

10. "Reflections on My Critics," p. 262.

11. See the discussions of *phronēsis* by David Wiggins and Gadamer, where these characteristics of practical reasoning are explored. Wiggins, "Deliberation and Practical Reason," reprinted in A. O. Rorty, *Essays in Aristotle's Ethics*; Gadamer, *TM*, pp. 278–89, as well as "Problem of Historical Consciousness," pp. 135–45. See also the perceptive discussions of practical reasoning by John McDowell, "Virtue and Reason," *Monist* 62 (1979):331–50; Charles Lamore, "Moral Judgment," *Review of Metaphysics* 35 (1981): 275–96; and Hilary Putnam's discussion of the role of "practical knowl-

edge" in science in his *Meaning and the Moral Sciences*, pp. 71–72. There are also aspects of Aristotle's analysis of *phronēsis* that are not (obviously) analogous to practical reasoning about theory-choice. A good scientist, even one who exemplifies the "virtue" of practical reasoning, is not necessarily a good man. But Aristotle concludes his discussion of *phronēsis* in *Nicomachean Ethics* by telling us, "These considerations therefore show that it is not possible to be good in the true sense without prudence [*phronēsis*] nor to be prudent without moral virtue" (6.13, 1144b, 30–32).

12. This essay is included in *Essential Tension*, pp. 320–39. On the relation between moral virtue (virtues of character) and practical intelligence, see MacIntyre, *After Virtue*, pp. 144–45.

13. "Objectivity," p. 326.

14. Ibid., p. 331.

15. Ibid., pp. 321–22.

16. Ibid., p. 322.

17. Ibid., p. 332.

18. Ibid., p. 336. See also Rorty's discussion of Kuhn on this point in *Philosophy and the Mirror of Nature*, pp. 336–42.

19. This concept of taste is a common one at present, but there is a tradition (which was particularly vital in the eighteenth century) in which "taste" was the name of a faculty shared in common by cultivated individuals. Kant speaks of taste as a *sensus communis*. Furthermore, this latter concept of taste was closely linked with the capacity for making reflective judgments. See the discussion of the concept of taste in Arendt, "Crisis in Culture," *Between Past and Future*; Gadamer, *TM*, pp. 33–39; and John Dewey, *The Quest for Certainty* (New York: Minton, Balch, 1929), p. 262.

20. Kuhn, "Objectivity," p. 337.

21. Ibid., p. 337.

22. Ibid., pp. 337–38. This passage is important for other reasons. Many of Kuhn's critics have taken him to be "against" scientific objectivity and progress. But this is a misreading (even though sometimes Kuhn's rhetoric invites such misinterpretation). His claim is that traditional (especially positivist) characterizations of the senses in which science is objective and progresses are inadequate and need to be reformulated to capture the way in which science actually "works." Thus, for example, in the final chapter of *Structure of Scientific Revolutions*, he is not "against" scientific progress or claiming that progress is not a distinguishing characteristic of science but rather groping for an adequate understanding of what we mean when we speak of scientific progress. Similar comments can be made concerning Kuhn's unfortunate remarks about truth in science. At times it sounds as if he is denying that the notion of truth is applicable to paradigm theories. But as I read Kuhn, his deeper point is that while one can say that science aims at truth or even that a true theory correctly "represents" the facts, such claims are not really very illuminating for clarifying how science works. Here Kuhn is pursuing the typical pragmatic strategy of shifting the emphasis to the effective procedures for establishing what are called "scientific truths" (and he gets himself into the typical pragmatic hassles whereby such a shift of emphasis is mistaken for a semantic analysis of the concept of truth). On this point too, Rorty's discussion is perceptive (*Philosophy and the Mirror of Nature*, pp. 333–42).

23. Kuhn consistently contrasts "rules" with "values." He does not fully explain what he means by "rules," although one can reconstruct what he means from the relevant contexts. A rule can be stated explicitly in a general or universal form (as, for example, Descartes' *Regulae*). A general rule is then applied to particular cases and, except for some "hard cases," there is no serious ambiguity or openness concerning the cases to which the rule does and does not apply. What is involved here is a *particular interpretation* of the "rule model." Although Kuhn was influenced by Wittgenstein, he does not fully appreciate that many of Wittgenstein's remarks about rules in the *Philosophical Investigations* challenge Kuhn's interpretation of understanding what is involved in following rules and the application of rules. Wittgenstein shows

us that in many cases the activity involved in following rules is close to what we have called "judgmental" activity—the activity Kuhn *opposes* to rules. See Stanley Cavell's "Availability of the Later Wittgenstein," in his *Must We Mean What We Say?* (New York: Charles Scribners Sons, 1969). John McDowell is particularly incisive in criticizing the "deep-rooted prejudice about rationality . . . that acting in the light of a specific conception of rationality must be explicable in terms of being guided by a formulable universal principle." He also relates the attack on this prejudice to Aristotle's insights about practical reasoning. See "Virtue and Reason," *Monist* 62 (1979):336–50.

24. P. 46. This is the theme that Kuhn develops in chap. 5, "The Priority of Paradigms."

25. This point is clearly made by Stegmüller. He calls it "the non-statement view." See *Structure and Dynamics of Theories*, pp. 10–14, 170–80.

26. See Michael Polanyi, *Personal Knowledge* (Chicago: University of Chicago Press, 1958).

27. This quotation is from p. 61 of the original typescript of an article, "Epistemological Crises, Dramatic Narrative and the Philosophy of Science," published in an abbreviated form in *Monist* 60 (1977):453–72.

28. "Objectivity," p. 335.

29. Ibid., p. 335.

30. Kuhn, "Reflections on My Critics," p. 264.

31. Kuhn, "Notes on Lakatos," *PSA 1970, in Memory of Rudolf Carnap*, ed. Roger C. Buck and Robert S. Cohen. Boston Studies in the Philosophy of Science, no. 8 (Dordrecht, Holland: D. Reidel, 1971), p. 144.

32. For an extremely helpful analysis of the background of these debates and an overview of the development of the philosophy of science in the twentieth century, see the introduction and afterword in *Structure of Scientific Theories*, 2d. ed., ed. Frederick Suppe (Urbana: University of Illinois Press, 1977).

33. See Suppe's discussion of the meaning and criticisms of the distinction between the "context of discovery" and "the context of justification" in *Structure of Scientific Theories*, 2d. ed., pp. 125–65.

34. *Philosophy and the Mirror of Nature*, p. 316.

35. Feyerabend, *Against Method: Outline of an Anarchistic Theory of Knowledge* (London: NLB, 1975), p. 21. Unless otherwise noted, all page references to Feyerabend refer to this work.

36. See Feyerabend on "true beliefs," in *Science in a Free Society*, pp. 156–63.

37. In making sense of Feyerabend's rhetorical and polemical stance, one not only has to see his affinity with the Dadaists that he so admires and the theater that he loves but one must also appreciate his Viennese background. Feyerabend shares the *esprit* of Viennese wit and irony that prevailed in the early part of the twentieth century, especially in the circle of artists associated with Karl Kraus. See the revealing self-portrait in "Origin of the Ideas of This Essay," in *Science in a Free Society*, pp. 107–24.

38. See the following characterization of "rationality":

> And as rules and standards are usually taken to constitute "rationality" I inferred that famous episodes in science that are admired by scientists, philosophers and the common folk alike were not "rational," they did not occur in a "rational" manner, "reason" was not the moving force behind them, and they were not judged "rationally." (*Science in a Free Society*, p. 14).

39. See Lakatos' discussion of the "three Poppers"—all of whom are to be distinguished from "the *real* Popper" ("Popper, Falsificationism and the 'Duhem-Quine Thesis'," in Lakatos and Musgrave, *Criticism and the Growth of Knowledge*, pp. 180–89). To see how bizarre the cross fire becomes among philosophers of science, one should also cite Popper on Lakatos. The following surely counts as one of the greatest put-downs in recent philosophy:

> After having been my student, he became my colleague in 1960, and he is

now one of my successors at the London School of Economics. It is for this very reason that I feel, unfortunately, obliged to warn the reader that Professor Lakatos has, nevertheless, misunderstood my theory of science; and that the series of long papers in which, in recent years, he has tried to act as a guide to my writings and the history of my ideas is, I am sorry to say, unreliable and misleading.

. . . .

Professor Lakatos has, in the course of his discussion of my work, introduced a large number of complications, distinctions, and epicycles; technical terms abound, and everything Professor Lakatos touches seems to sprout numbered subdivisions. All this is regrettable, for it will make it difficult for people to comprehend and to criticize what were originally some simple ideas of mine. ("Replies to My Critics," in *The Philosophy of Karl Popper*, 2 vols., ed. Paul Arthur Schilpp [LaSalle, Ill.: Open Court, 1974], pp. 999–1000)

40. For an excellent overview of Lakatos' brief intellectual career, see the critical study by Ian Hacking, "Imre Lakatos's Philosophy of Science," *British Journal of the Philosophy of Science* 30 (1979):381–402.

41. Concerning these two suggestions, there is not only essential agreement between Lakatos and Feyerabend but also agreement with Kuhn, Popper, and Toulmin—although each would interpret these "suggestions" in slightly different ways.

42. See Alan Musgrave, "Method or Madness," in *Essays in Memory of Imre Lakatos*, ed. R. S. Cohen, P. K. Feyerabend, and M. W. Wartofsky, Boston Studies in the Philosophy of Science, no. 39 (Dordrecht, Holland: D. Reidel, 1976).

43. Lakatos, "Replies to Critics," in Buck and Cohen, *PSA 1970*, p. 174.

44. Lakatos, "History of Science and Its Rational Reconstructions," in Buck and Cohen, *PSA 1970*, p. 104n.

45. Lakatos, "Falsification and the Methodology of Scientific Research Programmes," p. 164.

46. "Method or Madness," p. 476.

47. See the criticism of Feyerabend's interpretation of Galileo by Peter K. Machamer, "Feyerabend and Galileo: The Interaction of Theories, and the Reinterpretation of Experience," *Studies in the History and Philosophy of Science* 4 (1973):1–46, and Feyerabend's reply in *Against Method*, pp. 112–19.

48. *Philosophy and the Mirror of Nature*, p. 328.

49. Ibid., p. 328.

50. Ibid., p. 330.

51. Alasdair MacIntyre stresses the importance of the ability to give a "dramatic narrative" that explains what is right and wrong in a theory that is being replaced (see "Epistemological Crises"). Here, too, there is essential agreement among Kuhn, Lakatos, and Popper. Popper writes,

A new theory, however revolutionary, must always be able to explain fully the success of its predecessor. In all those cases in which its predecessor was successful, it must yield results at least as good as those of its predecessor and, if possible, better results. Thus in these cases the predecessor theory must appear as a good approximation to the new theory; while there should be, preferably, other cases where the new theory yields different and better results than the old theory. ("The Rationality of Scientific Revolutions," in *Problems of Scientific Rationality*, ed. Rom Harré [Oxford: Oxford University Press, 1975], p. 83)

Such a claim is compatible with a point stressed by Kuhn and Feyerabend, i.e., that when a new theory is first proposed, its predecessor may yield better results. Furthermore, there can be rational disagreements concerning which theory is more "successful" and in what respects, as well as concerning what constitutes "better results."

52. Rorty, *Philosophy and the Mirror of Nature*, p. 316.

53. See Mary Hesse's discussion of "the network model" in *The Structure of Scientific Inference* (London: Macmillan, 1974).

54. For a subtle analysis of the varieties of skepticism, see Stanley Cavell, *The Claim to Reason: Wittgenstein, Skepticism, Morality and Tragedy* (Oxford: Clarendon Press, 1979).

55. See Karl Popper, *Objective Knowledge: An Evolutionary Approach* (Oxford: Clarendon Press, 1972).

56. "Normal Science and Its Dangers," in Lakatos and Musgrave, *Criticism and the Growth of Knowledge*, p. 52.

57. Ibid.

58. See my discussion of the attack on and the alternative to foundationalism in pt. 3 of *Praxis and Action*. For a lucid statement and critique of foundationalism in a very different context, see Nicholas Wolterstorff, *Reason within the Bounds of Religion* (Grand Rapids, Mich.: William B. Eerdmans, 1976).

59. "Epistemological Crises," typescript, p. 59.

60. For discussions of the subtle relation between the history and philosophy of science, see Ernan McMullin, "The History and Philosophy of Science: A Taxonomy of their Relations," in *Historical and Philosophical Perspectives of Science*, ed. R. Stuewer, Minnesota Studies in the Philosophy of Science, no. 4 (Minneapolis: University of Minnesota Press, 1970), and "History and Philosophy of Science: A Marriage of Convenience?," in *PSA 1974*, edited by R. S. Cohen et al., Boston Studies in the Philosophy of Science, no. 32 (Dordrecht, Holland: D. Reidel, 1975). See also Richard M. Burian, "More than a Marriage of Convenience: On the Inextricability of History and Philosophy of Science," *Philosophy of Science* 44 (1977):1–42, and Mary Hesse, "Reasons and Evaluation in the History of Science," in her *Revolutions and Reconstructions*.

61. In this respect one can note the tendency in both Kuhn and Laudan to regard the notion of scientific truth with suspicion (at least insofar as such truth is supposed to illuminate how science works and progresses) and to fiercely defend the integrity and importance of historical truth when it comes to reporting what happened in the history of science.

62. For a discussion of the parallels between the dialectical development of the shapes of consciousness in Hegel's *Phenomenology of Spirit* and the development of analytic epistemology and the philosophy of science, see my *Praxis and Action*, pp. 230–304, and "Why Hegel Now?", *Review of Metaphysics* 31 (1977):30–60. See also Charles Taylor, "The Opening Arguments of the *Phenomenology*," in *Hegel*, ed. Alasdair MacIntyre (New York: Doubleday, 1972).

63. For a review of this stage, see Carl G. Hempel, "Empiricist Criteria of Cognitive Significance: Problems and Changes," in his *Aspects of Scientific Explanation* (New York: Free Press, 1965).

64. See Donald Davidson, "On the Very Idea of a Conceptual Scheme," in *Proceedings and Addresses of the American Philosophical Association* 47 (1973–74):5–20, and Rorty, "The World Well Lost," *Journal of Philosophy* 69 (1972):649–65.

65. P. 20.

66. "The Fertility of Theory and the Unit for Appraisal in Science," in *Essays in Memory of Imre Lakatos*, ed. R. S. Cohen, P. K. Feyerabend, and M. W. Wartofsky. McMullin, in this article, also gives a lucid account of the growing realization that the "unit for appraisal in science is a historical one."

67. "Epistemological Crises," p. 461.

68. Ibid. See my discussion of tradition in the context of hermeneutics, pt. 3.

69. *Collected Papers*, 5.311, pp. 186–87.

70. This is one of the main themes in the "transcendental pragmatics" of Karl-Otto Apel, whose own "transformation of philosophy" seeks to incorporate this Peircian theme. See Apel's *Towards a Transformation of Philosophy*.

71. For a discussion of the normative foundations of scientific inquiry, see my discussion of Peirce in *Praxis and Action*, pt. 3. Margareta Bertilsson has stressed this aspect of Peirce's work and related it to contemporary work in the philosophy of science. See her chapter, "The Community of Inquiry as a Normative and as a

Descriptive Concept" in her *Towards a Social Reconstruction of Science Theory*, University of Lund Studies in Sociology (Lund: University of Lund, 1978).

72. See Kuhn's discussion of "scientific progress" in "Progress through Revolutions," chap. 13 in *Structure of Scientific Revolutions*. Here, too, we find another motif shared by many postempiricist philosophers of science. Contrasted with the stress on the logical relations between theory and observation (or theoretical sentences and observation sentences), we find an emphasis on science as a problem-solving enterprise. Speaking of scientific communities and progress, Kuhn writes, "The nature of such communities provides a virtual guarantee that both the list of problems solved by science and the precision of individual problem-solutions will grow and grow" (*Structure of Scientific Revolutions*, p. 170). Too few commentators have noted that Kuhn combines an *evolutionary* account of scientific progress with his analysis of scientific *revolutions*. Despite the polemical attacks on Kuhn by Popper and Toulmin, there is a significant substantive overlap in their evolutionary accounts of scientific development. Furthermore, the pragmatic stress on understanding science as a distinctive type of problem-solving activity is just as fundamental for Popper as it is for Kuhn. In this respect I think Larry Laudan obscures matters when he argues that his stress on solving problems as the key for making sense of the notion of scientific progress is a new development (although he is helpful in classifying different types of scientific problems). Problem solving has been one of the major themes running through the postempiricist understanding of science. On the contrary, Laudan's analysis is retrogressive insofar as it invites us to think that there is (or can be) a permanent calculus for identifying, counting, and rating the importance of scientific problems. (See Ernan McMullin, "Discussion Review: Laudan's Progress and Its Problems," *Philosophy of Science* 46 [1979]:623–44.)

Old positivist myths and aspirations die hard, and it is instructive to see how the old positivist dream of discovering a fixed meta-scientific calculus for rating different theories crops up in new and strange places. This neopositivist strain is to be found not only in Laudan's idea of a calculus for counting and rating "problems" but in Popper's (unsuccessful) attempts to specify a decision procedure for rating the comparative verisimilitude of different theories and in Lakatos' attempt to find an "objective criterion" for distinguishing progressive from degenerating research programs by determining whether a new theory has some excess empirical content over its predecessor. We do not have a neutral framework or calculus in making such judgments. Scientists (and philosophers of science) do make such claims—e.g., that one theory solves more problems than another or that one theory has more empirical content than another, and they may indeed be warranted in making such claims, but their *judgments* are rationally contestable (which does not mean that they are arbitrary). To paraphrase Wittgenstein, we are on the very brink of misunderstanding, if we think that making and warranting such judgments requires or presupposes that there is (or must be) an unambiguous decision procedure or calculus for doing so. It is the suggestion that there is (or can be) such a permanent calculus that I take to be the neopositivist vestige in those who protest most vociferously against positivism.

73. Adolf Grünbaum, "Falsifiability and Rationality," unpublished typescript, 1971, p. 89.

74. Feyerabend, "Changing Patterns of Reconstruction," *British Journal of the Philosophy of Science* 28 (1977):363.

75. Kuhn, "Theory-Change as Structure-Change: Comments on the Sneed Formalism," *Erkenntnis* 10 (1976):190–91.

76. Feyerabend, "Changing Patterns," p. 363.

77. Ibid., p. 365.

78. See the excellent analysis and defense of Kuhn on incommensurability by Doppelt, "Kuhn's Epistemological Relativism."

79. Frederick Suppe gives a very lucid presentation of this received view, as well as of the primary criticisms advanced against it, in the introduction to his *Structure of Scientific Theories*.

80. "Normal Science and Its Dangers," p. 56.

81. One should always be cautious when the expression "radical" appears in discussions of incommensurability. Too frequently it is unclear precisely what is being claimed—how "radical" a radical difference really is.

82. Doppelt persuasively shows this in "Kuhn's Epistemological Relativism."

83. Kuhn, "Theory-Change as Structure-Change," p. 191.

84. It is primarily due to Feyerabend that the problem of incommensurability has been interpreted as a problem of meaning variance and invariance. I agree with Rorty when he argues that the focus on a "criterion of meaning-change" led to an intellectual dead end and to irrelevant charges of "idealism." This approach has also tended to obscure what is sound about the incommensurability thesis. See Rorty's discussion, *Philosophy and the Mirror of Nature*, pp. 273–84.

85. "Kuhn's Epistemological Relativism," p. 39.

86. See Doppelt's discussion of what is lost when a paradigm or theory replaces its predecessor, in "Kuhn's Epistemological Relativism."

87. One of Kuhn's clearest statements about the importance of scientific progress appears in his "Postscript—1969," in *Structure of Scientific Revolutions:*

> Though scientific development may resemble that in other fields more closely than has often been supposed, it is also strikingly different. To say, for example, that the sciences, at least after a certain point in their development, progress in a way that other fields do not, cannot have been all wrong, whatever progress itself may be. One of the objects of the book was to examine such differences and begin accounting for them. (p. 209)

88. In *Science in a Free Society,* Feyerabend tells us, "*A free society is a society in which all traditions have equal rights and equal access to the centres of power* (this differs from the customary definition where *individuals* have equal rights of access to positions *defined by a special tradition*–the tradition of Western Science and Rationalism)" (p. 9).

89. It is curious that in a book entitled *Against Method* Feyerabend does not hesitate to speak categorically about *the* anthropological method. If we actually examine the field of anthropology (as Feyerabend examines natural science), one discovers that there is as much diversity of opinion (and confusion) concerning methods in anthropology as there is about the methods of the natural sciences.

90. Compare this with my discussion of the hermeneutical circle in part III.

91. See n. 84.

92. "Comment on the Relations of Science and Art," in *Essential Tension,* p. 345.

93. "From the Native's Point of View: On the Nature of Anthropological Understanding," in Rabinow and Sullivan, *Interpretive Social Science.*

94. P. 226. Unless otherwise noted, all page references to Geertz refer to this article.

95. Like Gadamer, both Feyerabend and Geertz assert that in the studying of alien traditions and cultures, close attention to linguistic or symbolic expressions is more essential than any special psychic requirements of the investigator. We will see that a similar claim about the nature of hermeneutical thinking is one of Gadamer's main quarrels with nineteenth-century hermeneutics. Many critics—especially those in the positivist tradition—have assumed that *Verstehen* (understanding) refers to a special type of intuitive psychic act. Gadamer forcefully argues that such a "subjectivization" of *Verstehen* is a deformation of the "hermeneutical phenomenon." Geertz gives independent support to this claim from the field of anthropology.

96. For an illustration of the use of "experience-distant" concepts to account for symbolic forms, see how Geertz uses probability theory to analyze and understand the institution of betting in Balinese cockfights ("Deep Play: Notes on the Balinese Cockfight," in Rabinow and Sullivan, *Interpretive Social Sciences,* pp. 181–223).

97. This theme, too, is generalized and becomes dominant in Gadamer's philosophic hermeneutics. It is through the study of others (cultures, texts, traditions) that

one becomes aware of "blind prejudices." See my discussion of prejudice in part III.

98. For an example of what I mean by asking new sorts of questions about our concept of the person or self, see Charles Taylor, "Growth, Legitimacy and the Modern Identity," *Praxis International* 1 (1981):111–25. The type of ethnographic (hermeneutical) understanding that Geertz sketches can itself be applied to what he calls "the Western conception of the person." What Geertz describes is really a rather recent (modern) conception of the person. We must be careful not to reify this notion and must realize that it has developed historically. Hegel, especially in the *Phenomenology of Spirit*, brilliantly portrays changing historical conceptions of the self and the person in the West. Recently MacIntyre, in *After Virtue*, appropriating a Hegelian model of history, has argued that our failure to grasp what is distinctive about the tradition of the virtues is partly the result of our failure to understand how different the classical (Aristotelian) concept of the self is from the modern (post-Enlightenment) concept of the self and the person.

99. For a critique of Winch's understanding of the social sciences, see my *Restructuring of Social and Political Theory*, pp. 63–74.

100. "Understanding a Primitive Society," p. 41. Unless otherwise noted, all page references to Winch refer to this article.

101. "Understanding and Explanation in Sociology and Social Anthropology," in *Explanation in the Behavioural Sciences: Confrontations*, ed. Robert Borger and Frank Cioffi (Cambridge, England: Cambridge University Press, 1970), p. 246.

102. "Comment" on Jarvie's paper, in Borger and Cioffi, *Explanation in the Behavioural Sciences*.

103. There is also a further question to be faced. If we do compare beliefs and practices in primitive societies with Western science, what features of Western science are we stressing (and comparing)? See Robin Horton's extended comparison between African religious traditions and "theoretical" science. One of Horton's main theses is that a sophisticated understanding of the structure of theoretical explanation in science is the basis for an illuminating comparison with the structure of African traditional thought. See Robin Horton, "African Traditional Thought and Western Science," in Wilson, *Rationality*.

104. E. E. Evans-Pritchard, *Witchcraft, Oracles, and Magic among the Azande*, abridged with an introduction by Eva Gillies (Oxford: Oxford University Press, 1976), p. 65.

105. Ibid., p. 139.

106. Ibid.

107. See Steven Lukes, "Some Problems about Rationality," and Martin Hollis, "The Limits of Irrationality." Both essays are in Wilson, *Rationality*.

108. "Comment," p. 254.

109. "Rationality and the Explanation of Action," in his *Against the Self-Images of the Age* (New York: Shocken Books, 1971), pp. 252–53.

110. See "Mr. Louch's Idea of a Social Science," where he states, "I expressly insisted that my book was not intended as a contribution to methodology. I also remarked that any methodological inquiry would have to pay much more attention to the considerable differences between the procedures appropriate to different kinds of social study than I had deemed relevant to my philosophical purposes" (p. 316).

111. *Idea of a Social Science*, pp. 86–87.

112. Ibid., p. 89.

113. Geertz, "The Impact of the Concept of Culture on the Concept of Man," in his *Interpretation of Culture* (New York: Basic Books, 1973), p. 52.

114. See my criticism of Winch in *Restructuring of Social and Political Theory*, pp. 63–74.

115. See the essays reprinted in *Ethics and Action*.

PART THREE: FROM HERMENEUTICS TO PRAXIS

1. P. xv.
2. *The Genesis of Secrecy: On the Interpretation of Narrative* (Cambridge, Mass.: Harvard University Press, 1979).
3. One can trace the encounter between hermeneutics and literary studies in the articles published in the journal *New Literary History.*
4. "Interpretation and the Sciences of Man," p. 25.
5. See Quentin Skinner, "Meaning and Understanding in the History of Ideas," *History and Theory* 8 (1969):1–53; "Motives, Intentions and the Interpretation of Texts," *New Literary History* 3 (1972):393–408; and "Some Problems in the Analysis of Political Thought and Action," *Political Theory* 2 (1974):227–303. See Hayden White, *Metahistory* (Baltimore: Johns Hopkins Press, 1973).
6. Gadamer has been one of the few German philosophers to recognize the importance of Collingwood, especially Collingwood's idea of a logic of question and answer. Gadamer was responsible for the German translation of Collingwood's *Auto-biography.* See his discussion of Collingwood in *TM*, pp. 333–41; *WM*, pp. 351–60.
7. *Philosophy and the Mirror of Nature*, p. 315.
8. See Dilthey's essay, "The Rise of Hermeneutics," trans. Fredric Jameson, *New Literary History* 3 (1972):229–44. See also Paul Ricoeur, "The Task of Hermeneutics," in *Paul Ricoeur: Hermeneutics and the Human Sciences*, ed. and trans. John B. Thompson (Cambridge, England: Cambridge University Press, 1981).
9. *Meditations*, p. 174.
10. Hannah Arendt stresses this distinction between the *universality* characteristic of theoretical and practical reason and the *generality* or communicability of aesthetic judgments. See her discussion of the significance of this distinction in "Crisis in Culture." See also *Hannah Arendt: Lectures on Kant's Political Philosophy.*
11. *Critique of Judgment*, trans. J. H. Bernard (New York: Hafner Press, 1951), p. 52.
12. Kathleen Wright has pointed out to me that Gadamer's analysis of play can also be related to Heidegger's discussion of *Spiel* and *Spiegel.*
13. "Man and Language," in his *Philosophical Hermeneutics*, p. 66.
14. Although Gadamer's erudition is extremely impressive, there is no evidence in his publications that he has ever seriously encountered the American pragmatists. Yet there is a fundamental affinity between Gadamer's critique of Cartesianism and the critique developed by the pragmatic thinkers.

There are also basic similarities between Gadamer's understanding of play and the way in which we participate or share in works of art and Dewey's understanding of art as experience. Dewey, through his understanding of experience as situational and transactional, also seeks to overcome modern subjectivism and the "spectator theory of knowledge" without lapsing into relativism. In Gadamerian terms, Dewey's understanding of art as experience presents an alternative way of understanding our being-in-the-world. For Dewey, too, all *praxis* involves *pathos*, and all *pathos* involves *praxis*. In this respect both Gadamer and Dewey reflect the influence of Hegel's concept of experience (*Erfahrung*). There is, however, a major difference between Dewey and the American pragmatists, on the one hand, and Gadamer on the other. Gadamer typically emphasizes the differences between hermeneutical experience and science (despite his claims about the universality of hermeneutics). But the starting point for the pragmatists was a reinterpretation of science itself that brings out what Gadamer would call its "hermeneutical dimension." This difference of emphasis is of more than historical interest. The pragmatists were far more alert to the analogues and continuity between science (properly understood) and other dimensions of experience and human understanding. See my discussion of Peirce and Dewey in *Praxis and Action*, pt. 3.
15. The English word "passive" fails to capture Gadamer's nuanced meaning.

What Gadamer means is much closer to the Greek *pathos*. All *pathos* involves undergoing, experiencing, suffering. Just as the concept of *pathos* has been emasculated in many of its contemporary uses, Gadamer argues that this is also true of the concept of *praxis*. All genuine *praxis* involves *pathos*. The dialectical interplay of *praxis* and *pathos* is characteristic of all experience (*Erfahrung*). See Gadamer's discussion of *Erfahrung*, *TM*, pp. 310–25; *WM*, pp. 329–44. Fred R. Dallmayr has explored the relation of *praxis* and experience in a number of contemporary thinkers, including Gadamer. See Dallmayr's "*Praxis* and Experience" (forthcoming).

16. Gadamer claims that we can find anticipations of "a critique of the moral consequences of 'aesthetic consciousness' " in Plato's critique of mimetic poetry. See "Plato and the Poets," in his *Dialogue and Dialectic*, trans. P. Christopher Smith (New Haven: Yale University Press, 1980), p. 65. See also Smith's comment on the critique of "aesthetic consciousness," p. 65, n. 10. What Gadamer calls "aesthetic consciousness" can be directly related to MacIntyre's description of emotivism in *After Virtue*. MacIntyre also shows the relation of emotivism to aestheticism.

17. One of the travesties of Gadamer's thought in the English translation of *Wahrheit und Methode* is that the subtle and central distinction between *Erlebnis* and *Erfahrung* is obscured. Both German terms are translated as "experience." But Gadamer carefully shows not only how recent is the use of *Erlebnis* but also how its use is entwined with the emergence of "aesthetic consciousness." Gadamer tells us:

> Schleiermacher's appeal to living feeling against the cold rationalism of the enlightenment, Schiller's call for aesthetic freedom against mechanistic society, Hegel's contrasting of life (later, of spirit) with "positivity," were forerunners of the protest against modern industrial society which at the beginning of our century caused the words *Erlebnis* and *Erleben* to become almost sacred clarion calls. (*TM*, p. 57; *WM*, p. 55)

This distinctive meaning of *Erlebnis* is itself colored by the reaction against objectivism.

But *Erfahrung*, as Gadamer uses this concept, does not have the heightened subjectivistic resonances of *Erlebnis*. *Erfahrung* involves the dialectical interplay of *pathos* and *praxis*. *Erfahrung* always involves (as Hegel showed) negativity. To explain what he means by *Erfahrung*, Gadamer draws upon and blends motifs from Aeschylus, Aristotle, and Hegel. For the contrast between *Erlebnis* and *Erfahrung*, see *TM*, pp. 55–63; *WM*, pp. 56–66; and *TM*, pp. 310–25; *WM*, pp. 329–44.

18. Gadamer himself recognizes the affinity of his claims about the linguistic character of meaning and understanding with Wittgenstein's investigations of language games. See "The Phenomenological Movement," in Gadamer's *Philosophical Hermeneutics*, pp. 175–77. A similar emphasis on language and symbolic form is found in Geertz's analysis of understanding in "From the Native's Point of View." We find an analogous linguistic turn in Ricoeur's analysis of understanding. (See Thompson, *Paul Ricoeur: Hermeneutics and the Human Sciences*).

19. The German word which is translated as "prejudice" is *Vorurteil*. This can be translated as "prejudgment," in order to avoid the exclusively perjorative meaning that "prejudice" conveys in English. Gadamer's main point is that prejudices or prejudgments are preconditions for all understanding. But for Gadamer, both negative or unfounded prejudices and positive or justified prejudices are constitutive of understanding. See his discussion of the meaning of prejudice, *TM*, pp. 239–53; *WM*, pp. 255–69.

20. "The Universality of the Hermeneutical Problem," in his *Philosophical Hermeneutics*, p. 9.

21. Peirce, *Collected Papers*, 5.265, p. 156; see also Popper, "On the Sources of Knowledge and of Ignorance."

22. It is instructive to compare Gadamer's analysis of the concept of tradition with that of MacIntyre.

> A tradition then not only embodies the narrative of an argument, but is only to be recovered by an argumentative retelling of that narrative which will itself be in conflict with other argumentative retellings. Every tradition there-

fore is always in danger of lapsing into incoherence and when a tradition does so lapse it sometimes can only be recovered by a revolutionary reconstitution. ("Epistemological Crises," p. 461)

See also MacIntyre's discussion of the concept of tradition in *After Virtue*, especially chap. 15.

23. *Essential Tension*, pp. xi–xii.

24. Ibid., p. xii.

25. *Against Method*, p. 251.

26. "From the Native's Point of View," p. 239.

27. "Interpretation and the Sciences of Man," p. 65. See my discussion of Taylor in *Restructuring of Social and Political Theory*, pp. 109–12.

28. "Interpretation and the Sciences of Man," pp. 65–66.

29. Ibid., p. 67.

30. Taylor's claim may sound more subjectivistic than he intends it to be. There is plenty of ground for argumentation in evaluating different interpretations, and every interpretation is always open to further discussion and criticism. Nevertheless, Taylor does not want to deny or mitigate what can be seen as "a scandalous result according to the authoritative conception of science in our tradition" (p. 66). Ricoeur directs his attention to this crucial issue, in a manner that is closer to Gadamer, when he sketches a "dialectic of guessing and validation" in hermeneutical interpretation. See Ricoeur's discussion in "The Model of the Text: Meaningful Action Considered as a Text," in *Paul Ricoeur: Hermeneutics and the Human Sciences*.

31. "Interpretation and the Sciences of Man," pp. 67–68.

32. Ibid., p. 71.

33. Gadamer draws the explicit parallel between his investigation and the Kantian question in the foreword to the second edition of *Truth and Method:*

Thus the following investigation also asks a philosophic question. But it does not ask it only of the so-called human sciences. . . . It does not ask it only of science and its modes of experience, but of all human experience of the world and human living. It asks (to put it in Kantian terms): How is understanding possible? This is a question which precedes any action of understanding on the part of subjectivity, including the methodical activity of the "understanding sciences" [*verstehende Geisteswissenschaften*] and their norms and rules. (*TM*, p. xviii; *WM*, p. xvii)

34. "Problem of Historical Consciousness," p. 148.

35. Ibid., pp. 148–49.

36. Gadamer writes, "The best definition for hermeneutics is: to let what is alienated by the character of the written word or by the character of being distantiated by cultural or historical distances speak again. This is hermeneutics: to let what seems to be far and alienated speak again" ("Practical Philosophy as a Model of the Human Sciences," *Research in Phenomenology* 9 [1980]:83).

37. "Problem of Historical Consciousness," pp. 151–52.

38. See Gadamer's discussion of translation and his claim that "every translation is at the same time an interpretation," in *TM*, p. 346; *WM*, p. 361.

39. "Problem of Historical Consciousness," p. 107.

40. This is what Gadamer calls the "speculative" character of language. See his discussion, *TM*, pp. 423–31; *WM*, pp. 441–49. The meaning and significance of the speculative character of language is explored by P. Christopher Smith, *Hermeneutics as a Theory of Human Finitude* (forthcoming), and Kathleen Wright, "Gadamer on the Speculative Structure of Language" (forthcoming).

41. The expression "application" [*Anwendung*] is used to translate the Latin *applicatio*. But this translation can be misleading. For example, when we speak of "applied physics" or "applied mathematics" we normally want to distinguish between the pure or theoretical disciplines and their applications. We do not think of the applications as integral or internally related to the corresponding "pure" disciplines. We can call this the "technical" sense of application. But for Gadamer this is not what is distinctive about application as it pertains to understanding. Such application

is integral or internally related to all understanding. The English expression "appropriation" better conveys what Gadamer means, especially when we think of appropriation as transforming and becoming constitutive of the individual who understands. See Paul Ricoeur's discussion, "Appropriation," in *Paul Ricoeur: Hermeneutics and the Human Sciences*, pp. 182–93.

42. Gadamer, "Problem of Historical Consciousness," p. 107.

43. *Nicomachean Ethics*, chap. 3.

44. "Problem of Historical Consciousness," p. 140. Gadamer explores the distinctions between *phronēsis* and *technē* in the section of his essay entitled "The Hermeneutical Problem and Aristotle's *Ethics*." This is a restatement, with a slightly different emphasis, of the discussion in *TM*, pp. 283–89; *WM*, pp. 300–307.

45. "Problem of Historical Consciousness," p. 142.

46. Gadamer rejects the interpretation of Aristotle that claims that *phronēsis* and deliberation are only about "means" and never about "ends."

> Thus the whole problem is summarized in the fact that in moral actions there is no "prior" knowledge of the right means which realize the end, and this is so because, above all else, the ends themselves are at stake and not perfectly fixed beforehand. This also explains why in his discussion of *phronēsis* Aristotle constantly oscillates between defining it as the knowledge of the ends and the knowledge of means." ("Problem of Historical Consciousness," p. 143)

For independent support of this reading of Aristotle, see John Cooper, *Reason and Human Good in Aristotle* (Cambridge, Mass.: Harvard University Press, 1975), p. 19.

47. "Hermeneutics and Social Science," p. 312.

48. Ibid., pp. 313–14.

49. On the theoretical dimension of hermeneutics, see "Hermeneutics as a Theoretical and Practical Task," in his *Reason in the Age of Science*, trans. Frederick G. Lawrence (Cambridge, Mass: M.I.T. Press, 1981).

50. "Problem of Historical Consciousness," p. 113.

51. Concerning Hegel, Gadamer writes:

> For Hegel, it is necessary, of course, that the movement of consciousness, experience [*Erfahrung*] should lead to a self-knowledge that no longer has anything different or alien to itself. For him the perfection of experience is "science," the certainty of itself in knowledge. Hence his criterion of experience is that of self-knowledge. That is why the dialectic of experience must end with the overcoming of all experience, which is attained in absolute knowledge, i.e., in the complete identity of consciousness and object. We can now understand why Hegel's application to history, insofar as he saw it as part of the absolute self-consciousness of philosophy, does not do justice to the hermeneutical consciousness. The nature of experience is conceived in terms of that which goes beyond it; for experience itself can never be science. It is in absolute antithesis to knowledge and to that kind of instruction that follows from general theoretical or technical knowledge. The truth of experience always contains an orientation towards new experience. . . . The dialectic of experience has its own fulfillment not in definitive knowledge, but in that openness to experience that is encouraged by experience itself. (*TM*, pp. 318–19; *WM*, p. 337)

52. In his correspondence with Leo Strauss, Gadamer distances himself from Heidegger when he emphatically states:

> But where I otherwise still appeal to Heidegger—in that I attempt to think of "understanding" as an "event" [*Geschehen*]—[this thought] is turned however in an entirely different direction. My point of departure is not the *complete forgetfulness of being [vollendete Seinsvergessenheit]*, the "night of being," rather on the contrary—I say this against Heidegger as well as against Buber—the unreality of such an assertion. That holds good also for our relation to the tradition. (Gadamer and Leo Strauss, "Correspondence Concerning *Wahrheit und Methode*," *Independent Journal of Philosophy* 2 [1978]:8.)

This emphatic difference has consequences for Gadamer's understanding of truth. For

Gadamer places a much greater positive significance on "the claim to truth" that is always implicit in tradition.

53. Earlier (n. 14), I noted that there are a number of parallels between Gadamer and the pragmatists. But here we touch upon a significant difference. The issue of the validation of claims to truth is far more important for the pragmatists than it is for Gadamer. In part this is because the analysis of scientific inquiry plays a much more prominent role for them than for Gadamer. But Gadamer implicitly appeals to what is explicit in the pragmatists—the essential role of a *critical* community of inquirers in testing and validating claims to truth. See my discussion of the community of inquirers in *Praxis and Action*, pp. 165–229.

54. "Problem of Historical Consciousness," p. 159.

55. Ibid., p. 149.

56. For further discussion of the concept of truth, see "Wahrheit in den Geisteswissenschaften" and "Was ist Wahrheit?", in Gadamer's *Kleine Schriften*, vol. 1 (Tübingen: J. C. B. Mohr [Paul Siebeck], 1967).

57. "The Problem of Historical Consciousness," p. 108.

58. For a masterful and extremely subtle interpretation of the modern age, see Hans Blumenberg, *The Legitimacy of the Modern Age*, trans. Robert M. Wallace (Cambridge, Mass.: M.I.T. Press, 1983).

59. "Problem of Historical Consciousness," pp. 141–42.

60. Ibid., p. 142.

61. See *TM*, p. 289; *WM*, p. 306.

62. Gadamer approaches the problem of corruption indirectly. This can be seen in his perceptive interpretations of Plato's *Dialogues*, especially the *Republic*. The central "political" problem that Plato confronts is the corruption of the *polis*. Gadamer says the following about the *Republic:*

> Thus the exposition of this ideal state in the *Republic* serves in educating the political human being, but the *Republic* is not meant as a manual on educational methods and materials, and it does not point out the goal of the educational process to the educator. In the background of this work on the state is a real educational state, the community of Plato's academy. The *Republic* exemplifies the purpose of that academy. This community of students applying themselves rigorously to mathematics and dialectic is no apolitical society of scholars. Instead, the work done here is intended to lead to the result which remained unattainable for the current sophistic paideia, with its encyclopedic instruction and arbitrary moralistic reformulations of the educational content of ancient poetry. It is intended to lead to a new discovery of justice in one's own soul and thus to *the shaping of the political human being. This* education, however, the actual education to participation in the state, is anything but a total manipulation of the soul, a rigorous leading of it to a predetermined goal. Instead, precisely in extending its questioning behind the supposedly valid traditional moral ideas, it is in itself the new experience of justice. Thus this education is not authoritative instruction based on an ideal organization at all; rather it lives from questioning alone. ("Plato and the Poets," p. 52. See also "Plato's Educational State" in *Dialogue and Dialectic*)

The moral that can be drawn from this for our hermeneutical situation is that the political task of the philosopher is to help revive that sense of questioning that can lead to a "discovery of justice in one's own soul" and thus to "the shaping of the political human being." My quarrel with Gadamer is not that I think he is wrong about this, but rather to make the Hegelian point that the "discovery of justice in one's own soul" is only the beginning of "the shaping of the political human being." This process can become merely abstract and false unless one confronts the practical tasks of shaping or reshaping one's actual community in order to cultivate genuine dialogue among participants.

63. See the studies on Plato collected in *Dialogue and Dialectic*.

64. Gadamer's acknowledgment of the difference between a living dialogue where the other person can literally answer questions and the hermeneutical dialogue where "the text is expressed only through the other partner, the interpreter" opens a Pan-

dora's box of problems for philosophic hermeneutics. It is fundamental for Gadamer's understanding of philosophic hermeneutics that although we always understand and interpret differently, nevertheless we are interpreting the same text, the same "universal thing." "To understand a text always means to apply it to ourselves and to know that, even if it must always be understood in different ways, it is still the same text presenting itself to us in these different ways" (*TM*, p. 359; *WM*, p. 375). But if the interpreter not only must open himself or herself to what the text "says to us" and the "claim to truth" that it makes upon us but is also the linguistic medium for answering for the text, then this raises questions about in what sense, if any, we can speak of the same text, the same "universal thing." For it is not the text *an sich* that answers the interpreter, but only the text as understood, and all understanding is conditioned by our prejudices and prejudgments. This is a point that was pressed by Nietzsche and that has become a key idea in poststructuralist thinking. As Nietzsche showed, this problem can lead to a questioning of the very idea of truth and of the "claim to truth" that texts and tradition make upon us. It also raises problems in an ethical and political context concerning in what sense, if any, we can speak of the same universal principles, laws, or norms that are mediated by *phronēsis*, and who determines whether or not they are the same.

65. See *Die Idee des Guten*.

66. "On the Philosophic Element in the Sciences and the Scientific Character of Philosophy," in his *Reason in the Age of Science*, p. 9. There is another aspect of what I am calling the radical, indeed, the subversive quality of Gadamer's writing and rhetoric. Any careful reader of Gadamer cannot help being struck by the depth of his critique of all forms of dogmatism and fanaticism. He always seeks to elicit questioning. Thus, for example, publishing such an essay as "Plato and the Poets" in the context of Germany in 1934 must be seen as a politically subversive and courageous act. Viewed superficially, it might appear to be merely a scholarly paper. But consider the political significance of Gadamer's statements about Plato's *Republic* against the background of the coming to power of the Nazis.

> [The *Republic*] is intended to lead to a new discovery of justice in one's own soul and thus to *shaping of the political human being. This* education, however, the actual education to participation in the state, is anything but a total manipulation of the soul, a rigorous leading of it to a predetermined goal. Instead, precisely in extending questioning behind the supposedly valid traditional moral ideas, it is in itself the new experience of justice. Thus this education is not authoritative instruction based on an ideal organization at all; rather it lives from questioning alone. (*Dialogue and Dialectic*, p. 52)

Recently, I had an occasion to ask Gadamer if he was aware of the political significance of this article at the time of its publication. He told me that part of the reason for writing the article was the need to respond to what he was witnessing in Germany.

67. "Hegel's Philosophy and Its Aftereffects until Today," in *Reason in the Age of Science*, p. 37.

68. "What Is Practice? The Conditions of Social Reason," in *Reason in the Age of Science*, p. 80.

69. Ibid., p. 87.

PART FOUR: PRAXIS, *PRACTICAL DISCOURSE, AND JUDGMENT*

1. See Gadamer's autobiographical sketch, *Philosophische Lehrjahre* (Frankfurt am Main: Vittorio Klostermann, 1977).

2. Habermas, "Dialectics of Rationalization: An Interview," *Telos* 49 (1981):7. The original interview was published in *Ästhetik und Kommunikation* 45–46 (1981):126–57.

3. See the biography of Hannah Arendt by Elisabeth Young-Bruehl, *Hannah Arendt: For Love of the World* (New Haven: Yale University Press, 1982).

4. "A Review of Gadamer's *Truth and Method*," in Dallmayr and McCarthy, *Understanding and Social Inquiry*, p. 351.

5. For one of the clearest statements of Habermas's thesis that questions of meaning cannot be separated from questions of validity, see his *Theorie des kommunikativen Handelns* (Frankfurt am Main: Suhr Kamp Verlag, 1981), 1:152.

6. *Hegel* (Cambridge, England: Cambridge University Press, 1975), p. 218.

7. "What Is Universal Pragmatics?", in his *Communication and the Evolution of Society*, p. 24.

8. See Habermas's discussion of the differences between empirical-analytic sciences and reconstructive sciences in "What Is Universal Pragmatics?", pp. 8–20.

9. Although Habermas has always made a sharp distinction between *communicative* action, on the one hand, and *strategic* or *instrumental* action on the other hand, he has not always been clear about the relation between strategic and instrumental action. In his most recent writings Habermas classifies both strategic and instrumental action as types of action oriented toward success (as distinguished from communicative action, which is oriented toward reaching understanding). But he regards instrumental action as a form of *nonsocial* action and strategic action as a type of *social* action. See his discussion of the types of action in "A Reply to My Critics," in *Habermas: Critical Debates*, John B. Thompson and David Held (Cambridge, Mass.: M.I.T. Press, 1982), pp. 263–69.

10. "What Is Universal Pragmatics?", p. 3.

11. *Legitimation Crisis*, trans. Thomas McCarthy (Boston: Beacon Press, 1975), p. 110.

12. Ibid. See Steven Lukes' criticism of this claim and Habermas's reply in Thompson and Held, *Habermas: Critical Debates*, pp. 134–48, 254–60.

13. Throughout Habermas's writings, he returns again and again to critical reinterpretations of Weber and Marx. His most systematic reinterpretation of Weber is in *Theorie des kommunikativen Handelns*.

14. "Historical Materialism and the Development of Normative Structures," in *Communication and the Evolution of Society*, p. 117.

15. Ibid., pp. 119–20.

16. See MacIntyre's discussion of Aristotle's "metaphysical biology" in *After Virtue*, p. 139.

17. "Legitimation Problems in the Modern State," pp. 201–2.

18. See Habermas's remarks on neoconservatism and neo-Aristotelianism in "Legitimation Problems in the Modern State," pp. 119–204. For a recent analysis of conservatism and neoconservatism in the United States and West Germany, see his "Die Kulturkritik der Neokonservatism in den U.S.A. und der Bundesrepublik: über eine Bewegung von Intellectuellen in zwei politischen Kulturen," *Praxis International* 2 (1983):339–58.

19. *Theory and Practice*, p. 94.

20. "Historical Materialism," p. 97.

21. "A Reply to My Critics," p. 221.

22. Ibid., p. 228.

23. Ibid., pp. 261–62.

24. Thomas McCarthy and Steven Lukes both develop serious criticisms of Habermas's reliance on and appropriation of the developmental studies of Piaget and Kohlberg. See their contributions in Thompson and Held, *Habermas: Critical Debates*.

25. *Critical Theory of Habermas*, p. ix.

26. John B. Thompson, in his perceptive study of Habermas and Ricoeur, attempts to show how their positions contribute to a "critical hermeneutics." See his *Critical*

Hermeneutics (Cambridge, England: Cambridge University Press, 1981).

27. "Pragmatism, Relativism, and Irrationalism," *Proceedings and Addresses of the American Philosophical Association* 53 (1980):736.

28. Ibid., p. 734.

29. Ibid.

30. Ibid., p. 733.

31. Ibid., p. 734–35.

32. Ibid., p. 737.

33. Ibid.

34. For Rorty's interpretation and appropriation of Gadamer, see chap. 7, "From Epistemology to Hermeneutics," in *Philosophy and the Mirror of Nature*. See also his discussion of the difference between hermeneutics as a method and hermeneutics as an attitude in "A Reply to Dreyfus and Taylor," *Review of Metaphysics* 34 (1980):39.

35. Rorty, "Nineteenth Century Idealism and Twentieth Century Textualism," *Monist* 64 (1981):165.

36. Ibid., p. 167.

37. Feyerabend, *Science in a Free Society*, pp. 8–9.

38. "Pragmatism, Relativism, and Irrationalism," pp. 727–28. Rorty shares another trait with Feyerabend (and Derrida). All three have been extremely effective critics of prevailing philosophic orthodoxies when they have combined sharp argumentation with wit. This style was characteristic of Feyerabend's attacks on the received or orthodox philosophy of science during the 1950s and 1960s. We find the same type of trenchant criticism of phenomenology and Husserl in Derrida's writings in the 1960s. But all three have since moved to a philosophic style that is close to satire and borders on caricature. Recently, when I have sympathetically criticized Rorty in public discussions, I have discovered an enormous amount of hostility toward his work. He is frequently condemned for what some take to be the ultimate philosophic sin: failing to be "serious." Although I have been sharply critical of some of Rorty's claims, I think it is unfortunate that many philosophers are all too eager to dismiss him as an "irresponsible" relativist and fail to do justice to his eminently serious practical-moral vision.

39. "Nineteenth Century Idealism," pp. 167–68.

40. See my discussion of Rorty's disavowal of any "constructive" program in "Philosophy in the Conversation of Mankind."

41. "Nineteenth Century Idealism," p. 159.

42. See the concluding chapter, "Philosophy without Mirrors," in *Philosophy and the Mirror of Nature* and the introduction to his *Consequences of Pragmatism*, pp. xiii–xvii.

43. *Philosophy and the Mirror of Nature*, p. 354.

44. "Nineteenth Century Idealism," pp. 162–63.

45. "Pragmatism, Relativism, and Irrationalism," p. 727.

46. "Nineteenth Century Idealism," p. 173. See also "Method, Social Science, and Social Hope," in *Consequences of Pragmatism*, pp. 191–210.

47. "Pragmatism, Categories, and Language," *Philosophical Review* 70 (1961):197–223.

48. See Rorty's discussion of Dewey in the essays collected in *Consequences of Pragmatism*, especially "Method, Social Science, Social Hope." Rorty's fascination with metaphilosophy accounts in part for the thinness of his neopragmatism and indicates a sharp difference with one of his heroes, John Dewey. Rorty talks a great deal about "coping" but has very little to say about what this means concretely. One is not necessarily asking for blueprints about how to cope, but there is a form of discourse, which Dewey practiced very effectively in his time, that is completely lacking in Rorty. Dewey was concerned with illuminating what he called "the problems of men." Pragmatism becomes extremely thin when conceived of as a metaphilosophic "position." See my discussion of the way in which Rorty does violence to Dewey in "Philosophy in the Conversation of Mankind," pp. 766–76. See also

Garry Brodsky, "Rorty's Interpretation of Pragmatism," *Transactions of the Charles S. Peirce Society* 18 (1982):311–37.

49. "Creative Democracy—The Task before Us," *Classic American Philosophers,* ed. Max Fisch (New York: Appleton-Century-Crofts, 1951), p. 394.

50. My discussion of Arendt is primarily oriented toward understanding her contribution to the analysis of *praxis* and the role of judgment in the context of communal action. Arendt's analysis of action is itself embedded in a network of distinctions and categories, including the basic distinction of the *vita activa* and the *vita contemplativa.* Within the *vita activa,* she sharply distinguishes between labor, work, and action; and she distinguishes three mental activities—thinking, willing, and judging—that comprise the *vita contemplativa.* All of these distinctions raise numerous difficulties that I will not examine here. I find myself in basic agreement with Hanna Fenichel Pitkin, who has acutely and sympathetically pointed out a number of weaknesses in Arendt's analysis of action and politics. See Pitkin's discussion of Arendt in *Wittgenstein and Justice;* "The Roots of Conservatism: Oakeshott and the Denial of Politics," *Dissent* (1973):496–525; "Justice: On Relating Private and Public," *Political Theory* 9 (1981):327–52. See also Hanna Fenichel Pitkin and Sara Shumer, "On Participation," *Democracy* 2 (1982):43–59, and Jasminkz Udovicki "The Uses of Freedom and the Human Condition," *Praxis International* 3 (1983):54–61.

51. "Truth and Politics," in *Between Past and Future,* p. 241.

52. There are critical questions that can be raised about the adequacy of the categorial distinctions of labor, work, and action, and the related categorial dichotomy between the social and the political. See my discussion in "Hannah Arendt: The Ambiguities of Theory and Practice," in *Political Theory and Praxis: New Perspectives,* ed. Terrence Ball (Minneapolis: University of Minnesota Press, 1977). See also the way in which Arendt was pressed on these issues, and her responses, in *Hannah Arendt: The Recovery of the Public World,* ed. Melvyn A. Hill (New York: St. Martin's Press, 1979), pp. 301–39.

53. *Human Condition,* p. 158. Arendt consistently used masculine forms of speech when referring to human beings. For stylistic reasons I have followed her practice.

54. Ibid., p. 157.

55. Ibid.

56. *On Revolution* (New York: Viking Press, 1963), p. 23.

57. Ibid., pp. 120–21.

58. Ibid., p. 110.

59. See Arendt's discussion of these concepts in "On Violence," in her *Crises of the Republic* (New York: Harcourt Brace Jovanovich, 1969), pp. 142–55.

60. *On Revolution,* p. 174. For a critique of the limitations of Arendt's conception of power, see Habermas, "Hannah Arendt's Communications Concept of Power."

61. For subtle analysis of the place of political thinking in the gap between past and future, see her preface to *Between Past and Future.*

62. See my article "Hannah Arendt: The Ambiguities of Theory and Practice," where I criticize Arendt's reading of Hegel and Marx.

63. P. 296.

64. Gadamer, "What is Practice?", p. 80.

65. "Tradition and the Modern Age," in *Between Past and Future.* See my critical comments on her interpretation of Marx in "Hannah Arendt: The Ambiguities of Theory and Practice."

66. *Human Condition,* p. 160.

67. "Thoughts on Politics and Revolution," in her *Crises of the Republic.*

68. Ibid., p. 233.

69. See the discussion of the problem that the question of poverty poses for Arendt's theory of politics in Pitkin, "Roots of Conservatism," pp. 512–15, and Pitkin's

discussion of Arendt's neglect of the question of justice in "Justice: On Relating Private and Public."

70. See Pitkin and Shumer, "On Participation."

71. See Habermas, "Arendt's Communications Concept of Power."

72. See my discussion of this point in "Hannah Arendt: The Ambiguities of Theory and Practice," pp. 152–58.

73. See Arendt's comments in Hill, *Hannah Arendt: The Recovery of the Public World,* pp. 301–39.

74. See Habermas, "Hannah Arendt's Communications Concept of Power."

75. There are many scholarly problems in reconstructing Arendt's analysis of judgment. Prior to the essays published in *Between Past and Future,* there are only occasional references to judgment. "Judgment" was to be the third part of *Life of The Mind,* the part she did not live to write. The primary source for reconstructing Arendt's understanding of judgment as one of the primary mental activities is the lectures that she delivered at the New School of Social Research and the University of Chicago on Kant's political philosophy. Ronald Beiner has edited these lectures and written an extremely interesting interpretive essay drawing on all of the sources in which Arendt discusses judgment. His conclusion is that there are really two theories of judgment in Arendt. My own view is that the conflicting tendencies and apparent contradictions in what she does say stand in the way of our resolving the issue by speaking of an "earlier" and "later" theory of judgment. (I have explored these conflicts in "Judging—the Actor and the Spectator," in *Proceedings of History, Ethics, Politics: A Conference Based on the Work of Hannah Arendt,* ed. Robert Boyers [Saratoga Springs, N.Y.: Empire State College, 1982].) My discussion of opinion and judgment here is limited to the role that they play in action and politics. Ernst Vollrath first called my attention to this important dimension of Arendt's political thinking. In addition to Ronald Beiner's interpretive essay in *Hannah Arendt: Lectures on Kant's Political Philosophy,* see Ernst Vollrath, "Hannah Arendt and the Method of Political Thinking," *Social Research* 44 (1977):160–82, and Michael Dennery, "The Privilege of Ourselves: Hannah Arendt on Judgment," in *Hannah Arendt,* pp. 245–74.

76. "Truth and Politics," in *Between Past and Future.*

77. Ibid., p. 241.

78. *On Revolution,* p. 229.

79. "Crisis in Culture," p. 221.

80. That the capacity to judge is a specifically political ability in exactly the sense denoted by Kant, namely, the ability to see things not only from one's own point of view but in the perspective of all those who happen to be present; even that judgment may be one of the fundamental abilities of man as a political being insofar as it enables him to orient himself in the public realm, in the common world—these are insights that are virtually as old as articulated political experience. The Greeks called this ability φρόνησις, or insight, and they considered it the principal virtue or excellence of the statesman in distinction from the wisdom of the philosopher. (Ibid.)

81. Ibid.

82. Ibid.

83. Ibid.

84. I suspect that Arendt would have been surprised to discover how her understanding of taste was approximated and anticipated by John Dewey.

The word "taste" has perhaps got too completely associated with arbitrary liking to express the nature of judgments of value. But if the word be used in the sense of an appreciation at once cultivated and active, one may say that the formation of taste is the chief matter wherever values enter in, whether intellectual, esthetic or moral. Relatively immediate judgments, which we call tact or to which we give the name of intuition, do not preclude reflective inquiry, but are the funded products of much thoughtful experience. Expertness of taste is at once the result and the reward of constant exercise of thinking. Instead of there being no disputing about tastes, they are the one thing worth disputing about, if by "dispute" is signified discussion involving reflective inquiry. Taste, if we use the word in its best sense, is the outcome of experience brought cumulatively to bear on the intelligent appreciation of the real worth of likings and enjoyments. There is nothing in which a person so completely reveals himself as in the things which he judges enjoyable and desirable. Such judgments are the sole alternative to the domination of belief by impulse, chance, blind habit and self-interest. The formation of a cultivated and effectively operative good judgment or taste with respect to what is esthetically admirable, intellectually acceptable and morally approvable is the supreme task set to human beings by the incidents of experience. (*The Quest for Certainty* [New York: Minton, Balch, 1929], p. 262)

85. I explore this theme in my paper "Hannah Arendt: Judging—The Actor and the Spectator."

86. "Crisis in Culture," p. 222.

87. "Appendix: Judging," in *Life of the Mind*, 2:262.

88. "Crisis in Culture," pp. 220–21.

89. Although Arendt was strongly influenced by her reading and appropriation of Kant, she always was uneasy with Kant's moral philosophy and the *Critique of Practical Reason*. She was deeply skeptical of the role of rules and principles in moral philosophy (which, of course, are central for Kant's moral philosophy). It becomes clear in her later writings that she thinks that reflective judgment, which Kant discusses in the context of his analysis of aesthetic judgment (and which is to be sharply distinguished from the type of determinative or subsumptive judgment of practical reason), is far more important than rules and principles for understanding "matters of good and evil." This strain in Arendt's thinking was reinforced by her attempt to clarify the concept of the banality of evil. The faculty of judging particulars is applicable not only to making the judgment that "this is beautiful" and "this is ugly" but also to making the judgment that "this is right" and "this is wrong." In the introduction in *Life of the Mind*, she says that one of her motives for dealing with the mental activities (thinking, willing, and judging) was to raise the *questio juris* about the controversial concept of "the banality of evil," and asks, "Might the problem of good and evil, our faculty of telling right from wrong, be connected with our faculty of thought?" It is only near the end of the first volume of *Life of the Mind* (p. 193) that she indicates the relation between *thinking* and *judging*.

> The faculty of judging particulars (as brought to light by Kant), the ability to say "this is wrong," "this is beautiful," and so on, is not the same as the faculty of thinking. Thinking deals with invisibles, with representations of things that are absent; judging always concerns particulars and things close at hand. But the two are interrelated, as are consciousness and conscience. If thinking—the two-in-one of the soundless dialogue—actualizes the difference within our identity as given in consciousness and thereby results in conscience as its by-product, then judging, the by-product of the liberating effect of thinking, realizes thinking, makes it manifest in the world of appearances, where I am never alone and always too busy to be able to think. The manifestation of the wind of thought is not knowledge, it is the ability to tell right from wrong, beautiful from ugly. And this, at the rare moments when the stakes are on the table, may indeed prevent catastrophes, at least for the self.

90. "What Is Authority?", in *Between Past and Future*, p. 93.

91. For Arendt's understanding of tradition, see "Tradition and the Modern Age," in *Between Past and Future*.

92. Habermas does not make a sharp distinction between what Arendt calls "opinions" and "interests." But what he means by "generalizable interests," i.e., interests "that can be communicatively shared," parallels what Arendt means by opinions that are tested and purified through mutual debate. See Habermas's discussion of "generalizable interests" in *Legitimation Crisis*, p. 108, and in "A Reply to My Critics," pp. 250–63.

93. *Legitimation Crisis*, p. 108.

94. For a perceptive critical discussion of Habermas's conception of argumen-

tation as it pertains to theoretical and practical discourse, see Gunnar Skirbekk, "Pragmatism in Apel and Habermas," in *Contemporary Philosophy: A New Survey,* ed. G. Floistad; vol. 4, *Philosophy of Mind* (The Hague: M. Nijhoff, 1982).

95. Agnes Heller has also criticized Habermas for failing to stress the plurality of opinions in political struggles. Habermas does not really deny this irreducible plurality. I believe, however, that Arendt's and Heller's sensitivity to this issue can be related to their own experiences with totalitarian regimes. See Agnes Heller, "Habermas and Marxism," in Thompson and Held, *Habermas: Critical Debates,* pp. 21–41.

96. "On Participation," 47–48.

97. *Collected Papers,* 5.264.

98. "What Is Practice?", p. 86.

99. *Freedom and Independence* (Cambridge, England: Cambridge University Press, 1976), pp. 97–141.

100. *Hegel,* pp. 414–16.

101. "A Reply to My Critics," p. 222.

102. *After Virtue,* p. 244.

103. "Theses on Feuerbach," in *Writings of the Young Marx on Philosophy and Society,* ed. and trans. Loyd D. Easton and Kurt H. Goddat (Garden City, N.Y.: Anchor Books, 1967), p. 401.

APPENDIX

A Letter by Professor Hans-Georg Gadamer

[In the spring of 1982, I sent Professor Gadamer two papers dealing with his work. The first is a comparative study of Gadamer, Habermas, and Rorty, and the second is an explication and critique of philosophic hermeneutics. They were entitled, respectively, "What Is the Difference That Makes a Difference? Gadamer, Habermas, and Rorty," and "From Hermeneutics to Praxis." The contents of these papers have been modified and integrated into this book. The following letter is Gadamer's "first reaction" to these papers. Most of the criticisms that I made of Gadamer in these papers have been incorporated into the present book. Since Gadamer's letter is not only a response to some of my critical remarks but also represents a succinct and eloquent statement of his views, I asked his permission to publish his letter as an appendix. I want to thank Professor Gadamer for granting permission to reprint a personal letter which was not intended for publication. James Bohman translated the letter—R.J.B.]

1. Juni 1982

June 1, 1982

Lieber Herr Bernstein,

Schneller als erwartet fand ich die Zeit und das Interesse, die beiden mir gesandten Manuskripte zu lesen. Eine höchst interessante Lektüre für mich, zumal ich mit dem letzten Ihrer Themen in bezug auf literarische Texte aus Anlass einer Auseinandersetzung mit Derrida andauernd beschäftigt bin.

Ich las die beiden Manuskripte wohl in der von Ihnen auch gedachten Reihenfolge, das heisst, erst die vergleichende Studie und dann die speziell auf mich

Dear Mr. Bernstein,

I found the time and interest to read the two manuscripts you sent me sooner than I had expected. They proved to be extremely interesting reading, particularly since I have been concerned for some time with the last of your themes—that relating to literary texts—in the context of an exchange with Derrida.

I did read the two manuscripts in the order you suggested: first the comparative study and then the one dealing directly with my own work. The

gehende. Die Darstellung ist von bewundernswerter Klarheit, und es gibt nicht viele Punkte, an denen ich mich missverstanden fühle. So besteht eine gewisse Aussicht, dass meine Anmerkungen zu Ihre Aufstellungen für Sie auch verständlich sind. Im Ganzen ging es mir so, dass die Fragen und Gegeneinwendungen, die ich bei der Lektüre des ersten Manuskriptes notierte, fast alle in ausgezeichneter Weise in dem zweiten Manuskript ihre Auflösung finden.

Natürlich ist das erste Manuskript in manchen Aspekten für mich ausserordentlich nützlich. Im Grunde bin ich ja schon aus Altersgründen mit den beiden Vergleichspunkten nicht gleichzustellen und habe sozusagen mit Interesse zuzuhören, wie ein Jüngerer die Arbeiten von Habermas und Rorty liest und zu meinen eigenen Gedanken in Beziehung setzt. Mir wird dabei auch recht bewusst, wieviel mehr ich sozusagen in der Tradition der deutschen romantischen und nachromantischen Philosophie befangen bin. Ich lebe sozusagen in einem geschlossenen Horizont von Problemen und Fragestellungen, der doch noch Philosophie zu sein meint und weder eine sozialwissenschaftliche noch eine skeptische Hinterfragung derselben anerkennt. Aber vielleicht sollte ich vorsichtiger sein, dass dies nicht ganz für mein Verhältnis zu Habermas gilt. Er scheint mir eine eigene Aufgabe, die Sie sehr klar herausarbeiten, angepackt zu haben, und ich sehe nicht, warum ich meinerseits diese Aufgabe nicht anerkennen soll. Sie ist freilich nicht meine Sache, einmal, weil ich kein Aristoteles bin, den ein ausgeweitetes Interesse an Staatsverfassungen auszeichnet (aber bemerkenswerterweise nicht an den Problemen des Rechtswesens). Auf der anderen Seite gilt aber auch für Aristoteles *Politik*, dass sie nur deshalb von der Ethik ausbruchlos zu sich selbst kommt, weil sie die Resultate der *Ethik*, und das heisst vor allem: ein gemeinsames normatives Bewusstsein, voraussetzt. Sie entwirft sozusagen die Lehre von der Staatsverfassung für eine Gesellschaft, die noch weiss, was Ethos und Phronesis sind.

Ihr Argument und das von Habermas besteht aber gerade darin, dass wir das heute nicht mehr wissen. Damit verändert sich aber die Aufgabe eines

presentation is extraordinarily clear, and there are not many points on which I feel I have been misunderstood. Thus the prospects are good that my remarks on your views will also be intelligible to you. In general, the questions and counter-objections I noted in reading the first manuscript were almost all quite nicely resolved in the second manuscript.

Naturally, the first manuscript is in many respects extremely useful to me. By reason of age alone I cannot be put in the same category with either of the two thinkers to whom you compare me; but I listened intently, so to speak, to how someone from a younger generation reads the works of Habermas and Rorty and places them in relation to my ideas. At the same time, I become acutely aware of just how much I am caught up, one might say, in the tradition of German Romantic and post-Romantic philosophy. I live, as it were, in a closed horizon of problems and lines of questioning, which still understands itself to be philosophy, and which recognizes neither a social-scientific nor a skeptical questioning of philosophy itself. But perhaps I should be more cautious, for this is not wholly the case in my relation to Habermas. It seems to me that he has taken up a task of his own which you develop quite clearly, and I do not see why for my part I should not recognize this task. It certainly isn't my own concern: to begin with, for the reason that I am no Aristotle with an extensive interest in state constitutions (but not, surprisingly, in law and jurisdiction). On the other hand, it is also true of Aristotle's *Politics* that it comes into its own and makes the transition from ethics to politics only because it presupposes the results of the *Ethics:* first and foremost, a common, shared normative consciousness. The *Politics* proposes, so to speak, the doctrine of a political constitution for a society that still knows what *ethos* and *phronēsis* are.

Both your own and Habermas's argument assert that this is precisely the knowledge we no longer possess today. This fact fundamentally alters the task of the transition from ethics to politics; if I understand correctly, it now becomes the transition from practical philosophy to social science. But practical philoso-

Übergangs von der Ethik zur Politik grundsätzlich, und wenn ich recht sehe, wird sie zum Übergang von praktischer Philosophie zu Sozialwissenschaft. Praktische Philosophie aber besteht auf der führenden Funktion der Phronesis, die kein neues Ethos entwirft, sondern die gegebenen normativen Inhalte klärt und konkretisiert. Insofern teile ich nun geradezu Rortys Kritik an dem wissenschaftlichen Status, auf dem Habermas besteht. Ich kann nicht umhin, wie ich es ja auch gelegentlich formuliert habe, mit einer sogenannten wissenschaftlich disziplinierten Phronesis keinen Sinn zu verbinden, wohl aber mit einer durch Phronesis disziplinierten Wissenschaftlichkeit. Bei dieser Gelegenheit möchte ich den einzigen wirklichen Fehler, den ich in der Schilderung meiner Position vermute, aufklären. Sie sprechen dort von der Schlusswendung meines Buches, als ob ich mit Disziplin, die Wahrheit garantiert, meinerseits eine wissenschaftliche Methode meinte. Das ist aber ein Missverständnis. Ich meine Disziplin im moralischen Sinne des Wortes und mit "Garantieren" gerade nicht methodische Leistung. Ähnlich geht es mir manchmal, wenn Sie bei mir von Kritik der Tradition sprechen. Im Grossen und Ganzen verstehen Sie mich dort richtig, und das heisst, dass nicht die Tradition kritisiert wird, sondern dies oder jenes durch Tradition Vermittelte. Hier scheint mir Habermas von einem zu engen Begriff bestimmt, wenn er von kultureller Überlieferung redet. Unsere Erfahrung der Dinge, gerade auch der des täglichen Lebens, der Produktionsweise, ja, sogar der Vitalsphäre, ist eine hermeneutische. Weder das eine noch das andere geht darin auf, Objekt der Wissenschaft zu sein. Mit einer Wendung wie auf Seite 14 "Kritik der Tradition oder der gegenwärtigen Gesellschaft" ist ein "oder" gebraucht, das ich nicht verstehen kann.

Nun ist Ihr entscheidendes Argument der Zusammenbruch aller Prinzipien in der modernen Welt, und ich gebe Ihnen vollkommen recht, dass, wenn das richtig wäre, mein Bestehen auf der Phronesis reine Deklamation wäre. Aber ist das so? Verfallen wir nicht alle einem schrecklichen intellektuellen Hochmut, wenn wir die Antizipationen Nietzsches

phy insists on the guiding function of *phronēsis*, which does not propose any new ethics, but rather clarifies and concretizes given normative contents. To this extent, I share Rorty's criticism of Habermas's claim to scientific status. As I have put it elsewhere, I cannot really make sense of a *phronēsis* that is supposed to be scientifically disciplined, although I can imagine a scientific approach that is disciplined by *phronēsis*. I would like to take the opportunity here to clear up the only real mistake I find in your characterization of my position.* When you speak of the turn at the end of my book, it is as if what I had meant by a "discipline that guarantees truth" were a sort of scientific method. This is a misunderstanding. Here I mean "discipline" in the moral sense of the word, and by "guarantee" definitely not methodic achievement. Similar problems arise when you speak of my critique of tradition. On the whole you understand me correctly in this; that is to say, it is not tradition which is criticized but rather this or that particular element mediated by tradition. It seems to me that Habermas employs too narrow a concept when he speaks of cultural tradition. Our experience of things, indeed even of everyday life, of modes of production, and yes, also of the sphere of our vital concerns, are one and all hermeneutic. None of them is exhausted by being made an object of science. In your expression "critique of tradition or of contemporary society," "or" is then used in a way that I cannot understand.

Clearly your decisive argument is the collapse of all principles in the modern world, and I certainly agree with you that,

---

*[Gadamer is here referring to my interpretation and critique of the final paragraph of *Truth and Method* where he says, "Rather, what the tool of method does not achieve must—and effectively can—be achieved by a discipline of questioning and [inquiry], a discipline that guarantees Truth" (*TM*, p. 447). See my discussion of this in "From Hermeneutics to Praxis," p. 838. This specific criticism has been omitted in this book.—R.J.B.]

und die ideologische Verwirrung der Gegenwart mit dem wirklich gelebten Leben und seinen Solidaritäten gleichsetzen? Hier ist in der Tat meine Abweichung von Heidegger fundamental, und Sie machen einen seltsamen Gebrauch von meiner Wendung über das Konkrete, Reale, Machbare gegenüber der blossen Abstraktion. Das klingt so, als ob ich mit meiner philosophischen Arbeit in diese Konkretisierungsaufgabe hineinreden wollte. Das gerade will ich nicht und will nur die Theoretiker erinnern, dass es in Wirklichkeit darauf ankommt. Mit anderen Worten, wenn unter den Menschen, welcher Gesellschaft oder Kultur oder Klasse oder Rasse immer sie angehören mögen, keine Punkte der Solidarität mehr da wären, kann nur noch der Sozialingenieur oder der Tyrann, das heisst, die anonyme oder die direkte Gewalt, Gemeinsamkeiten konstituieren. Aber sind wir so weit? Werden wir je so weit sein? Ich glaube, dass die gegenseitige Vernichtung dann unvermeidlich bevorstünde. Das bedeutet umgekehrt, dass ich den Sozialwissenschaften auf ihrem Felde volle Anerkennung zolle, das heisst, Ihr Postulat eines Hinausgehens über die Hermeneutik durchaus teile, nur, dass ich dabei kein philosophisches Hinausgehen erkennen kann. Auch ich bin für Staatswesen und Politik, die Verständigung erlauben und Freiheit aller. Das ist keineswegs der Einfluss von Habermas. Seit der französischen Revolution, seit Kant und seit Hegel, ist das doch für jeden Europäer selbstverständlich. Aber ich rede nicht davon, was man tun muss, damit das wirklich wird, sondern davon, dass es keine noch so grosse Entstellung menschlicher Wirklichkeit gibt, in der nicht immer noch Solidaritäten bestehen. Plato hat das sehr gut gesehen: es gibt keine noch so verdorbene Stadt, in der nicht doch noch etwas von der wahren Stadt wirklich ist—und darauf beruht, meine ich, die Möglichkeit der praktischen Philosophie.

Ein Konflikt von Traditionen, wie wir ihn heute haben, scheint mir insofern gar nichts besonderes. Phronesis ist immer Unterscheidung und Wahl dessen, was man für das richtige hält.

if this were correct, my insistence on *phronēsis* would be nothing more than pure declamation. But is this really the case? Don't we all then run the risk of a terrible intellectual hubris if we equate Nietzsche's anticipations and the ideological confusion of the present with life as it is actually lived with its own forms of solidarity? Here, in fact, my divergence from Heidegger is fundamental. Thus the use you make of my expressions about the concrete, the real and the feasible, as opposed to pure abstraction, is odd. It sounds as if I wanted to interfere with this task of concretization through my philosophic work. This is precisely what I do not want; I only intend to remind the theoreticians that this is what it all hinges on in the final analysis. In other words, if it were the case that there were no single locus of solidarity remaining among human beings, whatever society or culture or class or race they might belong to, then common interests could be constituted only by social engineers or tyrants, that is, through anonymous or direct force. But have we reached this point? Will we ever? I believe that we would then be at the brink of unavoidable mutual destruction. Conversely, this means that I grant the social sciences full recognition in their field; that is, I completely share their postulate of going beyond hermeneutics; what I cannot see is that this amounts to a philosophic going-beyond. I too am in favor of a government and politics that would allow for mutual understanding and the freedom of all. But this is not due to the influence of Habermas. It has been self-evident to any European since the French Revolution, since Hegel and Kant. But I am not talking about what is to be done in order to realize this state of affairs. Rather, I am concerned with the fact that the displacement of human reality never goes so far that no forms of solidarity exist any longer. Plato saw this very well: there is no city so corrupted that it does not realize something of the true city; that is what, in my opinion, is the basis for the possibility of practical philosophy.

The conflict of traditions we have today does not seem to me to be anything exceptional. *Phronēsis* is always the

Sehr glücklich war ich über ihre überaus verständnisvolle Anwendung der Horizontverschmelzung auf meine eigene Aristoteles-Deutung. Sie sollten sie aber auch für das Problem des Naturrechts gelten lassen: es gibt keine eigene Sphäre des Rechtes in der griechischen Kultur, so wenig wie eine Freiheit aller, und doch haben wir daraus zu lernen, zum Beispiel, nicht auf dogmatischen Missbrauch von Naturrechtsargumenten hereinzufallen.

Vielleicht sollte ich noch eins hinzufügen: die Fortgeltung der philosophischen Tradition scheint mir bei allen Modifikationen, die ich vor allem Heidegger verdanke, auch für mich verbindlich. So gross die Bedeutung Heideggers und seiner Phronesisinterpretation 1923 für mich war: darauf war ich schon aus eigenem vorbereitet und zwar vor allem durch frühe Lektüre von Kierkegaard, durch den platonischen Sokrates und durch die gewaltige Wirkung des Dichters Stefan George auf meine Generation. (Letzteres war aber keine wirkliche Zustimmung zu der Esoterik um diesen Dichter.)

Doch ich will schliessen. Das alles bleibt ja eine erste Reaktion, und wenn ich Ihnen zum Schluss noch etwas sagen darf, was Sie gewiss befriedigen wird: jetzt werde ich erst wirklich anfangen, Habermas und Rorty neu zu lesen und vielleicht doch noch etwas in meinen alten Kopf hineinzubekommen. Freilich, aus mir einen Soziologen machen—das wird niemanden gelingen, auch nicht mir selbst.

Mit herzlichem Gruss, ihr
H. G. Gadamer

process of distinguishing and choosing what one considers to be right.

I was very pleased by your very insightful application of the fusion of horizons to my own interpretation of Aristotle. But you should also make use of it with regard to the problem of natural law. There is no independent sphere of law or right in Greek culture, just as there is no conception of freedom of all. Nevertheless we can learn something here—for example, not to fall prey to a dogmatic misuse of natural law arguments.

Perhaps I should add just one more thing: the continued validity of the philosophic tradition seems to me to have implications for my own thinking, even with all the modifications I owe primarily to Heidegger. As important as Heidegger and his 1923 *phronēsis* interpretations were for me, I was already prepared for it on my own, above all by my earlier reading of Kierkegaard, by the Platonic Socrates, and by the powerful effect of the poet Stephen George on my generation. (But I did not have any real sympathy with the esoteric atmosphere surrounding this poet.)

Now I would like to conclude. All this is by the way of a first reaction; and if, in closing, I may say something which you will certainly find satisfying, now I intend really to begin reading Habermas and Rorty again; perhaps I can still get something new into this old head. Admittedly, to make me into a sociologist is something no one will succeed in doing, not even myself.

All the best,

Yours,

H. G. Gadamer

BIBLIOGRAPHY

Adorno, Theodor W. *Against Epistemology.* Translated by Willis Domingo. Cambridge, Mass.: M.I.T. Press, 1983.

Apel, Karl-Otto. *Towards a Transformation of Philosophy.* Translated by Glyn Adey and David Frisby. London: Routledge & Kegan Paul, 1980.

Arendt, Hannah. *Between Past and Future.* New York: Viking Press, 1961.

———. *Crises of the Republic.* New York: Harcourt Brace Jovanovich, 1969.

———. *The Human Condition.* Chicago: University of Chicago Press, 1958.

———. *Lectures on Kant's Political Philosophy.* Edited by Ronald Beiner. Chicago: University of Chicago Press, 1982.

———. *The Life of the Mind.* 2 vols. New York: Harcourt Brace Jovanovich, 1978.

———. *On Revolution.* New York: Viking Press, 1963.

Aristotle. *Nicomachean Ethics.* Translated by H. Rackham. Cambridge, Mass.: Harvard University Press, 1926; rev. ed., 1934.

Ayer, A. J. *Language, Truth and Logic.* New York: Dover, 1946.

Ball, Terrence, ed. *Political Theory and Praxis: New Perspectives.* Minneapolis: University of Minnesota Press, 1977.

Bernstein, Richard J. "From Hermeneutics to Praxis." *Review of Metaphysics* 35 (1982):823–45.

———. "Hannah Arendt: The Ambiguities of Theory and Practice." In Ball, *Political Theory and Praxis.*

———. "Hannah Arendt: Judging—the Actor and the Spectator." In *Proceedings of History, Ethics, Politics: A Conference Based on the Work of Hannah Arendt,* edited by Robert Boyers. Saratoga Springs, N.Y.: Empire State College, 1982.

———. "Philosophy in the Conversation of Mankind." *Review of Metaphysics* 33 (1980):745–76.

———. *Praxis and Action.* Philadelphia: University of Pennsylvania Press, 1971.

———. *The Restructuring of Social and Political Theory.* New York: Harcourt Brace Jovanovich, 1976.

———. "What is the Difference That Makes a Difference? Gadamer, Habermas, and Rorty." In *PSA 1982,* vol. 2. Proceedings of the 1982 Biennial Meeting of the Philosophy of Science Association. Edited by P. D. Asquith and T. Nickles. East Lansing, Mich.: Philosophy of Science Association, 1983.

———. "Why Hegel Now?" *Review of Metaphysics* 31 (1977):29–60.

Bertilsson, Margareta. *Towards a Social Reconstruction of Science Theory: Peirce's Theory of Inquiry and Beyond.* Lund: University of Lund, 1978.

Betti, Emilio. *Die Hermeneutik als allgemeine Methodik der Geisteswissenschaften.* Tübingen: J. C. B. Mohr, 1962.

Bleicher, Josef. *Contemporary Hermeneutics: Hermeneutics as Method, Philosophy and Critique.* London: Routledge & Kegan Paul, 1980.

Blumenberg, Hans. *The Legitimacy of the Modern Age.* Translated by Robert M. Wallace. Cambridge, Mass.: M.I.T. Press, 1983.

Borger, Robert, and Cioffi, Frank, eds. *Explanation in the Behavioural Sciences: Confrontations.* Cambridge, England: Cambridge University Press, 1970.

Brodsky, Garry. "Rorty's Interpretation of Pragmatism." *Transactions of the Charles S. Peirce Society* 18 (1982):311–37.

Buck, Roger C., and Cohen, Robert S., eds. *PSA 1970, in Memory of Rudolf Carnap.* Proceedings of the 1970 Biennial Meeting of the Philosophy of Science Association. Boston Studies in the Philosophy of Science, no. 8. Dordrecht, Holland: D. Reidel, 1971.

Burian, Richard M. "More Than a Marriage of Convenience: On the Inextricability of History and Philosophy of Science." *Philosophy of Science* 44 (1977):1–42.

Caton, Hiram. *The Origin of Subjectivity: An Essay on Descartes.* New Haven: Yale University Press, 1973.

Cavell, Stanley. *The Claim to Reason: Wittgenstein, Skepticism, Morality and Tragedy.* Oxford: Claredon Press, 1979.

———. *Must We Mean What We Say?* New York: Charles Scribner's Sons, 1969.

Cohen, R. S., Feyerabend, P. K., and Wartofsky, M. W., eds. *Essays in Memory of Imre Lakatos.* Boston Studies in the Philosophy of Science, no. 39. Dordrecht, Holland: D. Reidel, 1976.

Cooper, John M. *Reason and Human Good in Aristotle.* Cambridge, Mass.: Harvard University Press, 1975.

Dallmayr, Fred R. "Praxis and Experience." Forthcoming.

Dallmayr, Fred R., and McCarthy, Thomas A., eds. *Understanding and Social Inquiry.* Notre Dame, Ind.: University of Notre Dame Press, 1977.

Davidson, Donald. "On the Very Idea of a Conceptual Scheme." *Proceedings and Addresses of the American Philosophical Association* 47 (1973–74):5–20.

Dennery, Michael. "The Privilege of Ourselves: Hannah Arendt on Judgment. In Hill, *Hannah Arendt: The Recovery of the Public World.*

Derrida, Jacques. *Speech and Phenomena.* Translated by David B. Allison. Evanston, Ill.: Northwestern University Press, 1973.

———. *Writing and Difference.* Translated by Alan Bass. Chicago: University of Chicago Press, 1978.

Descartes, René. *The Philosophical Works of Descartes.* 2 vols. Translated by Elizabeth S. Haldane and G. R. T. Ross. Cambridge, England: Cambridge University Press, 1969.

Dewey, John. "Creative Democracy—The Task before Us." In *Classic American Philosophers,* edited by Max Fisch. New York: Appleton-Century-Crofts, 1951.

———. *The Quest for Certainty.* New York: Minton, Balch, 1929.

Dilthey, Wilhelm. "The Rise of Hermeneutics." Translated by Fredric Jameson. *New Literary History* 3 (1972):229–44.

Doppelt, Gerald. "Kuhn's Epistemological Relativism: An Interpretation and Defense." *Inquiry* 21 (1978):33–86.

Dummett, Michael. *Truth and Other Enigmas.* London: Gerald Duckworth, 1978.

Edelman, Nathan. *The Eye of the Beholder.* Baltimore: Johns Hopkins Press, 1974.

Evans-Pritchard, E. E. *Witchcraft, Oracles, and Magic among the Azande.* Abridged, with an introduction by Eva Gillies. Oxford: Clarendon Press, 1976.

Feyerabend, Paul. *Against Method: Outline of an Anarchistic Theory of Knowledge.* London: NLB, 1975.

———. "Changing Patterns of Reconstruction." *British Journal of the Philosophy of Science* 28 (1977):351–69.

———. *Science in a Free Society.* London: NLB, 1978.

Foucault, Michel. *Discipline and Punish: The Birth of the Prison.* Translated by Alan Sheridan. New York: Vintage Books, 1979.

Gadamer, Hans-Georg. *Dialogue and Dialectic.* Translated by P. Christopher Smith. New Haven: Yale University Press, 1980.

———. *Hegel's Dialectic.* Translated by P. Christopher Smith. New Haven: Yale University Press, 1976.

———. "Hermeneutics and Social Science." *Cultural Hermeneutics* 2 (1975):307–16.

———. "Historical Transformations of Reason." In *Rationality Today,* edited by Theodore F. Geraets. Ottawa: University of Ottawa Press, 1979.

———. *Die Idee des Guten zwischen Platon und Aristoteles.* Heidelberg: C. Winter Universitätsverlag, 1978.

———. *Kleine Schriften,* vol. 1. Tübingen: J. C. B. Mohr [Paul Siebeck], 1967.

———. *Philosophical Hermeneutics.* Translated by David E. Linge. Berkeley: University of California Press, 1976.

———. *Philosophische Lehrjahre.* Frankfurt am Main: Vittorio Klostermann, 1977.

———. "Practical Philosophy as a Model of the Human Sciences." *Research in Phenomenology* 9 (1980):74–85.

———. "The Problem of Historical Consciousness." In Rabinow and Sullivan, *Interpretive Social Science: A Reader.*

————. *Reason in the Age of Science.* Translated by Frederick G. Lawrence. Cambridge, Mass.: M.I.T. Press, 1981.

————. "Summation." *Cultural Hermeneutics* 2 (1975):329–30.

————. *Truth and Method.* Translated and edited by Garrett Barden and John Cumming. New York: Seabury Press, 1975.

————. *Wahrheit und Methode.* 4th ed. Tübingen: J. C. B. Mohr [Paul Siebeck], 1975.

Gadamer, Hans-Georg, and Strauss, Leo. "Correspondence Concerning *Wahrheit und Methode.*" *Independent Journal of Philosophy* 2 (1978):5–12.

Geertz, Clifford. "Deep Play: Notes on the Balinese Cockfight." In Rabinow and Sullivan, *Interpretive Social Science: A Reader.*

————. "From the Native's Point of View: On the Nature of Anthropological Understanding." In Rabinow and Sullivan, *Interpretive Social Science: A Reader.*

————. *The Interpretation of Culture.* New York: Basic Books, 1973.

Giddens, Anthony. *Studies in Social and Political Theory.* New York: Basic Books, 1970.

Grünbaum, Adolf. "Falsifiability and Rationality." Unpublished typescript, 1971.

Habermas, Jürgen. *Communication and the Evolution of Society.* Translated by Thomas McCarthy. Boston: Beacon Press, 1979.

————. "Dialectics of Rationalization: An Interview." *Telos* 49 (1981):5–31.

————. "Dialektik der Rationalisierung." *Ästhetik und kommunikation* 45–46 (1981):126–55.

————. "Hannah Arendt's Communications Concept of Power." *Social Research* 44 (1977):3–24.

————. *Knowledge and Human Interests.* Translated by Jeremy J. Shapiro. Boston: Beacon Press, 1971.

————. "Die Kulturkritik der Neokonservativen in den U.S.A. und der Bundesrepublik: Über eine Bewegung von Intellektuellen in zwei politischen Kulturen." *Praxis International* 2 (1983):339–58.

————. *Legitimation Crisis.* Translated by Thomas McCarthy. Boston: Beacon Press, 1975.

————. "A Review of Gadamer's *Truth and Method.*" In Dallmayr and McCarthy, *Understanding and Social Inquiry.*

————. *Theorie des kommunikativen Handelns.* 2 vols. Frankfurt am Main: Suhrkamp Verlag, 1981.

————. *Theory and Practice.* Translated by John Viertel. Boston: Beacon Press, 1973.

Hacking, Ian. "Imre Lakatos's Philosophy of Science." *British Journal of the Philosophy of Science* 30 (1979):381–402.

Hegel, G. W. F. *Phenomenology of Spirit.* Translated by A. V. Miller. Oxford: Oxford University Press, 1977.

Heidegger, Martin. *Basic Writings.* Edited by David Farrell Krell. New York: Harper & Row, 1977.

――――. *Being and Time.* Translated by John Macquarrie and Edward Robinson. London: SCM Press, 1962.

Hempel, Carl G. "Criteria of Cognitive Significance: Problems and Changes." In his *Aspects of Scientific Explanation.* New York: Free Press, 1965.

Hermeneutik und Ideolgiekritik. Mit Beiträgen von Karl-Otto Apel, Claus v. Bormann, Rüdiger Bubner, Hans-Georg Gadamer, Hans Joachim Giegel, Jürgen Habermas. Frankfurt am Main: Suhrkamp Verlag, 1971.

Hesse, Mary. *Revolutions and Reconstructions in the Philosophy of Science.* Brighton, England: Harvester Press, 1980.

――――. *The Structure of Scientific Inference.* London: Macmillan, 1974.

Hill, Melvyn A., ed. *Hannah Arendt: The Recovery of the Public World.* New York: St. Martin's Press, 1979.

Hirsch, E. D., Jr. *Validity in Interpretation.* New Haven: Yale University Press, 1967.

Hollis, Martin. "The Limits of Irrationality." In Wilson, *Rationality.*

Hollis, Martin, and Lukes, Steven, eds. *Rationality and Relativism.* Oxford: Basil Blackwell, 1982.

Horkheimer, Max, and Adorno, Theodor W. *Dialectic of Enlightenment.* Translated by John Cumming. New York: Herder & Herder, 1972.

Horton, Robin. "African Traditional Thought and Western Science." In Wilson, *Rationality.*

Hoy, David Couzens. *The Critical Circle: Literature and History in Contemporary Hermeneutics.* Berkeley: University of California Press, 1978.

Husserl, Edmund. *The Crisis of European Sciences and Transcendental Phenomenology.* Translated by David Carr. Evanston, Ill.: Northwestern University Press, 1970.

James, William. *The Works of William James: Pragmatism.* Edited by Fredson Bowers and Ignas K. Skrupskelis. Cambridge, Mass.: Harvard University Press, 1975.

Jarvie, I. C. "Understanding and Explanation in Sociology and Social Anthropology." In Borger and Cioffi, *Explanation in the Behavioural Sciences: Confrontations.*

Jay, Martin. "Should Intellectual History Take a Linguistic Turn? Reflections on the Habermas-Gadamer Debate." In *Modern European Intellectual History,* edited by Dominick LaCapra and Steven L. Kaplan. Ithaca: Cornell University Press, 1982.

Kant, Immanuel. *The Critique of Judgment.* Translated by J. H. Bernard. New York: Haffner Press, 1951.

――――. *The Critique of Pure Reason.* Translated by Norman Kemp Smith. London: Macmillan, 1929.

Kennington, Richard. "'Descartes' 'Olympica'." *Social Research* 28 (1961):171–204.

Kermode, Frank. *The Genesis of Secrecy: On the Interpretation of Narrative.* Cambridge, Mass.: Harvard University Press, 1979.

Kolakowski, Leszek. *Husserl and the Search for Certitude.* New Haven: Yale University Press, 1975.

Kuhn, Thomas S. *The Essential Tension: Selected Studies in Scientific Tradition and Change.* Chicago: University of Chicago Press, 1977.

———. "Notes on Lakatos." In Buck and Cohen, *PSA 1970.*

———. "Reflections on My Critics." In Lakatos and Musgrave, *Criticism and the Growth of Knowledge.*

———. *The Structure of Scientific Revolutions.* 2d. ed. enl. Chicago: University of Chicago Press, 1970.

———. "Theory-Change as Structure-Change: Comments on the Sneed Formalism." *Erkenntnis* 10 (1976):179–99.

Lakatos, Imre. "Falsification and the Methodology of Scientific Research Programmes." In Lakatos and Musgrave, *Criticism and the Growth of Knowledge.*

———. "History of Science and Its Rational Reconstructions." In Buck and Cohen, *PSA 1970.*

———. "Replies to Critics." In Buck and Cohen, *PSA 1970.*

Lakatos, Imre, and Musgrave, Alan, eds. *Criticism and the Growth of Knowledge.* Cambridge, England: Cambridge University Press, 1970.

Lamore, Charles. "Moral Judgment." *Review of Metaphysics* 35 (1981):275–96.

Laudan, Larry. *Progress and Its Problems: Towards a Theory of Scientific Growth.* London: Routledge & Kegan Paul, 1977.

Lukes, Steven. *Essays in Social Theory.* New York: Columbia University Press, 1977.

———. "Some Problems about Rationality." In Wilson, *Rationality.*

McCarthy, Thomas M. *The Critical Theory of Jürgen Habermas.* Cambridge, Mass.: M.I.T. Press, 1978.

McDowell, John. "Virtue and Reason." *Monist* 62 (1979):331–50.

Machamer, Peter K. "Feyerabend and Galileo: The Interaction of Theories, and the Reinterpretation of Experience." *Studies in the History and Philosophy of Science* 4 (1973):1–46.

MacIntyre, Alasdair. *After Virtue: A Study in Moral Theory.* Notre Dame: University of Notre Dame Press, 1981.

———. *Against the Self-Images of the Age.* New York: Schocken Books, 1971.

———. "Epistemological Crises, Dramatic Narrative and the Philosophy of Science." *Monist* 60 (1977):453–72.

McMullin, Ernan. "Discussion Review: Laudan's Progress and Its Problems." *Philosophy of Science* 46 (1979):623–44.

———. "The Fertility of Theory and the Unit for Appraisal in Science." In Cohen, Feyerabend, and Wartofsky, *Essays in Memory of Imre Lakatos.*

———. "History and Philosophy of Science: A Marriage of Convenience?"

In *PSA 1974*, edited by R. S. Cohen, C. A. Hooker, A. C. Michalos, and J. W. Van Evra. Proceedings of the 1974 Biennial Meeting of the Philosophy of Science Association. Boston Studies in the Philosophy of Science, no. 32. Dordrecht, Holland: D. Reidel, 1976.

————. "The History and Philosophy of Science: A Taxonomy of Their Relations." In *Historical and Philosophical Perspectives of Science*, edited by Roger H. Stuewer. Minnesota Studies in the Philosophy of Science, no. 5. Minneapolis: University of Minnesota Press, 1970.

Makkreel, Rudolf A. *Dilthey: Philosopher of the Human Studies*. Princeton: Princeton University Press, 1975.

Marx, Karl. *Writings of the Young Marx on Philosophy and Society*. Edited and translated by Loyd D. Easton and Kurt H. Guddat. Garden City, N.Y.: Anchor Books, 1967.

Mendelson, Jack. "The Habermas-Gadamer Debate." *New German Critique* 18 (1979):44–73.

Misgeld, Dieter. "Critical Theory and Hermeneutics: The Debate between Habermas and Gadamer." In *On Critical Theory*, edited by John O'Neill. New York: Seabury Press, 1976.

Musgrave, Alan. "Method or Madness." In Cohen, Feyerabend, and Wartofsky, *Essays in Memory of Imre Lakatos*.

Palmer, Richard. *Hermeneutics: Interpretation Theory in Schleiermacher, Dilthey, Heidegger, and Gadamer*. Evanston, Ill.: Northwestern University Press, 1969.

Peirce, Charles Sanders. *Collected Papers of Charles Sanders Peirce*. Edited by Charles Hartshorne and Paul Weiss. Cambridge, Mass.: Harvard University Press, 1931–35.

Pitkin, Hanna Fenichel. "Justice: On Relating Private and Public." *Political Theory* 9 (1981):327–52.

————. "The Roots of Conservatism: Oakeshott and the Denial of Politics." *Dissent* (1973):496–525.

————. *Wittgenstein and Justice*. Berkeley: University of California Press, 1972.

Pitkin, Hanna Fenichel, and Shumer, Sara M. "On Participation." *Democracy* 2 (1982):43–54.

Polanyi, Michael. *Personal Knowledge*. Chicago: University of Chicago Press, 1958.

Popper, Karl R. *Conjectures and Refutations: The Growth of Scientific Knowledge*. 4th ed. rev. London: Routledge & Kegan Paul, 1972.

————. *Objective Knowledge: An Evolutionary Approach*. Oxford: Clarendon Press, 1972.

————. *The Open Society and Its Enemies*. 5th ed. rev. 2 vols. London: Routledge & Kegan Paul, 1966.

————. *The Philosophy of Karl Popper*. 2 vols. Edited by Paul Arthur Schilpp. LaSalle, Ill.: Open Court, 1974.

————. "The Rationality of Scientific Revolutions." In *Problems of Scien-*

tific Revolutions, edited by Rom Harré. Oxford: Oxford University Press, 1975.

Putnam, Hilary. *Meaning and the Moral Sciences*. London: Routledge & Kegan Paul, 1978.

———. *Reason, Truth and History*. Cambridge, England: Cambridge University Press, 1981.

Rabinow, Paul, and Sullivan, William M., eds. *Interpretive Social Science: A Reader*. Berkeley: University of California Press, 1979.

Ricoeur, Paul. *Paul Ricoeur: Hermeneutics and the Social Sciences*. Edited and translated by John B. Thompson. Cambridge, England: Cambridge University Press, 1981.

Rorty, Amelie Oksenberg, ed. *Essays on Aristotle's Ethics*. Berkeley: University of California Press, 1980.

Rorty, Richard. *Consequences of Pragmatism*. Minneapolis: University of Minnesota Press, 1982.

———. "Nineteenth Century Idealism and Twentieth Century Textualism." *Monist* 64 (1981):155–74.

———. *Philosophy and the Mirror of Nature*. Princeton: Princeton University Press, 1979.

———. "Pragmatism, Categories, and Language." *Philosophical Review* 70 (1961):197–223.

———. "Pragmatism, Relativism, and Irrationalism." *Proceedings and Addresses of the American Philosophical Association* 53 (1980):719–38.

———. "A Reply to Dreyfus and Taylor." *Review of Metaphysics* 34 (1980):39–46.

———. "The World Well Lost." *Journal of Philosophy* 69 (1972):649–65.

Scheffler, Israel. *Science and Subjectivity*. Indianapolis: Bobbs-Merrill, 1967.

Shapere, Dudley. "The Structure of Scientific Revolutions." *Philosophical Review* 73 (1964):383–94.

Shklar, Judith N. *Freedom and Independence: A Study of the Political Ideas of Hegel's "Phenomenology of Mind."* Cambridge, England: Cambridge University Press, 1976.

Skinner, Quentin. "Meaning and Understanding in the History of Ideas." *History and Theory* 8 (1969):1–53.

———. "Motives, Intentions and the Interpretation of Texts." *New Literary History* 3 (1972):393–408.

———. "Some Problems in the Analysis of Political Thought and Action." *Political Theory* 2 (1974):227–303.

Skirbekk, Gunnar. "Pragmatism in Apel and Habermas." In *Contemporary Philosophy. A New Survey*. Vol. 4, *Philosophy of Mind*, edited by G. Floisted. The Hague: M. Nijhoff, 1982.

Smith, P. Christopher. *Hermeneutics as a Theory of Human Finitude: Studies on H.-G. Gadamer*. Forthcoming.

Stegmüller, Wolfgang. *The Structure and Dynamics of Theories.* New York: Springer-Verlag, 1976.

Stevenson, Charles L. *Ethics and Language.* New Haven: Yale University Press, 1944.

Strauss, Leo. *Natural Right and History.* Chicago: University of Chicago Press, 1953.

Suppe, Frederick, ed. *The Structure of Scientific Theories.* 2d. ed. Urbana: University of Illinois Press, 1977.

Taylor, Charles. "Growth, Legitimacy and the Modern Identity." *Praxis International* 1 (1981):111–25.

———. *Hegel.* Cambridge, England: Cambridge University Press, 1975.

———. *Hegel and Modern Society.* Cambridge, England: Cambridge University Press, 1979.

———. "Interpretation and the Sciences of Man." In Rabinow and Sullivan, *Interpretive Social Science: A Reader.*

———. "The Opening Arguments of the *Phenomenology.*" In *Hegel,* edited by Alasdair MacIntyre. New York: Doubleday, 1972.

Thompson, John B. *Critical Hermeneutics.* Cambridge, England: Cambridge University Press, 1981.

Thompson, John B., and Held, David, eds. *Habermas: Critical Debates.* Cambridge, Mass.: M.I.T. Press, 1982.

Toulmin, Stephen E. "Does the Distinction between Normal and Revolutionary Science Hold Water?" In Lakatos and Musgrave, *Criticism and the Growth of Knowledge.*

———. *Human Understanding.* Vol. 1. Princeton: Princeton University Press, 1972.

Tugenhat, Ernst. "The Fusion of Horizons." *Times Literary Supplement,* 19 May 1978.

Udovicki, Jasminkz. "The Uses of Freedom and the Human Condition." *Praxis International* 3 (1983):54–61.

Vollrath, Ernst. "Hannah Arendt and the Method of Political Thinking." *Social Research* 44 (1977):160–82.

Watkins, John. "Against 'Normal Science'." In Lakatos and Musgrave, *Criticism and the Growth of Knowledge.*

Wellmer, Albrecht. *Critical Theory of Society.* Translated by John Cumming. New York: Herder & Herder, 1971.

White, Hayden. *Metahistory.* Baltimore: Johns Hopkins Press, 1973.

———. *Tropics of Discourse.* Baltimore: Johns Hopkins Press, 1978.

Wiggins, David. "Deliberation and Practical Reason." In Rorty, *Essays on Aristotle's Ethics.*

Wilson, Bryan R., ed. *Rationality.* Oxford: Basil Blackwell, 1970.

Winch, Peter. "Comment" on Jarvie's paper. In Borger and Cioffi, *Explanation in the Behavioural Sciences.*

———. *Ethics and Action.* London: Routledge & Kegan Paul, 1972.

————. *The Idea of a Social Science and Its Relation to Philosophy.* London: Routledge & Kegan Paul, 1958.

————. "Mr. Louch's Idea of a Social Science." *Inquiry* 7 (1964):202–8.

Wittgenstein, Ludwig. *Culture and Value.* Oxford: Basil Blackwell, 1980.

————. *Philosophical Investigations.* Translated by G. E. M. Anscombe. New York: Macmillan, 1953.

Wolin, Sheldon. "Political Theory as a Vocation." In *Machiavelli and the Nature of Political Thought,* edited by M. Fleisher. New York: Atheneum, 1972.

Wolterstorff, Nicholas. *Reason within the Bounds of Religion.* Grand Rapids, Mich.: William B. Eerdmans, 1976.

Wright, Kathleen. "Gadamer on the Speculative Structure of Language." Forthcoming.

SUBJECT INDEX

INDEX OF NAMES